Self and World
in
Schopenhauer's Philosophy

Self and World
in
Schopenhauer's Philosophy

Christopher Janaway

CLARENDON PRESS · OXFORD
1989

Oxford University Press, Walton Street, Oxford OX2 6DP

Oxford New York Toronto
Delhi Bombay Calcutta Madras Karachi
Petaling Jaya Singapore Hong Kong Tokyo
Nairobi Dar es Salaam Cape Town
Melbourne Auckland
and associated companies in
Berlin Ibadan

Oxford is a trade mark of Oxford University Press

Published in the United States
by Oxford University Press, New York

© Christopher Janaway 1989

British Library Cataloguing in Publication Data
Janaway, Christopher
Self and world in Schopenhauer's
philosophy.
1. German philosophy. Schopenhauer, Arthur
1788–1860
I. Title
193
ISBN 0–19–824969–1

Library of Congress Cataloging in Publication Data
Janaway, Christopher.
Self and world in Schopenhauer's philosophy / Christopher Janaway.
Bibliography: p. Includes index.
1. Schopenhauer, Arthur, 1788–1860. I. Title.
B3148.J36 1989 193—dc19 88–28631 CIP
ISBN 0–19–824969–1

Set by Hope Services, Abingdon
Printed and bound in Great Britain by
Biddles Ltd, Guildford and King's Lynn

*To
Fiona*

PREFACE

ARTHUR Schopenhauer was born on 22 February 1788. The
present book happily coincides with his bicentenary, though I
had not originally intended it to do so. If I offer it as a
celebration of Schopenhauer, it is in the spirit, not of
adulation, but of fair, critical assessment. Schopenhauer
himself, who craved celebration all his life, was wise and
honest enough to know that this is the only worthwhile kind.

The writing of this work, from my first interest in
Schopenhauer's philosophy as a postgraduate student, through
the completion of a doctoral thesis, to the finished book, has
stretched over ten years, and I would like to thank the
following people for reading and discussing its various stages
with me: David Hamlyn, Patrick Gardiner, Charles Taylor,
David Pears, Stuart Hampshire, Albert Landau, Peter Bieri,
and Reiner Wiehl. I am also most grateful to my family,
friends, colleagues, and students for their interest and
support.

When I began to think about Schopenhauer, there was very
little published about his philosophy in English, and his
preoccupations seemed—refreshingly or tediously, according
to one's preference—remote from 'our' way of doing philosophy.
Since then things have changed: a number of books on
Schopenhauer have appeared, and, for whatever reasons,
philosophy seems better equipped to engage with him again.
It is perhaps more fashionable now than it was to debate the
larger metaphysical questions—What is the self? What is the
will? What is the world?—which are pre-eminently Schopenhauer's domain. I have found in the recent writings of Thomas
Nagel and Brian O'Shaughnessy two specific instances where
not only Schopenhauer's deepest problems, but even some of
his answers, are strongly echoed.

I hope, too, that philosophers have become a little more
sophisticated in their expectations of the history of philosophy.

It cannot be enough to raid the past for the odd nugget that can be reshaped into a present-day jewel. Only a proper appraisal of the context in which, and the aims with which, Schopenhauer was arguing can bring out the true philosophical interest in studying him. That his metaphysics is flawed, as I shall argue it is, does not detract from his historical importance or from the worth of the problems he raises. If I have succeeded in showing this at all, it is a fitting celebration.

C. J.

Birkbeck College, London
May 1988

CONTENTS

Abbreviations and References   xi

Introduction   1

PART ONE

1. The Development of Schopenhauer's Philosophy   21

2. Kantian Objects   37

    Space, Time, and the Categories   37
    Kant and Berkeley   53
    Appearance and Thing in Itself   67

3. Kantian Subjects   84

    Transcendental Freedom   84
    Self and Knowledge   98

PART TWO

4. Subject and Object in Schopenhauer   117
5. Idealism   140
6. Materialism   172
7. Knowing the Thing in Itself   188
8. Willing and Acting   208
9. Determinism and Responsibility   230
10. The Primacy of Will   248
11. Freedom from Will   271

PART THREE

12. Self and World   291
13. Remarks on Wittgenstein and Nietzsche   317
14. Conclusions   358

    Bibliography   366

    Index   375

ABBREVIATIONS AND REFERENCES

I. *Works by Schopenhauer*

FMW	*Über die Freiheit des menschlichen Willens* [*On the Freedom of the Will*]
GM	*Über die Grundlage der Moral* [*On the Basis of Morality*]
*HN*1–*HN*5	*Der handschriftliche Nachlass* [Unpublished manuscripts], ed. Arthur Hübscher, vols. 1–5
*PP*1, *PP*2	*Parerga und Paralipomena* [*Parerga and Paralipomena*], vols. 1 and 2
VW	*Über die vierfache Wurzel des Satzes vom zureichenden Grunde* [*On the Fourfold Root of the Principle of Sufficient Reason*]. Referred to in the text as *On the Fourfold Root*.
*W*1, *W*2	*Die Welt als Wille und Vorstellung* [*The World as Will and Representation*], vols. 1 and 2
WN	*Über den Willen in der Natur* [*On the Will in Nature*]

With the exception of the *Nachlass*, references are given as follows: work—page number of German text—(page number of English translation). Thus: *W*1 p. 29 (3). For all references of this type, the number in brackets refers to a page in the relevant English translation, as listed in the Bibliography. The first page number refers to the text of the 10-volume edition by Diogenes (Zürich, 1977), which reproduces in a more accessible form the text of Arthur Hübscher (ed.), *Schopenhauers sämtliche Werke* (3rd edn.; Wiesbaden: Brockhaus, 1972), though unfortunately not its pagination.

II. *Works by Other Authors*

(a) *Kant*

Ak.	*Kants gesammelte Schriften*, ed. by the Königlich Preussische Akadamie der Wissenschaften. References are by volume and page number.
Gr.	*Grundlegung zur Metaphysik der Sitten* [*Groundwork of the Metaphysic of Morals*]. References by volume and page of

Ak. edition, which are usually given as marginal numbers in other editions.

KdrV   *Kritik der reinen Vernunft* [*Critique of Pure Reason*]. References are by standard A and B marginal numbers, indicating page numbers of 1st (1781) and 2nd (1787) editions.

Prol.   *Prolegomena zu einer jeden künftigen Metaphysik, die als Wissenschaft wird auftreten können* [*Prolegomena to any Future Metaphysics*]. References to Ak. edition (see *Gr.* above).

(b) Nietzsche

ASZ   *Also Sprach Zarathustra* [*Thus Spoke Zarathustra*]
Gen.   *Zur Genealogie der Moral* [*The Genealogy of Morals*]
JGB   *Jenseits von Gut und Böse* [*Beyond Good and Evil*]
WM   *Der Wille zur Macht* [*The Will to Power*]

All references to Nietzsche's works are by numbers of section and/or aphorism.

(c) Wittgenstein

NB   *Notebooks 1914–16*
PI   *Philosophical Investigations.* References by part and section numbers.
TLP   *Tractatus Logico-Philosophicus.* References by proposition number.

Translations from the German are in all cases my own, unless otherwise stated. I have, however, frequently consulted and benefited from existing translations. These are listed in the Bibliography.

Introduction

How must we conceive the self? In recent years this essentially metaphysical question—what kind of being must each of us regard him- or herself[1] to be?—has received renewed attention from philosophers. In English-speaking analytical philosophy the question has often seemed to be that of how the word 'I' refers, or of what relation self-conscious thought bears to its object (oneself). Sometimes the motivation is to see to what extent 'I' fits into wider contemporary theories about how speaking and thinking manage to refer to things in general. Yet there often lurks in the background a sense of continuity with historical figures whose primary philosophical concerns were in each case somewhat different. There is Descartes's conception of the self as an immaterial substance distinct from the body. This view is generally regarded as deeply erroneous, but it is still present in our thoughts almost as a temptation to be warded off—as if in part one yearned to believe that 'I' refers to a separate soul. Then there is Hume's confessedly troubled attempt to dissolve the self into a mere series of 'perceptions', a stream of events—thoughts, sensations, memories—occurring without any substantial underpinning. And there is Kant's sophisticated notion of the 'transcendental unity of apperception': the self as the single subject of a multiplicity of experiences, aware to itself of its own unity (without which no objective experience would be possible), yet not a substantial entity, nor encountered at all within experience. On the other hand, it is natural to ask: Why might I not be something substantial by being

[1] Where possible, I shall not use cumbersome locutions such as this. In quotations from Schopenhauer, whose virulent attitude to women is well known, it would be a distortion to use anything other than 'he', 'him', etc. In my own text, to redress this imbalance, I shall use 'she' etc. where I discuss an indefinite person. But there will be many occasions when, in discussing 'the subject', I shall use 'it', which follows the gender of the German *das Subjekt*, and, more importantly, retains the crucial implication that the subject may not be identifiable with a person as such.

something material? Yet to many, a purely materialist conception of the universe, which in other respects may seem unobjectionable and perhaps unavoidable, founders over the suggestion that I am straightforwardly part of that universe. Surely I *really* am a single unified centre of experience and action. But at the same time, how can I not be included in whatever objective description is true of the world at large? If a material description—probably the leading contender—is true, how can I fail to be a material constituent of the world?

In some strands of nineteenth-century thought these problems became particularly acute. The rapid development of physiology as a science, and the rise of evolutionary theory, brought increased evidence that the nature of the mind must in some sense be organic. Although the sheer mechanism of earlier thought might not be enough, there were new ways of exploring the claim that the basis of human consciousness could be material. Yet at the same time, especially in German philosophy, the nineteenth century began with idealism in full flight. For Kant and his idealist successors, experience depended on the unifying self that was conscious to itself of being the *subject* of experience. Furthermore, they held that the world was in some sense constituted by this subject, whose active imposition of fundamental classifications on experience allowed it to confront a world of distinguishable *objects* other than itself. The world of objects was there only *for* some active, classifying 'I'. The 'I' itself resisted any theoretical absorption into nature—the objective realm—and as such inhabited the realm of freedom. This was not a return to the conception of an immaterial substance, but an attempt to save the 'I' from being seen as an objectively existing thing at all.

While acknowledging that the idealist conception of the 'I' is highly problematic, we may keep alive the interesting thought that idealism brings to light here questions which might otherwise have been overlooked, and which can continue to have a bearing far beyond the systems of thought in which they were first posed. This thought is not new; in 1845 Karl Marx wrote:

The chief deficiency of all materialism up till now . . . is that objectivity, reality, the sensible world is conceived only in the form of the object or of observation; not, however, as sensible human activity, or practice, not from the aspect of the subject. Hence, in opposition to materialism, the active side developed in abstract fashion by idealism, which naturally knows no real sensible activity as such.[2]

One broad interpretation of this passage runs as follows: idealism is driven to produce an account of the self as subject which does not reduce it to the level of a 'mere object'; but its drawback is that it fails to incorporate the subject in the objective world at all. Materialism, on the other hand, runs the risk of nullifying the self in the very attempt to locate it as an object within the world. Thus the task is to produce a brand of materialism which reappropriates from idealism the central notion of a subject of experience and action.

One year before this famous passage was written, Schopenhauer's main work, *The World as Will and Representation*, was reprinted in a second, greatly extended edition. Schopenhauer had worked on the first edition during the second decade of the century, and had published it in 1819. He shared some of the background assumptions and some of the preoccupations of the young Marx, despite the great divergence of their views.[3] The central task Schopenhauer set himself was to incorporate both the idealist conception of the subject as the non-worldly focal point of objective experience, and a vision of the self as a material, organic product of nature, within one all-embracing metaphysical system. His key thought was that essentially we are active, striving beings. Although to be human necessarily involves the capacity for objective knowledge, our conception of the self must undergo a fundamental reorientation. We must accommodate the thought that we are embodied as subjects of action, and that our essential organic nature—what we are 'in ourselves'—brings with it pre-rational strivings for survival and reproduction, while at the same time not losing sight of the idealist conception of ourselves as subjects of a wholly objective conception of the world, as if from outside it. The interplay between these competing accounts of the self generates enormous tensions

---

[2] 'Theses on Feuerbach', 1.
[3] For comparative studies of Schopenhauer and Marx, see Hans Ebeling and Ludger Lütkehaus (eds.), *Schopenhauer und Marx: Philosophie des Elends—Elend der Philosophie?*, and Alfred Schmidt, *Drei Studien über Materialismus*.

which Schopenhauer strains, often unsuccessfully, to control within a single metaphysical construct. Nevertheless, in the process he raises extremely important questions—which it is my prime task to articulate—about the nature of the self, its relation to the world, and the possibilities of its misery or salvation.

It is my belief that a reading of Schopenhauer greatly and happily broadens our understanding of the questions that should be debated by philosophers with an interest in 'the self'. Hence my aim is both to give a coherent interpretation of Schopenhauer, placing him as much as possible in his own intellectual context, and to pursue a philosophical argument through his system in a way that will impinge upon present-day discussion of the same broad issues. Rather than approaching the texts with a secure conviction that I know what problems there are for philosophy to address in this area, I have tried as far as possible to let Schopenhauer himself, whose aims and presuppositions were in some respects very far removed from those of today, determine my agenda. On the other hand, it would be naïve to think that I could slough off without trace the terms of reference of my own time and place. This, if it were possible, would be to speak out of, and into, a vacuum. So I acknowledge that my endeavour has throughout both a historical and a philosophical dimension, and that some degree of tension between the two is probably inevitable.

In Part One, the historical predominates. I attempt to set Schopenhauer in an intellectual context that will make most sense of his philosophy. Here I give pride of place to Kant, the only philosopher with whom Schopenhauer really engaged—through studying his writings—in protracted and serious dialogue, and in Schopenhauer's own eyes the greatest of his predecessors. I have striven to understand what the nature of that dialogue was for Schopenhauer when he encountered Kant in the second decade of the nineteenth century. Yet the fact that it is Kant who has pre-eminent importance for Schopenhauer already suggests in a tentative way the possibility of some common ground with today's English-speaking philosophy, where Kant is likewise accorded great status. As I shall reveal later, Schopenhauer goes on to offer a profound challenge to Kant's conception of the self and its relation to the world of objects. Indeed, the challenge was there from the beginning. For Schopenhauer's ultimate goal was never to produce an extended version of Kant's epistemologically based philosophy, but merely to incorporate large portions of it into a metaphysics that would solve the 'riddle' of the self and the world.

In Part Two, I move on to a consideration of Schopenhauer's philosophy itself, the core of which, I suggest, is the interplay between his different conceptions of the self and its relation to the world.

Schopenhauer once made a note to the effect that his whole philosophy could be summed up in the words, 'The world is the self-knowledge of the will'[4]—an enigmatic statement which in a way rephrases the title of his main work, *The World as Will and Representation*. Since this work contains Schopenhauer's thought in all its essentials and with most of its ramifications, a short systematic summary of it will give us an initial picture of the single, great vision to which he lays claim. The work is in two volumes, each divided in parallel into four books. (In its first edition the work had only one volume; the essays in Volume 2 were written much later and are there to provide commentary on the corresponding passages of Volume 1.[5]) I shall present in outline here what I consider to be the main thread of the argument as it unfolds through these four books.

Book I. The world of which we can have knowledge is a world of *appearance*: we cannot know anything of *things in themselves*. This is what is meant by saying, as Schopenhauer does at the outset, that 'The world is my representation'. This part of his philosophy is based squarely, though with some divergences, on Kant's transcendental idealism. Schopenhauer, too, calls himself a transcendental idealist, assuring us that he does not want to deny that there is a real empirical world composed of spatio-temporal objects. But he insists that this world is exhausted by what appears as object before the representing subject. For Schopenhauer, all objects presuppose

---

[4] *HN*1 p. 462.
[5] Apart from the first (1819) and second (1844) editions, a third edition appeared in 1859, the year before Schopenhauer's death.

some subject, and in fact he seems to equate being an object with being an object for some subject. All modes of connectedness among objects in the empirical world are accordingly equated with modes of connectedness among our representations. Or should it be *my* representations? Schopenhauer does not intend to be a solipsist, although he does assert that the world is 'my representation'; I shall argue later that his dismissal of solipsism is perfectly consistent.

A great deal depends here on the nature of the *subject* to which the world ('as representation') is tied, and for Schopenhauer the subject of representation is decidedly not equated with any one individual situated within the empirical world. Rather, it is merely the necessary correlate of all objects, and as such never an object itself. This is connected with his claim that the subject of representations is unknowable, like an eye that cannot see itself. So far, the self is something of a riddle to itself, but Schopenhauer is content for the moment that it should remain so, the riddle being solved only later through the realization that our primary role in the world is not as mere representers of it. The world, too, he presents as a riddle, in the sense that we can never know the thing in itself, but only a set of representations. Having established the central distinctions between representation and thing in itself, and between subject and object, Schopenhauer next proposes to solve both riddles in one highly original stroke.

Book II. We now discover that the thing in itself is, after all, knowable, but in a special way. It is important first of all to realize that because nothing beyond the realm of empirical representations can partake in spatial or temporal properties or relations, there can be no distinct individuals beyond that realm. There is therefore just one undivided thing in itself, which Schopenhauer now argues to be *the will*. In a sense requiring heavy qualification later, he argues that there is one will which underlies the whole world and manifests itself in the multiplicity of things we can come to know in experience. His argument begins, perhaps unexpectedly, from a point about self-knowledge. He first establishes that there is one kind of knowledge which must be sharply differentiated from our knowledge of objects, and which he hopes will provide the 'key' to an otherwise impregnable reality beyond the world as representation. This key is to be found in our knowledge of our own willed actions, which is 'immediate' in a unique way: we do not observe ourselves acting and infer from this what we will; rather, we know what we will because our action itself expresses our will. Willing, for Schopenhauer, is acting. He denies any causal connection between act of will and bodily movement, arguing that there is no inner or purely mental act of will preceding an action, no act of will at all except the action itself, which is the will expressed in bodily movement. Subjects of will are thus embodied. My immediate access to my willing gives me a special kind of knowledge of an event (my action) and an object (my body) within the empirical world. Action situates the subject. But it also provides us, in Schopenhauer's eyes, with access to the underlying thing in itself, in ourselves. Given this, the heart of the great vision, the rest of Schopenhauer's thought falls quite naturally into place.

It is central to Schopenhauer that we are not (as his own Book I may have suggested) passive, disembodied spectators of the world of objects, but are essentially embodied and active. The will in us is primary, not the intellect. This one thought is extremely fruitful for Schopenhauer, and he uses it to mount a sustained attack on the notion of the purely rational and self-transparent subject of perspectiveless knowledge. The human body, not only in its actions but in all its functions and in its very growth and formation, is a manifestation of will. The latter term comes to signify any end-directed process, whether conscious or not. Thus Schopenhauer presents us with an extraordinary panoramic view of the whole world as springing into empirical object-hood out of one and the same essence, the all-permeating, unconscious striving force which he continues, perhaps misleadingly, to call 'will'. In us, the will is a primary element which can also be called the 'will to life', an urge both to go on living and to produce new life, to reproduce. It exhibits itself especially strongly in the form of sexual desire, but it is also in evidence in a number of ways throughout our conscious life, interfering constantly with the workings of the fragile self-conscious intellect with which philosophers are wont to equate the self. Intellect and will must be clearly distinguished, Schopenhauer argues, and the 'I' seen as a kind of composite of the two, but with the will in many respects the dominant partner. In fact, since it is conditional on the growth of an organism complete with brain and nervous system, the intellect is as much a natural manifestation of the will as anything else in organic nature. This is how Schopenhauer can claim that in us the will becomes conscious of itself.

As I have said, this is the heart of Schopenhauer's great vision. But as he writes it, this is not merely a neutral description of the way things ultimately are: it turns into a lament on the human condition, for which Schopenhauer has earned the title 'the philosopher of pessimism'. In the vividly drawn picture that he gives us, we are doomed to be tormented by powerful desires that we can neither control nor ever fully satisfy, to be swayed by unseen forces within us that we can never fully comprehend, and to swing like pendulums between anguish and a fleeting, stale satiety. Throughout, we bolster up our own precarious egos, destroying others if necessary when they get in our way. All this, for Schopenhauer, is the dictate of the will, and the will is what, along with the rest of the greedy, self-devouring world, we really are. Schopenhauer is thus unusual among metaphysicians in that he presents us with an ultimate reality which we are meant to abhor rather than wonder at or venerate. I shall suggest that the pessimistic attitude is much more closely linked with Schopenhauer's central argument about the nature of the self than has sometimes been suspected.

Book III. Yet another dramatic reversal now takes place: Schopenhauer tells us that all hope should not be abandoned, for there are ways in which we can escape from the will. One of these is provided by aesthetic experience, which Schopenhauer sees as resulting from a qualitative change in both the experiencing subject and its object. We can be so taken up with an object we are contemplating that we cease to have desires, and cease to evaluate the object according to our own ends and needs. We can cease to be attracted or repelled by things as objects of any practical import. In short, in this, the aesthetic experience, we cease to will. Schopenhauer speaks—one imagines from first-hand experience—of a state of inner tranquillity brought about by immersion in the arts, that for him forms an all too brief respite from a daily life oppressed by base desires and the struggle against them. ('Happiness? It would be rest. But that is not possible for the subject of willing.'[6]) But in straight philosophical terms, Schopenhauer's view is that in aesthetic experience the subject of experience ceases to be a subject of will, and becomes a merely passive receptor of the object presented to the senses. The subject becomes, as Schopenhauer puts it, a mirror of the world. In this state of being a 'pure', will-less subject, one is no longer conscious of one's individuality, because one is not conscious of oneself at all, only of present experience as it flows in, and therefore only of each immediate object of experience. In becoming a disinterested percipient, one merges entirely with that which is contemplated. Our normal 'way of regarding things', as beings with interests which motivate our actions, involves us in an experience whose objects have a significance relative to those interests. Consequently, the fundamental modes of organization among objects as we ordinarily perceive them are interest-relative. Aesthetic experience frees us from will, from interest, and in thereby freeing objects from their mind-imposed interrelations, it enables us to view each of them as a unique and separate individual. Schopenhauer finds his view well reflected in Spinoza's dictum: *mens aeterna est, quatenus res sub aeternitatis specie concipit*—'the mind is eternal in so far as it conceives things from the standpoint of eternity'.[7]

However, a further qualification is needed. In Schopenhauer's account of aesthetic experience, there is not just a change in the *subject*, but also one in the *object*. We are aware, in this pure contemplative state, not of an individual empirical thing, but of *an Idea* (*Idee*), a term which Schopenhauer intends to be taken in a Platonic sense. Plato would have objected to his *ideai* being made objects of purely *perceptual* contemplation, to the exclusion of conceptual thought. Yet the motivation here is deeply Platonic: the search for something more real than the ever-changing realm of phenomena, something that the mind can mirror in a state of 'timeless, will-less, painless' calm. Like Plato, Schopenhauer thinks that this calm is reached at the

---

[6] Thomas Mann, 'Schopenhauer', in Gerd Haffmans (ed.), *Über Arthur Schopenhauer*, p. 99.

[7] Spinoza, *The Ethics*, part v, prop. 31.

moment of the greatest knowledge—in aesthetic experience we are the 'pure subject of *knowing*'. Ideas for Schopenhauer are a series of 'grades of the will's objectification' in nature, something like universals, as opposed to particular natural objects. Part of his thought here is that an Idea is a universal which we see embodied in a particular perceived object. Thus a particular statue might embody for us the essence of a horse—or of *the* horse, or of what a horse is in general. Although we can never experience the true reality or 'in itself' of anything, we come as close to it in the Ideas as we can by way of mere representation; and this, paradoxically, by liberating ourselves from that very will which is our essence.

Schopenhauer's doctrine of Ideas is remarkable and full of difficulties. Though it was not exceptional in his time, we must find it striking that it is in *aesthetic* experience that he sees the human subject as coming closest to an adequate view of reality, in distinct contrast both to everyday experience and to science. This fact alone might help to explain the great influence Schopenhauer has had on the theory and practice of the arts. But we must also take into account his extended discussions of each of the arts, where he displays great knowledge and insight. Particularly influential has been his view of music, which he regards as the direct, unmediated expression of the will—not the individual will of the artist or composer, but the will in itself that permeates nature.

Book IV. Schopenhauer has argued that the individual is the product of a somewhat uneasy alliance between the will and the self-conscious intellect. Yet, he thinks we all tend to be egoists, we all treat our 'I' as the centre of the world, and seek power, pleasure, and property for this individual above all else. Schopenhauer regards this view of ourselves as the source of all immorality. While holding that it is in the nature of things for human beings to think this way, he nevertheless believes that it rests on a fundamental error. For a little reflection reveals the *illusory* nature of the individual experiencing subject. In our essence we are all identical, appearances of the one world-will; as creatures with brains and other cognitive apparatus we are among its objective manifestations in nature. We are individual organisms within the empirical realm. But as subject of experience none of us is an individual, since the subject is not an item there, within the world, to be individuated. The person who realizes this is on the way to becoming morally better, as she is less likely to set up an insuperable barrier between herself and the rest of the world. To be morally bad is to have a distorted view of one's own importance as an individual, arising from a tacitly accepted but mistaken metaphysical account in which one figures as something qualitatively different from the rest of the world. To be morally good is to regard oneself as essentially belonging to the whole, and to see others as 'I once more'. Thus the morally good life is one in which I impose my will as little as possible on the course of events. Schopenhauer is adamant—and in this he is strongly opposed to Kant—that morality is in no way to be achieved or guaranteed by the grasp of ethical precepts. He even holds that morality is not acquired at all by any inculcation that appeals to rational thought—concepts, as he puts it, are as unfruitful in ethics as they are in aesthetics. Thus we may say that for Schopenhauer ethics is incommunicable, and rests on 'seeing the world aright'.

If this seems to border on the outright mystical, then so much the better as far as Schopenhauer is concerned. For it is with a commitment to the life and vision of the mystic that he ends his book. Since the only hell to which we are consigned is in fact our present life, it is in the here and now that we must seek salvation. And the answer for Schopenhauer is to cease to will altogether, to turn and deny the will that is our essence. At best we should lead a life of self-imposed abstinence in which all desire is stilled, looking for guidance to the ascetic practices of various Eastern religions. (In view of the comfort of his own high-bourgeois lifestyle, some have doubted the sincerity of Schopenhauer's advocacy of asceticism. Lukács memorably describes the Schopenhauerian system as a beautiful and comfortably equipped hotel on the edge of an abyss, adding that 'the daily sight of the abyss, between the leisurely enjoyment of meals or works of art, can only enhance one's pleasure in this elegant comfort.'[8])

Ultimately for Schopenhauer we are to reach a point where

---

[8] *The Destruction of Reason*, p. 243 (also at Michael Fox (ed.), *Schopenhauer: His Philosophical Achievement*, p. 193).

we become so detached from practical concerns and purged of
all will that we cease to regard ourselves as individuals at all,
and see our true self as co-extensive with the universe as a
whole. His views here are presented with undeniable power
and eloquence, though whether philosophy can have anything
to say about their content is another question. Schopenhauer
himself believed that he could only delimit the ultimate truth
negatively, and that the mystical experience that would show
him to be right could not be communicated in words.
Philosophy, he thought, must stop at the brink of these
unchartable waters.

Schopenhauer's great book is surely a consummate work of
art. It has been likened to a symphony in four movements,[9]
and I have sought above to present the flow of its thought in a
way which reveals this aspect of it. The book is built of
dramatic reversals, deliberately sustained tensions, and later
variations on earlier themes. This bears on how it must be
read. It has unity, but it is a dynamic unity through change
and conflict, as indeed we would expect from a great
symphony. At odds, I suspect, with his own expectation
of building a coherent and static metaphysical system,
Schopenhauer has presented us with a series of oppositions
and self-underminings which disallow the assumption that
'What is the self?' and 'How are self and world related?' will
be given any single answer. The answer is likely to have many
different facets, and to consist of the acknowledging and
balancing-out of tensions between them. For this, I will
suggest, we can be thankful to Schopenhauer.
   But these remarks raise the question of how we are to
approach Schopenhauer's writings from the point of view of
philosophy, as I have set myself to do. In part there are
historical reasons for our needing to ask this question. Some
general features of Schopenhauer's thought make it as close to
the twentieth century as to the first part of the nineteenth—

---

[9] Cf. Arthur Hübscher, *Schopenhauer: Biographie eines Weltbildes* (hereafter *Biographie*),
p. 64. For comments on the dramatic structure of Schopenhauer's work, cf. Erich
Heller, *Thomas Mann: The Ironic German*, ch. 2. Also noteworthy is Royce's judgement:
'in form the most artistic philosophical treatise in existence, if one excepts the best of
Plato's "Dialogues" ' (*The Spirit of Modern Philosophy*, p. 250).

the absence of God, the concern with unconscious drives, the pessimism about the possibility of human progress, the absurd and strenuous predicament of the individual subject. On the other hand, no major school of philosophical thought in the twentieth century has regarded Schopenhauer as an important predecessor. In some cases his opposition to German academic philosophy and to Hegel in particular may have something to do with his neglect; in others his smugly bourgeois political stance, and the suspicion that he provides what Lukács calls 'indirect apologetics' for the status quo of his day, will have taken their toll of admirers. It is true that in 1809, at the age of 21, Schopenhauer inherited a fortune which enabled him to live for the rest of his life without undertaking paid work.[10] His attitude to Hegel and his like contains an element of contempt on the part of a man of leisure for those who must toil within the university system. But these facts are hardly a guide to his philosophical worth. Lukács recounts with relish the anecdote in which, during the revolutions of 1848, Schopenhauer passes his opera-glasses to a Prussian officer, so that the latter can take better aim at the rebelling populace;[11] yet he manages to distort Schopenhauer's philosophy grotesquely in the attempt to reveal him as a 'bourgeois irrationalist'. To take but one example: the suggestion that Schopenhauer straightforwardly 'glorifies the individual' is at odds with his central claim that individuality is fundamentally illusory and to be transcended. Furthermore, the very crux of Schopenhauer's philosophy is the thought that our existence as subjects of thought and knowledge is explicable in terms of the satisfaction of material needs and drives—the place where some have sought parallels with Marx. Thus for the schools of thought that look to Marx or Hegel as their ancestors, the obstacles to reading Schopenhauer are in part a matter of historical prejudice.

But what of English-speaking analytical philosophers? Here there is also prejudice, though of a much more narrowly methodological kind. At its worst, the orthodox argument that supports this prejudice runs like this: we cannot easily persuade ourselves that Schopenhauer is addressing the precise questions which we regard as the genuine philosophical ones,

---

[10] Cf. Hübscher, *Biographie*, p. 33.
[11] *The Destruction of Reason*, p. 200.

still less that he formulates his answers in the rigorous manner to which we are accustomed; a historical philosopher is worth studying only if it is easy to present him as answering our questions by our methods; therefore, Schopenhauer is not worth studying. As far as I am concerned there are no good reasons for accepting the second premiss of this argument—it is a mere prejudice, and one that can be overcome. Nevertheless, there is some truth in the first premiss, concerning Schopenhauer's methods and the questions he addresses. As long as we do not regard some highly specialized portions of the present and the recent past as having a monopoly on the discovery of philosophical problems, we can be prepared to enlarge our conception of what problems there are through a reappraisal of historical works. With the question of methods, however, there are limits to the latitude we may allow and still be able to recognize a writer as philosophical.

It must be acknowledged that Schopenhauer presents some potential difficulties in this regard. He is highly idiosyncratic, and in a strange way aloof from debate. His work was the product of intellectual solitude, and there are parts of it where he weaves into his great metaphysical framework self-indulgent personal observations on life whose effect is to diminish philosophical interest. He can be very wise and perceptive, but he is not consistently so. In the course of the discussion he will turn aside to consider anything, from the Spanish Inquisition to the sex-life of glow-worms, and his judgement of what is relevant is often questionable. His independence from academic conventions has its refreshing side, but it also brings with it a streak of obstinate crankiness, and an unreadiness to argue thoroughly. Again, the brilliant literary qualities for which he is justly praised, and the great skill with which he enlivens his text with allusions to Homer, Dante, Shakespeare, Byron, and hundreds of others, threaten to crowd out a more sober philosophical approach. Metaphor, rhetoric, and allusion can complement the virtues of precise formulation, clear exposition, and reasoned argument—as they undoubtedly do in Plato—but they should not replace them.

Having said this, it is far from true that Schopenhauer offers philosophers nothing to go on. The basic questions he addresses, and the line of argument he pursues in answering them, are always crisply stated—and they are serious and difficult philosophical questions. What is more, Schopenhauer is extremely knowledgeable about the history of philosophy, keen to make contact with many of his predecessors, and, as we have seen, involved in close critical debate with Kant. It was as a philosopher that Schopenhauer expected to be read, and it is thus that I shall read him. He is perhaps nearer to the limits of what conventionally counts as philosophical than Kant, or Descartes, or Hume, but he is still well within them, and in need only of a little tolerance from a present-day philosophical audience.

In expounding Schopenhauer's philosophy in Part Two, I shall approach him selectively and critically. I shall develop some arguments further than he takes them and inquire into their coherence, while ignoring parts of his work which are not relevant to the broad, central theme of 'self and world'. But in the process I shall be concerned not to falsify Schopenhauer, and to locate and understand the dynamic tensions which are at the very centre of the problems as he conceived them.

The issue of *rapprochement* between Schopenhauer's thought and contemporary philosophy is by no means straightforward, but, as one contribution to it, Part Three offers a more systematic summary of the philosophical problems of self and world which I argue to be especially illuminated by Schopenhauer. Then I enter some fairly extended 'Remarks on Wittgenstein and Nietzsche'. Schopenhauer is not widely read now, either by professional philosophers or by the general public. The same could be said for the greater part of his own lifetime. But we should not forget that during a period beginning in the 1850s and ending around the First World War, Schopenhauer rose to become one of the dominant voices in philosophy and more widely in German culture— and that during that time both Nietzsche and Wittgenstein read him with some degree of commitment. Part of Schopenhauer's 'relevance' for us may lie in his influence on these figures slightly nearer to home, each of whom has played a great part in shaping twentieth-century philosophy.

A full account of Schopenhauer's influence during this period would include discussions of Wagner and Thomas

Mann, of Burckhardt, Wundt, Vaihinger, and von Hartmann.[12] It would note that Freud found in Schopenhauer's views about the will and the intellect a prefiguring of his own conception of the unconscious. Schopenhauer did not play a direct role in the genesis of Freud's thought, but a proper study would ask to what extent he contributed to a prevailing climate of receptivity towards the notion of an unconscious essence to the self, and to the linking of it with sexuality.[13] That von Hartmann's *The Philosophy of the Unconscious* of 1869 was deeply indebted to Schopenhauer is likely to be relevant here. A single quotation sums up Schopenhauer's position at this time: 'by the 1890s it could confidently be asserted before an audience at Harvard that he was generally better known than "any other modern continental metaphysician, except Kant" '.[14]

To complete the picture it would be necessary to assemble a mass of facts about his general cultural influence. In Viennese high society we find, for example, that he was Margarete Wittgenstein's 'favourite philosopher', and that at Christmas 1894, while a guest at the Wittgenstein family house, Mahler gave Bruno Walter Schopenhauer's collected works as a present.[15] On coming to read Schopenhauer around 1905, when he was 16 years old, Wittgenstein himself can scarcely have regarded him as other than vitally important, both as a philosopher and as a central figure in contemporary culture. Some of those around him were under the same prevailing influence. Fritz Mauthner, whose conception of philosophy as *Sprachkritik* Wittgenstein alludes to in the *Tractatus*, was in his own estimation thoroughly imbued with the Schopenhauerian system; and Otto Weininger, the author of *Sex and Character* (1903), whom Wittgenstein is known to have admired, also claimed Schopenhauer among his influences.[16]

---

[12] For brief accounts, cf. Frederick Copleston, *A History of Philosophy*, vol. 7/ii, pp. 55–9; Bryan Magee, *The Philosophy of Schopenhauer*, pp. 276 ff.

[13] Cf. remarks by Freud in 'History of the Psychoanalytic Movement', sect. 1; and *Collected Papers*, vol. 4, p. 355. Also remarks in Ernest Jones, *Sigmund Freud: Life and Work*, vol. 2, p. 461 (quoted, along with some other sources, by Magee, *Schopenhauer*, pp. 283–5).

[14] Patrick Gardiner, *Schopenhauer*, p. 21, citing Josiah Royce, *Modern Philosophy*, p. 228.

[15] Allan Janik and Stephen Toulmin, *Wittgenstein's Vienna*, pp. 172, 18.

[16] Ibid. pp. 123–5 (Mauthner), 71–2 (Weininger).

Thus it is not at all surprising that both Wittgenstein and, earlier, Nietzsche should have been swept up in this trend of popularity briefly enjoyed by 'the philosopher of the will'. My remarks in Part Three do not purport to give a general intellectual and cultural history, however, but concentrate once again on philosophical questions about the self. In 1885–6 Nietzsche wrote in his notebooks: 'The assumption of one single subject is perhaps unnecessary; perhaps it is just as permissible to assume a multiplicity of subjects, whose interaction and struggle is the basis of our thought and consciousness in general?; and: 'The will to power *interprets* . . . In fact, interpretation is itself a means of becoming master of something.'[17] Thirty years later, Wittgenstein wrote in his notebooks: 'Good and evil enters only through the *subject*. And the subject does not belong to the world, but is rather a limit of the world. One could (in a Schopenhauerian way) say: it is not the world of representation that is either good or evil, but the willing subject.'[18] As I make clear by an examination of their writings, their reactions to Schopenhauer were crucial to the work of both philosophers, and carry forward the debate which Schopenhauer's works initiate. It is perhaps a testimony to the many-faceted nature of Schopenhauer's thought that Nietzsche and Wittgenstein fashioned two such diametrically opposed conceptions of the self from materials he supplied. Nietzsche dissolves the self into a multiplicity of essentially organic drives directed towards mastering the environment by imposing partial, perspectival interpretations on it. Wittgenstein, at the other extreme, casts the individual body and soul into the realm of mere facts in the world, and looks to 'the philosophical "I" ' which mirrors the world from no point of view within it. Having seen how each resolves the central tension, we may in the end respect Schopenhauer the more for holding on to it.

---

[17] Incorporated into *WM* as sects. 490, 643.
[18] *NB* p. 79.

PART ONE

I

The Development of Schopenhauer's Philosophy

IN our study of Schopenhauer, the greatest single influence to consider is that of Kant. Schopenhauer would not have described himself as a 'Kantian', and was highly critical of many aspects of Kant's philosophy, but he was ready to acknowledge that Kant provided the basis without which his own work would have been inconceivable. In striving to place Schopenhauer in his intellectual context, therefore, we shall turn to Kant both for the basic ground-plan against which Schopenhauer operates, and for most of the detailed points of controversy which give his system its life. Such an emphasis echoes that of Schopenhauer's main work, *The World as Will and Representation*, at the end of which we find an appendix, one-quarter the length of the work itself and entitled 'Critique of the Kantian Philosophy', where Schopenhauer gives us the penetrating analysis of Kant's strengths and weaknesses which he sees as a prerequisite for justifying his own philosophy.

In general terms, Schopenhauer mentions as Kant's chief merits his distinction between appearance and thing in itself, his claim that the moral significance of actions concerns the thing in itself, and his overthrow of 'scholastic' philosophy. Of these, the first two will be dealt with fully in subsequent chapters. With regard to the third, Schopenhauer has in mind the freeing of philosophy from its domination by the Christian religion during the seventeenth and eighteenth centuries—a liberation which he sees as consequent upon Kant's bold attempt to place metaphysical speculations, including those of religious dogma, outside the sphere of what can be known.[1] That 'university professors' of the nineteenth century still strive to accommodate their philosophy to received religious

---

[1] *W*I p. 521 (423–4).

tenets does not, in Schopenhauer's view, detract from Kant's achievement.[2]

It is sometimes said of Kant that he was opposed to all metaphysics, and that his critical procedure aimed to show that metaphysics was impossible. Schopenhauer, at any rate, takes this general view of Kant. According to him, Kant's fundamental line of thought run like this:[3] (1) Metaphysics is a body of knowledge (*Wissenschaft*) concerned with that which lies beyond the possibility of all experience. (2) Such knowledge cannot be based on principles derived from experience, but must be entirely a priori. (3) We really have a priori principles of this kind, which can be called knowledge of pure reason. So far metaphysics escapes any drastic criticism. But now Kant asks: *How* is metaphysics possible? And it turns out that metaphysics is possible only if it restricts itself to knowledge of the world as it appears to us, and restrains itself from venturing into the realm beyond all experience to seek knowledge of things as they are in themselves. There can be no knowledge beyond the possibility of experience. But since metaphysics is supposed to be a body of just such knowledge, we can conclude, in Schopenhauer's words, that 'metaphysics is impossible, and the critique of pure reason replaces it'.[4]

The overall aim of Kant's *Critique of Pure Reason* might indeed be summarized thus: to answer the question of how there could be substantive truths about the world which can be known to us other than by confirmation through experience. Such truths are what Kant calls synthetic truths known a priori, and they are possible, according to him, only if they pertain to the conditions under which we, as subjects, experience the world. To take the most important examples: we can know a priori, Kant claims, that something in the world must endure through time whenever there is change, and that all change is according to the principle of cause and effect; but we can know this only of the world inasmuch as it can be presented to us in experience. If we abstract from the conditions under which the world presents itself to us in experience, and consider it 'in itself', independently of these

---

[2] *W*1 p. 521 (423–4).   [3] Cf. ibid. p. 524 (426).
[4] Ibid. p. 525 (427).

conditions, we can know nothing of it. We can know the principles of substance and causality a priori, rather than by empirical observation. Unlike analytic truths, however, which are known to be true because their denial involves a contradiction, these principles advance our knowledge, and tell us something informative about the world. They can do this because the basis of our knowing them to be true is that they are necessary conditions of our having a coherent experience of the world at all. Thus we would be left with no route by which we could arrive at knowledge of how the world must be, if we were to prescind entirely from our nature as experiencing subjects. But if instead we give an account of the way things must be for us to have experience of them, then the enterprise of metaphysics can be set on a sure footing which it has not previously enjoyed. It is an over-simplification, then, to say that Kant thought all metaphysics impossible. We must distinguish between metaphysics as it has been in the past, and metaphysics as it could become, once subjected to the Kantian critique. Metaphysics hitherto Kant regards as 'a battle-ground quite peculiarly suited for those who desire to exercise themselves in mock combats, and in which no participant has ever yet succeeded in gaining so much as an inch of territory, not at least in such manner as to secure him in its permanent possession'.[5] From now on such combats can be superseded, according to Kant, since any metaphysical speculation which proceeds intrepidly beyond the limits of possible experience can be shown to have forfeited its claim to yield knowledge. Yet at the same time we do not deny the possibility of metaphysical knowledge altogether, nor lapse into scepticism with regard to any and every claim to such knowledge.

For reasons of his own, it is important to Schopenhauer that metaphysics be possible. So, thinking as he does (not quite accurately) that Kant had declared all metaphysics impossible, he must find some way of disputing the point. What he suggests is that Kant's initial assumption (cf. *Prolegomena*, sect. 1) that the source of metaphysics can never be in experience is unfounded. This is how Schopenhauer puts the matter:

[5] *KdrV* Bxv (Norman Kemp Smith's translation).

The world and our own existence present themselves to us necessarily as a riddle. But now it is simply assumed that the solution to this riddle could not proceed from the thorough understanding of the world itself, but must be sought in something entirely distinct from the world (for that is the meaning of 'beyond the possibility of all experience').[6]

If metaphysics must consist exclusively of a priori knowledge, then (Schopenhauer thinks) it is no wonder that there has been no progress in metaphysics, or that Kant was able to show that metaphysics must fail. But to justify the identification of metaphysics and a priori knowledge,

one would have to have proved first that the material for the solution to the riddle of the world could not be contained within the world itself, but was to be sought only outside the world, in something to be reached only under the guidance of those forms known to us a priori. But as long as this is not proved we have no reason, in this most important and difficult of tasks, to stop up those sources of knowledge which are richest in content—inner and outer experience —and operate solely with forms that are empty of content. Therefore I say that the solution to the riddle of the world must proceed from an understanding of the world itself; and so the task of metaphysics is not to soar above the experience in which the world is presented, but to understand it thoroughly—experience, inner and outer, being indeed the source of all knowledge. Hence it is only through the connection of outer experience with inner, completed properly and at the right point . . . that the solution to the riddle of the world is possible.[7]

Here in outline are some of Schopenhauer's most central themes: the self and the world; the dichtomy of inner and outer experience; and the 'in itself' as a riddle for philosophy to solve. The self and the world are alike riddles to us, but we can in the end know what both are in themselves, arriving at what is for Schopenhauer the ultimate metaphysical truth, that both are *will*. The Kantian attitude to metaphysics he regards as 'despair' (*Verzweiflung*),[8] and counters with a more positive doctrine—yet without going back on Kant's critique of a dogmatic metaphysics which attempts to gain knowledge beyond all possible experience.

---

[6] *W*1 p. 525 (427).   [7] Ibid. p. 526 (427–8).
[8] Ibid. p. 526 (428).

It is important at this stage, before a more detailed examination of the Kantian doctrines which shape so much of Schopenhauer's work, to guard against any misconceptions about the importance of Kant to Schopenhauer. In the first place, it should not be thought that Schopenhauer was ever a slavish or unduly reverent disciple of Kant. As we shall see, he makes forceful criticisms of many central aspects of his predecessor's work. But apart from his many challenges to Kant's authority on substantive issues, Schopenhauer's attitude is also well summed up in his more general criticisms of Kant's way of writing philosophy, with which it is hard to disagree. Firstly, though Kant's style is clearly that of a lofty intellect, Schopenhauer regards it as a major failing, with all its obscurities, ambivalences, repetitions, and overblown technicalities. True, Kant's subject-matter is not the most elementary; but, as Schopenhauer bitingly puts it, a man who writes as Kant so often does cannot really be thinking clearly.[9] And then there is the seeming obsession with symmetry, which lets purely architectonic considerations dominate over the natural flow of the argument. Here Schopenhauer's well-documented and characteristically lucid exposé of Kant is scarcely to be bettered[10]—and though it retains many Kantian terms, his own writing is always free from mere jargon and the peculiar cramping influence that Kant's love of order can exert.

The view that Schopenhauer was merely a follower of Kant has to be qualified further in the light of some of his own utterances about other influences. Thus at the beginning of the Critique of the Kantian Philosophy he writes: 'I confess that, next to the impression of the world of intuition [*Anschauung*], it is to the impression of Kant's works, as well as to the sacred writings of the Hindus and Plato, that I owe the best in my own development'.[11] Before discussing the Hindus and Plato, the reference to intuition deserves some comment. (I have adopted the translation 'intuition' to conform to standard usage in Kantian contexts.) What Schopenhauer is referring to is immediate awareness, through the senses, of particular empirical objects. He prided himself on having

---

[9] Ibid. p. 527 (428–9).   [10] Ibid. pp. 528–33 (430–4).
[11] Ibid. p. 513 (417).

been influenced to a great extent by the world as he directly experienced it. We saw earlier how he criticized Kant's conception of metaphysics for neglecting the testimony of the senses. A further claim that Schopenhauer often makes is that being influenced by the data of intuition marks out the true philosopher from someone whose thought is merely a reaction to a previous philosophical system laid out in a book. Fichte's philosophy was related to Kant's in this way, he thinks, and was therefore artificial and out of touch with reality.[12] His own developed out of Kant's also, but it was never, he claims, a mere bookish response to it, but always had a sense of relevance to empirical reality, whether to ordinary experience, scientific findings, or what was contained in written testimony of other kinds. Schopenhauer does to a certain extent live up to this claim in constantly seeking empirical confirmation for his metaphysical doctrines from a wide variety of sources.

The allusion to the 'impressions of intuition' may also hark back to experiences he gained in his youth, when he travelled widely throughout Europe and began to form attitudes which stayed with him when he later studied philosophy systematically. Particularly noteworthy is an incipient conviction that life is inherently full of suffering. The sights of Europe in 1804–5 were not all pleasant, and Schopenhauer was deeply affected by the poverty and cruelty which he witnessed. Looking back on this time, he was later to write:

In my seventeenth year, without any academic schooling, I was gripped by the sorrow of life, as was Buddha in his youth when he saw illness, age, pain, and death. The truth that spoke loud and clear from the world overcame the Jewish dogmas that had been inculcated into me, and the result for me was that this world could not be the work of any being that was all-good, but must be that of a devil, who had called creatures into this world to feast himself on their torment.[13]

The inevitability of suffering, and the question of how one could free oneself from it, played a very important role in Schopenhauer's later thought, providing the backbone for his theory of the will. Some fragments written during the next few

---

[12] *HN*1 p. 74.
[13] *HN*4/i p. 96, written in 1832. Cf. Hübscher, *Biographie*, p. 19.

years (1805–9) show Schopenhauer, partly under the influence of Wackenroder's *Phantasien über die Kunst*, finding in music access to a realm higher than that of trivial, miserable, everyday life which otherwise 'presses down everything that strives upwards'.[14] He also begins to think in terms of an extreme polarization between the ordinary external world and a 'spirit-world' to which the 'higher person' can aspire, and to conceive of philosophy as embodying the consoling thought that we can inhabit this higher realm, and in some way leave behind the painfulness of corporeal reality.[15] These are early thoughts, written before Schopenhauer had studied philosophy properly, but something of the same aspiration remains with him as a university student and beyond.

In Göttingen, at the beginning of his philosophical training, Schopenhauer was advised by G. E. Schulze (then famous as the author of *Aenesidemus*, a sceptical attack on Kant) to concentrate his initial efforts principally on Kant and Plato, and although he read many other books too he did follow this advice. What then of the influence of Plato? It was the theory of Ideas (*Ideen*) that was of overwhelming importance for Schopenhauer. As early as 1810, his first year as a philosophy student, he sees clearly that the Ideas are *realities*, in an important way distinct from abstract concepts which are merely human artefacts. In the Ideas we glimpse, as he puts it, a divine order that is distorted by the physical world.[16] He values the Ideas as providing an unchanging reality behind the ever-changing and illusory world of individual empirical objects, but he is mainly concerned to adapt them to his own preoccupations—particularly what he now calls the 'better consciousness' (*besseres Bewusstsein*), and the elevation brought about by aesthetic experience.

The better consciousness is throughout opposed to the inferior empirical consciousness, the consciousness of particular objects. The latter is dealt with in a basically Kantian way in his dissertation of 1813, *On the Fourfold Root*: empirical objects are a species of the subject's representations; they are organized in space and time, and they are universally subject

---

[14] *Arthur Schopenhauer: Mensch und Philosoph in seinen Briefen*, pp. 15, 16; cf. Hübscher, *Biographie*, pp. 23–5.
[15] *HN*1 pp. 7–8.   [16] Ibid. p. 11.

to causality. The better consciousness, which makes no appearance in the dissertation, is an eternal or timeless consciousness, divided sharply from the empirical and attainable only as an exception. It is clear from his notebooks that Schopenhauer's early philosophical aspirations lay in this direction. He worked intensively on his conception of the better consciousness during 1813–14, and around it there came together a rich pattern of ideas that provided the basis for much of his major work. The timeless better consciousness is associated with happiness, consolation, freedom from pain, and with more explicitly religious notions, such as sanctification (*Heiligung*) and even (surprisingly, given his claim that he had lost his faith by this stage) the peace of God.[17] The better consciousness is seen as the source of all virtue, and the state of mind characteristic of the saint.[18] But the calmness and elevation of this timeless state are also to be found in the artist or genius, whose contemplation lifts him out of the mere empirical consciousness to a clear vision of underlying realities. As early as 1813, Schopenhauer puts Plato's Ideas to use as the objects of this timeless contemplation,[19] thus giving him the core of the aesthetic theory that he elaborated at much greater length in *The World as Will and Representation*. Stimulated by the Platonic version of the divide between timeless reality and the realm of mere empirical objects, Schopenhauer makes use of it for a purpose entirely his own.

Certainly this stimulus seems to have been crucial in the process of crystallizing and developing his thought; and the same may be said, I think, if we turn to his reference to 'the Hindus'. Schopenhauer is often said to be the first, or indeed the only, modern Western philosopher of any note to attempt any integration of his work with Eastern ways of thinking. That he was the first is surely true, but the claim that he was *influenced* by Indian thought needs some qualification. There is a remarkable correspondence, at least in broad terms, between some of the central Schopenhauerian doctrines and Buddhism: notably in the views that empirical existence is suffering, that suffering originates in desires, and that

[17] Cf. *HN*i pp. 79, 104–5.
[18] Ibid. pp. 122, 149 ff.
[19] Ibid. p. 47.

salvation can be attained by the extinction of desires. These three 'truths of the Buddha' are mirrored closely in the essential structure of the doctrine of will.[20] However, the early days of Schopenhauer's acquaintance with Eastern thought came at a time when European knowledge of it was in general very rudimentary—a fact which Schopenhauer later used to deny any Buddhist influence as such, emphasizing how gratifying it was to find his own views arrived at independently by the religion he had come to respect more than any other.[21]

If Buddhism may be discounted as an influence during the years of the formation of *The World as Will and Representation*, something still remains to be said about the oriental interests during that time which led to the tribute to 'the Hindus'. Schopenhauer's involvement with Eastern thought is generally said to have begun when he met an oriental scholar, Friedrich Majer, in his mother's intellectual circle in Weimar. This was late in 1813, after his dissertation had gained him his doctorate. References reflecting oriental reading begin in the notebooks in 1814, and are concentrated mostly around the Upanishads, which Schopenhauer cites under the title *Oupnek'hat*.[22] This work made a very deep impression on him, and continued to provide him with spiritual fulfilment throughout his life. Seeking out whatever oriental literature he could find, for six months in 1815–16 he worked through the available issues of the English journal, *Asiatic Researches*. He continued such studies, and by the time of his death he had accumulated a library of more than two hundred items of 'orientalia'.[23] However, if we take seriously his claim that his full system of thought was already complete in 1814, it can be only the early stimulus of the Upanishads that contributed to the development of his philosophy, dovetailing with the rest of his thoughts towards the end of the process of completion. Once again, as with Plato, there is a single Upanishadic doctrine which catches Schopenhauer's imagination, the doctrine of *māyā*,

---

[20] On this, see Dorothea W. Dauer, *Schopenhauer as Transmitter of Buddhist Ideas*. Note also the discussion by Bryan Magee, *The Philosophy of Schopenhauer*, pp. 14–15, 316–21.

[21] *W*2 p. 197 (169).

[22] Schopenhauer's *Oupnek'hat* was a Latin version, by Anquetil Duperron, of a Persian translation of the Upanishads. Cf. *HN*5 p. 338 for further details.

[23] Ibid. pp. 319–52 documents the surviving items. Details of *Asiatic Researches* are on pp. 319–20.

which becomes for him a leitmotiv, pregnant with significance, and used whenever he wants to evoke the fleeting and illusory nature of the empirical world. Here is how he uses the notion of *māyā* in 1814:

> As long as a human being lives . . . he is not only prey to sin and to death, but to *delusion* [*Wahn*], and this *delusion* is as real as life, as the sensible world itself, indeed it is one with these (the *māyā* of the Indians): on it are based all our wishes and addictions, which in turn are merely the expression of life, as life is merely the expression of delusion. As long as we live, will to live, are human, the delusion is truth; only in comparison with the better consciousness is it a delusion.[24]

His doctrine, he writes, 'could never have arisen until the Upanishads, Plato, and Kant were able to cast their rays simultaneously into the mind of one human being'.[25] By uniting these strands, Schopenhauer does indeed create a uniquely rich set of resonances around his original dichtomy between the empirical and the better consciousness. But he goes further than mere synthesis: 'The "*māyā*" of the Vedas, Plato's "*aei gignomenon, on de oudepote*" [that which is always becoming, and never is], and Kant's "appearance" are one and the same; they are the world in which we live, and we ourselves, in so far as we belong to it.'[26] The nature of Schopenhauer's indebtedness to his sources is clear from the fact that he sees these various doctrines as simply the same. What concerns him is not whether they are really the same, but whether they can be pressed into the same role in his own scheme of things.

The seal is set on this pattern of thought by Schopenhauer's conception of the will—as the source of suffering associated with the empirical realm, and as the essence that underlies both the subject and the object of empirical consciousness. The term 'better consciousness' is dropped from now on, and Schopenhauer works out his conceptions of the suspension and denial of the will as the road to liberation from suffering. He has a number of problems to deal with, however, some of which stem from his close association of disparate philosophical

---

[24] *HN*i p. 104.   [25] Ibid. p. 422.
[26] Ibid. p. 380 (written 1816).

doctrines. One difficulty is that release from willing is supposed to come from knowing, but the (originally Kantian) conception of a pure knowing subject confronted by its objects is associated already with the empirical rather than with the timeless consciousness.[27] Another is that while the equation of Kant's 'appearance' with Plato's realm of 'that which is becoming and never is' may have some plausibility, the same cannot be said of the Ideas and the Kantian thing in itself. Schopenhauer at first equates them, then has some intricate disentangling to do.[28] Schopenhauer worked for four years to overcome such inconsistencies and to give his thought a unified presentation. The result was *The World as Will and Representation*, finished in 1818 and published in December of that year with the date 1819 on the title-page.

So much for those sources of inspiration, other than Kant, which Schopenhauer acknowledges. A more difficult issue is raised by those contemporaries whom he vilifies, especially Fichte and Schelling. It would be unwise to suppose that Schopenhauer's philosophy 'followed on' quite unproblematically from Kant's. The Critical works for which Kant was, and still is, most famous were brought before the public largely in the 1780s. Schopenhauer, as we have seen, began his study of philosophy (in which reading Kant played an important part) in 1810, and developed his own system of thought during the next decade. We perhaps tend to forget that the Kantian philosophy had been controversial from the start, and that Schopenhauer learned about it against the background of nearly thirty years of discussion, during which it had been criticized, reinterpreted, revised, and rejected by many thinkers. The methodological implication of these facts is that we should try to assess which post-Kantian thinkers were known to Schopenhauer and which he considered important. Certainly he could not claim to be unaware of the major developments during these years: he learned of them to some extent through Schulze, but most directly through attending Fichte's lectures in Berlin, and through some considerable effort spent reading the works of Fichte and Schelling. We know of this because of the preservation of early manuscript

---

[27] Cf. ibid. pp. 166–7.
[28] Cf. ibid. pp. 187, 188 n., 225.

notes and annotations to books in Schopenhauer's possession.[29] His blunt and often witty remarks debunking the pretensions both of style and of content in which Fichte and Schelling indulge, make the most immediate impression. He dubs their approach 'windbaggery' (*Windbeutelei*), and thinks they use obscurity, execrable style, and sheer tedium to conceal from the reader the thinness and absurdity of their thought. But at the same time he does appear to have taken in their doctrines fairly thoroughly.

We should not be deflected by Schopenhauer's own injunction to forget this part of history entirely: 'People are generally becoming aware that real, serious philosophy still stands where Kant left it. At any rate, I do not acknowledge that anything at all has happened in it between him and myself; which is why I take my departure from him.'[30] For even if, as is the case, Schopenhauer reacted negatively to the work of Fichte and Schelling, that in itself counts as an influence which must be acknowledged. There have been suggestions that he was much more positively indebted to them than he claimed. One distinguished reviewer wrote in 1820 that from the title alone he expected Schopenhauer's work to be Fichtian, and on reading it he judged that: 'Mr Schopenhauer belongs to the class of people who, taking the Kantian philosophy as their starting-point, occupy themselves with trying to improve it according to their own mind, while departing a long way from its doctrines. Of these Reinhold is the first, Fichte the most profound, Schelling the most comprehensive. But Schopenhauer is the clearest, the cleverest, and the most approachable.'[31]

One of my concerns will therefore be to assess Schopenhauer's debt to his more immediate philosophical environment. I shall postpone any more detailed discussion of this until later chapters, where it can be linked thematically with Schopenhauer's position, and understood in the light of Kant's.

[29] For Schopenhauer's early notes on Fichte, Schelling, Schleiermacher, Jacobi, Schulze, and others, see *HN2*. For his marginal annotations, see *HN5*.

[30] *W1* pp. 512–13 (416).

[31] J. F. Herbart, review (1820) of *W1*, reprinted in Volker Spierling (ed.), *Materialien zu Schopenhauers 'Die Welt als Wille und Vorstellung'* (hereafter *Materialien*), p. 109.

Furthermore, I shall be selective in my treatment of Fichte and Schelling, since even a modestly comprehensive summary of their views is far beyond the scope of this book. What I shall suggest specifically, however, is that Schopenhauer's use of the distinction between subject and object, his views about the question of deriving one from the other, and his conception of the subject as essentially willing owe a great deal to the formulations of Fichte and Schelling among others. The problems he addresses here are Kantian, but as well as being illuminated by a study of Kant's works, they are mediated by what had happened between Kant and himself. Schopenhauer is much more of his time than he would like to think.

The dismissal of those intervening years as irrelevant, and indeed the way he uses his very disparate sources, are symptoms of Schopenhauer's general contempt for history, which truly put him at odds with what was to become the dominant movement in the German philosophical world. Any reader of Schopenhauer will be struck by the fact that he groups together three philosophers as the recipients of his most venomous attacks. Always included with Fichte and Schelling is Hegel, whom he hated most of all. Schopenhauer's deliberate ahistoricism, his disaffection from Christianity, his love of elegance and clarity, his dislike of the university system, and his well-established views about Fichte and Schelling placed Hegel for him in a uniquely adversarial position. But when it comes to the question of influences on Schopenhauer's development, Hegel is (perhaps surprisingly) simply not among them at all. An examination of Schopenhauer's unpublished manuscripts reveals no mention of Hegel until 1830, just one year before Hegel's death, and, most importantly, a full twelve years after Schopenhauer had completed his system of thought in *The World as Will and Representation*. The years between 1810 and 1818 were the genuinely creative years in Schopenhauer's life, as the manuscripts once again testify. As we have partly outlined above, he reacts to a great range of intellectual stimuli, assimilating, modifying, picking and choosing, then gradually constructing his master-work. Hegel is not among the stimuli, so Volume 1 of the work owes nothing to him, either positively or negatively. Schopenhauer had heard of Hegel—he sent a copy of his *Logik* back to the

booksellers in November 1813[32]—but it is worth emphasizing
that Hegel did not become widely renowned until after 1818,
when he took up the chair in philosophy at Berlin. Schopenhauer arrived in Berlin two years later, and attempted to
lecture at the same hour as Hegel, with the predictable result
that Schopenhauer had no audience. What dominated his
attitude to Hegel from then on was the disparity of their two
reputations: Schopenhauer's master-work remained completely
neglected, while Hegel was hailed as one of the great
philosophers. During the period 1830–44, a large proportion
of Schopenhauer's manuscript references to Hegel occur in
reworkings of a preface to the planned second edition of *The
World as Will and Representation*. They show Schopenhauer
obsessed with his eclipse by someone whom he could only see
as a pompous charlatan, and despairing of the intellectual
community which could make, as he saw it, such a stupendous
error of judgement. Any references to Hegel in the apparently
earlier Volume 1 of the main work and in *On the Fourfold Root*
are in fact later interpolations dating from this period. In the
main, Schopenhauer involves himself hardly at all in discussing
substantive issues in Hegel's philosophy. Sometimes he
complains at his mangling of the German language, but
mostly he indulges over and over again in pungent and
brilliantly written abuse. So, even considering the later
Schopenhauer as an 'opponent of Hegel' produces little of
philosophical interest. (Consequently, when Karl Popper uses
Schopenhauer as a 'man of supreme integrity' to bear witness
against Hegel, it is Popper's own case against Hegel that is
devalued.[33])

In its final form, Schopenhauer's great book presents itself
to the reader as falling fairly squarely within a Kantian frame
of reference. Not only the lengthy Appendix, but the opening
book, where Schopenhauer presents a transcendental idealist
account of the world as representation, leave no doubt about
the work's Kantian origins. Though I too shall give Kant
prominence, I have tried to enter a number of qualifications to

---

[32] Cf. Hübscher, *Biographie*, p. 51. Schopenhauer's accompanying comment was:
'I would not have kept this so long, if I had not known that you read such books as
little as I do.'

[33] *The Open Society and its Enemies*, vol. 2, *Hegel and Marx*, p. 32.

the view that *The World as Will and Representation* grew plainly and simply out of Kant. First, Schopenhauer accepts the basic structure of Kant's Critical philosophy, but always on his own terms. He was never a disciple, and never subordinated his own ends to those of Kant. Secondly, he does not merely produce his book as a reaction to Kant's, as he accused Fichte of doing. He tries to reflect his own direct experience of the world within the terms provided by Kantian philosophy. Thirdly, he had learned far more from Fichte and Schelling than he ever acknowledges (or perhaps ever realizes), so that to some extent his vision of Kant is mediated by them. And finally, there is a lesson to be learned from Schopenhauer's involvement with Plato and the Hindus. The point is not that Schopenhauer was influenced by them in anything like the way he was by Kant; rather, it is that they excited him because they fuelled his thinking about the suffering of life, the illusory nature of the world, and the ways in which both might be overcome by a kind of insight that went beyond empirical reality. And it is these concerns that remain the real driving force of his philosophy. In his presentation, the starting-point (Book I of *The World as Will and Representation*) is firmly Kantian, and firmly epistemological. This has made it easy to expect Schopenhauer to 'fit in' rather too neatly as the next station on the grand epistemological line stretching back to Descartes,[34] when in fact the story is more complicated than that. If we assume that Schopenhauer's main motivation as a philosopher was to be a Kantian epistemologist, the remaining three-quarters of the work can begin to seem a bizarre, quirky abberration. It is much better to realize that the doctrine of the will, with its attempt to give an account of the nature of human beings, their relation to the world, and the possibility of their happiness within it, was not merely a secondary by-product of the Kantian doctrine of representation, but a centre of Schopenhauer's concern in its own right. I hope to bring out the extent to which Schopenhauer tried to marry his own vision of the world, and of the self's relation to it, with the Kantian epistemology-based account, and to reveal the great

[34] Magee does this explicitly (*Schopenhauer*, pp. 15, 56 ff.). To a lesser extent, such an approach is implicit in the emphasis of both D. W. Hamlyn and Patrick Gardiner in their respective books entitled *Schopenhauer*.

tensions that arose for him as a result. In particular, I argue, the Kant-inspired notion of the pure knowing subject is fundamentally at variance with the account of the self as manifestation of will. Schopenhauer does not succeed in producing a smoothly unified system of thought; he does not fit neatly into any 'tradition' that existed before him, and he would be less historically important and less philosophically interesting if he did. Having entered these qualifications, we may now turn to examine the Kantian influence on Schopenhauer in some detail.

2

Kantian Objects

KANT couched his philosophical claims in terms of the position which he called *transcendental idealism*. From the start, there was controversy about the viability and the correct interpretation of the position with this name. Today many people would say that transcendental idealism in any form, and certainly in Kant's, is untenable; yet recently others have thought it defensible if one reinterprets Kant's utterances in one way or another. The debate occasionally threatens to dissolve into the question of whether we should clean up Kant by removing transcendental idealism, or rescue transcendental idealism by leaving Kant behind. But, after more than two hundred years, a prior task is still to seek an understanding of what Kant's transcendental idealism is. For us this is especially important because Schopenhauer also describes himself as a transcendental idealist, and presents himself as Kant's direct successor. My immediate aims, then, are restricted to the following: to give a brief account of Kant's position from the way he sets it out; to indicate some of the problems that attach to it; and to try to make clear the view taken by Schopenhauer.

SPACE, TIME, AND THE CATEGORIES

The first claim that is of importance to us concerns the ideality of space and time. This was Kant's way into transcendental idealism, developed in his *Inaugural Dissertation* of 1770,[1] and placed at the beginning of the *Critique of Pure Reason*, in the section entitled 'Transcendental Aesthetic'. Here, as indeed throughout, Kant makes prominent use of the term *Vorstellung*, which has a very wide sense, and might be paraphrased as

---

[1] *De mundi sensibilis atque intelligibilis forma et principiis*, sect. 3 (Ak 2 pp. 398–406).

'something that comes before, or is presented to, the mind'.
'Presentation' would in some ways be the best translation, but
I follow the current practice of most translators and use
'representation'. (This standard rendering might be taken,
wrongly I think, to commit Kant to an inherently relational
understanding of any *Vorstellung* as a 'representation *of*'
something else, in the way that a portrait is. In favour of it as a
translation, on the other hand, is Kant's Latin equivalent for
Vorstellung, which is *repraesentatio*.) Representation, for Kant,
is taken very widely. Thus everything that comes before
the mind, be it a sensation, a perception, a thought, a
consciousness of oneself, or an awareness of space and time, is
a representation. Sometimes a representation is explained
as a 'modification of the mind' belonging to 'inner sense',
the temporal sequence of a subject's mental states (A99).
Elsewhere, and without making a clear distinction, Kant
requires us to understand the term as signifying whatever
content or object is thought of or perceived when the mind is
in a state of perceiving or thinking. But in general—or so I
shall assume for the moment—to call something a representation is to indicate its mind-dependence, whether as state of
mind or as content presented to it.

Now in the Transcendental Aesthetic, Kant contends that
space and time are not 'determinations or relations of things',
but that they belong only to the 'subjective constitution of our
mind', or that they are forms of representation only, not of
things in themselves. In a series of compressed arguments,
Kant seeks to show, first, that our representations of space
and time are a priori, in that (*a*) they do not come before the
mind by way of abstraction from experience of temporally and
spatially organized objects and events, but are preconditions
of any experience of such objects and events; and (*b*) we
cannot imagine the absence of space and time—experiencing
them is necessary if we are to experience anything. Secondly,
he seeks to show that our representations of space and time
are what he calls intuitions (*Anschauungen*), which is to say that
they are presented to the mind as particular objects of
immediate awareness. In the case of space, he adds an
argument to the effect that the synthetic a priori truths of
geometry could not be truths about space unless we had 'pure

intuition' of space; unless, that is, we had awareness of space as a particular, 'prior to any perception of an object' given to us by the senses.

The conclusions that follow these arguments—and it is with these conclusions that I shall be most concerned—are surprisingly far-reaching. Space is to be viewed as nothing more than the form of outer sense, a condition of our becoming aware of particular objects which we 'represent as outside us'; time as nothing more than the form of inner sense, a condition of our becoming aware both of particular states of ourselves and of external objects. But, Kant thinks, before we can regard them as such, we must embrace the conclusion that space and time originate *in the subject of experience*. We must hold that we bring space and time, as subjective forms, to bear upon the raw material (whatever it is, of which more later) that we receive through the senses. Kant's message seems pretty clear in such passages as this: 'if we remove ourselves as subject, or even merely the subjective constitution of the senses in general, the whole constitution and all the relations of objects in space and time, nay space and time themselves, would vanish. As appearances they can exist, not in themselves, but only in us' (A42/B59).

Schopenhauer is highly impressed both with these conclusions and with the supporting arguments. The latter we need not discuss in detail. They have been given sufficient attention by recent commentators on Kant, who have often found them unconvincing as arguments. Schopenhauer's appraisal here is at the other extreme: 'The Transcendental Aesthetic is a work of such outstanding merit that it alone would suffice to immortalize Kant's name. Its proofs have such complete power of conviction that I number their propositions among the incontrovertible truths.' Yet Schopenhauer goes on to put his finger accurately on the most powerful assumption behind the Aesthetic as a whole:

The fact—strictly proven by Kant—that we are conscious a priori of a part of our cognitions [*Erkenntnisse*], admits of no other explanation than that these constitute the forms of our intellect: indeed, this is not so much an explanation as the clear expression of the fact itself. For a priori means nothing other than 'not gained by way of experience, and hence not come into us from without'. But what is present in the intellect, but has not come from without, is just that which belongs originally to the intellect itself, its own nature [*Wesen*].[2]

Kant argues that space and time are 'a priori representations', presupposed by, rather than derived from, experience. But in order to support the transcendental idealist conclusion that space and time are forms of intuition having their origin in the subject of experience, Kant must rely on the principle which (in the Preface to the second edition of the *Critique*) he puts forward as his 'new method of thought', namely, 'that we can know a priori of things only what we ourselves put into them'.[3] In the Preface, Kant famously advocates a change in our point of view (the 'Copernican revolution'), whereby instead of assuming that our knowledge must conform to objects, we assume that objects must conform to our knowledge, or to our mode of representation. Here, he states, this procedure is presented hypothetically, but in the main text 'it will be proved, apodeictically not hypothetically, from the nature of our representations of space and time and from the elementary concepts of the understanding'. If we make the initial assumption that objects must conform to our modes of representation, then we can show that on this assumption, synthetic a priori knowledge is possible. But what we are promised is, in effect, a demonstration that objects must indeed conform to our modes of representation. What we get in the Aesthetic is the claim that the spatio-temporality of objects is to be explained by their conforming to those two modes of our representation which Kant calls the forms of intuition. And why? Because our representations of space and time are intuitions, and because our representations of space and time are a priori, rather than belonging to the received, a posteriori content of our awareness. All this can demonstrate what is promised—namely, that objects must conform to certain of our modes of representation—only if the subjective origin of space and time is assured. Unless space and time have been shown to be modes of our representation, the Aesthetic takes Kant no nearer to his intended proof that objects must conform to our modes of representation. But

[2] *W*1 p. 537 (437).
[3] Passages referred to in *KdrV* Preface (B), Bxviii, Bxvi, Bxx, Bxxii n.

what guarantees that they *are* modes of our representation seems to be simply the assertion that we can know a priori of things only what we contribute to them.

Here Kant would argue that, given that his theory of the ideality of space and time provides a *possible* account of the nature of our knowledge of space and time, we must consider whether there are any possible alternative accounts. The alternatives with which he was familiar were the traditionally opposed Newtonian and Leibnizian accounts, according to which space and time were, respectively, absolutely real 'containers' of spatio-temporal objects, or sets of relations between objects. According to either view, space and time exist in absolute independence of the experiencing subject. For Kant this indicates that a priori knowledge of space and time should be ruled out. But since, as he sets out to establish, we have such knowledge, no view of space and time as absolutely real is tenable. Once again, however, to dismiss the Newtonian and Leibnizian alternatives in this way, Kant must rely on the crucial principle that we can know a priori of things only what we ourselves put into them. So Schopenhauer is right to see this principle as of fundamental importance to Kant, though he is perhaps uncritical in his acceptance of its role.

As one might expect from his approbation of Kant, Schopenhauer never questions the truth of the doctrine that space and time are subjective forms of intuition rather than determinations of things in themselves. This is an important part of his transcendental idealist position, though (as we shall see in Chapter 5) he primarily advances more general considerations in favour of transcendental idealism, and turns to space and time only when it is a question of specifying the details of the manner in which our representations are ordered.

With the complementary theory in Kant, however, according to which objects of our experience are ordered by a priori *concepts*, Schopenhauer has a number of serious quarrels. Indeed, he regards the whole of the Transcendental Analytic in the *Critique*, where that theory is developed, as begotten of deep confusions—a fact to which (he thinks) its tortuous exposition bears witness. Before we see why, let us attempt a

brief account of Kant's doctrines. Our having experience, or
(equivalent to this (B147)) empirical knowledge, requires for
Kant that we have both *intuitions* and *concepts*. Cognition of
objects requires the presence-to-mind both of particular
objects of awareness, and of general concepts whose function
is to apply to more than one particular. Correspondingly,
Kant discerns in the mind a capacity for receiving particular
items of awareness, and an active capacity of thought which
produces concepts applicable to classes of objects, and
operates with them by combining them to make judgements.
Objective experience would be impossible, Kant maintains, if
either of these mental functions was lacking. Without reception
of particular items of awareness, there could be no empirical
content for our mental operations to work on. However much
we might combine concepts in thought, we would not then
have experience of objects. Without the application of
concepts and the formation of judgements, we might receive
all manner of data through the senses, but they would lack
that organization, introduced by conceptual thought, which is
requisite for us to build up a picture of an objective world. In
the words of one of Kant's more succinct and frequently
quoted sentences: 'Thoughts without content are empty,
intuitions without concepts are blind' (A51/B75).

Having established to his satisfaction that space and time
are the a priori forms of intuition, Kant moves on to consider
whether there are a priori forms of thought. Is there anything
which necessitates our having certain fundamental modes of
applying concepts to the multiplicity of data of which we can
be aware? Kant's answer is that there are certain 'categories of
the understanding', or 'a priori concepts'. These are a priori
firstly in the sense that they constitute the ways in which
objects must be ordered, as a condition of our having
experience—or objective knowledge—at all. But, as in the
Transcendental Aesthetic, Kant also uses 'a priori' to indicate
that the categories are of subjective origin. Thus, in the first
edition at any rate, he is led to say that 'the order and
regularity in the appearances, which we entitle *nature*, we
ourselves introduce. We could never find them in appearances,
had we not ourselves, or the nature of our mind, originally set
them there' (A125). Because the order, or unity, exhibited by

the phenomena we call nature 'has to be a necessary one', Kant continues, 'that is, has to be an a priori certain unity of the connection of appearances', it must have 'subjective grounds . . . contained a priori in the original cognitive powers of our mind'. The general picture that emerges is of the mind being constrained to contribute certain basic modes of organizing the material received in empirical intuition (or present in a priori intuition) so as to make possible an experience of objects, as opposed to a mere play of subjective states of mind. Very detailed interpretation, especially of the notoriously difficult Transcendental Deduction of the Categories, risks being controversial and would be out of place here. But a few words must be said about what is, after all, at the very core of the *Critique of Pure Reason*.

Kant is clearly concerned to establish a close connection between self-consciousness and objectivity, though it is less clear precisely what this amounts to. Indeed, it may be that Kant has no one single view, but rather a host of problems, illuminated (or not!) from a variety of angles. Among recent interpretations of the Transcendental Deduction, the most popular has probably been that associated particularly with Strawson,[4] according to which the Deduction's main thrust is to argue from self-consciousness to objectivity. Kant's major project is presented as that of 'answering the sceptic aout the external world'. The sceptic claims: 'Anything beyond my subjective experience, and in particular the supposed existence of an independent world of objects, is in doubt.' Kant supposedly answers this by means of an argument which shows that it is a condition of one's having 'subjective experience' that one can ascribe a multiplicity of mental states to oneself in a unified manner, and that it is a condition of this that one perceives items which constitute an objective world— objects enjoying an order and regularity independent of that exhibited by one's own experiential states. It is undeniable that Kant wishes to oppose scepticism about external objects, but questionable whether Strawson's interpretation of Tran- scendental Deduction as such is accurate. As others have pointed out,[5] in seeking the conditions of experience, Kant

---

[4] Cf. P. F. Strawson, *The Bounds of Sense*, part ii, ch. 2.
[5] Cf. Ralph C. S. Walker, *Kant*, pp. 75–6. On problems of interpretation here, see

starts out with a conception of experience that tends to equate it with 'empirical knowledge' (B147, within the Deduction itself), or 'objective knowledge of appearances' (B246). And he surely aims to finish up with the *conclusion* that concepts of the understanding apply a priori to all objects of possible experience, rather than with the Strawsonian conclusion that all experience must be objective. Intentionally, I think, Strawson abstracts from the Deduction a direction of argument moving from self-consciousness to objective experience—which is undoubtedly there in the Kantian structure—at the expense of a more careful look at the whole web of arguments, tangled or otherwise, which surrounds it.

Kant certainly wants to establish the converse of the Strawson argument along the way—namely, that self-consciousness is a condition of the objectivity of experience. Suppose that I, an experiencing subject, am confronted with an ordinary physical object—a pencil, an apple, or a house; part of Kant's project is to discover what is required for me, the subject, to be able to be aware of any such object *as an object*, or as something distinct from my representations (taken here as mental states which form a sequence immediately present to my mind). What is required is, first, that all the various representations be united in one consciousness, since otherwise no single objective 'picture' could arise. However, the way in which the received 'data' are combined is not dictated by the data, but is actively imposed by the mind. So the unification of representations in one consciousness must proceed according to rules set by the mind of the subject, and such rules are the concepts with which the subject thinks. Thus, for Kant, experience of objects (in general) is the being present of a multiplicity of representations to one single subject which organizes that multiplicity in certain ways. Some of these ways are merely contingent. The concepts *pencil*, *apple*, and *house* provide rules for tying representations together in ways which are dispensable; there could still be objective experience without our structuring the data in precisely these ways (even if the data remained the same). But Kant is more interested in necessities. First, he wants to establish the necessity for a concept of an

Karl Ameriks, 'Recent Work on Kant's Theoretical Philosophy', *American Philosophical Quarterly* 19 (1982), pp. 12–13.

object in general, and secondly, to argue that a limited number of categories provides slightly more specific ways of structuring the data which are necessary to any possible experience.

There are passages where Kant explicitly equates (*a*) the relation of a subject's mental states to an object distinct from them, with (*b*) the subject's awareness of the unity of its own consciousness throughout the multiplicity of its mental states. For example, at B137, after discovering that '*object* is that in the concept of which the manifold of a given intuition is *united*', we are told quite clearly that 'it is the unity of consciousness that alone constitutes the relation of representations to an object'. Kant's thought on the unity of consciousness has been highly influential, despite its impenetrability. (Schopenhauer, who had sat through Fichte's lectures, would have been inclined here to substitute 'because of' for 'despite'.) In outline, Kant argues, as I have mentioned, that if representations are to amount to an experience of objects, they must be brought into a unity by a single mind. But he further suggests that such a unity requires that the subject of representations be self-conscious, or at least have the possibility of becoming self-conscious, with regard to each of its representations. Precisely what unifies a set of representations is, for him, there being a subject which can ascribe them severally to itself. The notion of a representation which no subject could think of as being its own Kant regards as highly problematic: 'The "I think" must *be able to* accompany all my representations; for otherwise something would be represented in me which could not be thought at all, which amounts to the representation's being either impossible, or at least nothing for me' (B131–2). For a representation to belong to me is for me to be able to ascribe it to myself, i.e. for any representation to belong to any subject is for that subject to be able to ascribe it to itself self-consciously. But if representations are to be united into a single set capable of constituting a picture of an objective world, they must belong to a single subject. So a condition of a set of representations constituting a picture of an objective world is that a single subject be able to ascribe to itself each of the set.

This, then, is the direction of argument which I suggested was clearly present in the Transcendental Deduction: from the objectivity of experience to self-consciousness of the subject of experience. This self-consciousness is qualified in certain important ways, and goes under the imposing name of the 'transcendental unity of apperception' (among others). To see how Kant strives towards the conclusion that the categories apply to all objects of experience, we have to note the great stress laid on the unification of representations in one consciousness. I am conscious of myself as that which unites representations, Kant says. Such consciousness is not a matter of my passively receiving some data, but rather is a consciousness of myself as actively combining representations —what Kant often refers to as the act of _synthesis_. Arguing that the capacity for combining representations (in judgements) must precede experience as its condition enables Kant to reach his conclusion that there must be a priori concepts (the categories) governing any combination of representations which is to amount to objective experience. Representations could not constitute objective experience without being united in one consciousness, nor, according to Kant, without there being fundamental rules originating in the subject that govern the combinations of representations made. Much in Kant's account is tenuous and ill-defined, especially when it comes to the doctrine of synthesis, but I do not propose to enter into intricacies which are not relevant here. I shall have more to say in Chapter 3 about Kant's conception of the self, whose consciousness he makes here the highest principle of his philosophy.

So far we have not mentioned any of the specific categories, which is not wholly out of tune with Kant's procedure: although he announces the categories in a list before the Transcendental Deduction, that section itself is an attempt to establish their legitimacy in entirely general terms. What, then, of the individual categories? Kant arrives at them by setting out twelve functions of judgement, which are supposed to constitute the most fundamental formal characteristics of all thought, and then argues that to each there corresponds a concept 'applying a priori to objects of intuition in general', in which case it is called a category.[6] In common with many

---

[6] Cf. A70–83/B95–109.

commentators, Schopenhauer regards the list of twelve categories and its derivation from the functions of judgement as highly artificial. Most of the twelve have come to be treated as having little importance, the two great exceptions being those of *substance* and *causality*. As we shall see, Schopenhauer even argues that one of these is dispensable.

The role of substance and causality can be understood as that of providing an answer to either of the following two questions: (1) What modes of organizing the multiplicity of data do our minds necessarily engage in as a condition of our having experience? (2) What, as a condition of our having experience, are the necessary modes of organization of a world of objects? Among answers, strong contenders at least have seemed to be: (1) Our minds must combine the data such that properties and states are ascribed to a substance whose properties and states they are, and such that all changes are understood to be causally conditioned; or (2) a world of objects must consist of enduring substances, and must be subject to causal laws. Without even going into any of the qualifications needed to round out these claims, we must remark on the obvious gap between the first question–answer pair and the second. To put it crudely, the first pertains to the way we must think the world is, the second to the way the world must be. The suggestion has been made recently that transcendental arguments (which attempt to demonstrate a conclusion on the grounds that, unless it were true, experience would not be possible); can only take us as far as conclusions about how we must think the world is, given that we make certain other judgements, such as 'I have experiences'.[7] Now whether or not this is so, it should be noted that, for Kant, it is transcendental idealism that is supposed to bridge the gap— or rather, is supposed to preclude the gap's arising. To the extent that he is an idealist, Kant's answer to the question: How must we think the world is?, is in effect an answer to the question: How must the world be? as well.

If we are asking about how the world constituted of empirical objects must be, Kant takes the question to be one about what is 'appearance' for us. Thus, if he can establish

[7] See especially Barry Stroud, 'Transcendental Arguments', *Journal of Philosophy* 65 (1968), pp. 241–56.

that space, time, and the categories are the necessary forms governing the way the world must come before us in appearance, he will claim to have arrived at knowledge of how the world must be. This is, moreover (according to Kant), the only 'knowledge of how the world must be' that we could attain, because if we demand knowledge of how things in themselves must be, beyond any possibility of our experiencing them, we demand the impossible. Here, then, we see the crucial role of Kant's transcendental idealism, which claims that we have no knowledge of things in themselves, and that (in Kant's wording) 'all objects of any experience possible to us are nothing but appearances, that is, mere representations'.[8] We shall in due course examine what these claims amount to, and what Schopenhauer made of them. But before tackling such wider issues, there are a number of detailed areas of divergence between the two philosophers which are no less important.

Schopenhauer's attitude to the intricate procedure of the Transcendental Analytic is iconoclastic. For example, eleven of the twelve categories are simply to be thrown out. Only *causality*, Schopenhauer argues, need serve as a subjective form of the understanding. For *substance*—or, as he would rather say, *matter*—is reducible to spatial, temporal, and causal concepts; and as for the rest of the categories, their only *raison d'être*, Schopenhauer finds, is the entirely spurious one of filling a vacancy in the grand architectonic scheme. More heretical still, in his view (which I discuss more fully in Chapter 5) that the way in which our minds connect up representations as cause and effect is not a matter of its operating with concepts at all, but a matter of immediate intuition.

The removal of the sole remaining category from the realm of concepts reflects a wider conviction on Schopenhauer's part that Kant neglects intuition at the expense of conceptual thought, and that he gives no adequate account of either because he never makes a clear enough distinction between intuitive and abstract cognition (*anschauliche und abstrakte Erkenntnis*[9]). To appreciate the most serious aspect of the

---

[8] Cf. A490–1/B518–19.   [9] *W*1 p. 530 (431).

problem here, consider the question: What is the content of intuition? Space and time are its forms, but what is it that they give form to? I somewhat glibly wrote earlier of the 'data' of experience, but it is unclear what this is supposed to amount to. Schopenhauer considers, quite reasonably, that the content of intuition should be particular spatio-temporal objects (or, in the case of time alone, particular temporally organized representations). Kant in fact says, if somewhat obscurely, that in intuition we are *given an object* (A50/B74). But (Schopenhauer's line of thought goes), this surely means that empirical intuition, with its given content organized according to a priori forms, is sufficient for experience of objects. Indeed, empirical intuition is just that: experience of particular spatio-temporal objects. And yet Kant goes to great lengths to show that thought involving the use of concepts is required in addition to intuition before we can have experience of objects. Schopenhauer's criticism seems to miss the possibility that a spatio-temporally ordered multiplicity (or 'manifold') of intuitions could be present to a subject's mind without constituting an experience of objects as such, and that concepts and judgement might be needed for this. But he would no doubt claim to be going simply by what Kant says, the implication of which is often that intuition is sufficient to present an object (in some sense) before the mind.

Schopenhauer in fact charges Kant with the sins of omission and self-contradiction. Kant omits to give any account of the content of intuition; all we get is 'the oft-repeated, empty phrase: "The empirical in intuition is *given* from outside" '.[10] But, more seriously, he is involved in an all-pervading contradiction over experience of objects. Schopenhauer cites a dozen passages in the *Critique of Pure Reason* and in other works which present the following picture: the function of the understanding is to think, employing concepts, and not to receive intuitions, whereas intuition proceeds without any admixture of thinking. From this it follows, Schopenhauer suggests, 'that this intuited world would be there for us even if we had no understanding'. He then goes on to cite more than a dozen further passages which represent

[10] Ibid. p. 538 (438).

Kant's overall doctrine of the understanding, where, as we have seen, experience of objects is made conditional on the unification of representations according to concepts, and even 'the *intuition* of objects' is said to stand necessarily under the categories. Filtering out the surrounding exposition, we thus find two trends in strident opposition to one another. It is clear that the latter trend predominates, and that Kant places his emphasis on the categories as conditions of experience of objects. To follow this through consistently, however, he would again have to make much clearer exactly what the content of intuition as such is when considered independently of what the understanding does to it.

After marshalling his evidence, Schopenhauer makes a judgement of Kant which shows some insight:

I am convinced that this proven contradiction, which runs through the whole of the Transcendental Logic, is the real reason for the great obscurity of exposition in that section. For Kant was obscurely conscious of the contradiction, struggled internally with it, yet would or could not bring it clearly to consciousness, and so concealed it from himself and others, circumventing it by all manner of devious routes.[11]

Schopenhauer is of the opinion that instead of bringing thought into intuition and intuition into thought (as he puts it[12]), Kant should have made a clear division between intuitive cognition (immediate perceptual awareness of particular spatio-temporal objects) and abstract cognition (discursive thought by way of the combination of concepts). The former, for Schopenhauer, does not presuppose the latter, while the latter (discursive thought) is the function of reason (*Vernunft*) properly so called. The view is not without its problems, which I shall discuss in Chapter 5, but it has the virtue of clarity when compared with Kant's. It also has the truly destructive consequences for Kant's architectonic which Schopenhauer claims: we no longer need the majority of the Transcendental Analytic, for example. At one point Schopenhauer goes so far as to suggest that the only real discovery in the first *Critique* is that we have a priori knowledge of space and time, and that the whole doctrine of a priori concepts

---

[11] *W*1 p. 542 (441–2).   [12] Ibid. pp. 539–40 (439).

applying to objects of experience is in there primarily for the sake of symmetry: by hook or by crook, Kant has to find a priori concepts that will balance out the a priori forms of intuition.[13] Though this is an over-cynical caricature, it does correspond to the direction of Kant's development from the *Inaugural Dissertation* to the *Critique*, and provides a tempting explanation of why parts of the Analytic seem so strained. Another clarification Schopenhauer introduces concerns the demarcation between reason and understanding—something which Kant never achieved very neatly, despite his declared intentions. Schopenhauer reserves the title *reason* for the capacity to operate with concepts, yet retains for the understanding a (concept-free) role in empirical intuition. So, by the same move empirical cognition is purified of any taint of strictly conceptual thought, and reason and understanding are very clearly separated.[14] One corollary of this is Schopenhauer's distinctive view that animals are equipped with understanding, enabling them to perceive a world composed of particular spatio-temporal objects, but that reason and discursive thought involving general concepts are exclusively human propensities.

It is thus a heavily modified version of Kant's transcendental idealism that Schopenhauer presents. Even in the case of the one retained category, causality, he rejects Kant's attempted proof of its a priori nature in a well-argued passage in *On the Fourfold Root* (sect. 23). In the Second Analogy, Kant undertook, as Schopenhauer succinctly puts it, a 'proof of the a priori nature and necessity of the law of causality from the fact that only through its mediation did we recognize the objective succession of changes, and that to that extent it was a condition of experience'.[15] Seeking to clarify the distinction between subjective and objective succession of representations, Kant introduces his two examples of the house and the ship. My representations of a house, as I survey it visually from top to bottom or vice versa, have no necessary ordering and so do not form an objective sequence. In contrast, my representations of a ship moving steadily downstream occur in an irreversible, or necessary, order. The argument then strives towards the

---

[13] Ibid. pp. 550–1 (448–9).
[14] Cf. ibid. pp. 531–2 (431–2); ibid. sect. 8. [15] *VW* p. 106 (128).

conclusion that such a distinction between subjective and
objective time-orderings could not be made at all if change
were not invariably an instance of an effect's following a cause
with necessity derived from a law.

Schopenhauer makes two interesting points against Kant.
One is that it is arbitrary to view the 'house' example as an
instance of purely subjective change and the 'ship' example as
one of objective change. Both can equally be seen as courses of
events in which objects change with respect to one another. In
the first case, it is merely the eye itself that moves relative
to the house. To say that the order of representations here is
irreversible amounts to no more than saying that it is up
to me, the subject controlling the eye, which sequence of
objective movements it makes. But, given that a particular
sequence occurs, that is no less irreversible than the progress
of the ship relative to the observer. Again, I cannot reverse my
representations in the ship case, but I might if I had a power
to move the ship analogous to my power to move the eye. The
force of this objection is debatable. What is at stake is not
whether objective change of one thing with respect to another
is occurring, but whether the sequence of my representations
constitutes an experience of objective change occurring. In the
house case it does not; in the case of the ship it does. That I
might also perceive the objective sequence of movements of
my eye with respect to the house does not seem immediately
relevant. Still, the objection at least shows that Kant needs to
be more precise about the distinction he is trying to illustrate
with these two examples.

In his second point, Schopenhauer alleges that Kant
regards all objective succession as an instance of the cause–
effect relation, and states that to hold this would be absurd.
The sequence of notes in a piece of music, and the following on
of night and day are cases of objective succession where the
succeeding items are not related as cause and effect. They may
indeed depend on a common cause, and this may have
something to do with the objectivity of their succession, but it
is true that Kant does not give an adequate explanation of
this. It is doubtful whether Kant intended to equate 'sequence
with consequence' as starkly as Schopenhauer alleges; but if
this is not what he intended, the text of the Second Analogy

leaves even more doubt as to how the route from the possibility of objective succession to the necessity of the principle of causality is to be traced. Schopenhauer's objection is a decisive one against what is perhaps the most straightforward reading of a not very straightforward argument.

KANT AND BERKELEY

Aside from the modifications just dealt with, Schopenhauer follows Kant in being an idealist and in calling his position 'transcendental idealism'. So we must at last broach the question of what this position involves, and indeed, ask whether it involves the same for both thinkers. That it does not is suggested initially by a difference in their attitudes to the reputed arch-idealist, Berkeley. For while Kant expends considerable energy in trying to convince his readers that his own kind of idealism is opposed to that associated with Berkeley, Schopenhauer regards Berkeley as an important forerunner. It is worthwhile examining this issue, because it is close to the heart of Schopenhauer's interpretation of what transcendental idealism is—an interpretation which I shall argue to be broadly correct.

Berkeley had maintained that whatever we perceive through the senses (including what are ordinarily called 'bodies') was an *idea*, and that ideas existed only inasmuch as they were perceived by, or were in, some mind. The existence of bodies is for him equated with their being perceived; and 'all those bodies which compose the mighty frame of the world, have not any subsistence without a mind'.[16] It is not easy to state precisely what Berkeley means by 'in the mind' when he claims that bodies exist only thus, nor have commentators been able to agree on a stable interpretation of 'idea'. This, however, is not the place to settle such issues: I shall simply assume that to call the world of bodies a collection of ideas is to assert that it is mind-dependent, and hence that, according to Berkeley's central thesis, without minds to which they are present, there would be no bodies. Schopenhauer's summary

---

[16] *Principles of Human Knowledge*, 6 (*Philosophical Works*, pp. 78–9).

of Berkeley is often limited to the bald and anachronistic comment that he discovered the truth of 'No object without subject', and did nothing more of any lasting merit.[17] However, this fuller statement does reflect Berkeley's central point quite well:

Berkeley achieved the position of genuine idealism, i.e. the realization that the spatially extended world, that is, the objective, material world in general, as such exists only in our *representation*; and that it is false, indeed absurd, to attribute to it, *as such*, an existence outside all representation and independent of the knowing subject, in other words to assume matter as simply present with an existence in itself.[18]

Schopenhauer makes the implicit assumption that Berkeley's 'idea' and Kant's *Vorstellung* are equivalent terms—unwisely, given the different historical circumstances in which the terms are used. Nevertheless, provided it is true that 'idea' and *Vorstellung* agree in involving a commitment to mind-dependence, we need not quarrel with Schopenhauer's version of Berkeley for the purposes of discussing his view that Kant and Berkeley are similarly committed to idealism.

It would be wrong to suggest that the views of Kant and Berkeley coincide in fine-grained detail. On the other hand, the slogan 'No object without subject' seems too ill-defined to provide scope for a useful discussion. There is, however, an idealist thesis which is clear and still very general in character, namely: if there were no subject of experience, spatio-temporal particulars of the kind which we experience would not exist. It is the attribution of this general idealist thesis to both Kant and Berkeley that I shall discuss.

The claim leaves open (*a*) whether the objects of *my* experience depend for their existence on *my* experiencing them—which in fact neither Kant nor Berkeley hold; and (*b*) whether the objects that any human subject experiences are some kind of strictly mental entity (sensation, sense-datum, mental act or state)—which it is at best dubious whether Kant or Berkeley ever believed. It further leaves open (*c*) whether objects depend for their existence on actually *being perceived*—which Berkeley does hold, but Kant does not; and

---

[17] *W*1 pp. 533–4 (434).　　　[18] *W*2 p. 11 (4).

finally, (*d*) whether the required perceiver may be an infinite spirit, or only a human or sufficiently similar subject—over which, again, Berkeley and Kant differ crucially. Thus the idealist view under discussion is that there are particular spatio-temporal things which we experience, but that their existence depends on there being some subject of experience. I shall refer to this sometimes as the thesis of the mind-dependence or subject-dependence of empirical things, but it will be important to remember that it is a general thesis which is non-committal on each of the points (*a*) to (*d*). In terms of the general idealist thesis, I shall argue that Schopenhauer's assessment of Kant and Berkeley is broadly right.

There is no mention of Berkeley in the first edition of the *Critique*—what led Kant to his disclaimers was the interpretation placed on the first edition, in particular by two of its reviewers, Garve and Feder, who attacked it for espousing an idealist position of the Berkeleian kind.[19] Kant considered this a radical misunderstanding, and was provoked into clarifying his position. His *Prolegomena* accordingly contains passages which take his critics to task, contrasting his own theory, transcendental (or 'critical') idealism, with idealism pure and simple, and the same stance is continued in the second edition of the *Critique*. The clearest complaint against Berkeley is that he denies the existence of a world of bodies altogether, and holds that the senses convey to us only an illusory appearance. Thus Kant urges us not to confuse him with the kind of idealist who asserts that there are none other than thinking beings, and who holds 'the rest of the things which we believe we perceive in intuition' to be 'only representations in the thinking beings, to which in fact no object existent outside them corresponds'. Idealism can be defined, Kant says, as the casting of doubt on the existence of things—something which it never occurred to him to do. Berkeley, on the other hand, is alleged to be a true idealist according to the definition: he 'degrades bodies to mere illusion', and 'maintains that space, with all the things of which it is the inseparable condition, is something which is in itself impossible; and he therefore regards the things in space as merely imaginary entities'. In

---

[19] For references to the reviews, see *Prol.* pp. 372 ff., and Arnulf Zweig (ed.), *Kant: Philosophical Correspondence 1759–99*, pp. 98–105.

another place Kant suggests that all idealists, including
Berkeley, believe that 'all knowledge through the senses and
through experience is nothing but illusion, and only in the
ideas of pure understanding and reason is truth'.[20]

Kant is of course wrong to suggest that Berkeley denied the
existence of a world of bodies, and there has been much
debate as to how he came to do so. There are two factors
which support the claim that Kant was genuinely in error
about this aspect of Berkeley's views, but not through his own
fault. One is that his knowledge of Berkeley's earlier views was
based on a translation of the latter's *Dialogues* in which
'material substance' was systematically rendered as 'corporeal
substance', and 'idea' as 'thought'.[21] This had the effect of
exhibiting to the reader a Berkeley who denied the existence of
a world of bodies, and of hiding the extent to which, for him,
the senses conveyed the truth. Kant's remark that idealists
make truth reside not in the senses but in the understanding is
now thought to reflect his reading of the later *Siris*.[22] But the
translation of the *Dialogues* would make it easy for Kant to
read some such doctrine into the earlier Berkeley's position as
well. Kant was correct in his claim that Berkeley denied
absolute space (*à la* Newton),[23] but again he was misled into
thinking that the *Dialogues* provided for no real things in space
at all. The second factor is that of the wider understanding of
Berkeley in Kant's day. A standard definition of idealists had
been given by Christian Wolff: 'those who allow only an ideal
existence of bodies in our minds, and thus deny the real
existence of the world and of bodies', and Berkeley was cited
as an instance. In fact, Berkeley had an almost universal
reputation in the eighteenth century as a sceptic, a solipsist,
and an absurd denier of the existence of the world.[24] This

---

[20] Cf. *Prol.* pp. 288–9, 293, 374; *KdrV* B71, B274.

[21] The translation was by Eschenbach, and was in fact derived not from Berkeley's
original, but from a French translation of it. See G. J. Mattey, 'Kant's Conception of
Berkeley's Idealism', *Kant-Studien* 74 (1983), p. 164. (Schopenhauer, incidentally,
read English fluently, and occasionally cites from an English edition of Berkeley
(e.g. *W*i p. 71 (38)). This may partly explain his more sympathetic treatment of
Berkeley.)

[22] Cf. *Siris*, 264.

[23] Cf. Berkeley, *De motu*, 52 ff. (*Philosophical Works*, pp. 222–3).

[24] A reputation well documented by H. M. Bracken in *The Early Reception of
Berkeley's Immaterialism*. The Wolff definition is in *Psychologia rationalis*, sect. 36.

prevailing view conspired with the distortions of the available texts to obscure Berkeley's true position from Kant.

In this light we can understand why Kant was so shocked to be associated with Berkeley, and why he was so anxious to clear his name. But if we look beyond Kant's misunderstanding, Schopenhauer's contention seems to be right: whatever their further differences, Kant argues for the dependence on the subject of the world of objects in space and time, and he is unjust to Berkeley who had argued for the same basic point. Schopenhauer sees clearly that rather than denying the existence of a world of objects, Berkeley contends that such a world really exists, but that it is mind-dependent. He wants to be both an idealist and an empirical realist, to put the matter in Kantian terms. I shall discuss Schopenhauer's interpretation of Berkeley no further, and I shall now turn to the more complicated matter of his reading of Kant.

For Schopenhauer, Kant is an idealist in that he asserts the mind-dependence of the empirical world. But he discerns a marked difference between the first edition of the *Critique*, where he finds Kant to be genuinely committed to idealism, and the second, where he finds great confusion. For a long time Schopenhauer was familiar with the *Critique* only in the second and subsequent editions, and thought that on idealism it completely fudged the issue: it seemed idealist, but it was simultaneously entangled in a vehement denial of that very position. When he later had access to the first edition, he found it in this respect a vastly superior work in which Kant, 'with just as much decisiveness as Berkeley and I, explains the external world lying before us in space and time as mere representation of the subject that knows it'. He admires particularly some of the passages that Kant saw fit to eliminate:

Thus, for example, he says there on p. 383, without reserve: 'If I take away the thinking subject, the whole world of bodies must fall away, as it is nothing but the appearance in the sensibility of our subject and a species of its representations.' But the whole passage pp. 348–92 [in the Paralogisms section], where Kant presents his decided idealism with great beauty and clarity, was suppressed by him in the second edition, while on the other hand a number of pronouncements were brought in which conflict with it. In this way

the text of the *Critique of Pure Reason*, as it was in circulation from
1787 to 1838, became disfigured and spoilt, and the book became a
self-contradictory one, whose sense, for this very reason, could not
be completely clear and intelligible to anyone.[25]

Schopenhauer goes on to relate how he prevailed upon
Rosenkranz to print the neglected first-edition version in the
collected works published in 1838.

Kant himself tells us that there are no doctrinal changes
between the two editions, only changes of exposition.[26] What
he regards as the only really new section is indeed entitled
'Refutation of Idealism', but the newness is supposed to
concern solely the 'method of proof'—again no substantive
change of mind. It is worth noting that the Refutation is not
directed at Berkeley, but at the oddly named 'problematic
idealism of Descartes', which holds the existence of objects in
space outside us to be doubtful and indemonstrable. Berkeley's
idealism, by contrast, is called 'dogmatic' in considering the
existence of things in space as 'false and impossible', or
'imaginary'. Kant remarks fairly casually at B274 that the
view here attributed to Berkeley has already been undermined
in the Transcendental Aesthetic. He thinks that his doctrines
of space and time are sufficient to dispense with dogmatic
idealism, and, if they are, then Berkeley has effectively been
dealt with in the first edition, despite not being mentioned
there by name. Schopenhauer's view does not go directly
against Kant's claim that he did not change his mind between
editions; rather, it is the view that Kant set out to be an idealist,
but in the second edition, while still professing to be an
idealist, his nerve failed him under the threat of assimilation
to Berkeley. Our task will be to assess both the claim of an
initial commitment to idealism, and that of a subsequent
failure of nerve.

Let us turn first to the Paralogisms section of the first
edition of the *Critique*. It is not surprising that Schopenhauer
mentions this section specifically—to this day, that is the
standard move of those who press for an assimilation of Kant

---

[25] *W*1 p. 534 (435). According to Hübscher, Schopenhauer first read the first
edition of *KdrV* in 1826 (Cf. *HN*5 p. 94).

[26] *KdrV* Bxxxvii–xlii, and esp. Bxxxix–xli n., on the 'Refutation of Idealism'.

and Berkeley.[27] Here Kant is criticizing a kind of idealism, which he calls *empirical* idealism, and contrasting it with his own *transcendental* idealism. The view criticized is clearly that of scepticism about the existence of a world of objects 'outside us', and the grounds for criticism are these: if you suppose (1) that external objects must be something existing (as things in themselves) in total independence of us, and (2) that we could never experience such objects, only their effects in us, then since (3) for any effect, the inference to any thing's having been its cause is uncertain, you arrive at the view (4) that the existence of external objects is uncertain. Step (1) is what Kant calls *transcendental realism*, and step (4), to which it leads, is the sceptical position he here calls *empirical idealism*.

Kant does not question steps (2) and (3), and thus presents (1) as an erroneous assumption that leads inevitably to (4): 'It is the transcendental realist who later plays empirical idealist' (A369), and, even more clearly, 'transcendental realism necessarily becomes embarrassed, and sees itself forced to give way to empirical idealism' (A371). The way to avoid the sceptical, empirical idealist conclusion of step (4) is thus to deny (1), the transcendental realist assumption. And the position which makes this denial is precisely Kant's own transcendental idealism, 'the doctrine according to which we view [appearances] as a whole as mere representations and not as things in themselves' (A369). In denying that external objects are transcendentally real, which is to say, in affirming that they are our representations, we deprive scepticism about external objects of any foundation. This is spelt out at A370–1:

I am conscious of my representations; therefore they exist as do I myself who have these representations. But external objects (bodies) are mere appearances, and so nothing other than a species of representations, whose objects are something only through these representations, but nothing in separation from them. Therefore external things exist just as much as I myself exist, and both indeed

[27] For a detailed 'assimilating' reading of the Fourth Paralogism, see Colin Turbayne, 'Kant's Refutation of Dogmatic Idealism', *Philosophical Quarterly* 5 (1955), pp. 225–44. Also Norman Kemp Smith, *A Commentary to Kant's Critique of Pure Reason*, pp. 304–5. H. E. Allison, 'Kant's Critique of Berkeley', *Journal of the History of Philosophy* 11 (1973), pp. 48–9, concedes an affinity between Kant and Berkeley here, in the context of an article arguing for their differentiation.

on the immediate testimony of my self-consciousness, only with this difference: that the representation of myself, the thinking subject, is related merely to inner sense, while the representations which denote extended beings are related to outer sense as well.

The identification of external objects with 'representations' surely has some parallel with Berkeley, as does the assertion that external things certainly exist on the testimony of my self-consciousness. Cf. Berkeley's *Third Dialogue*, 238: 'I am as certain as of my own being, that there are bodies or corporeal substances (meaning the things I perceive by my senses)'. Berkeley's diagnosis of the origins of scepticism is also the same: 'You indeed said, the reality of sensible things consisted in an *absolute existence* out of the minds of spirits, or distinct from their being perceived. And pursuant to this notion of reality, you are obliged to deny sensible things any real existence: that is . . . you profess yourself a *sceptic*' (*Second Dialogue*, 211–12). In fact, the *Dialogues*' character Hylas (here addressed) is a transcendental realist who later plays empirical idealist.

Kant claimed that he had suppressed the Paralogisms section because of the 'misunderstandings' that it had suffered. But it surely cannot be a misunderstanding to view this argument against scepticism as relying on a thesis of the mind-dependence of external objects. For the argument could not work at all unless the representations that were known with immediate certainty were mind-dependent, and unless external things were explicitly equated with representations. Nor is the mind-dependence thesis confined to the suppressed Paralogisms section. Kant writes earlier: 'We have then meant to say: that all our intuition is nothing but the representation of appearance . . . and that if we remove ourselves as subject, or even merely the subjective constitution of the senses in general, the whole constitution and all the relations of objects in space and time, nay space and time themselves, would vanish' (A42/B59). Here is an assertion of the mind-dependence of the spatio-temporal world, which as such fits securely into Kant's argument about the nature of space and time. This passage was not omitted, or even altered, in the second edition. We have some evidence, then, that Kant was a genuine idealist in the first edition of the *Critique*, and some that he retained a commitment to idealism in the second.

Whatever the affinity of his idealism with Berkeley's, there is nevertheless a major difference between the two, which Kant himself emphasizes. For Berkeley, unlike Kant,

regarded space as a mere empirical representation which, like the appearances in it, only becomes known to us, together with all its determinations, by means of experience or perception; I on the contrary show first that space . . . with all its determinations can be known by us a priori because it . . . is present in us before all perception or experience as a pure form of our sensibility, and makes possible all intuition of sensibility, and hence all appearances. From this it follows that as truth rests on universal or necessary laws as its criteria, experience with Berkeley can have no criteria of truth because nothing was laid (by him) a priori at the ground of appearances in it, from which it then followed that they are nothing but illusion; whereas for us space and time . . . prescribe their law a priori to all possible experience, and this yields at the same time the sure criterion for distinguishing truth in it from illusion.[28]

Kant commonly says that his transcendental idealism is combined with empirical realism. Space and time are said to be both transcendentally ideal and empirically real. This means that while (for the purposes of explaining the possibility of a priori knowledge of objects) we must regard space and time as subjective forms existing only in us, space and time are the criteria of the reality of objects of experience. Thus space is the condition under which we must, the only condition under which we can, experience objects 'outside us': 'Apart from space there is no other subjective representation, referring to something *outer*, which could be called objective a priori [*die a priori objektiv heissen könnte*]' (A28/B44). As one recent commentator has put it: 'spatial characteristics are regarded as inseparable from body, while the so-called secondary qualities are "connected with the appearances only as effects accidentally added by the particular constitution of the sense organs". This is essentially the Cartesian, Lockean, Newtonian doctrine, now viewed as holding within the phenomenal realm.'[29]

It would not be entirely wrong, therefore, to say that Kant

[28] *Prol.* pp. 374–5.
[29] Allison, 'Kant's Critique of Berkeley', p. 55.

operates with a distinction between primary and secondary representations, the former not pertaining to things in themselves, but being the necessary forms of representation. We can interpret some of the accusations against Berkeley in the light of this distinction. Kant thinks that it is a consequence of not making this distinction that one cannot speak intelligibly of our experiencing real objects existing outside us—unless, that is, one ascribes an absolute, transcendentally real existence to space. Since Berkeley also rejects absolute space, as Kant rightly thought, he is left with no adequate criterion of the reality of external objects. Let us consider Berkeley's well-known contention that the traditional distinction between primary and secondary qualities is unfounded: this leaves us with a position in which both colours and spatial qualities are 'ideas existing in the mind' (cf. *Principles*, 9), and in which no distinction is made between those ideas which are necessary to something's being a body existing outside us, and those which we contingently have through experience and the mere habits of thought associated with it.

We can see Kant as striving to answer the question: What makes representations objective? in a way that is fundamentally idealist (in holding the objective world to be mind-dependent), but radically distinct from Berkeley in using the a priori modes of organization among representations to provide a criterion of their objectivity. This is essentially Schopenhauer's interpretation, but it is also put forward clearly in this passage from Kant's disciple, J. S. Beck:

Even if we assume that the *Critique* should not even have mentioned the distinction between things in themselves and appearances, we should still have to recall that one must pay attention to the conditions under which something is an object. Appearances are the objects of intuition, and they are what everybody means when he speaks of objects that surround us. But it is the reality of just these objects that Berkeley denies and that the *Critique*, on the other hand, defends. If one once sees that space and time are the conditions of the intuiting of objects and then considers what the conditions of the thinking of objects are, one sees easily that the dignity that representations achieve in referring to objects consists in the fact that the synthesis of the manifold is thus thought as necessary.[30]

[30] Letter from J. S. Beck, 10 Nov. 1792 (Zweig (ed.), p. 195).

The notion of representations 'achieving the dignity of referring to objects' occurs in the *Critique* itself at A197/B242: Beck is undertaking to summarize Kant's own position. According to Beck, the 'dignity' of objectivity is to be achieved without invoking anything other than mind-dependent representations. Like Kant, he takes Berkeley effectively to deny that the mind-dependent can be objective, but goes on to suggest that, in the Kantian view, the necessary modes of synthesis according to space, time, and the categories provide the criterion of objectivity, without any need to invoke mind-transcendent objects. Later in the same passage Beck in fact glosses 'necessary' with 'valid for everyone' (*für jedermann gültig*): the necessary conditions of thinking and intuiting are supposed to provide intersubjective criteria for something's being an object.

Kant speaks of a criterion for distinguishing truth from illusion (*Kriterium . . . Wahrheit von Schein zu unterscheiden*). It should be clear that he is not looking here for an epistemological criterion, which one could apply to certain experiences one had in order to ascertain whether they were veridical. If an experience has spatial characteristics—if it is *as of* a spatially extended object, for example—this is insufficient in itself to mark it as a veridical experience. When Kant says that spatiality is a criterion of the reality or objectivity of representations, 'criterion' should be taken in a *constitutive* sense: being spatial is constitutive (or at least co-constitutive with other things) of being objective. Knowing this will not of itself distinguish illusory from veridical representations, but this is not the point that Kant is trying to make. His point is rather that *it could not be an illusion that objective reality as such was spatial*. If all representations are merely empirical, nothing can serve to delineate the way in which the world that falls within our representations must be. For an idealist who tries, without any a priori rules, to give an empiricist account of the way ideas are collected together to result in experience of objects, which objects there are will have to depend entirely on contingent facts about how our minds work. The only possible idealist account of objectivity is that which uses a priori rules for the combination of representations, and thereby (the claim is) discerns the necessary structure of the (mind-dependent) world.

Thus Kant has pin-pointed a crucial difference between himself and Berkeley here. Even if Berkeley does not want to deny the existence of a world of bodies (as, in fact, he does not), he has no mechanism within the field of ideas with which to discriminate the features constitutive of objective reality from those which merely depend on contingent properties of the mind to which the ideas are present. It might, however, be objected that Kant has overlooked Berkeley's most important candidate for the role of constitutive criterion of reality, namely, God. In the *Dialogues*, Berkeley's world of real things exists independently of its being perceived by you or me, but in the mind of God. God causes (or wills to bring about) ideas in us in regular ways—which Berkeley equates with the laws of nature—so as to give us a perception of the real world. It is their relationship to God, both as their perceiver and as their cause, that constitutes the reality of ideas for Berkeley. Is Kant further in error about Berkeley, then, to the extent of missing the role of God in his argument?

The answer to this is that Kant is well aware of this aspect of Berkeley, and critical of it. Another name which he attaches to Berkeley's position is 'visionary' or 'mystical' idealism, and the introduction of God into the argument will help us to see why. Kant addresses the problem in this passage which he wrote while preparing *Prolegomena* but left out of the final text:

Berkeley found nothing permanent, nor could he find anything that the understanding grasped in accordance with a priori principles; therefore he had to look for another [kind of] intuition, namely the mystical intuition of the divine ideas, which [presupposes] a twofold understanding: one which combines appearances in experience, the other which has cognition of things in themselves. I need only one sensibility and one understanding.[31]

If the ideas which constitute reality simply exist in God's mind, this can be of no consequence for the achievement of objectivity on the part of the ideas in our various human understandings. No individual human subject could *have* God's ideas. But this leaves us without anything to say about the objectivity of *our* ideas, so we find ourselves forced to provide for some kind of access to God's. We might posit a

[31] Ak. 23 p. 58.

cognitive access to the divine mind by which we attain to knowledge of things in themselves, but it is unclear how this adjunct to our normal cognitive abilities (derided by Kant as 'mystical intuition') is supposed to operate. So, the price of making objectivity cognizable is an *ad hoc* and mysterious facility for knowing the contents of God's mind. One might object that it would be sufficient if we could know the pattern of God's causing of our ideas, rather than have insight into the divine ideas themselves. But then the even more straightforward objection by Kant would be that God's mind lies beyond the world of appearance, and is therefore unknowable to us. If their resulting from the action of God's mind in a certain way is to be definitive of the objectivity of our ideas, then objective reality once again transcends our minds completely, and we can know only its effects.

In the light of our discussion, Kant's claim to superiority over Berkeley can be summarized as follows. Kant's account provides for a constitutive criterion of the objectivity that can be achieved by our representations. It does so by (*a*) relying on nothing external to the realm of representations themselves, and (*b*) seeking those a priori rules which must govern the experience of any subject. Berkeley, on the other hand, faces the dilemma either of making objectivity depend solely on contingent facts about our minds (which Kant thinks deprives it of its right to be called objectivity at all), or of seeking his criterion beyond representations in the realm of the thing in itself. The latter option makes objectivity transcend our minds altogether, unless we add the purely 'mystical' notion of an insight into the divine. Kant makes objectivity both accessible to our minds without any mystical intuition, and independent of our own particular subjective constitution. In all this, however, we have not seen Kant retract his claim that the world of spatio-temporal objects depends on the subject. At the time of his strongest criticisms of Berkeley, he can even write the following: '[S]pace and time, together with everything they contain, are not things of their properties in themselves, but merely belong to appearances of them; and so far I am of one confession with the idealists' (*Prolegomena*, 374). So he even seems to concede precisely the affinity with Berkeley which Schopenhauer maintains.

The account I have given goes beyond what Schopenhauer says, but the framework of it can be found in his appraisal of the relationship between Kant and Berkeley. As Schopenhauer sees it, Berkeley should be given credit for the general thesis that the world of objects is the world as representation for a subject, and Kant should be regarded as making this same general point—clearly when he had no fear of assimilation to Berkeley, less so when it became imperative to him to counter that assimilation. (Here there is some over-simplification: as we shall see, Kant's commitment to idealism was never entirely clear cut.) Kant does differ from Berkeley in Schopenhauer's view, but not over this general idealist claim. Rather, he differs in that he *adds* to the general claim the doctrine of a priori representations, which delineates the necessary modes of organization of any set of representations which are to achieve the dignity of referring to objects, or, in other words, to count as experience of an objective world. As Schopenhauer puts it: 'Thus to the simple or *Berkeleian* idealism, which concerns the *object in general*, is directly added the *Kantian*, which concerns the specially given *mode and manner* of being an object.'[32]

For Schopenhauer, the sum of the addition Berkeley + Kant is transcendental idealism. It allows empirical reality to the material world we experience, in that this world necessarily and for all subjects conforms to the subjective conditions of space, time, and causality. Yet the world so organized does not exist independently of 'the subject' and the conditions of its experience. In view of what we have seen, this is at least a highly plausible interpretation, and I would argue that it is broadly correct. Kant might not be satisfied with it, and might wish to differentiate himself from Berkeley in more radical ways; but in Berkeley's view, as we shall see, Kant's attempts to do this only bring out inconsistencies which threaten to explode transcendental idealism completely. This brings us to Schopenhauer's contentions about the confused position reached in the second edition of the *Critique*. To appreciate his interpretation here we will need a closer examination of the Kantian *thing in itself*. Schopenhauer admires Kant's distinction

---

[32] *W*2 p. 15 (8).

between appearance and thing in itself as being one of his greatest achievements; but that does not prevent him from criticizing the role which the latter is made to play. In the next section, I will look at Schopenhauer's allegation that the way in which Kant uses the thing in itself signals a failure of his idealist nerve, and I will also consider a more recent suggestion that the distinction between thing in itself and appearance can be read so as to fend off Kant's assimilation to Berkeley altogether.

APPEARANCE AND THING IN ITSELF

Returning to Schopenhauer's characterizations of the fundamental idealism which he thinks is shared by Kant and Berkeley, we may note that he is careful to ascribe a subject-relative existence only to 'the visible world', or to 'the external world that lies before us in space and time'. He says—with a perhaps puzzling emphasis—that it is false to attribute to the spatially extended world *as such* an existence independent of the knowing subject. The point is that idealism is a claim that the things that compose the *empirical* world are mind-dependent, and this is the world of spatio-temporal objects that we experience. But it is not incompatible with this idealism that there should be things that exist *in themselves*. To see this, one need only think of Berkeley. He is an idealist because he holds that the entire *sensible* world has no 'subsistence without a mind'. But there are for him entities other than those that compose the sensible world, namely, finite minds or spirits and the infinite spirit, God. These entities do not depend for their existence on being perceived or even being perceivable (since for Berkeley they are neither), and they are in Kant's sense things which have an existence in themselves.

For Schopenhauer too the empirical world is mind-dependent, consisting of representations—but far from excluding the world's existing in itself, Schopenhauer's philosophy has at its centre the claim that the world in itself is will. Thus as far as the Schopenhauerian view is concerned, to say that Kant shares a commitment to idealism with Berkeley is not to deny his right to a belief in things in themselves, i.e. things whose existence is mind-dependent. But could he, or anyone, have a consistent position composed of idealism about the empirical world and a belief in things in themselves? There are two basic thoughts here which are coherent and compatible. One is that ultimately the world ('what there is') cannot depend for its existence on its falling within the conditions of our having knowledge of it. The other is that the experienced order of spatio-temporal objects must fall within these conditions, and does only have a subject-dependent existence. The two thoughts taken together yield the view that the experienced order of spatio-temporal objects is not what there (ultimately) is. But this is surely what Kant himself intends when he says at A26/B42 that 'It is . . . solely from the human standpoint that we can speak of space, of extended things, etc.'

This combination of views must be handled fairly carefully, and there are two mistakes which destroy its coherence altogether. One is to try to maintain that the very same particulars which exist 'only as representations' exist also in themselves. The other is to try to assure the objectivity of our experience by linking it causally with things in themselves. Either of these moves conflicts with the idealist claim about the objects of the empirical world. The first does so through the straight contradiction of asserting that the same objects both are and are not mind-dependent. The second misapplies the principle of causality beyonds the limits of possible experience, and at the same time undermines the idealist claim that an account of our knowledge of objects can be given wholly from within the resources of the subject. In his own system, Schopenhauer is scrupulous to make neither mistake. The criteria of identity of objects—space and time—strictly lapse beyond the limits of experience, and so there is no plurality of things in themselves that are identical, or even isomorphic with spatio-temporal objects. It is simply an undifferentiated 'reality as a whole', simply 'the world', that can be conceived as existing in itself. Furthermore, the undifferentiated world as it is in itself is not causally related, for Schopenhauer, to the representations we experience. Rather, it merely 'manifests' or 'objectifies itself' as these representations, or objects. Kant, however, does make both mistakes, and this is the basis of Schopenhauer's claim that he fails to produce a coherent position.

What Kant should have done, according to Schopenhauer, was to ally himself explicitly to Berkeleian idealism, which was incorporated in his own transcendental idealism. Instead, he is bent on showing that his theory has a place for external objects, in a way that Berkeley's does not. In the last section it was suggested that, assuming 'external things' to be empirical objects, Kant can differentiate between himself and Berkeley over the objectivity of external things without invoking anything mind-transcendent. However, Kant has a tendency to view his task as that of showing that he affirms the existence of *things in themselves*, conceived as causes of our sensations— and it is precisely this way of introducing the thing in itself that Schopenhauer finds to be 'in undeniable contradiction to the decisive idealist view so clearly expressed in the first edition'.[33] This, he adds, was no doubt the reason why Kant suppressed the Paralogisms section, and came out so strongly against Berkeley.

Some passages can indeed be found where Kant seems to rely on things in themselves to distinguish himself from 'the idealists'. Thus in *Prolegomena* he says that making the so-called primary, as well as the secondary, qualities belong to appearances does not detract from the *existence of the thing*, 'but shows only that we cannot through senses have any cognition of it at all as it is in itself' (289); and later (314–15) he argues in the same vein that:

If, as is proper, we regard the objects of the senses as mere appearances, we are thereby conceding at the same time that a thing in itself lies at their ground, although we do not know it as it is constituted in itself, only its appearance, that is, the way in which our senses are affected by this unknown Something.

Kant wants to assure us of the existence of a thing in itself causing in us those appearances which, as an idealist, he equates with the world of objects. The resulting confusion into which he falls is exemplified in this longer extract from *Prolegomena*:

---

[33] *W*1 p. 535 (435).

[Unlike the 'idealists' I say that] there are things given to us as objects of our senses existent outside us, only we know nothing of what they may be in themselves, but are acquainted merely with their appearances, that is, the representations which they cause in us by affecting our senses. Consequently, I do indeed admit that there are bodies outside us, that is, things which, though unknown to us in respect of what they may be in themselves, we are acquainted with through the representations which their influence on our sensibility brings about, and to which we give the name of body—a word signifying merely the appearance of that to us unknown, but none the less real, object. Can this be called idealism? It is surely the very opposite.[34]

Though the confusion Schopenhauer complained of was specifically in the second edition of the *Critique*, it is certainly apparent in this troubled passage. Kant still asserts, as a genuine idealist should, that bodies are appearances in us; but at the same time he goes out of his way to assert the existence of a real but unknown object as the cause of those same appearances. To be an idealist, one must (for whatever reason) have confidence in the possibility of accounting for objectivity wholly within the realm of the mind-dependent. Kant now reveals that he lacks that confidence. He is not a consistent idealist, therefore, despite retaining an official commitment to certain aspects of idealism. This is the core of Schopenhauer's criticism of Kant.

For Schopenhauer, the introduction of things outside us with an existence in themselves, causing representations in us, is doubly mistaken. It is mistaken because it conflicts with a decisive idealism; but, more seriously, it is mistaken because it had always been the 'major defect', which Kant should have removed, and which 'was soon recognized as the untenable point in Kant's system'.[35] Kant's contemporary, Jacobi, was famous for his remark about the doctrine of affection by the thing in itself: '*without* this presupposition I could not enter the system, and *with* this presupposition I could not remain in it'.

---

[34] *Prol.* p. 289. I follow Adickes' reading of Kant's 'things' here as things in themselves (*Kant und das Ding an sich*, p. 31). This interpretation is resisted by Gerold Prauss, *Kant und das Problem der Dinge an sich*, pp. 202 ff., who takes them to be 'empirical things'. Prauss concedes that Kant becomes confused, however, and explains this through Kant's not having fully understood his own position.

[35] *W*I p. 535 (435–6).

Schopenhauer's teacher G. E. Schulze, had also attacked the same doctrine in his work *Aenesidemus*—and others who claimed in one way or another to be following Kant, such as J. S. Beck and Fichte, had argued that transcendental idealism had to get rid of this piece of baggage if it was to be made viable.[36]

Schopenhauer's view is thus not unusual, but he gives a concise summary of Schulze's objection:

Kant founds the presupposition of the thing in itself, albeit in a manner concealed beneath all kinds of twists and turns, on an inference in accordance with the law of causality—the inference that empirical intuition, or more correctly the *sensation* in our organs of sense from which the intuition proceeds, must have an external cause. But now, according to his own correct discovery, the law of causality is known to us a priori, is consequently a function of our intellect, and therefore of *subjective* origin. Moreover, the sensation itself, to which the law of causality is here applied, is undeniably *subjective*, and finally even space, in which by way of this application we place the cause of the sensation as an object, is an a priori given, and thus a *subjective* form of our intellect. Hence the whole of empirical intuition remains throughout on a *subjective* basis, as merely a process in us, and nothing entirely distinct from and independent of it can be introduced as a *thing in itself*, or demonstrated as a necessary precondition.[37]

Things in themselves, which must be non-spatial, non-temporal, and subject to none of the categories, do seem spectacularly unsuited to their proposed role. In particular, the principle of causality has no application, in Kantian thought, beyond the limits of possible experience, while the thing in itself is beyond those limits. Kant cannot coherently claim that things in themselves cause anything, and therefore cannot claim that they cause sensations in us, let alone assert their existence on the basis of such a claim. Someone might

[36] Cf. Friedrich Heinrich Jacobi, *David Hume über den Glauben*, in *Werke*, vol. 2, p. 304; Beck's letter to Kant, 20 June 1797 (Zweig (ed.), pp. 227–31); and (also from 1797) Fichte's Second Introduction to the *Wissenschaftslehre*, *Sämtliche Werke*, vol. 1, pp. 480–6. The translation of the *Wissenschaftslehre* by Peter Heath and John Lachs (*The Science of Knowledge*) includes both introductions, and gives marginal references in line with the *Sämtliche Werke*.

[37] *W*1 pp. 535–6 (436). At *PP*1 p. 105 (90), Schopenhauer makes reference to pp. 374–81 of Schulze's *Aenesidemus* as the source of the objection discussed in the text.

reply that Kant can allow the intelligibility of the causal claim about things in themselves, but that what he cannot do is present it as a claim to knowledge. This, however, scarcely leaves him in a tenable position, for now, like the transcendental realist, he will end up having to profess himself a sceptic with regard to his own claim. On the other hand, the notion of affection, in which the senses passively receive some modification, is too central to be abandoned by Kant—and it depends on the assumption that something causes this received modification. From the outset, therefore, Kant must have some view as to what this cause is.

If Kant's position thus amounts to idealism combined with the awkward claim of affection by things in themselves, Schopenhauer's assessment is highly attractive: the position is incoherent, and it would have been better to stick consistently to a 'decided idealism'. But before accepting Schopenhauer's judgement, we should consider whether there might not be a different way of interpreting transcendental idealism which both saves it from inconsistency and clearly removes it from the Berkeleian camp.

It has been suggested recently that Kant's all-important distinction between appearances and things in themselves should be viewed not as a distinction between two kinds of object, but as a distinction between two different aspects under which objects can be considered.[38] There are many passages which suggest this 'two-aspect' view. In the Transcendental Aesthetic, to take just one example, we find at B69 that: 'in appearance the objects, nay even the properties that we ascribe to them, are always regarded as something actually given—except that in so far as this property depends only on the subject's mode of intuition in the relation of the given object to the subject, this object as *appearance* is distinguished from itself as object *in itself*.' The 'two-aspect' view allows Kant to make his central points about the limitations of knowledge, but without the troubling ontological claim that there is a species of things existing outside space and time, not

---

[38] Cf. H. E. Matthews, 'Strawson on Transcendental Idealism', in Ralph C. S. Walker (ed.), *Kant on Pure Reason*, pp. 132–49; H. E. Allison, 'Things in Themselves, Noumena, and the Transcendental Object', *Dialectica* 32 (1978), pp. 41–76; Prauss, *Kant und das Problem der Dinge an sich*.

subject to causality, and so on. On this reading, Kant's position can be paraphrased thus: we can have knowledge of things only if we consider them under a certain restricted aspect, namely, as they can appear to us in experience. We cannot have knowledge of things if instead we consider them apart from the conditions of our experiencing them—if we consider them, that is, 'in themselves'. Nevertheless, that things have an existence in themselves is something we can coherently think; and, moreover, it is something we must be able to think if we are to consider them as appearances. Recognizing the 'restricted aspect' under which we can have knowledge of them presupposes the conceivability to us of their not being subject to this restriction.

The hope is that, interpreted in this way, Kant's idealism can affirm (unlike Berkeley's) that empirical things exist in themselves—and can do so without generating those mysterious entities 'things in themselves', for which he has so often been pilloried. It is, it must be said, unclear to what extent the 'two-aspect' interpretation corresponds with Kant's own under-standing of the appearance/thing-in-itself distinction. At best, he wavers between the 'two-aspect' and the 'two-object' readings. Let us consider the following extracts from letters he wrote in 1783:[39] 'all objects that can be given to us can be interpreted in two ways: on the one hand as appearances; on the other hand, as things in themselves'. And, only nine days later:

the a priori knowledge of which we are capable extends no farther than to objects of a possible experience, with the proviso that this field of possible experience does not encompass all things in themselves; consequently there are other objects in addition to objects of possible experience—indeed they are necessarily presupposed, though it is impossible for us to know the slightest thing about them.

There are numerous passages which support, more or less clearly, each of the opposed readings. But let us disregard Kant's waverings for the moment, and adhere for the sake of argument to the 'two-aspect' reading. Let us accept that the point of the appearance/thing-in-itself is to make an

---

[39] Letters to Garve (7 Aug. 1783) and Mendelssohn (16 Aug. 1783) (Zweig (ed.), pp. 103, 106–7).

epistemological claim: considered in one way the world is unknowable, considered in another it is knowable. Calling things 'appearances', then, is innocent of any connotation of their mind-dependence, and merely serves to remind us that the things of which we can claim any knowledge are things *as they appear to us*, or empirical things. In support of this we may recall the extract from Beck in the previous section, in which he takes it for granted that what everyone means by 'appearances' is 'the things that surround us'. (Or as T. D. Weldon puts it: 'it makes sense to say that *Erscheinungen* have backs and insides; that they are solid and obey the laws of mechanics'.[40]) Accepting all this, do we have enough to discredit Schopenhauer's view that Kant is committed to a basic idealism that is also found in Berkeley? H. E. Matthews clearly thinks so:

Whereas Berkeley [in his doctrine of ideas] was making an ontological point about the types of things there are, Kant was making an epistemological point about the limits of human knowledge. . . . If this is right, then Kant does not mean by an 'appearance' or a 'representation' a particular type of *thing*, such that it only exists in the mind. To talk about 'appearance' is rather to talk about things *from a particular point of view*, namely, as they are experienced by human beings. In saying 'objects are nothing but representations', Kant is not denying, as Berkeley would, the existence of extra-mental objects, but simply asserting that the way we experience objects, and the kind of knowledge we can have of them, depends on the nature of our human experience.[11]

However, I believe it is important to question an implicit assumption made in this passage, which is that 'appearance' and 'representation' can be treated as synonyms. Kant very often writes that things are 'appearances, i.e. representations', thereby suggesting a mere terminological equivalence. But there are a number of places where he sets store on the supposedly substantive thesis that appearances are our representations, and even sets out to prove it. This would be absurd if the two were merely interchangeable terms. So what can Kant mean by the claim that appearances are our

[40] 'Kant's Perceptual Vocabulary', in Terence Penelhum and J. J. MacIntosh (eds.), *The First Critique*, p. 35.
[11] Matthews, 'Strawson', pp. 136–7.

representations? I suggest that he must mean that empirical objects (the ordinary bodies that surround us) are mind-dependent, at least in the sense of the general idealist thesis, and thus parallel with Berkeley's view that real things are ideas.

Now it will be protested that Kant's use of the term 'representation' is so vague that such a thesis cannot be pinned on him—in particular, that he does not distinguish clearly between a state of mind and the content of such a state. This is perfectly true; but rather than fending off the 'mind-dependence' charge, it points to the nub of the problem. Vague though Kant's conception of representations is, nearly everything he says about them commits him in a general way to their mind-dependence. He speaks continually of 'mere' representations, explains representations as modifications or determinations of the mind, says that they are 'in us' and that they have only 'subjective reality'. Furthermore, he tells us that it is impossible for representations to exist outside the mind, and a contradiction to suppose that 'mere representations exist before they are encountered in the representing faculty'.[42] I am not suggesting that Kant must be read as equating empirical things with mere modifications of the mind (any more than Berkeley must be read that way). In this context, representations are objects present to the mind which provide the content of thoughts and perceptions. Yet Kant gives us no grounds whatever for supposing that such objects or contents could exist independently of the mind. Nowhere are we assured that there is a special class of representations which are unlike 'mere' representations, in that they exist, or can exist, outside the mind, and have objective reality. Indeed, he frequently asserts precisely of empirical objects that they are 'mere representations'. Therefore, the 'two-aspect' view, if correct, does not falsify Schopenhauer's claim that Kant was an idealist in a way parallel to Berkeley. For the two-aspect view merely establishes that to claim (1) that we can have knowledge only of appearances, not of things in themselves, implies no ontological duality. But Kant's unsatisfactory conception of representations is such that the distinct claim

---

[42] *Prol.* p. 342. For other attributions, see *KdrV* A491 f./B519 f., A98–9, A101, A197/B242, A372–3.

(2) that appearances are our representations, is most plausibly read as committing him to the general idealist thesis of the mind-dependence of the empirical objects that surround us.

Clearly, if we read (2) in this idealist way it is incompatible with the 'two-aspect' interpretation of (1). For if appearances are dependent for their existence on some subject, it cannot be that under a different aspect they exist independently of the subject. And yet it is precisely this inconsistent position that we find Kant putting forward sometimes. An example is this passage which is present unchanged in both editions (A42/B59):

> We have then meant to say: that all our intuition is nothing but the representation of appearance, that the things which we intuit are not in themselves what we intuit them as being, nor their relations constituted in themselves as they appear to us, and that, if we remove ourselves as subject [*unser Subjekt*] or even merely the subjective constitution of the senses in general, the whole constitution and all the relations of objects in space and time, nay space and time themselves, would vanish. As appearances they can exist, not in themselves, but only in us. How it may be with objects in themselves and apart from all this receptivity of our sensibility remains completely unknown to us. We know nothing but our way of perceiving them, which is peculiar to us. . . .

Here Kant says that the things we intuit, which are appearances that can exist only in us, are, unbeknown to us, constituted in such-and-such a way in themselves. However, if they can exist only in us, they cannot be constituted in any way in themselves. Kant seems, as Schopenhauer alleges, to be an idealist who is also committed to a view that conflicts with idealism—and here he manages it within the same sentence. The presence of this passage in the first edition is enough to discredit Schopenhauer's suggestion that Kant was a decisive idealist at one stage, and a lapsed or confused idealist later. The inconsistency was there from the beginning. Rather than being a committed idealist who changed his mind radically, Kant was an idealist whose position was not coherent. When confronted with the charge of Berkeleianism, he did not change his basic position, but went out of his way to emphasize those elements in it that conflicted with idealism, while keeping the major idealist elements intact. Thus the substance of Schopenhauer's criticism remains true, even if his joy at discovering the first edition of the *Critique* had blinded him to its defects.

Another objection to the two-aspect view is that it fails to remove the problem about things in themselves as causes. For even if it makes sense to say that empirical things, considered apart from the conditions of our experiencing them, cause sensations in us, it is extremely doubtful whether Kant could say this. The category of causality must surely apply only to objects considered as they can appear to us, and Kant would not have wanted to make the causal connection between object and sensation a matter that was not empirically discoverable to us. Things in themselves cannot be causes without major surgery to Kant's conception of transcendental idealism.

Why not make empirical objects the causes of those sensations out of which our objective experience arises (as Beck in fact urged)? It is this move which Kant appears to resist in (for example) the passage from *Prolegomena* discussed above. Empirical objects are themselves representations in us, according to transcendental idealism, so if they are made the causes of our sensations, nothing mind-transcendent enters the picture of objective experience. Had he been consistently idealist, this consequence would not have troubled Kant, but he seems to have feared that unless some wholly mind-transcendent real object played a role in the account of experience, he would be open to the charge of denying the reality of things altogether. According to this view, he retreats from idealism under pressure not to lapse into the absurdity credited to him under the title of 'Berkeleianism'. And this is precisely the reason that Schopenhauer gives for Kant's insistence on the thing in itself in a causal role: 'The causal law is subjective in origin, as is the sensation itself, and moreover one's own body, inasmuch as it appears in space, already belongs in the class of representations. But Kant's fear of Berkeleian idealism prevented him from admitting this.'[13]

This is, I suggest, an acute insight into the difficulties that Kant makes for himself. He clearly feels that only a

---

[13] *W*1 p. 548 (447).

thoroughly realist conception of the real can clear him of the charge of denying real things altogether. Thus it must be part of what constitutes appearances that they are appearances of something beyond themselves. Only if there is a Something that is unknown but has an existence that transcends the mind can reality be safely assured to things. Clearly, Schopenhauer is right in maintaining that this signals a failure of nerve for someone who set out to be an idealist, for, as we have seen, the materials already exist within Kant's idealism for him to construct a reply both to the charge of having denied the existence of empirical things, and the charge of being no nearer to a criterion of objectivity than Berkeley was. I conclude that Schopenhauer's account of the relationship between Kant and Berkeley is correct on all of the following points:

1. In a number of passages in the first edition of the *Critique*, Kant propounds an idealism which shares with Berkeley the general thesis that the empirical world is mind-dependent.
2. Kant's repudiation of Berkeley is unfair to Berkeley.
3. Kant adds to the general thesis of mind-dependence his account of the a priori structures constitutive of anything's being an object.
4. Later, Kant remains officially committed to the same idealist doctrine as before.
5. Kant also explains objective experience as essentially involving the causation of appearances by things in themselves, which conflicts with his idealism.
6. After the criticisms of the first edition, he uses this realist doctrine to resist assimilation to Berkeley.
7. The resulting position is incoherent: an idealism which is simultaneously opposed to itself, as it always had been, and which emphasizes its anti-idealist aspects.

Even though we may go this far with Schopenhauer, the assessment of Kant's achievement cannot end there. We should, I think, give Kant credit for wrestling with the question of the objectivity of experience in a quite unprecedented way. Schopenhauer is merciless towards Kant's deep unclarity about what the 'object of representations' is supposed to be. But while Kant surely senses, however dimly, that there are enormous philosophical difficulties here for which his terminology of 'representation' is really not adequate, Schopenhauer's somewhat shallow criticism marks a retrograde step to the view that no distinction should or can be made between 'object of representation' and 'representation' itself.

We have seen that in some sense empirical objects are a species of our representations, and that Kant is driven to seek some object beyond representations as a condition of the objectivity of experience. In this context he often introduces the *transcendental object*, which is conceived as 'something in general', 'a mere something', an unknown quantity (' = x').[44] Now Schopenhauer interprets Kant as saying that the object to which the categories apply is distinct both from empirical objects in space and time (which are representations), and from the thing in itself. It is an object of thought, not of intuition, and so it is not subject to space and time, which are the forms of intuition. But it is not the completely unknowable thing in itself (to which the categories cannot apply), but rather its 'closest relative' which Schopenhauer calls the 'object in itself' [*Objekt an sich*], the 'object of representation' [*Gegenstand der Vorstellung*], or the 'absolute object'. Schopenhauer regards this somewhat shadowy entity as 'the source of all Kant's errors', itself resulting from a conflation of features belonging to representation and those belonging to the thing in itself. Kant should have realized that something could only be an object of our experience if it is a representation—'as Berkeley had already shown'—and that beyond representations the only 'object' there could be is the unknowable thing in itself:

If one did not want to count the object of representation in with representation and identify it with it, then one would have to place it with the thing in itself: in the end this depends on the sense one gives to the word 'object'. But what always holds is that, on clear reflection, nothing is to be found except representation and thing in itself.[45]

The possibility of our representations having objective

---

[44] Cf. (e.g.) *KdrV* A250–1; A277/B333.
[45] *W*1 p. 545 (444). The full discussion covers *W*1 pp. 543–6 (442–5).

content is such a delicate issue, approached so painstakingly by Kant, that we must surely query Schopenhauer's blunt assertion that everything is either representation or thing in itself. However, is not Kant committed to some such view, unless he throws off the conception of 'representation' that he has used throughout? Certainly Kant should agree that whatever we can experience is a representation, and hence that the object of representations, if it is experienced, must itself be a representation.

To press Kant any further on this is to enter into an area of enormous difficulty, as we can appreciate if we look at the passage Schopenhauer cites, A108–9 of the *Critique*. Here Kant says:

All representations have, as representations, their object, and can in turn be objects of other representations. Appearances are the only objects which can be given to us immediately, and that in them which relates immediately to the object is called intuition. But these appearances are not things in themselves but rather they are themselves only representations, having in turn their object, which thus cannot be intuited by us, and hence may be called the non-empirical, that is, transcendental object $= x$.

In saying that representations must have an object, Kant seems to recognize implicitly that a distinction must be made between mental states and their contents. There is then the question of how these contents of mental states can constitute information about an objective world. But Kant phrases that question in the same terminology as he used to make the distinction between mental states and their contents—in terms of 'representations having their objects'. He is perhaps on the brink of making a clear distinction between mental states and their intentional objects, and between intentional objects and material objects, but he achieves neither of them unequivocally. So one can agree with Schopenhauer that Kant seems on the one hand to hold that there is no distinction to be made between 'representation' and 'object', and on the other hand to be struggling hard for just such a distinction. But to recognize this difficulty for Kant is not to agree with Schopenhauer that there is nothing wrong with the fairly primitive conception of representation as it stands.

The famous Refutation of Idealism raises a related point.

The Refutation ostensibly shows that it is a condition of my awareness of my own mental states that there be objects in space outside me. To be aware of my own mental states as succeeding one another in time, I must be able to perceive something with a continuous existence. But this, Kant argues, is 'possible only through a *thing* outside me and not through the mere *representation* of a thing outside me' (B275). On the face of it, if the argument is sound, it refutes idealism in the sense required, namely scepticism about external objects. But how is this idealism to be refuted within Kant's system? What is the status of the 'thing outside me'? If, as he implies, this thing is not a representation at all, then Kant is, as Schopenhauer claims, postulating a perceived 'object of representations' which is neither thing in itself nor representation. But since the perceived thing outside me is explicitly spatial, the assertion of its existence in these terms would be at the expense of Kant's own previous claim that things in space are a species of our representations. In effect, then, Kant would be abandoning transcendental idealism, just as Schopenhauer charges, by requiring an object of experience that was not a representation. If Kant is not abandoning transcendental idealism here, then the 'thing outside me' which he mentions must in some sense be a representation, which would seem to involve him in a contradiction. To convince us that a thing could be a representation, without thereby dwindling to 'a mere representation of a thing', Kant would then have to differentiate between two senses of 'representation'. One possibility would be to hold that things in space are the contents of mental states, as opposed to these states themselves. But then the most that the Refutation of Idealism would show would be that it is a condition of my ascribing mental states to myself that some of my mental states have a spatial content—i.e. pertain to putatively spatial objects. This is less than Kant sets out to show, for his statement at the outset (B275) includes a claim that the *existence* of objects in space outside me will be proved. It is hard to think of any interpretation of 'representation' which would enable Kant both to prove what he wants and to hold on to the claim that objects outside me (in space) are representations. So it seems that if the Refutation is successful,

Kant will be committed to something incompatible with transcendental idealism.[46]

The view that Kantianism led to such a fundamental inconsistency (a view which I have argued to be substantially correct) was not in all its aspects of Schopenhauer's own devising. Immediately after Kant, there was a strong trend towards a position in which, unequivocally, the subject actively constructed the objective world in its own consciousness. If the question was: How can representations achieve the dignity of referring to objects?, the Kantian answer suggested on the one hand that a subject's representations achieved objectivity by being combined in necessary ways by the subject, according to a priori rules that originated in the subject. But it also wanted to account for objectivity in terms of the subject's representations containing an element that was given, i.e. produced in the subject by some object that did not number among the subject's representations and lay outside the mind completely. Since this combination of answers proved unstable, many understandably turned to the view that the a priori modes of the unification of representations were necessary and sufficient conditions of the subject's representations achieving objectivity. As Schelling was to put it in his *System of Transcendental Idealism*: 'On seeing how an objective world with all its determinations develops out of pure self-consciousness without any external affection, there will surely be nobody who finds necessary an additional world independent of self-consciousness.'[47]

This radically subjectivist reinterpretation of transcendental idealism came hard on the heels of the *Critique of Pure Reason*, being first stated in no uncertain terms by Fichte in his *Wissenschaftslehre* of 1794. The Kantians of the day were struggling with a position castigated by Fichte as 'a reckless juxtaposition of the crudest dogmatism, which has things in themselves making impressions on us with the most decided idealism, which has all existence arising solely through the

[46] Here I am indebted to Eckart Förster, 'Kant's Refutation of Idealism', in A. J. Holland (ed.), *Philosophy: Its History and Historiography*, pp. 287–303.

[47] *Sämtliche Werke*, vol. 3, p. 378. This work is available in a translation by Peter Heath, *System of Transcendental Idealism*, which gives marginal references to the *Sämtliche Werke*.

thinking of the intellect, and knows nothing of any other existence'.[48] Fichte lays down a challenge: we must make a choice between dogmatism, defined as the philosophical position which takes the thing in itself as its starting-point in the explanation of objective experience, and idealism, which eschews the thing in itself and takes the self or the intellect as its starting-point.

He adopts the latter as his explanatory basis, and aims for a 'complete deduction of all experience from the possibility of self-consciousness', with the self actively positing itself and positing all objects as limits of its own activity. Fichte claims to bring out the true import of Kant's philosophy—which is certainly a wild claim. But we have seen enough to be able to understand why he thought he was clarifying rather than distorting the doctrine of transcendental idealism. The rudiments (at least) of Fichte's views are present in Kant's taxing reflections on the transcendental 'I' as active in bringing about a combination of representations capable of referring to objects, and in his account of the freedom of the self.

Schopenhauer, too, claims to be developing a line of thought contained within Kant's philosophy. He also rejects the doctrine that things in themselves cause sensations in us—but he shrewdly observes that Fichte was too hasty in dismissing the thing in itself completely for its lack of such a causal role.[49] For Schopenhauer it is of the greatest importance to show that, though the Kantian use of the thing in itself as cause of sensations in us is illegitimate, there is nevertheless a thing in itself whose nature we can establish in a startling way. If the conception of the thing in itself left by Kant is something of a riddle, Schopenhauer portrays himself as the possessor of its solution, using materials latent in Kant's own thought.[50] Ironically, given his contempt for Fichte, Schopenhauer's foothold in Kant's philosophy is similar to Fichte's—for it too lies in Kant's account of the spontaneous activity of the subject, and it is to this that we shall now turn.

[48] *Sämtliche Werke*, vol. 1, p. 483; following references are to pp. 425 ff., 469 ff., and 462 of the same volume (see n. 36 above for system of references to the *Wissenschaftslehre*).
[49] Cf. *W*1 p. 536 (436).   [50] Cf. ibid. pp. 612–13 (501–2).

3

Kantian Subjects

FOR a transcendental idealist, the world revolves around the subject. In Schopenhauer's formulations, the world is what is object for the subject, the world is my representation. But what is the subject, the 'I' for which the world is supposedly there? And how does this subject relate to the world of objects? Schopenhauer's answer to these questions derives most of its elements from Kant. Like many of his contemporaries, Schopenhauer was particularly impressed by the Kantian conception of the self as spontaneously active, which I shall consider first as it occurs in Kant's account of freedom—one of his truly great and lasting achievements, according to Schopenhauer. As before, I shall say something about Kant's views in their own right, and about Schopenhauer's reception of them. Then I shall return to the problem of the subject of thought and experience, and Kant's wary account of what we can know of ourselves in this capacity. As we shall see, this is a part of Kant's work which, though he trumpets its merits far less, Schopenhauer equally comes to rely on.

TRANSCENDENTAL FREEDOM

One way of regarding the problem of free will would be to see in it an instance of the difficulty of finding a satisfactory theoretical *rapprochement* between the self and the world. It might be said that the difficulty is this: we must consider ourselves as part of the objective world, while simultaneously resisting a threat that thereby we shall have to regard ourselves as 'mere objects' rather than as self-conscious subjects of rational thought and action. We cannot give an exhaustive account of Kant's intricate handling of the problem here, nor can we discuss at all fully the role of freedom in his moral philosophy. However, the best place to start is undoubtedly the Third Antinomy in the *Critique of Pure Reason*, particularly since this passage figures prominently in Schopenhauer's consciousness of his relation to Kant: 'Here of all places,' he writes, 'is the point where Kant's philosophy leads on to mine, or where mine issues from his as from its stem.'[1] Just why he makes this claim will become clear later.

The Third Antinomy is concerned with overcoming the apparent opposition beween the principle of causality and human freedom, and at A444–5/B472–3 we find its two initial propositions stated as follows:

Thesis: The causality in accordance with the laws of nature is not the only one from which the appearances of the world can as a whole be derived. It is necessary to assume further a causality through freedom to explain them.

Antithesis: There is no freedom, but rather everything in the world happens solely in accordance with the laws of nature.

The solution to this antinomy is supposed to be found in the recognition that thesis and antithesis do not really stand in opposition to each other after all. Clearly, if this is to be possible, we must omit from the antithesis the clause 'there is no freedom', and be prepared to assert both (*a*) everything in the world happens in accordance with the laws of nature, and (*b*) it is necessary to assume further a causality through freedom to explain the appearances of the world.

What the thesis of the Antinomy seeks to prove is more closely specified as 'an *absolute spontaneity*, to begin spontaneously [*von selbst*] a series of appearances which runs according to natural laws, and thus transcendental freedom'.[2] The example Kant gives a little later makes it clear that *action* is the main problem area for whose explanation the introduction of absolute spontaneity is urged:

We speak here not of the *absolutely first* beginning in terms of time, but in terms of causality. If I now (for example) completely freely, and without the necessary determining influence of natural causes, stand up from my chair, there begins in this event . . . a completely

---

[1] *W*I p. 612 (501). [2] *KdrV* A446/B474.

new series, although in terms of time this event is only the continuation of a preceding series.[3]

This example, as presented, is not very convincing. In standing up, I may begin a series of events, but this does not license the view that I act 'without the necessary determining influence of natural causes'. It may seem to me that there are no causal influences on my action, but (*a*) this seeming is no guarantee that there are none, and (*b*) if my action is an event in the empirical world, we have no right to assume its exemption from natural causes. But the problem remains of how to do justice to the intuition that in standing up I 'begin a series of events'.

Kant's demand is for an 'absolute spontaneity'. We might also call the process which is supposed to be involved 'radical initiation'. Radical initiation is to be understood as the beginning of a series of causes and effects by an element which itself is not the effect of any cause. This first element, whatever it is, might be called a 'radical initiator'. Of course, we are normally entitled to assume of anything that initiates a causal chain that it is itself the effect of some cause or causes either unknown or disregarded for the sake of explanatory convenience. Normally speaking, that is, the antithesis of the Third Antinomy admits of no dispute in its claim that everything that happens, happens according to causal laws. But Kant's claim is that in addition we must assume radical initiation— transcendental freedom—to be possible.

Kant makes an important distinction between transcendental freedom and practical freedom. About the latter he says: '*Freedom in the practical understanding* is the independence of the will [*Willkür*] from coercion by impulses of sensibility.'[4] In other words, I am practically free if I am able to act otherwise than I am inclined to as a result of sensory stimuli. Thus, if I am hungry and have strong visual and olfactory sensations of food but because of some overriding motivation decide not to eat, this exhibits practical freedom. Animals lack practical freedom, because their sensations of hunger and their sensations of food invariably cause them to eat. Kant says that the *Willkür* of animals is 'pathologically necessitated', whereas the

---

[3] A450/B478.   [4] A534/B562.

Willkür of humans is free—they can decide not to act. Of course, since the sensations of human beings very often do cause them to eat, the claim must also be made that if they do eat in these circumstances, they were nevertheless free not to eat, i.e. they could have acted otherwise. According to Kant, 'practical freedom can be proved through experience'.[5] Our common experience that there are no external obstacles to either course of action, our experience of deciding (e.g.) to eat or not to eat although we are aware that nothing coerces us to do so—these experiences are sufficient, in Kant's view, to prove that we have practical freedom in this sense, even in cases where we do not actually go through the process of deciding.

Practical freedom is thus supposed to be a matter of empirical fact. But it requires further explanation. To this end, Kant introduces the concept of reason (*Vernunft*), saying that practical freedom is 'one of the natural causes, namely a causality of reason in the determination of the will'.[6] The notion of reason as causing free actions is crucial to Kant's moral philosophy, just as the motivation of wanting to 'rescue' freedom of the will is largely a concern for the possibility of morality, the assumption being that only if freedom of the will is possible can there be attribution of responsibility or moral accountability for actions. Kant's moral philosophy revolves around 'pure reason', the following of whose dictates is equated with moral freedom; but he makes it quite clear that in the *Critique of Pure Reason* his concern is merely to establish that the conception of freedom is not ruled out by the rest of his theory of our experience of the objective world. For example, he says in the Preface to the second edition (Bxxix):

As I thus need nothing more for morality than that freedom simply is not self-contradictory, and so may at least be conceived, without need of further insight into it; and that freedom thus places no obstacle in the way of the natural mechanism at work in the very same action . . . so the doctrine of morality claims its place, and the doctrine of nature its place also.

So, in the first *Critique* Kant sets himself to show simply the following two things: (1) that 'causality through freedom' is

---

[5] A802/B830. [6] A803/B831.

not an impossible concept, i.e. one ruled out by its own internal inconsistency; and (2) that 'causality through freedom' does not as such conflict with ordinary empirical causality. He ends the discussion slightly confusingly by saying that he has sought to show neither the *reality* of freedom nor its *possibility*, but only to treat it as a 'transcendental idea'.[7] Some light will be shed on this in what follows. There is some unclarity as to whether Kant later wants to found the doctrine of freedom on the legitimacy of morality, or vice versa.[8] But either way, as regards his aims in the *Critique of Pure Reason*, failure to establish either (1) or (2) will clearly have disastrous consequences for his account of morality.

Transcendental freedom is, according to Kant, distinct from practical freedom but connected with it as its ground.[9] That is, it is a condition of the possibility of our making effective rational decisions contrary to mere sensory stimuli—which we in fact do—that there can be 'causality through freedom', or radical initiation of causal chains. Unless we can guarantee the possibility that there is such radical initiation, Kant believes, we will not be able to explain how reason can bring about decisions 'of itself' over and above sensory stimuli.

As regards the ascription of ethical predicates, Kant shows that we make ethical judgements irrespective of our knowledge of the causal history behind the action or the agent which we judge. One example he uses is that of the malicious liar. First of all, in attempting to explain the behaviour of the liar, 'One goes through his empirical character right back to its source, which one seeks in bad upbringing, bad company, and also partly in the wickedness of a nature insensitive to shame'.[10] The precise nature of what one finds in this search is unimportant; what is important is that 'one proceeds as generally in the investigation of the series of determining conditions for a given natural effect'. Whatever causes one finds for the action in question, 'even though one believes the action to be determined by them, one nevertheless blames the doer'.[11] It is important to note here that Kant does not try to say that the action which is blamed is not empirically

[7] A557–8/B585–6.   [8] Cf. *Gr.* p. 450.   [9] *KdrV* A533/B561.
[10] A554/B582.   [11] A554–5/B582–3.

conditioned, or in other words that it does not have causes. The implication is rather that knowledge of the full causal history behind an action does not entail inability to apply moral predicates. But if this is so, why does there seem to be such a clash between moral freedom and causality?

Kant sees our persistence in applying moral predicates, in the face of knowledge of the full causal history of the action, as an indication that we regard the action 'as if the doer began with it a series of effects completely spontaneously [*von selbst*]'.[12] Thus, even though within the empirical world exemption from causality is not theoretically acceptable, we must proceed *as if* some kind of radical initiation takes place, otherwise we leave no room for moral accountability. Practical freedom is grounded in transcendental freedom: treating the person who lies as having been able to do otherwise is a precondition of moral accountability, and has as its pre-condition, according to Kant, the conceivability of radical initiation. The 'as if' in the formulation is of great importance. We cannot know—or Kant cannot consistently say that we know—that the agent is the radical initiator of a series of events. Our knowledge is, after all, restricted to the empirical world, in which every event must have a cause and in which, therefore, radical initiation could not possibly occur. But Kant thinks we can evade the problem by assigning the spontaneous element to a world other than the empirical world, one which transcends our knowledge but which we are nevertheless able to conceive in pure thought. This Kant calls the *intelligible* world.

Here we must go carefully. Kant's distinction between two 'worlds', the empirical and the intelligible, or the phenomenal and the noumenal, sounds mysterious and ontologically extravagant if taken with a dead-pan literalness. But it is highly probable that once again we are dealing with two *aspects* here. Kant is concerned with two viewpoints from which we can regard ourselves, and links his claim with more general reflections on two viewpoints from which everything may be regarded. The essential point can be grasped from the following passage:

[12] Ibid.

Man is one of the appearances of the world of sense, and as such one of the natural causes, whose causality must stand under empirical laws. As such an appearance, he too must accordingly have an empirical character, as do all other things in nature. We notice this character in powers and faculties, which are expressed in his actions. In lifeless nature, or nature with merely animal life, we find no ground for conceiving any faculty other than as purely sensibly conditioned. But man, who otherwise is acquainted with the whole of nature solely through the senses, also knows himself through pure apperception, and moreover in actions and inner determinations, which he can in no way assign to the impression of the senses. He is to himself on the one hand phenomenon, but on the other hand, namely in respect of certain faculties, a purely intelligible object, because his action can in no way be assigned to the receptivity of sensibility. We call these faculties understanding and reason . . .[13]

In a similar passage in the later *Grundlegung* Kant writes: 'Thus he may assign himself, with regard to mere perception and receptivity of sensations, to the *world of sense*, but in respect of what in him may be pure activity (that which reaches consciousness not at all through affection of the senses, but immediately) he must assign himself to the *intellectual world*, which however he knows no further'.[14] This could legitimately be regarded as an alternative way of expressing the same thought. Kant himself says that 'The concept of an intellectual world [*Verstandeswelt*] is . . . only a *standpoint*, which reason sees itself constrained to adopt outside appearances, *in order to think of itself as practical*'.[15] Thus the point of talking of 'two worlds' is essentially this: we can view ourselves as 'purely intelligible objects', or as something over and above that which we experience ourselves to be in inner and outer sense. The distinction between appearance and thing in itself applies in our own case just as it does for the world at large, and, as with the more general account, we can have no knowledge of ourselves as we are in ourselves. The application of this distinction to the problem of freedom and determinism is stated in no uncertain terms in *Prolegomena*:

If the objects of the world of sense were taken for things in themselves . . . the contradiction would be unavoidable. In the same way, if the subject of freedom were represented like other objects as

---

[13] A546–7/B574–5.   [14] *Gr.* p. 451.   [15] Ibid. p. 458.

mere appearance, then the contradiction could likewise not be avoided; for exactly the same thing would simultaneously be affirmed and denied of one sort of object in the same meaning. But if natural necessity is merely related to appearances, and freedom merely to things in themselves, then there arises no contradiction if one at the same time assumes or concedes both kinds of causality, however difficult or impossible it may be to make the latter kind conceivable.[16]

Kant's procedure here raises a great many questions. He may at one stage have thought that he could prove freedom straightforwardly from the reflection that we are aware of a spontaneity of thought which is incompatible with our being merely natural objects subject to natural causality.[17] But in the *Critique* and subsequently, the strategy appears to be this: independently of the question of free will, we must make the distinction between ourselves as we appear to ourselves and ourselves as what we are over and above that. This is so because we are aware of ourselves other than empirically, as subjects of thought. Considered as appearances, we are no more free than any other empirical object, but we do no violence to the notion of universal causality within the world of empirical objects if we attribute freedom to ourselves in our non-empirical aspect. The main questions which this raises are surely: (*a*) What precisely are we to do when asked to consider ourselves as 'purely intelligible objects'?; and (*b*) How is freedom to be 'related' to ourselves so considered?

While in some ways the status of intelligible objects is as doubtful in Kant's philosophy as that of things in themselves (with which they seem to be sometimes identified, sometimes not), we may be sure that they are called 'intelligible' because they are supposed to be objects only for the intellect or understanding and not for sense-perception. Kant speaks of positing in addition to phenomena 'other possible things, which are in no way objects of our senses, thought as objects only by the understanding', which we can call 'intelligible entities (noumena)' (B306). He then goes on to distinguish a positive and a negative sense of 'noumenon'. In the negative sense, we understand a noumenon to be 'a thing, inasmuch as it is not an object of our sensible intuition, in that we abstract

[16] *Prol.* p. 343.   [17] Cf. Karl Ameriks, *Kant's Theory of Mind*, pp. 189–91.

from our way of intuiting it' (B307). On the other hand, a noumenon in the positive sense would be 'an object of non-sensible intuition'. Kant clearly rejects this positive sense here, for if we accept it, 'we accept a special mode of intuition, namely the intellectual, which is not ours, and whose very possibility we cannot even grasp'. Our intuition (and hence our imaginative powers) remain bound to the reception of impressions through outer and inner sense. A little further on, Kant says that 'our understanding is not restricted by sensibility, but rather restricts it, by calling things in themselves noumena' (A256/B312). In a sense, then, noumena are to be equated with things in themselves. If we abstract from our mode of intuiting an object, this is to consider it as it is in itself. But it remains an *object of thought*, and so acquires the title of 'intelligible object' or 'noumenon'. Since what Kant needs to invoke with regard to the question of freedom is a conception of ourselves gained by abstracting from our way of intuiting ourselves, it is fairly clear that he hopes to solve the Third Antinomy by using the negative conceptions of 'intelligible object', 'noumenon', and 'thing in itself'.

The concepts of all these 'things' have what Kant calls 'problematic' status. They contain no contradiction, but cannot achieve objective reality; they can serve as 'limiting concepts', enabling us to clarify ways in which our knowledge is restricted, but they cannot play a part in any positive assertions which make a claim to knowledge. This means, of course, that anything attributed to ourselves as intelligible objects will also be merely problematic for Kant. And it is in accordance with this that he refers to our spontaneity as 'a pure transcendental idea'. An idea is, for Kant, the concept of something completely unconditioned, which reason is bound to form. Reason must form the concept of spontaneity, though this has no basis in empirical reality, since otherwise 'the whole field of experience' is 'transformed into a sum of mere nature [*Inbegriff blosser Natur*]', where there can be only what is causally conditioned.[18] It is not clear whether we must think in this way independently of the view that we have free will, and, if so, why. But the point to emphasize is that, for Kant,

---

[18] *KdrV* A533/B561.

our freedom is not a matter about which we can claim to have knowledge. That we are free is something that we can consistently think, and must think if morality is to have a foundation; but it is not something which we can claim to know: 'I had to remove *knowledge*', he comments, 'to make room for *belief*' (Bxxx).

Once these qualifications are entered, the question still remains to be asked: What does it mean to say that freedom is related to things in themselves? Surely *actions*—which were the original area of interest—cannot be things in themselves, nor for that matter can they be 'events in themselves', since they are part of the world of objective experience. Actions must take place in time—at a particular time or during a particular time—and, since time is for Kant a form of inner sense, not a form of the world as it is in itself, anything which takes place in time must be reckoned to sensibility and cannot belong to the noumenal world. There can be no particular events in the noumenal realm. What Kant intends, however, is not that actions belong to the noumenal world, but rather that actions must be seen as if they were *caused by* something belonging to the noumenal world. We must posit ourselves as we are in ourselves as existing in the noumenal world; therefore it is at least not impossible that we ourselves (as we are in ourselves) cause our phenomenal actions. We in ourselves could thus be radical initiators, and the freedom of our actions could be transcendentally guaranteed. Though we could never know that our actions are thus free, all Kant requires is our acquiescence that *it is not impossible*. But, as we shall see, it is hard to agree even this far.

The noumenal self is one's 'intelligible character', to be distinguished from one's 'empirical character'. A person's empirical character is simply one of the causal factors determining her actions. Every person's *Willkür* has a character, so that what a person wills at a given time is determined partly by causal factors external to the person, partly by the person's character. This is intuitively plausible. If I offer somebody £1,000 to let me pass my driving test, a variety of actions may follow. It clearly depends who it is I attempt to bribe; but if I know the person's character well enough, it could serve as a factor in my prediction of the outcome. Kant's account implies further that this is not different in principle from the role played by my knowledge of the empirical character of an ice-cube in my production of its behaviour when placed in warm water. A wooden cube, for example, would behave differently in identical circumstances because it has a different character:

> Thus a person's actions in appearance are determined by his empirical character and the other co-effective causes according to the order of nature, and if we could investigate all appearances of his will [*Willkür*] right to the bottom, there would be no single human action which we could not predict. . . . So in respect of this empirical character there is no freedom; but it is only according to this character that we can consider a person when we merely *observe* . . .[19]

Again, Kant's phrase, 'when we merely *observe*', indicates his conviction that if we consider ourselves as items within the objective world, there is no place in the picture for freedom.

However, in Kant's view, our empirical character is not our only one. Our *intelligible* character is conceived as that which grounds our empirical character, as the way we are in ourselves which explains the way our will makes its appearance. But a major problem is that 'the way we are in ourselves' can never actually be explanatory of our empirical character, because it is forever inaccessible to us. We are left with the conception of something to be viewed neither spatially, nor as occurring in time, nor as a member of any causal chain, something which determines our empirical character but is not itself determinable. This intelligible character is said to coincide with reason as 'the permanent condition of all willed actions',[20] and also with 'the transcendental subject, which is empirically unknown to us', or with 'the acting subject as *causa phenomenon*'.[21] In the *Grundlegung*, Kant adds that: 'A rational being counts himself, as intelligence, as belonging to the intelligible world, and solely as efficient cause belonging to this world does he call his causality *will* [*Wille*].'[22] But the basis for these alternative characterizations of our (unknowable) intelligible character is obscure.

Clearly, Kant wants the noumenal self to act. The same

---

[19] A550–1/B578–9.
[20] A553/B581.
[21] A545/B573.
[22] *Gr.* p. 453.

acting subject is supposed to have both an empirical and an intelligible aspect:

> But according to its intelligible character . . . the same subject [i.e. the active subject] would have to be pronounced free of any influence of sensibility and any determination of appearance; and, since in it, inasmuch as it is *noumenon*, nothing *happens*, and no change is encountered which requires a dynamic temporal determination . . . therefore this active being would to this extent be independent and free in its actions from all natural necessity. . . . One could say of it with all correctness, that it began its effects in the world of sense *of itself*, without the action itself beginning *in it*.[23]

If 'this active being' refers to the subject under its intelligible aspect, the account is clearly incoherent, as there can be no noumenal events, let alone actions. But then, if 'this active being' refers to the subject under its empirical aspect, the claim that it could be independent of all natural necessity is false. It is hard to imagine a coherent explanation of how something could be both temporally indeterminable and an active subject. Thus, though the empirical subject may be active, and the intelligible subject may be free, it seems that Kant is unable to show how one and the same thing could *both* act *and* be free.

Nor can it be said that Kant overcomes all the problems of the 'difficult or impossible' conception of intelligible causality. According to him, the application of the category of causality is restricted to that which has a temporal determination (cf. A144/B183, for example), so it is obvious that if an intelligible object is a cause, we are dealing not with ordinary causality but with something else. The only way to characterize this something else is to say that it is the necessary conditioning of an empirical causal chain by an intelligible object. What this conditioning *is* remains unclear, and there seems to be no good reason for calling it 'causality' at all. Kant would say that he is using the category of causality in a way which would be illegitimate if we were concerned with a claim to knowledge—since the category is applied in a case where no object is given in intuition—but is legitimate here in that we are concerned with what can be thought, not what can be

---

[23] *KdrV* A541/B569.

known. Thus we have a 'pure' use of the category. But to say
this is not to provide an explanation of how intelligible objects
can be the causes of events without themselves being subject
to causal influence. The abiding interest of Kant's attempt to
solve the problem of free will is probably in his suggestion that
it arises from a conflict between two viewpoints which we can
adopt with regard to ourselves, and his implication that our
not being subject to ordinary empirical causality would be
neither necessary nor sufficient for freedom. In detail, though,
it is hard to see how it could be made to work.

This discussion will enable us to present Schopenhauer's
views about freedom and determinism in their proper context
(for which see Chapter 9). His comments on the proposed
solution to the Third Antinomy reveal the great importance to
him of this part of Kant's thought. Remember that he singles
out Kant's connection of freedom with the thing in itself as
one of his greatest achievements, and proclaims the Third
Antinomy as the 'stem' from which his own philosophy grows.
The chief point for Schopenhauer is that Kant is constrained
to say more about the thing in itself here than he does
anywhere else; but he thinks that Kant failed to work out fully
what he meant, and that it falls to himself to complete the task
and to 'answer the riddle' with the clear statement that the
thing in itself is *will*.[24] For the distinction between empirical
and intelligible characters, Kant receives nothing but praise:
'I include this among the most admirable things ever said by
man'.[25] But all this does not prevent Schopenhauer from
adopting his customary critical stance. Some of his criticisms
are highly acute. For one thing, Schopenhauer does not think
that Kant can claim to have shown, as he wants to, that both
the thesis and the antithesis of the Antinomy are true, 'each in
a different sense'. What is shown is that the antithesis is right:
everything in the world of phenomena must have its cause.
The thesis must be rejected because, like the antithesis, it
'does not speak in any way of the thing in itself, but entirely of
appearance, of the objective world, of the world as representation'. Thus what Kant takes it upon himself to prove
possible is not what is stated in the thesis: 'the transcendental

---

[24] *W*1 p. 612 (502).   [25] Ibid. p. 616 (505).

freedom of the will which is expounded is in no way the unconditioned causality of a cause asserted by the thesis, because a cause must be essentially appearance, not something *toto genere* different that lies beyond all appearance'.[26]

The more general point here is one that we made earlier: the connection between appearance and thing in itself cannot be one of causality. Just as the positing of things in themselves as causing representations in us involved a mistaken use of the concept of causality, so now the attempted account of freedom illegitimately applies the same concept to the connection between ourselves as intelligible objects and sequences of empirical events. Consistent with his criticism of Kant, Schopenhauer uses the concept in neither of these ways.

Some of Schopenhauer's other criticisms of Kant's 'solution' of the problem of free will arise more directly out of views Schopenhauer himself had developed. Two can be simply mentioned here in order to give a foretaste of how different Schopenhauer's view of the will is from Kant's. The first is Schopenhauer's suggestion that Kant was quite wrong to equate the will with reason; the second is his complaint that Kant should have extended his insight about the thing in itself to other animals.[27] By what right does Kant single out human beings for special treatment, assuming that causal explanation according to empirical laws suffices to explain the behaviour of other species? Indeed, why stop at animate nature: if our actions are on a par with other empirical events, why should we not consider the whole of nature as in itself analogous to ourselves? In effect, as we shall see, this is what Schopenhauer does. However, we have yet to complete our account of the Kantian background. We have seen how Kant thinks that we must regard ourselves from two distinct viewpoints, and we have made some remarks earlier about his conception of self-consciousness. But before leaving Kant it will help to examine systematically the various strands in his work about the self as subject of thought and knowledge, the inheritance of which provides Schopenhauer with some of his central problems.

[26] Ibid. p. 618 (506).
[27] Ibid. p. 617 (505-6).

SELF AND KNOWLEDGE

In the previous section we saw one use which Kant makes of the contrast between the self as appearance and the self as noumenal or intelligible object. The latter might also be referred to (a little clumsily) as 'the self as it is in itself'. Something Kant is clear about is that there can be no knowledge of the self as it is in itself. On the one hand this should come as no surprise, given his general doctrine about things in themselves; but on the other hand it might be thought to have troubling consequences. We may feel that Kant is denying the possibility of self-knowledge altogether, perhaps implying that we cannot even know we exist—an uncomfortable conclusion from any point of view, but especially so for a transcendental idealist, who requires the existence of the subject of experience as that which unites representations into one consciousness and thereby, in some sense, constructs the world.[28] What we shall find is that Kant's position on the self avoids these difficulties. Though it is presented in an over-intricate way, and suffers from some serious internal peculiarities, it contains some philosophical thought of great subtlety and lasting value.

When he is discussing the self, and in particular the knowledge we can have of ourselves, Kant commonly confines such knowledge to what we can call the empirical self, or the self as appearance. But he further restricts the empirical self to what is presented in *inner* sense, with outer sense providing access exclusively to objects other than the self. (Cf.: 'The representation of myself, the thinking subject, is related merely to inner sense' (A371); and: 'I, represented by inner sense in time, and objects in space outside me, are . . . entirely distinct appearances' (A379–80).) This distinction holds, even though we are not thereby committed to thinking that the transcendental object that underlies the appearing self is distinct from the transcendental object which underlies outer appearances. In other words, when it comes to the 'in itself', I may be identical with whatever lies behind objects outside me.

[28] Cf. Ralph C. S. Walker, *Kant*, p. 133.

Perhaps (Kant speculates) we might even be entitled to say that 'the very same thing which, as outer appearance, is extended, is internally (in itself) a subject, which is not composite, but is simple and thinks' (A360). Then we would be able to say that spatially determinate human beings (*Menschen*), rather than souls, are the subjects of thoughts. In company with many philosophers, however, Kant finds some difficulty in settling for this latter, apparently common-sense alternative (referred to in the passage under discussion as a 'hypothesis' and not pursued). Why there should be this difficulty in seeing objectively located human beings as subjects of thought is one of the main questions that I want to examine in this book.

In Kant's case, of course, even if some of the objects presented to outer sense are in themselves subjects, or if I am in myself identical with what some external objects are in themselves, none of this can be known, because knowledge is restricted to the level of appearance. But now, which among appearances are appearances *of myself* and enable self-knowledge on my part, and which are appearances of something other than myself? In practice, as I have said, Kant's answer is that that which belongs to inner sense is appearance of myself, and that which belongs to outer sense is appearance of things 'outside me' and thus distinct from me. This may seem to commit Kant to a Cartesian dualist position, in which the 'I' that thinks and perceives a world of objects is an immaterial soul, an object of some kind, but one distinct from anything bodily. After all, anything bodily is an object (or a possible object) for outer sense, and so 'outside' the 'I'; and this must include what I call 'my body'. Kant does not address first and foremost the question of whether my body as it appears (as an object in space) is wholly distinct from, part of, or identical with my 'empirical self'. He would certainly—and correctly—assume that my knowledge of myself is not simply exhausted by my knowledge of my body. But he often seems to be making the stronger assumption that 'what I am' (in any sense) does not even include the body. Clearly, the problems here are not peculiar to Kant, but, as we shall see, he takes a more balanced view than some of his predecessors, a more sophisticated view than many of his successors, and he is by no means a Cartesian dualist.

Because Kant in practice restricts 'myself as appearance' to what appears in inner sense, 'myself as appearance' is to be equated with a temporal sequence of representations of which I am aware. But now a pressing problem arises. Here am I, a subject aware of certain inner states ordered in time; I call these states 'myself as I appear to myself'. But what is there to guarantee that it is *myself*, the subject of awareness, that I have knowledge of 'as appearance'? The 'I' that is aware of all these states is not itself one of them, so how can we claim that the subject has intuition of *itself* here? Kant is troubled by this question; that he has no real answer to it is suggested by his comment that 'this is a difficulty common to every theory' (B68), and by this later passage:

How the I who am thinking [*das Ich, der ich denke*] may be distinct from the I that intuits itself (since I can imagine another mode of intuition at least as possible), and yet be identical with it as the same subject, how, that is, I could say: 'I, as intelligence and *thinking* subject, know *my*self as *object of thought* [*gedachtes Objekt*], inasmuch as I am given to myself over and above what is in intuition, but, as with other phenomena, not as I am for the understanding, but as I appear to myself'—this has no more nor less difficulty about it than how I could be an object for myself at all, even an object of intuition and inner perceptions.

This (from B155–6) is a notable example of the kind of passage where, as Schopenhauer says, Kant cannot really have been thinking clearly. But what lies behind it?

The general problem here is how I, a subject, can be an object for myself. If I, an actively thinking subject, am to be an object of thought for myself, I must think of myself as an actively thinking subject. However, for Kant, mere thought of myself is not sufficient for knowledge of myself, I require in addition some experience, some intuition of myself. But since that of which I can have intuition—the 'manifold in me' (B158)—does not contain the actively thinking subject that I must think of myself as being, it becomes hard to see how genuine *self*-knowledge, where knower and known are identical, can be possible. One may charge Kant not only with obscurity of exposition, but with departing from an unnecessarily complicated set of assumptions—though in fairness it must be said that he is acutely aware of the difficulties he faces. Some of these difficulties could be circumvented by rejecting the doctrine of inner sense. In common with many of his predecessors, Kant assumes that my experience of my perceptual states in temporal sequence is analogous with my experience of objects in the physical world: my states are arrayed before me temporally as objects are both spatially and temporally, and my relation to both is conceived in terms of some kind of receptive awareness. I can discover my perceptual states by an 'internal' empirical examination, just as I can discover objects by an 'external' one. This kind of model engenders the conviction that there is on the one hand a set of quasi-objects, 'my perceptions', and on the other hand myself as that which is surveying them, while at the same time paradoxically presupposing that in surveying them it is precisely myself (as opposed to the external world) that I am coming to know.

Kant, however, takes the analogy between inner and outer sense to even more uncomfortable lengths, and encounters yet another problem of affection:

> if we make the assumption about outer sense that through it we know objects only in so far as we are externally affected, we must also concede in the case of inner sense that through it we intuit ourselves only as we are internally affected *by ourselves*, that is, as far as inner intuition is concerned, know our own subject only as appearance, but not according to what it is in itself.[29]

In outer sense we supposedly function as passive receptors of sensations caused in us by things in themselves with an existence outside us. We saw in previous sections how problematic this notion is in Kant's philosophy—but surely, the attempt to extend the same notion to inner sense is bound to be even more hazardous. The idea is that we passively receive quasi-sensations caused in us by the activity of our own minds, working at the unknown noumenal level.[30] All the problems about noumenal causality rear their ugly heads again, together with the sceptical charge that since all causal inferences are uncertain, I must doubt whether it is *myself* at all causing the contents of inner sense, rather than something

[29] B156.   [30] Cf. B153–4.

else. It may be that Kant thinks that the doctrine of inner self-affection can help to explain what it is that makes inner appearances appearances of myself. But if so, he is surely mistaken, for it only compounds the problem by making this very fact unknowable to me.

Kant has three discernible conceptions of the self, which continually threaten to become conceptions of three selves, each distinct from the others. There is, first, the empirical self—the collection of mental states appearing in inner sense. Secondly, there is the self as it is in itself—that *of* which those states are an appearance. And thirdly, the self as pure subject—that *for* which those states are there, and which can think of them as its own. We have already noted the difficulties Kant encounters in assuring the identity of the empirical self with the subject, and of the empirical self with the self as it is in itself. It should also be said, however, that there is nothing at all in what Kant says that vouchsafes the identity of the self as it is in itself with the self as subject. Whatever it is that produces appearances in me by inner affection, I surely have no grounds for supposing it to be identical with that 'I' *for* which its effects occur as mental states. The notion of *self*-knowledge seems to fall apart again, because the conception of the self is hopelessly fragmented.

To pursue any further the internal inconsistencies and embarrassments to which Kant's theory may be prone is scarcely a fruitful exercise. Rather, I wish to concentrate on the philosophically more valuable aspects of his view of the self; and, perhaps surprisingly, we can approach these best by considering precisely those three distinct conceptions of the self which I mentioned above.

Kant was of course familiar with the traditional, rationalist conception of the soul as a simple, immaterial substance. He must have known it intimately, having espoused it himself early in his career.[31] There is also evidence to suggest that he knew of Hume's views on personal identity.[32] In terms of the conceptions of the self introduced above, we may say that the

---

[31] Cf. Ameriks, *Kant's Theory of Mind*, esp. pp. 27–32.

[32] Cf. Robert Paul Wolff, 'Kant's Debt to Hume via Beattie', *Journal of the History of Ideas* 21 (1960), pp. 117–23; and Patricia Kitcher, 'Kant on Self-Identity', *Philosophical Review* 91 (1982), pp. 41–72.

rationalist doctrine attempts to state what the self is in itself, whereas the Humean position, which equates the self with 'a bundle or collection of different perceptions',[33] attempts to get by without any other conception of the self than the Kantian 'empirical self' given in inner sense. Put bluntly, Kant's attitude in the *Critique of Pure Reason* is that the rationalist view is excessive, the Humean view deficient. Both are criticized from the standpoint of the third conception, what I have called 'the self as pure subject'. This fragile but all-important conception must be kept distinct from the others and carefully examined, if Kant's achievement in this area is to be appreciated.

The doctrine that comes first, both historically and in a plausible account of the way Hume's and Kant's arguments develop, is that of the self as a simple, immaterial substance which is identical with itself over different times, and is that in us which thinks. One of Hume's major points, with which Kant agrees, is that what is presented in inner sense (to use the Kantian term) yields no perception at any one time of a single, non-composite thinking thing, nor of oneself as a substance enduring from one time to another: 'There is properly no *simplicity* in it [the mind] at one time, nor *identity* in different [times]; whatever natural propension we may have to imagine that simplicity and identity.' So the first point is that, among the data of inner sense, there is no such self as the rationalist doctrine requires, only 'successive perceptions'. But Hume's next step is to say that these successive perceptions 'constitute the mind' or the self. (The assumption is still that questions about the self are questions about the mind; Hume switches easily from one to the other.) So the view we are now confronted with is that myself, what I am, is exhausted by the temporal sequence of mental states in inner sense. Each item in the sequence is distinct from the others, though there are ways, apart from mere succession, in which they may be related. The relations which Hume allows to pertain between perceptions are those of *resemblance* and *cause and effect*. With only these relations to go on, the mind nevertheless has a habit (the 'propension' referred to above) of

[33] *A Treatise of Human Nature*, p. 252.

running together what is distinct yet related, and assuming instead that there is experience of a single enduring entity: 'Thus we feign the continu'd existence of the perceptions of our senses, to remove the interruption; and run into the notion of a *soul*, and *self*, and *substance*, to disguise the variation.'[34]

Though Kant does not explicitly present his argument (in the Transcendental Deduction) as an answer to Hume's, it functions at least in part as such an answer. Both Kant's agreement and his disagreement with Hume are reflected in a comment in a later passage (A402): 'I cannot know as an object that which I must presuppose in order to know any object.' The point of agreement is that, in terms of the empirical self of inner sense, Hume is right to say: 'I never can catch *myself* at any time without a perception, and never can observe any thing but the perception.'[35] The point of disagreement arises with Kant's argument that the sequence of perceptions must nevertheless be unified by attribution to a single subject. It is a presupposition of talking about experience that one conceive of the self as a self-conscious subject unifying perceptions.

Unless I am able to think of a collection of perceptions, all of which together are *mine*, there will be no sense in which perceptions are the contents of a mind at all. 'A collection of perceptions' means presumably some subset of all the perceptions that have ever occurred. When Hume said that 'they are the successive perceptions only that constitute the mind', he did not mean that there was at most one mind, constituted by the succession of all perceptions. But what is to be the principle by which we sort perceptions into distinct collections or 'heaps' (as Hume at one point graphically puts it)? Kant's answer involves the fundamental idea that a number of perceptions belong to the same collection if, and only if, they are contained within one and the same consciousness. But this amounts to saying that they belong to the same collection if, and only if, there is a subject that is conscious of them all. We noted earlier Kant's famous statement that 'The "I think" must *be able to* accompany all my representations' (B131). This can be interpreted as

---

[34] *A Treatise of Human Nature*, pp. 253, 260, 254.   [35] Ibid. p. 252.

meaning simply that a condition of each single representation's belonging to me is that I must be able to judge it as mine (though I may not in fact make such a judgement about each). Kant's point, however, is not simply that each representation must have a subject, but that the subject must be (or must be able to be) conscious of itself as that *single* unifying element common to *all* the representations which it can call its own: 'For the multiplicity of representations which are given in a particular intuition would not collectively be *mine* if they did not collectively belong to one self-consciousness' (B132). And it is quite clear that, for Kant, this collective unity in one consciousness is the only thing that can save us from a purely Humean conception of the self: 'It is only through my being able to comprehend the multiplicity of representations in one consciousness that I call them collectively *my* representations; for otherwise I would have a self as many-coloured and diverse as the representations I have of which I am conscious' (B134).

Hume's position only seems to make sense (and even Hume had his doubts about it[36]) to someone who bypasses completely the question: 'What makes a collection of perceptions mine?' Kant's answer to this question, despite the many pages of tortuous exposition, really amounts to this: 'The possibility of my judging self-consciously that I am the subject of all of them collectively.' It is hardly an informative answer—but Kant recognizes this: 'Now admittedly this principle, that of the necessary unity of apperception, is itself identical, and so an analytic proposition' (B135). What the principle does reveal is that if I set out to talk intelligibly about 'my experience' or 'my perceptions', I must over and above this think of myself not as identical with the totality of my perceptions, but as their subject. Any awareness of an item of my experience as such presupposes a kind of *self*-consciousness on my part: the possibility of my thinking of myself as subject of a unified set of perceptions. Kant calls this particular kind of self-consciousness 'pure apperception'—since it is a non-empirical consciousness of oneself. The unity among representations which is guaranteed by pure apperception he calls 'the

---

[36] Ibid. pp. 633–6.

transcendental unity of apperception', because such unity is an a priori condition of experience, and 'the synthetic unity of apperception', because (he argues) it is to be regarded as effected only by a spontaneous act of synthesis or combination on the part of the understanding. (Cf. B135: 'without [synthesis] the uniform identity of one self-consciousness cannot be thought. For through the "I" nothing multiple is given. It can be given only in intuition, which is distinct from the "I", and thought only through *combination* in one consciousness.')

Kant is scrupulously careful to distinguish the self-consciousness associated with this unity of apperception from self-*knowledge*. As far as the former is concerned, 'I exist as an intelligence that is conscious solely of its power of combination' (B158). The importance of keeping separate the conception of the self as subject from the other two conceptions mentioned earlier now becomes clear, as can be seen from the following passage:

as far as inner intuition is concerned, we know our own subject only as appearance, and not according to what it is in itself.

As against this, in the transcendental synthesis of the multiplicity of representations in general, and thus in the synthetic original unity of apperception, I am conscious not of myself as I appear to myself, nor as I am in myself, but only that I am. This *representation* is an act of *thought*, not of *intuition*. For knowledge of ourselves we require, in addition to the action of thinking, which brings the multiplicity of every possible intuition to the unity of apperception, a determinate mode of intuition, in which this multiplicity is given. So, although my own existence is not appearance (still less mere illusion), the determination of my existence can only come about in conformity with the form of inner sense, according to the particular way in which the multiplicity which I combine is given in inner intuition. Consequently I have no knowledge of myself *as I am*, but merely as I appear to myself. The consciousness of oneself is thus far from being a knowledge of oneself.[37]

I can know that I exist, as the subject of those thoughts that present themselves in my consciousness. This is essentially the point about the 'I think' which Descartes made in the *Meditations*. But, Kant insists, simply being aware that I exist

---

[37] *KdrV* B156–8.

is not enough to tell me what kind of thing I am. Having dismissed the Humean alternative as inadequate, Kant skilfully resists any slide back to the positive rationalist doctrine by holding apart the conception of the self as self-conscious unifying subject and the conception of the self as in itself a simple, immaterial substance.

The metaphysical excesses documented in the second half of the *Critique*—those of cosmology and theology as well as psychology (the doctrine of the soul)—are supposed to be inevitable, according to Kant. They rest on inferences which are 'sophistications not of people, but of pure reason itself',[38] and which lead us on, in search of 'the unconditioned', into a realm beyond the limits of experience. Here we form 'pure transcendental ideas', which (as we saw with the case of freedom) are such that we can have no knowledge of any object corresponding to them (although, as Kant says, we may have a merely 'problematic' concept). In the section of the *Critique* called the 'Paralogisms of Pure Reason', Kant suggests that we are led to form the rationalist conception of the soul (whose proponent he calls the 'rational psychologist') by fallacious but inevitable processes of reasoning, although all we are strictly entitled to is the notion of the 'I' as the necessary unifier of experience in apperception. In detail, Kant is not always entirely clear as to the nature of the false inferences involved, but the overall points are clear enough.

If what we seek is knowledge of the self, we require some intuition of the self. It is only of something that is a possible object of experience that we can know what it is or what kind of thing it is. Experience reveals to me the empirical contents of my mind, but not the 'I' that unites them. For the 'I' is not to be identified with any of those contents, and not even with all of them collectively. So it is a mistake (albeit, as Kant thinks, an inevitable one) to hold that knowledge-claims can be made about the 'I' as if it were determinable as some kind of object. Kant tries to show this by breaking down the rational psychologist's claim about the soul into separate components. The first component (and the most important, judging by the way in which the whole section is recast in the

---

[38] A339/B397.

second edition) is the claim that 'I, as thinking being (soul) am *substance*' (A348). This is otherwise stated as 'a thinking being exists only as substance' (B411). Now on one reading of this proposition, Kant not only agrees with it but regards it as analytically true. 'Substance' can be taken to mean something that is only a subject to which predicates are applied, and not itself predicable of anything else. The analytically true proposition, then, is this: 'I who am thinking [*Ich, der ich denke*] must count in thought always as *subject*, and as something which cannot be regarded as attaching to thought merely as a predicate' (B407). Kant's point is that in any thought in which 'I' occurs, it refers to the thinker of that thought and to nothing else, and that this is analytically true. But in saying 'I, as thinking being, am substance', the proponent of the rationalist doctrine is trying to make a statement about the existence of a kind of entity which endures through time while states of it change—namely, that a particular thinking being is such an entity. Indeed, Kant says that unless the concept of the substantiality of the thinking subject could deliver the conclusions 'that I continue to exist' and 'that I neither come into being nor perish', it would be of no use, and one might as well forget about it (A349). Kant's position is entirely consistent here: it is analytically true that 'I, as thinking being, am substance', i.e. subject of my thoughts; but one might as well forget about this truth, if, like the rational psychologist, one seeks knowledge of the self. The only things we could ever know to be substances that endure, and that neither perish nor come into being, are things of which some intuition is possible.

Kant deals similarly with other components of the rational psychologist's position. According to that position, the soul is a *simple* substance. But Kant shows that the simplicity which the 'I' enjoys cannot be used to support the claim that there are in the world two kinds of substances—one divisible (matter), and one indivisible or simple (soul). In a sense the 'I' is simple: given *my* thoughts collectively, they cannot have a plurality of subjects; and, moreover, 'this representation "I" includes in itself not the least multiplicity' (A355), in that it refers not to any collection of perceptions, but to the subject. But the true proposition, 'the "I" is simple', is uninformative about what kind of object the subject is, which is why Kant talks not only of 'the simplicity of the representation of the subject', but of 'the expression "I" which is totally devoid of content' (A355). Once again, then, nothing follows from these reflections about simplicity that is of any use in building up a doctrine of what kind of thing the soul is. Kant goes on to apply the same point (though less clearly) to the views that the conception of the soul as a substance can help with the problem of personal identity, or establish whether the soul can exist apart from the material world.[39]

As a summing up of Kant's general point in the Paralogisms, his own words (B409) are admirably concise: 'Thus, through the analysis of the consciousness of myself in thought in general, not the slightest gain is made with regard to knowledge of myself as an object. The logical exposition of thought in general is taken for a metaphysical determination of the object.' The conception of the self-conscious subject of thought which Kant develops can support no claim to knowledge of the self as an item existing objectively in the world—whether it be as an immaterial soul, or as a material object. This might be regarded as a weakness of his position, but that would be to mistake his aims. Kant's concern is not to state definitive (or, indeed, any) criteria of personal identity, but rather to explore the conception of a subject, starting from the minimum 'functional' requirements for something's being a subject, and trying to demonstrate how these very minimum requirements can be misunderstood as licensing informative statements about the manner in which these requirements are 'realized'.[40] This is worth stressing, because it might be thought that in arguing against an essentially Cartesian position, Kant had implicitly committed himself to a view which equates the self with some component of the empirical world. Strawson, for example, assumes this to be the thrust of Kant's argument, and then takes him to task for not following it through far enough.[41] It is true that Kant entertains the idea that the thinking subject is simply the human being (*Mensch*),

---

[39] B408–9; cf. A361–6 on personal identity.
[40] For this way of putting the point, cf. Patricia Kitcher, 'Kant's Paralogisms', *Philosophical Review* 91 (1982), pp. 530–1.
[41] Cf. *The Bounds of Sense*, pp. 164, 169.

and hence an object of outer sense (B415). But equally he elsewhere commends the idea of an immaterial substance soul for at least 'destroying entirely all materialist explanations of the inner appearances of our soul'.[42] He does argue that the rational psychologist cannot establish that I could exist 'merely as a thinking being (i.e. without existing in human form)', but in the previous sentence he states that the proposition, 'I distinguish my own existence as that of a thinking being from other things outside me (*including my body*)', expresses an analytic truth.[43] The latter passage is somewhat obscure, but anyone who can write that it is analytically true that I am distinct from my body, and who can show such determined opposition to materialism, is probably not opposing the immaterialist view in the way Strawson suggests.

We should recognize, then, that at best Kant's account leaves open the question of the relation of the self-conscious thinking subject to the world of empirical objects. It is intentionally negative, and makes problematic the view that the subject is a constitutent of the world presented in its own experience. Surrounding Kant's central argument is a rich assortment of paradoxes and unexplored pathways, some of which are of dubious value, but some of which are worthy of more attention than they can be given here. We tend to think of Kant solely as the great systematizer, but particularly in his discussion of the self he is as much an acute raiser and articulator of problems. Some of these problems stick with the conception of the pure subject through its elaborations by Fichte and Schelling, and are central difficulties for Schopenhauer too. Some, as I shall suggest, are still with us today.

Schopenhauer's thought on the self as subject of knowledge or of representation is built on distinctly Kantian foundations. Thus his naïve-sounding comment on the synthetic unity of apperception—that it is 'a very strange thing, very strangely presented'[44]—does not really reflect the extent to which he relies on a closely related notion in his own theory. (In fact, he goes on to concede that what Kant means 'is what I call the

---

⁴² *Prol.* p. 334.   ⁴³ B409 (my emphasis).   ⁴⁴ *W*I p. 554 (451).

subject of knowing, the correlate of all representations'.) We can surely excuse Schopenhauer's exasperation at the 'strange' mode of presentation of this part of Kant's theory. On the other hand, his reaction to the famous sentence: 'The "I think" must be able to accompany all my representations', is a little short-sighted. Because of its close juxtaposition of necessity ('must') and possibility ('be able to'), he accuses the sentence of being 'a problematic-apodictic enunciation; in plain language, a sentence which takes with one hand what it gives with the other'—and is at a loss to know what it means at all. This raises questions which we shall address later. One is whether Schopenhauer entirely appreciates what Kant is struggling with in his account of the subject; another is whether he merely uses a simplified version of Kant's view of the subject for his own distinct ends.

That Schopenhauer is Kant's heir is clear from his opposition to the doctrine that the self is an immaterial soul, combined with a reliance on the notion of the subject of representations which cannot be an object of representations. Kant duly receives approval from Schopenhauer for his critique of rational psychology, though with a qualification:

This refutation has as a whole great merit and much that is true. However, I am of the opinion that it is merely for the sake of symmetry that Kant derives the concept of the soul as necessary from that paralogism, by applying the demand for the unconditioned to the concept *substance*, which is the first category of relation.[45]

The supposedly systematic origin of the Paralogisms gives Kant his basis for asserting that 'the concept of a soul arises in this way in every speculative reason'. But Schopenhauer has serious reservations. He has already made an acerbic (and almost Nietzschian) point at the expense of Kant's views on the unconditioned in general. It is supposed to be inherent in pure reason itself not only to search for the unconditioned, but moreover to arrive at just three species of the unconditioned: the soul, the world existing in itself as a totality, and God. But it is highly suspicious, Schopenhauer finds, that the deliverances of reason itself should turn out to coincide with the basic tenets of one religious tradition—Christianity. 'In fact,' he

[45] Ibid. p. 597 (488).

says elsewhere, 'all the talk about the absolute . . . is nothing but the cosmological proof *incognito*'.[46] To see if such concepts are universal, we should require historical research into 'whether the ancient and non-European people, in particular those of Hindustan, and many of the oldest Greek philosophers, in fact arrived at these concepts too; or whether it is merely we who, over-generously, attribute them to these peoples'.[47] He clearly thinks that the latter is the case, and that Kant's a priori reasonings are simply not borne out by fact.

This observation provides Schopenhauer with a general ground for not accepting that reason itself constrains us to think of the soul as an immaterial substance. But he has further points to make. For one thing, he argues that if reason demanded an unconditioned subject for all predicates, this should apply to all things, not just persons. Kant does not explain why we do not as a matter of necessity posit a soul for every object. A further point Schopenhauer makes is that Kant's talk of something 'being able to exist only as subject and not as predicate' is irregular: 'Nothing exists as subject and predicate: for these expressions belong exclusively to logic, and designate the relations of abstract concepts one to another. In the intuited world their correlates or representatives are supposed to be substance and accident.' But then the only *substance* existing in the empirical world—something that 'remains when all its properties are taken away'—is *matter*.[48] We shall discuss Schopenhauer's conception of matter along with his attitude to materialism in Chapter 6. For the present, however, let us look at his alternative explanation of how the concept of an immaterial substance arises in philosophy.

Schopenhauer suggests that the very concept *substance* was formed, redundantly, to act as the genus of which *matter* is a species. Its formation was redundant because matter is in fact the sole species in question. But, having formed the higher concept, philosophers could then with the semblance of legitimacy invent a second species parallel with matter, but minus the qualities of extension, impenetrability, and divisibility. Normally, generic concepts are formed by abstraction from more than one species, but in this case 'the concept of substance was merely invented to be the vehicle for the surreptitious introduction of the concept of an immaterial substance'. Here one might object that it is Schopenhauer's turn to provide some historical evidence (which he does not attempt to do). But it is more important to ask whether the concept *immaterial substance* is one which every rational being is constrained to use, or a tenuous hybrid serving a particular function within a particular school of thought. And Schopenhauer's point is surely correct: rather than arriving at the concept of an immaterial substance by a faulty piece of syllogizing to which they had an in-built propensity, philosophers were driven to invent it by one pressing philosophical concern, which Schopenhauer goes on to isolate:

The opposition which gave rise to the assumption of two fundamentally distinct substances, body and soul, is in truth that of the objective and subjective. If man apprehends himself objectively in outer intuition, he finds a spatially extended and in general entirely corporeal being. If on the other hand he apprehends himself in mere self-consciousness, that is, purely subjectively, he finds a merely willing and representing being, free of all forms of intuition, and thus also without any of the properties accruing to bodies. Now he forms the concept of the soul, in the manner of all the transcendent concepts, which Kant calls ideas—by applying the principle of [sufficient] reason, the form of all object, to that which is not object, and here indeed to the subject of cognition [*des Erkennens*] and willing. He regards cognition, thinking, and willing as effects, whose cause he seeks. He cannot take the body as this cause, and so posits for these effects an entirely distinct cause. It is in this way that dogmatists, from first to last, prove the existence of the soul. . . . It was only after the concept of an immaterial, simple, indestructible being had thus arisen by the hypostasizing of a cause corresponding to an effect, that the school developed and demonstrated this concept from that of *substance*.[49]

Schopenhauer may differ with Kant over details, but Kant's legacy is apparent: while no longer being able to regard ourselves as simple, immaterial souls, we are nevertheless conscious of ourselves as subjects, and this presents problems for any straightforward view of ourselves as objects. I shall argue that the opposition between the subjective and the objective, and consequent problems about the place of the self with respect to the world of objects, are of vital importance to Schopenhauer's thought, and make it of considerable philosophical interest. If Schopenhauer's reactions to Kant's various conceptions of the subject have not been explored at great length in this chapter, it is because those reactions form the very core of his own philosophy, and will occupy us for the rest of this book.

PART TWO

4

Subject and Object in Schopenhauer

'THE world is my representation' is the opening sentence of Schopenhauer's main work, and one whose repercussions are heard throughout what follows. There are unclarities about what a representation is for Schopenhauer, as there were in the case of Kant. But one thing is clear, and should come as no surprise after the discussion of Kant and Berkeley, and that is that in saying 'The world is my representation', Schopenhauer intends to assert the dependence of the world on the experiencing subject. 'Everything at all that belongs or can belong to the world', he writes, 'is unavoidably affected by this being conditioned by the subject, and is there only for the subject.'[1] Schopenhauer's central idealist thesis is that objects depend on, are conditioned by, or are there only for the subject. I shall examine his idealism as such in Chapter 5, but the present chapter will be concerned with his conceptions of subject and object, which make up the structure of representation, and determine so much of the pattern of his philosophy as a whole.

The notion that subject and object are the essential components of consciousness was widespread in the decades following the publication of Kant's *Critique*, and we shall have recourse to discussions of this wider background at a number of points in this chapter and the next. But we can begin with Schopenhauer's own characterization of knowledge, experience, or conscious awareness in terms of the simple relation between the two halves of this dichotomy: 'Our knowing consciousness . . . divides into subject and object, and contains nothing besides. To be object for the subject, and to be our representation, is the same thing. All our representations are objects of the subject and all objects of the subject are our representations.'[2] Schopenhauer is prepared to put great

[1] *W*I p. 29 (3).   [2] *VW* p. 41 (41–2).

weight on the succinct slogan 'No object without subject', which he often chooses as the vehicle of his idealism (and which, as we saw, he also thinks summarizes what is of any worth in Berkeley's philosophy[3]). However, there are a number of questions that need to be asked about the central thesis as thus formulated. First, what are the 'objects' that are said to depend on, or to be conditioned by, or not to be possible without the subject? Secondly, what is the nature of this dependence or conditioning? (More generally, how are subject and object related?) Thirdly, what (or perhaps who?) is this 'subject' on which the world depends?

Let us begin by posing this third question: What—who—is the subject? Schopenhauer tells us that the subject, by which he means solely the subject of *representation*, is 'that which knows everything and is known by none', adding that 'It is accordingly the bearer of the world, the condition of all appearance, of all object.'[4] One can read the proposition 'the subject is the condition of all appearance' as an expression of the relatively innocent assumption that all experience requires an experiencer. (The syntax carries the suggestion that a single point is being made in different ways, although in calling the subject 'the bearer of the world' Schopenhauer goes much further than the relatively uncontentious point that a subject of experience is presupposed by any experience.) Here, then, we meet again the notion—familiar from our earlier discussion of Kant—of the subject as a necessary presupposition of experience. This is surely what Schopenhauer has in mind when he writes of the subject as that which 'knows everything', as well as when he calls it 'the condition of all appearance'. But the question to ask now is: Why must this subject itself be unknown, and not an object of possible experience? This view seems to go against some very commonplace assumptions—that among the objects of one being's experience there can be other experiencing beings, for example; and that a being can be an object of experience for itself. What reasons does Schopenhauer have, then, for this statement that the subject is known (or experienced) by none?

Sometimes Schopenhauer's reason for holding this view

---

[3] Cf. *W*1 pp. 30(3), 533–4 (434); *W*2 p. 11 (4).
[4] Ibid. p. 31 (5).

appears to be that it is self-evidently so, that it is in the logic of the concepts *subject* and *object* that nothing can be an instance of both. Again and again he states this conviction, reinforcing his message with a number of striking similies, one of which has become especially well known through its appropriation by Wittgenstein: 'Our knowledge, like our eye, only sees outwards and not inwards, so that, when the knower tries to turn itself inwards, in order to know itself, it looks into a total darkness, falls into a complete void.'[5] In other words, the subject of representation cannot represent itself. The same image is elaborated in the following passage to make the same point, but here an explicit connection is made between this point and the notion of the subject as condition of experience:

Since the representing I, the subject of knowing, as the necessary correlate of all representations, is their condition, it can never itself become representation or object; but of it holds the fine saying of the holy Upanishad: *id videndum non est: omnia videt; et id audiendum non est: omnia audit; sciendum non est: omnia scit; et intelligendum non est: omnia intelligit* [this is not something to be seen: it sees all; and it is not to be heard: it hears all; it is not to be known: it knows all; and it is not to be understood: it undertands all].[6]

Apparently, then, the subject's being the condition (or 'necessary correlate') of objects of experience is the reason for its unknowability. But as it stands this is inadequate. We may grant that experience requires an experiencer without thereby being committed to the impossibility of one experiencing subject being experienced by another, or of a subject experiencing itself.

Part of Schopenhauer's motivation for keeping subject and object so clearly distinct was that he wanted to counter the recent treatment which those concepts had received, particularly at the hands of Fichte and Schelling. I said in Chapter 1 that Schopenhauer was more of his immediate time than he liked to think, and here is a case in point. It is not that his treatment of subject and object is the same as that of his contemporaries; more important is the way in which his own views are shaped by the need to reject what he saw as pernicious errors made by Fichte and Schelling.

[5] *PP*2 p. 54 (46).   [6] *VW* pp. 157–8 (208).

A recurrent theme for Fichte and Schelling is the identity of subject and object. Both of them seem to have begun with a notion that consciousness necessarily involves a separation of subject and object, of what represents and what is represented. But then they proceed to establish that subject and object are identical in a particular case, that of intellectual intuition. Kant had claimed that there could be no such state, but Fichte and Schelling had in mind a special kind of awareness in which instead of knowing an object distinct from oneself, one becomes directly but non-empirically aware of oneself as that which knows. From the start, Schopenhauer objected to this procedure. 'What is the I?', asked Fichte in his lectures, and answered: 'an absolutely immediate intuition of the identity of the intuiter and the intuited [*des Anschauenden und des Angeschauten*]'. Schopenhauer, in the audience, appended to his notes the comment: 'There is only *one* intuiter, the I: and this is for that very reason never something intuited.'[7] Similar remarks on Schelling's explanation of the 'I' as 'the subjective becoming object for itself' show Schopenhauer already fully assured of his own position in 1812:

That the subject should become object for itself is the most monstrous contradiction ever thought of: for subject and object can only be thought one in relation to the other. This relation is their only mark, and when it is taken away the concept of subject and object is empty: if the subject is to become an object, it presupposes as object another subject—where is this to come from?[8]

One element in Schopenhauer's objection is his conviction that to make the subject an object is to turn it into some quasi-empirical thing, instead of the pure ('empty') subject to be found in Kant. The very expression 'the I', surreptitiously introduced (so he alleges) by Fichte, leads one in this direction. By distorting the use of 'I' we invent a spurious entity, as if all Kant's warnings were in vain.[9] One might object that talking of 'the subject' as Schopenhauer does is hardly less innocent of ontological suggestions than Fichte's 'the I'. Furthermore, Schopenhauer seems not to have recognized the lengths to which both Fichte and Schelling

---

[7] *HN*2 p. 68.   [8] Ibid. p. 334.   [9] Cf. *PP*2 p. 46 (38).

went to prevent 'the I' being interpreted as a quasi-thing. They repeatedly assert it to be a pure act ('that act which does not and cannot appear among the empirical states of our consciousness, but rather lies at the basis of all consciousness and alone makes it possible'[10]—really quite Kantian). This said, there is of course room for puzzlement of a familiar kind about how 'acting' is possible beyond the empirical realm—a point to which we shall return later.

This may explain the vehemence of Schopenhauer's stand against identifying subject and object, but we still have to assess the extent to which his position is coherent, and ask what reasons he has for holding it. The question of whether the subject can be an object is really the same for him as the question of its knowability. The knower, he holds, cannot be known. One point here is that I do not know myself (primarily) as I know other objects: my awareness of being a subject of experiences is unlike my awareness of objects in that it does not require me to identify a particular individual item in the empirical realm as myself. Here 'knowledge of *x*' is being used to mean something like 'experiential acquaintance with *x*': I am not acquainted with my myself in experience in the way that I am with spatio-temporal objects, or (perhaps) with some of my own mental states. However, Schopenhauer also seems to want to rule out propositional knowledge concerning the subject of representations. Thus one objection to his own position which he considers is this: 'I do not just know [*erkenne*], but I also know [*weiss*] that I know'.[11] His reply is that 'I know that I know' is only apparently distinct from 'I know [*Ich erkenne*]', and the latter says no more than 'I'. In view of the two German words for 'know' involved here, I shall use 'cognition' for *Erkennen* in discussing the remainder of this passage, which runs as follows:

If your cognition and your knowledge of this cognition are two in number, then just try to have each on its own, either to have the cognition without knowing about it, or again, merely to know about the cognition without this knowing being at the same time the cognition. True, one can abstract from all *particular* cognition and thus arrive at the proposition 'I have cognition'. This is the final

---

[10] Fichte, *Sämtliche Werke*, vol. 1, p. 91.
[11] *VW* p. 158 (208).

abstraction we are capable of, but it is identical with the proposition 'There are objects for me', and this is identical with 'I am a subject', which contains no more than 'I'.[12]

The suggestion is that the attempt to set up an instance of knowledge of oneself as a knower collapses. What Schopenhauer says about the 'abstracted' proposition 'I have cognition' carries conviction. To know this about myself is ultimately to know only that I am a subject, which presumably I already know in knowing that I am. But it cannot be right, surely, to say that my knowing that I have a particular cognition (*c*) is not distinct from my having *c*. For here we have two cognitive states with different propositional contents, which surely ought to make them distinct cognitive states, even if it is true that I cannot have *c* without knowing that I do so (which is by no means uncontestable). And if it is perfectly legitimate to say that I know that I have a particular cognition (at a particular time), then in one sense I can have knowledge of myself as a knower. The general assumption that Schopenhauer makes is that if I know about a state I am in, then the state known about and the state of knowing must be distinct. However, the two states that he cites can perfectly well be regarded as distinct, so the claim that we can have self-knowledge does not fall foul of the general assumption.

It begins to look as if Schopenhauer does not have any good arguments for holding that the subject of knowing and the object known must be distinct. As I said earlier, he usually proceeds on the basis that this is a self-evident truth—in at least one place he says quite tersely that the knowing subject is completely unknowable *because it is that which knows*.[13] To all intents and purposes, he treats as an assumption the following proposition: necessarily, if *x* is an object for *y*, then *x* and *y* are not identical.

We can perhaps make more sense of Schopenhauer's remarks here if we return to the Kantian position discussed earlier. Simplifying greatly, we can say that two key propositions in Kant's account are:

(*a*) The 'I' is not experienced.
(*b*) The 'I' is a condition of experience.

---

[12] *VW* p. 158 (208–9).   [13] *W*2 p. 23 (15).

(*a*) can be seen in effect as a concession of Hume's point that introspection reveals only states of mine, not any unitary entity which is *myself* as opposed to any of these states. Schopenhauer's image of the eye looking into a void is clearly an expression of essentially the same point as this. (*b*) can be explained by saying that experience presupposes the unification of representations as belonging to a single subject capable of self-consciousness. Kant combines these two points when he says: 'I cannot know as an object that which I must presuppose in order to know any object' (A402). In effect, it is these two points that Schopenhauer is also making in the above passage, using the most abbreviated of Kant's expressions of them. But how does this deal with the unnerving implication that (*a*) might be the case simply *because* (*b*) is the case? Well, arguably there is a sense in which, suitably qualified, the Kantian position could be expressed in this way too. For Kant held that precisely in so far as I am considered as the transcendental subject of representations, I can have no knowledge of myself, because knowledge of myself requires experience (intuition) of myself, and the consciousness of myself in the transcendental unity of apperception is a matter not of intuition, but of thought (B157). So one might say that as a pure transcendental subject of experiences I am merely 'the condition of all appearance', and hence not an object of experience. Schopenhauer is merely expressing this central Kantian thought in a rather bald and provocative fashion.

Schopenhauer's acceptance of Kant's doctrine of the subject has to be qualified by taking account of his criticisms of Kant. As I mentioned in the previous chapter, Schopenhauer is disparaging towards Kant's conception of the transcendental unity of apperception, and scornful of the obscurity in Kant's exposition of it. It is, as he says, 'a very strange thing, very strangely presented'. Moreover, he finds fault with the renowned sentence 'The *I think* must be able to accompany all my representations', whose confusing juxtaposition of necessity and possibility he thinks 'takes away with one hand what it gives with the other'.[14] What could this sentence mean in plain language?, he asks: 'That all representing is thinking?—that is

[14] *W*1 p. 554 (451).

not so; and it would be hopeless, for then there would be nothing but abstract concepts . . . And again animals would in that case have to think, or not represent at all.' The interpretation with which Schopenhauer toys here results from his inability to comprehend the structure of the Kantian sentence: he thinks that Kant is claiming that every representation must in fact be accompanied by a thought. However, his last point is still surely a strong one against Kant. On any reading, Kant's proposition seems to imply that animals, if they are not capable of self-conscious *thought*, cannot be said to have representations; and it is, to say the least, unclear that that is an acceptable consequence.

Perhaps though, Schopenhauer continues, Kant's proposition is intended to express the thought 'No object without subject'. If that is so, 'it would be a very bad way of putting the point, and would come too late'. Presumably it would be too late because Kant has already used other arguments (notably in the Transcendental Aesthetic) to establish that the world of objects would disappear without the subject. It is less clear why it would be—other than stylistically—a bad way of expressing the Schopenhauerian 'No object without subject'. Consider the concession with which Schopenhauer rounds off the discussion: 'If we summarize Kant's utterances, we will find that what he understands by the synthetic unity of apperception is, as it were, the extensionless centre of the sphere of all our representations, whose radii converge towards it. It is what I call the subject of all knowledge, the correlate of all representations'.[15] This, I think, enables us to disregard the quibbles about Kant's exposition. For Schopenhauer considers his conception of the representing subject to be essentially the same as the Kantian conception of the transcendental subject. And in essence, I would like to argue, it is. Schopenhauer fails to appreciate the subtle point that Kant is trying to make about the necessity of the potential self-ascription of any experience, but, despite this, he captures in more figurative language the two important points: first, that the subject is to be treated as the condition of all appearance, the 'focal point' to which all representations must

---

[15] *W*1 p. 554 (451–2).

be related; and secondly, that of such a subject there can be no experience (only its representations can be experienced), nor any knowledge beyond that of its mere existence.

It is time now to confront Schopenhauer's claim that the subject of representations knows but is not known, either by itself or by others, with the commonplace assumptions that subjects can be known both to themselves and to each other. What does Schopenhauer have to say in defence of such an apparent deviation from common sense? First, we must note that his claim is not that persons are unknowable or not possible objects of experience. 'Person' and 'subject' are not equivalent. Persons he will allow to be objects of experience, inasmuch as they are bodily entities:

That which knows everything and is known by none is the *subject*. . . . Everyone finds himself as this subject, yet only in so far as he knows, not in so far as he is object of knowledge. However, his body is already object, and it too we therefore, from this standpoint, call representation. For the body is object among objects, and falls under the laws of objects.[16]

Sometimes Schopenhauer appears to use 'person' and 'body' as equivalent terms, while more frequently his view is that a person is bipartite, falling into subject and object components. Both views are represented in the following passage:

[T]he existence of my person or of my body, *as something extended and effective*, always presupposes some *knowing thing* distinct from it: because it is essentially an existence in apprehension, in representation, thus an existence *for another*. In fact it is a brain-phenomenon, no matter whether the brain in which it presents itself belongs to one's own person or to another. In the first case one's own person divides into knower and known, into subject and object, which here, as everywhere, stand inseparably and incompatibly opposed to each other.[17]

For the moment I shall ignore Schopenhauer's view that the representation of object to subject takes place in the brain, though this is anything but a minor point in his theory as a whole and must be attended to later on. What concerns me here are the relations between Schopenhauer's conceptions of subject, object, person, and body. Clearly, my body is an

[16] Ibid. p. 31 (5).   [17] *W*2 p. 13 (6).

object, so that if I am at least in part a bodily being, I am at least in part an object. So, in line with common sense, Schopenhauer can say that I am an object either for myself or for others, and that this is an instance of a *person* being an object. A person, then, can be both subject (*qua* knowing or representing) and object (*qua* bodily)—which so far sounds straightforward.

However, this conception of a person is ineliminably dualist. The dualism is of a post-Kantian nature, in that it does not pertain between two substances: Schopenhauer is clear that the subject, 'though simple (being an extensionless point) is not for that reason a substance (soul), but a mere state'.[18] Nevertheless, he is committed to the views that each person is to be analysed into subject and object, and that subject and object must be distinct from one another. Thus he has an answer to the objection that, using his theory, persons would be unknown to themselves and to others; but the answer leaves him in the position of not being able to identify the subject of experiences with any individual object in the empirical world.

The empirical world (which for him is the world as representation) is, according to Schopenhauer, governed by laws which connect representations together. He amends somewhat Kant's account of the a priori categories and forms of intuition, but retains the essentially Kantian view that the forms which constitute the connectedness among empirical representations are space, time, and causality. Thus all objects which make up the world of representation are spatio-temporal and governed by causal laws. But Schopenhauer must hold that the subject of representations is not spatio-temporal and not governed by causal laws, because spatio-temporality and causal regularity are, for him, not only necessary conditions of object-hood, but sufficient conditions as well. Anything that is at some place, at some time, or subject to causal interaction with other things is an object, a representation for some subject (or at least a possible representation). But of course, as we have already seen, the subject of representations cannot be an object at all. So, given

---

[18] *W*2 p. 325 (278).

these assumptions, and the requirement that all experience have a subject, Schopenhauer is committed to the existence of a non-temporal, non-spatial, non-causal subject.

The subject of representation, therefore, has from the start an entirely problematic status, which Schopenhauer not only acknowledges but capitalizes upon later, when he considers how such a subject could be in any way related to a physical organism, and argues that it is only as *willing* beings (in a broad sense) that we can appear as individuals in the world. The problematic status of the representing subject for Schopenhauer can be brought out most dramatically by considering his own oft-repeated remarks about the principle of *individuation* (*principium individuationis*). His initial statement will serve the purpose as well as any: '[I]t is only by means of time and space that something which in its nature and in its concept is one and the same appears as differentiated, as a plurality of coexistent and successive things: they [space and time] are consequently the *principium individuationis*'.[19] The notion that individuals in the world of objects are to be distinguished one from another by their location in space and time is a familiar one. To this Schopenhauer adds the doctrine that the world as it is in itself, independently of its appearing to any subject, is an entirely undifferentiated whole, with differentiation occurring only at the level of representation. But the subject is to be thought of neither as a thing in itself, nor as one object among others in the world—rather, it is simply that for which there appears a multiplicity of objects, bound by the forms of space, time, and causality. Thus it is that while 'the body, like all objects of intuition, lies within the forms of all knowledge, space, and time, through which there is plurality', the subject on the other hand 'does not lie within these forms, but rather is always presupposed by them: thus to it belongs neither plurality, nor its opposite, unity'.[20]

One might have expected that Schopenhauer would say there can be only one subject, but here he is mysteriously asserting that there are neither many, nor one. What does he mean? He expands on his position a little here:

The world as representation . . . has two essential, necessary, and

[19] *W*1 p. 157 (113).   [20] Ibid. p. 31 (5).

inseparable halves. The one is the *object*, whose forms are space and time, and through these plurality. The other half, however, the subject, does not lie in space and time: for it is whole and undivided in every representing being; hence a single one of these with the object completes the world as representation as fully as the millions which there are in existence.[21]

Is Schopenhauer demanding that, strictly, one should treat an individual experiencing being as an *instance of subject*, with *subject* now being taken as a kind of universal? Or is it that 'experiencing being' is to be taken as an ordinary countable noun, and 'subject' as something more like a mass term? There is no clear answer to these questions. But one perfectly intelligible thought here is that if the world of objects requires an experiencer, it is no particular individual that is required. Rather, the requirement is simply that objects be experienced. Some experiencing being must exist, but each and every experiencing being is alone sufficient to satisfy the requirement, i.e. each individual experiencing being provides an instance of objects being experienced. The necessity that all experience should have some subject with an interconnected set of experiences, whose connecting principle is precisely their being the experiences of one and the same subject, does not lead us to the conclusion that the world exists only for this or that individual experiencing being, nor to the conclusion that this or that individual experiencing being is the only one in existence. What Schopenhauer, with his graphic style, brings out more starkly than Kant is that the conception of a mere subject of representations is not the conception of one empirical experiencing being among others. Thus it is a wholly inadequate tool for any account of oneself as an individual. Whilst arguing for the necessity of this conception of the subject of representations, Schopenhauer is quite prepared to present it as problematic and inadequate, because this clears the way for his central argument that a full account of ourselves as subjects can only be attained by giving prominence to our nature as subjects of will.

The notion of the self as willing is tied in with dissatisfaction with the view that, as subject, I am unknowable to myself. In

---

[21] *W*1 p. 32 (5).

the following passage he recognizes (albeit again in a fairly picturesque manner) the demand for a unitary subject of experiences:

It is a wonder that we do not become thoroughly confused by such a heterogeneous mixture of fragments of representations and thoughts continually criss-crossing again and again in our heads, but rather are always able to find our way and to fit everything together. Plainly there must exist a simple thread on which everything strings itself together: but what is this?

After commenting that memory will not suffice, he goes on to reject a number of characteristic Kantian answers as unhelpful: The *logical I*, or indeed the *transcendental synthetic* unity of *apperception*—are expressions and elucidations, which will not readily serve to make the matter comprehensible . . . Kant's proposition: "The *I think* must accompany all our represen- tations" [*sic*] is insufficient: for the I is an unknown quantity, i.e. a secret to itself.'[22]

We may well find this surprising, since for all his irritation at Kant's obscurity, Schopenhauer has said that Kant's doctrine of the unity of apperception amounts to the same as his own doctrine of the subject of representations as that which unifies them or focuses them into one point. Here he is looking for a 'thread' to unify representations; elsewhere he uses the same image, saying that representations are strung together like pearls in a necklace, with the 'theoretical I, which is precisely Kant's synthetic unity of apperception', providing the thread.[23] But what he goes on to say in the present passage is that our representations can ultimately be unified only by the thing in itself which underlies consciousness as its substratum, and this he equates with the *will*: 'It is therefore the will that gives [consciousness] unity and holds together all its representations and thoughts, accompanying them, as it were, as a continuous ground-bass.'[24] Reverting to familiar imagery, Schopenhauer adds that without the will the intellect would have no more unity than a mirror which receives successive images, or the 'imaginary point' in which a convex mirror concentrates light rays. It is important to realize, Schopenhauer is telling us, that the subject of

[22] *W*2 p. 162 (139).   [23] Ibid. p. 293 (251).   [24] Ibid. p. 162 (139).

representations *is no more than* an extensionless point. We can say it is that which unifies a multiplicity of representations, but, in the absence of any further specification of the nature of the subject, the assertion is an empty one. For any kind of account of myself as a continuing individual, to whom a multiplicity of experiences belong in common, the conception of the transcendental subject is wholly inadequate. (It might be said that Kant went out of his way to make this point himself in the Paralogisms section.[25]) Schopenhauer thinks a positive account can and must be given of the self as it is in itself (as will), that this account also explains the nature of the thinking subject, and that without the account of the will, the self is left as an entirely problematic and shadowy appendage to the world of objects. Thus he finds the notion of the representing subject to be at one and the same time entirely necessary to his theory and seriously deficient if treated as any kind of full account of the self. Schopenhauer's denial of self-knowledge applies only to myself as subject of *representation*, or as *knowing* subject. His position does not deny self-knowledge outright, but holds that 'the subject knows itself only as a *willing* being, not as a *knowing* one'.[26] With this doctrine the spectre of Fichte arises once again—but this time to agree with Schopenhauer. For in his *Sittenlehre* Fichte had argued strenuously for the parallel conclusion that it is only as willing that I 'find myself'.[27] In his review of 1820, Herbart used this passage in Fichte to support his assessment of Schopenhauer as an unoriginal thinker, though he alleges, wrongly, that Schopenhauer had not concerned himself with the *Sittenlehre*.[28]

The doctrine that self-knowledge is always of the self as willing is an early one for Schopenhauer. He incorporates it into *On the Fourfold Root*, where the will is made a *sui generis* object for the subject of knowing, and it is more than likely that reading the *Sittenlehre* the previous year had played some role in crystallizing his thoughts on the matter. However, there is an importance divergence of views. Fichte insists that the object and the subject in this instance of consciousness are

---

[25] Cf. esp. A346/B404.   [26] *VW* p. 157 (208).

[27] *Sämtliche Werke*, vol. 4, pp. 18–22. for Schopenhauer's notes on the *Sittenlehre*, see *HN*2 pp. 347–52.

[28] Cf. Volker Spierling (ed.), *Materialien*, pp. 114–15.

one and the same—and why not, since we are supposedly talking of self-consciousness? Fichte's argument is hard to follow, but it looks as if his premisses include: (1) In all consciousness there is a necessary opposition between subjective and objective. (In all thinking there is something *thought* which is not the thinking itself.) (2) The 'I' is such that it both acts and is that which is acted upon. Fichte then wants to argue that if the object of my thinking must be distinct from the thinking itself, it must be 'a real determining of the self by the self'. The self must think *of* itself as doing something other than merely thinking. The kind of 'doing' involved must be 'real acting' with some objective dimension that takes it beyond pure thinking. But such 'real acting' is (he tells us) what is meant by *willing*. So he concludes that if I am to have knowledge of myself by thinking of myself, what I know must be myself as willing. Amid some obscurity, Fichte appears to assume both that the object in self-consciousness must be identical with the subject, and that it must be distinct. Schopenhauer, however, even when he read this passage, was convinced of the necessary distinctness of subject and object. Thus his summation of Fichte's argument is as follows: 'If I want to think of myself, I must think of myself as *willing*. For although *thinking* is the second predicate (after willing) of the I, yet I cannot think of myself as what thinks, because then I am actually still what thinks, and subject and object would flow together here, violating the fundamental condition of all thought'.[29]

If Fichte really must keep subject and object distinct, he is contradicting himself when he assumes that one can talk of the 'I' being conscious *of itself*. But by making explicit the non-identity of subject and object, Schopenhauer encounters the same problem in even more clear-cut form, and he never really resolves it. Later I shall argue that his persistence with the view that representing subject and willing subject are distinct, even in the face of these difficulties about self-knowledge, is but one symptom of the incompatibility of his two conceptions of the subject. He sets up the conception of the representing subject, brings in an essentially competing

[29] *HN*2 p. 348.

account of the subject as willing, and then tries vainly to incorporate the one account into the other, as if they were not competing but complementary conceptions. Despite this, I shall argue that we can learn something philosophically important from Schopenhauer once we realize that the two accounts are in conflict.

Having discussed the Schopenhauerian subject at some length, we must return to the two outstanding questions that were posed at the beginning of the chapter: What does Schopenhauer understand by the term 'object'? And what is the nature of the dependence he alleges between object and subject?

We must be alert to the fact that Schopenhauer often uses the term 'object' as roughly equivalent to 'intentional object'. In this sense, of course, a thought or a quasi-perceptual experience can 'have an object' in the absence of any really existing object corresponding to it. This is the sense in which Macbeth's state of mind had a dagger as its object, although in another sense no such object as the dagger existed. I want to argue that Schopenhauer frequently, though not always, uses 'object' in the former, intentional, sense. (In the interests of clarity, I shall sometimes use expressions such as 'content of a subject's experience', 'subjective content', or simply 'content' instead of 'object'.)

Consider first this passage from Schopenhauer's doctoral dissertation, *On the Fourfold Root of the Principle of Sufficient Reason*: 'Our knowing consciousness . . . divides into subject and object, and contains nothing besides. To be object for the subject, and to be our representation, is the same thing. All our representations are objects of the subject and all objects of the subject are our representations.'[30] Consciousness divides into subject and object for the subject. Objects, if they are simply objects for the subject, are equivalent to representations, or to whatever comes before the mind. If we recall the ambiguity we noted earlier in Kant's usage of the term 'representation', as between a mental state and the content of a mental state, we may suspect that Schopenhauer is making the seemingly uncontroversial point here that experience

[30] *VW* p. 41 (41–2).

requires both an experiencer and an experienced content. On the other hand, given that he wants to make so much of the dichotomy of subject and object, and the dependence of the one on the other, it is hardly likely that this is all that he means.

There are a number of indications that at crucial places in his argument Schopenhauer does take the dichotomy of subject and object to be simply that of experiencer and experienced content, and the relation between them to be a straightforward matter of logical interdependence between the concepts *subject* and *object*. In at least one passage Schopenhauer says that the most general form of all appearance or representation is 'being-object-for-a-subject [*das-Objekt-für-ein-Subjekt-sein*]', suggesting that Kant would have rescued himself from inconsistency about the thing in itself if he had taken this principle more seriously.[31] This passage, and the one quoted in the previous paragraph, surely give a strong clue as to how we should read the term 'object' elsewhere. But in addition I shall mention three pieces of evidence that are dispersed quite plentifully throughout Schopenhauer's pages. First, there is his confidence about the unassailability of his key slogan 'No object without subject'. Secondly, his division of 'objects' into a number of classes, which contain disparate items whose principle of unity is merely that they appear as the contents of mental states. Thirdly, his insistence on the self-evidence of the proposition 'No subject without object' as the exact correlative of 'No object without subject'. Let me now say a little about each of these pieces of evidence in turn.

We have already seen that Schopenhauer makes the categorical assertion that there can be no object without subject. Very often he does not feel any compulsion to argue his point, and merely states it as if it could be taken as a fixed and unarguable premiss. It is true that there are some arguments for idealism (or against realism), and I shall consider these in the next section. It must also be conceded that Schopenhauer is not a philosopher who is always scrupulously careful about inserting an argument where one might be demanded. But on the other hand it is noteworthy

---

[31] *W*1 p. 227 (174–5).

that he should give so little argument for such a pivotal proposition. The interpretation of 'subject' and 'object' that I am offering can help to explain this significant fact, for if Schopenhauer treats 'No object without subject' as expressing the thought that there could not be a subjective content of experience without an experiencer, one can easily understand how he could consider it incontestable. This is not to say that one could not conceivably demand an argument for the proposition thus interpreted, but simply that, thus interpreted, the proposition could easily seem obvious. The 'content' reading would also explain why Schopenhauer can write: 'No object without a subject can be thought of without contradiction',[32] and elsewhere speak of 'the simple, so accessible, undeniable truth "No object without subject".'[33] My contention, then, is that Schopenhauer is supremely confident about his slogan because he regards it as expressing a proposition whose denial involves a contradiction, and that this is readily understandable if he took the slogan to be equivalent to something like 'No experienced content without an experiencer'.

For the second point we can turn once again to Schopenhauer's doctoral dissertation, which he updated after writing *The World as Will and Representation*, and to which he refers us, in the latter work, on this very point. In section 16 of *On the Fourfold Root* he starts off with the passage quoted above: 'Our knowing consciousness . . . divides into subject and object, and contains nothing besides. To be object for the subject, and to be our representation, is the same thing [etc.].' Next he introduces the important idea that a representation can be an object for us only if it stands to other representations in a relation of law-like connectedness, whose form is determinable a priori. The importance of this idea for Schopenhauer should not be underestimated: it provides the very core of *On the Fourfold Root*, as is reflected in Schopenhauer's remark that 'It is this connectedness that the principle of sufficient reason, in its general form, expresses.' The most general form of the principle of sufficient reason, Schopenhauer has previously assured us, is that enunciated by Wolff, and it is on the basis of this that he himself proceeds: '*Nihil est sine ratione cur potius*

---

[32] *W*1 p. 42 (15).　　　　[33] Ibid. p. 533 (434).

sit, quam non sit. Nothing is without a reason [*Grund*] for its being.'[34] Everything, then, that is an object for us must exhibit some kind of law-like connectedness to some other object(s) as its reason or ground.

The main burden of *On the Fourfold Root* is to show that there are four, and only four, such kinds of connectedness between objects, corresponding to four basic divisions in kind among objects themselves.[35] The first class of objects is that of empirical representations by way of intuition. Schopenhauer deals here with ordinary, concrete spatio-temporal representations, and finds that the law of their interconnection is that of causality (the 'principle of the ground of becoming'). The second class comprises concepts, or 'abstract representations', which, in opposition to representations of intuition, are in the province of reason (*Vernunft*). The principle of sufficient reason finds a place here in relating a conceptual judgement to its grounds (the 'principle of the reason of knowing'). The third class is familiarly Kantian, being made up of a priori intuitions of space and time. Schopenhauer speaks here of the 'principle of the reason of being', pointing out that for a numbers of truths about space and time (e.g. those concerning the relations of a triangle's sides to its angles, or the unidimensionality of time), a principle of explanation is required which is distinct both from that which relates effects to causes and from that which relates true empirical judgements to their justifications. The fourth class is unusual in having only one object as member, namely 'the willing subject' experienced as object which we encountered above. The principle here is that of the 'sufficient reason of acting', a special instance of the law of causality, with the difference that here causality is 'seen from within' by the subject. What the various classes of objects have in common, apart from the claimed unifying element of the principle of sufficient reason, is that they are contents of a subject's consciousness, or objects for the subject. The organization of *On the Fourfold Root* bears out the suggestion that Schopenhauer's 'object' can to a large extent be interpreted as equivalent to 'content'.

---

[34] *VW* p. 17 (6).
[35] Ibid. p. 41 (42). The following account of the four classes of objects is a very brief summary of chs. 4–7 of *VW*.

My third piece of evidence brings us into contact with what Johannes Volkelt, writing at the turn of the century, called Schopenhauer's 'correlativism'.[36] Representation, for Schopenhauer, is essentially bipolar: it involves both a subject and an object, which are not only such that one cannot be identified with the other, but such that one cannot be thought away without thinking away the other: 'The world as representation . . . has two essential, necessary, and inseparable halves. . . . Thus, these halves are not to be separated, even in thought: for each of them has meaning and existence only through the other, is there with it, and disappears with it. They limit one another immediately: where the object begins, the subject ceases.'[37] Subject and object are related to one another as 'necessary correlates' for Schopenhauer, and he goes out of his way to show that not merely 'No object without subject', but also the correlative 'No subject without object' express a simple, undeniable truth. Thus he writes that although he began by stating that the object was conditioned by the subject,

[o]n the other hand the subjective point of departure and the original proposition 'the world is my representation' has its inadequacy too . . . partly inasmuch as it only expresses the being conditioned of the object. For just as false as the proposition of the raw understanding 'The world, the object, would still be there, even if there were no subject' is this one: 'The subject would still be a knowing thing [*ein Erkennendes*], even if it had no object, i.e. no representation at all.' A consciousness without object is no consciousness.[38]

In the light of this passage, it seems clear that 'No subject without object' is intended to express the thought that for any experiencer there must be something *of* which it has experience. In fact, if we take the two 'correlative' slogans together, assuming each of them to express something which Schopenhauer could plausibly claim as obvious and undeniable, then their most natural interpretation is simply that consciousness must be both *of* something and *for* something (somebody). This further bears out my claim that the primary sense of

[36] Johannes Volkelt, *Arthur Schopenhauer: Seine Persönlichkeit, seine Lehre, sein Glaube*, pp. 89–101.

[37] *W*1 p. 32 (5). [38] *W*2 p. 23 (14–15).

'object' for Schopenhauer is something like 'content of consciousness', or 'experienced object', or 'object for some subject'.

However, this is by no means all that Schopenhauer's 'correlativism' amounts to. One of the more surprising features of his exposition is that he combines a vehement advocacy of idealism, in which the world of objects is held to depend for its very existence on the subject, with the assertion, made less frequently but still unequivocally, that idealism is merely a one-sided picture. He often ridicules the materialist claim that the subject of experience is to be explained exclusively in objective terms as nothing but a modification of matter; but he then seems to retreat to the position that materialism is as acceptable as idealism, although, taken on its own, just as one-sided. What is ultimately required is that idealism (whose starting-point is the subject) and materialism (whose starting-point is matter) should each recognize the legitimacy of the other. Here we have probably the most important instance of 'correlativism'; in even countenancing the notion that the subject can be explained as a modification of matter, Schopenhauer seems to deviate markedly from the idealist standpoint which he lays down initially. Whether this is in fact so is one of the issues I shall be discussing in Chapters 5 and 6. Here I merely want to comment on a crucial confusion which Schopenhauer makes, between the correlativism of subject and object and the correlativism of idealism and materialism. The two are clearly very different cases. Since a subject of experience without any experienced content is surely just as inconceivable as an experienced content without a subject, an idealist may cheerfully accept the proposition that subjects presuppose objects—and then go on to say that the objects of our experience are mind-dependent entities not things in themselves, and so on. Conversely, one has to be neither an idealist nor a denier of the proposition that everything is a modification of matter in order to be able to agree that (in the sense discussed) objects presuppose a subject.

Nevertheless, Schopenhauer does regard the 'simple, undeniable truths' about the mutual dependence of subject and object as bearing directly on the issues raised by both idealism and materialism. He makes the conflation easier for himself by couching what he sees as the correlativity of idealism and materialism in terms of the claim that subject and matter are correlates. At one memorable point, subject and matter are personified in a short dialogue: the conversation begins in an unpromising way, with each of the participants asserting 'I am, and besides me there is nothing', but ends with the reassuring unison: 'So we are inseparably connected as necessary parts of one whole, which includes us both and exists through us both.'[39] The most fatal aspect of Schopenhauer's conflation is that he thinks he can use the obvious-sounding principle of the dependency of the object on the subject to support his idealist case. But this involves a slide from the principle that an experienced content requires an experiencer, through the claim that anything experienced by a subject exists only inasmuch as it is experienced by a subject, to the ultimate position according to which the whole world of material objects depends for its existence on being experienced.[40] It can be asserted without hesitation that Schopenhauer commits himself to this position—although precisely what Schopenhauer's idealism involves, and what further arguments he uses for it, are issues I reserve for the next chapter.

At the beginning of the present chapter I posed three questions of interpretation about Schopenhauer's central claim that the world of objects is conditioned by the subject: they concerned the nature of the subject, the nature of objects, and the nature of the dependence of the latter on the former. In answer to the first question, we saw that, for Schopenhauer, the subject is something presupposed by all experience but not itself a possible object of experience, and furthermore something to which he gives a deliberately problematic extra-worldly status. On the second question, I argued that a primary sense of the term 'object' for Schopenhauer is something like 'content of an experience', with this representing, I suggested,

---

[39] *W*2 pp. 25–7 (17–18).

[40] I speak here of a 'slide' from one sense of 'object' to another, although from Schopenhauer's point of view there is clearly only one sense. Because of this, and because he allows no distinction at all between 'representation' and 'object of · representation', he regards 'No object without subject' as simply encompassing the claim that ordinarily perceivable things are mind-dependent. (I am grateful to David Hamlyn for help in clarifying this point.)

the significance of his phrase 'object for the subject'. Objects in this sense are to be divided into four classes, only one of which comprises ordinary material objects. We saw that experience for Schopenhauer is essentially bipolar, with subject and object being conceived as necessarily distinct but at the same time presupposing one another. On the final question, it must be said that while for much of the time Schopenhauer understands the notion of the dependence of objects on the subject in terms of the ('undeniable') proposition that any content of experience is so for some subject, he also wants to claim that the whole world of material objects depends for its existence on being experienced by some object. It is far from obvious that *this* proposition is undeniable without contradiction. A convincing case for idealism cannot be built solely on what is contained in the slogan 'No object without subject'. If that slogan can be expanded to mean something obviously true, it does not give any argument for idealism; if it is read as a statement of idealism, it is highly contentious.

5

Idealism

No truth is more certain, more independent of all others and less in need of proof than this: that everything which is there for knowledge, hence the whole world, is only object in relation to the subject, perception of the perceiver, in a word, representation.[1]

PART of the opening page of *The World as Will and Representation*, this reads like a warning not to expect any arguments, and to some extent Schopenhauer is true to this warning. On many occasions he gives us to understand that any alternative to idealism is flatly inconceivable. For example, near the beginning of his most extended defence of idealism (*W2* ch. 1), which does contain some arguments, he says that ' "The world is my representation" is, like the axioms of Euclid, a proposition which everyone must recognize as true as soon as he understands it.' (Although, he adds, it is also not one which everyone 'understands as soon as he hears it'.[2]) We may suspect that there is a proposition lurking somewhere of which this might plausibly be held, but that this proposition is not, as such, an expression of idealism. On the following page he accuses realism of ignoring something which he describes as 'the surest and simplest truth':

that the *objective existence* of things is conditioned by something which represents them, and that consequently [*folglich*] the objective world exists only *as representation*, is no hypothesis, still less an authoritarian pronouncement, or even a paradox set up for the sake of argument; rather, it is the surest and simplest truth, recognition of which is made harder only by its being too simple, and by the fact that not everyone has sufficient power of reflection to go back to the first elements of their consciousness of things.[3]

Schopenhauer claims to be saying something simple and

[1] *W1* p. 29 (3).
[2] *W2* p. 10 (3).
[3] Ibid. pp. 11–12 (5).

incontestable. But there is a 'simple' truth here only if 'objective existence' and 'objective world' are taken as equivalent to 'existence as object for a subject' and 'world existing as object for a subject'. The world existing as object for a subject only exists as representation. But this does nothing to convince us that there are not, or could not be, things (let us not for the moment call them objects) existing independently of subjects altogether. In expecting to gain this consequence from his 'simple truth', Schopenhauer is once again begging the question. Besides, the presence of the word 'folglich' (*consequently*) in the above passage is troubling. Suppose we grant that something can be objective, in the sense of being an object for a subject, only if there is a subject; it is true then that books and tables can be objects for a subject only if there is a subject. But it is not a 'consequence' of that that books and tables exist only as representations.

To some extent we can explain Schopenhauer's complacency about the idealist starting-point of his philosophy in historical terms. It is probably true in general that better arguments are likely to be produced in the face of radical controversy, and although many in the German academic community were opposed to idealism, it had become the dominant trend by Schopenhauer's time, so that the reading public would have taken less convincing than at many other times and places. Related to this is the fact that Schopenhauer's defence of idealism is really very un-Kantian, showing again how wrong he was to think that he was taking his departure directly from Kant and that any intervening links were irrelevant. Kant had used the terms 'representation', 'subject', and 'object' of course, but the idea that idealism could be proved more or less by exhibiting what one was committed to by using these terms is alien to Kant. A major change, however, was brought about by Karl Leonhard Reinhold's attempts to popularize Kant in the 1790s. Reinhold formulated a 'principle of consciousness' which reads: 'Representation is distinguished in consciousness by the subject from both subject and object, and is referred to both;' or, in another version: 'We are all compelled by *consciousness* to agree that to every representation there pertains a representing subject and a *represented* object, and that both must be distinguished from the representation to which they pertain.'[4] Reinhold saw the prime task of philosophy as being an analysis of consciousness. One must isolate consciousness and consider it apart from its objects in order to discern its necessary structure. What is revealed, according to Reinhold, is that for all consciousness *representation* is the primitive concept, and that it necessarily pertains to both a subject and an object. This object is distinct from representation and falls outside the subject's consciousness altogether, but the latter is supposed to be related necessarily to it. That Reinhold still wants to retain an essential distinction between representation and object signifies an important difference between his account of consciousness and Schopenhauer's superficially similar view that 'our knowing consciousness . . . divides into subject and object, and contains nothing besides'. But Schopenhauer here shows himself as the heir of subsequent arguments. For it was out of Reinhold's version of Kantianism that there came, within a few years, the developments mentioned in Chapter 2: the sceptical attack (led by Schulze) on the weak notion of 'objects' existing in themselves, and Fichte's bold determination to avoid this difficulty by giving a complete account of experience which invoked only objects that lay within the realm of self-consciousness.

Though he came on the scene ten or more years after these controversies were at their height, Schopenhauer was personally acquainted with Reinhold, Schulze, and Fichte (if attending the latter's lectures counts as personal acquaintance), and was well aware of the way philosophy had progressed since Kant. (It is worth entering this reminder again, if only to counteract the impression he sometimes gives that all this had happened on another planet.) The marks of these developments are clearly discernible in Schopenhauer's position, even when he thinks he is returning directly to Kant. Thus it is apparently not open to question for him that the structure of representation should be the starting-point for an account of knowledge. There is also no question that the analysis of representation is fundamentally in terms of subject and object. Moreover, as we saw from his attacks on Kant in Chapter 2, he finds it

---

[4] Cf. George di Giovanni and H. S. Harris, *Between Kant and Hegel*, pp. 70 and 99 n. 29. I owe my outline of Reinhold and his influence to the succinct account in this book, pp. 9–32.

inconceivable that there should be a distinction between representation and object of representation. To be an object is to be a representation for him: 'object' cannot refer to anything existing outside what is present in the subject's consciousness, and 'representation' is not a term which raises the question of a relation to any such object. Beyond this, the theme of the mutual dependence of subject and object, and the posing of the question of whether the subjective should be derived from the objective or vice versa—both pivotal in Schopenhauer—have very explicit parallels in both Fichte and Schelling.[5] Thus part of the *inevitability* of idealism for Schopenhauer lies in the pervading influence of his own immediate predecessors on the shape of philosophy—an influence which in many respects makes him as much of a post-Kantian idealist as they were.

Schopenhauer was prone to take a wider view of his own place in the history of philosophy (when he did so at all). And here we do find him offering some justification for his confidence in the truth of idealism. He declares that Descartes is rightly seen as the father of modern philosophy, because his scepticism of the senses revealed immediate subjective consciousness as the true foundation of philosophy, and that it was as an ultimate consequence of the Cartesian train of thought that Berkeley arrived at idealism. Thus, for Schopenhauer, idealism can be defended on the grounds that it is the culmination of post-Cartesian philosophy, and, within that historical context, the only form for philosophy to take. Thus we find the following argument:

1. It is only of what lies within consciousness that there is immediate certainty.
2. The foundations of any body of knowledge (*Wissenschaft*) must have immediate certainty.

[5] e.g. in the *Wissenschaftslehre* (*Sämtliche Werke*, vol. 1, p. 218), Fichte asserts his leading principle to be: 'das Ich setzt sich als bestimmt durch das Nicht-Ich' (*the I posits itself as determined by the not-I*), and appends to his explanation the parentheses 'No object, no subject' and 'No subject, no object'. Schelling's *System des Transzendentalen Idealismus* opens with the claim that 'in knowledge . . . objective and subjective are united in such a way that one cannot say which has priority', and then poses as its central question whether philosophy should give primacy to the subjective or the objective (*Sämtliche Werke*, vol. 3, pp. 339–42).

3. Philosophy must concern itself with the 'first and original' foundations of knowledge.
4. Therefore the basis of philosophy must be what lies within consciousness.
5. Therefore philosophy is essentially idealistic.[6]

Given the assumptions of 'foundationalism', steps 2 and 3, and the familiar assumption of step 1 (all of which, though now somewhat discredited, are obviously far from unique to Schopenhauer), we can make the inference to step 4 without much difficulty. But the point at issue is whether idealism can be supported on the basis of these assumptions; and it seems that it cannot. For steps 1–4 are consistent with a position according to which inference may be made to the existence and nature of a world fully outside consciousness. It could be objected that this position collapses inevitably into scepticism. But then scepticism too is compatible with steps 1–4, and Schopenhauer, like Berkeley and Kant before him, wants his idealism to be clearly demarcated from scepticism. The upshot is that the present argument cannot be said to secure Schopenhauer in his conclusion that idealism is the only possible philosophical standpoint, although it does reveal some of the presuppositions which help to make idealism the leading contender for him.

At first sight, and to the untutored mind, Schopenhauer admits, realism seems highly plausible. People generally do tend to think that the world has an objective existence independently of its being presented to some conscious subject. But, he thinks, there are arguments which show this view to be untenable. According to one of these, it is contradictory to suppose that one could successfully imagine the existence of an objective world without the knowing subject, because the world that one would then imagine would exist after all in the imagination of a knowing subject.[7] In essence, this argument is the same as one used by Berkeley,[8] whether or not Schopenhauer consciously took it from that source. It is no more convincing in either author. Of course anything I imagine exists as such 'only in my imagination' if

⁶ *W*2 pp. 10–11 (4–5).   ⁷ Ibid. p. 12 (5).
⁸ *Principles of Human Knowledge*, 23; *Three Dialogues*, 200 (*Philosophical Works*, pp. 83–4, 158).

one is talking in terms of the content of my imaginings (perhaps a mental picture, a thought of some kind, or a description). But that in no way addresses the question of whether any object exists which corresponds to the picture, thought, or description. Schopenhauer also asserts that 'everything with which we are acquainted [*kennen*] lies within our consciousness'[9]—but here a similar point applies. That we must *be conscious of* something in order to be acquainted with it is presumably true, but it is a very different thing to say that *that with which we are acquainted* lies *within our consciousness*, either in the sense of being purely mental or in that of depending for its existence on a subject of consciousness. Schopenhauer nevertheless thinks that his assertion constitutes a devastating blow for the unsophisticated realist outlook: 'Never can there be an objective existence absolutely and in itself; indeed, such a thing is completely unthinkable: for the objective, as such, always and essentially has its existence in the consciousness of a subject'.[10] The context tells us, though, that we are back to the problems discussed above: first, that in making 'objective' mean that which is object for a subject Schopenhauer begs the question in favour of subject-dependence; and secondly, that by an equivocation over two kinds of subject-dependence, he illegitimately concludes from the necessity of a subject for any experienced content that anything experienced exists only for a subject.

Two other arguments which Schopenhauer gives for idealism are worth mentioning briefly. In one he suggests that unless the spatio-temporal world were a product of the human intellect, there would be no way of explaining our being so fully at home in it. Indeed, he says that it would be *impossible* from the start for us 'to find our way about in' a world whose fundamental order did not depend on us.[11] Besides being a mere assertion, this might be said to overstate the case. The converse is perhaps true: if the fundamental laws governing the world proceed from us, we could not but understand that world. But while our understanding an independently ordered world is less probable than that, more is required to show it to be impossible. Furthermore, it might be questionable whether

---

[9] *W*2 p. 11 (5).   [10] Ibid. p. 12 (5).   [11] Ibid. p. 16 (9).

we do understand the world's fundamental order at all fully. Schopenhauer's view appears to be motivated by an excessively sharp dichotomy: either we fully comprehend the world, in which case it must somehow originate in us, or it is external to us, and in the process irretrievably alien to our understanding.

In the other argument Schopenhauer suggests that idealism is a simpler theory than realism, on the grounds that the latter posits two distinct spatio-temporal worlds, one existing prior to being apprehended by the subject, and another existing in the mind of a subject once apprehension is held to have taken place.[12] Schopenhauer may be thinking here of Leibniz's doctrine of pre-established harmony, which he criticizes on similar grounds elsewhere. Leibniz, he says, 'felt the conditioning of the object by the subject, but yet could not free himself from the thought of an existence for objects in themselves', and thus was led to assume a world of objects in themselves 'exactly the same as and running parallel with the world of representation, connected to it, however, not directly but only externally, by way of a *harmonia praestabilita*—obviously the most redundant thing in the world, since the world itself never enters into perception and the exactly similar world in representation takes its course just as well without it'.[13] Schopenhauer apparently makes the assumption that the realist view he is attacking *includes* the essentially Kantian position that the spatio-temporal world as we experience it is constituted solely by representations. This is especially clear in the discussion of Leibniz, whose first assumption is said to have been that of the conditioning of the object by the subject. If we can take this idealist premiss as read, then indeed the assumption of a further spatio-temporal world existing beyond representations is problematic, if not redundant. But of course, an argument for idealism which has to include an assumption of idealism is not highly satisfactory.

Thus, without being anachronistic or patronizing, we can conclude our discussion of Schopenhauer's arguments for idealism by remarking that they are poor arguments. To some extent this is explicable in terms of his belief that 'No truth is more certain . . . and less in need of proof'. In effect, he makes

---

[12] *W*2 pp. 16–17 (9).   [13] *VW* p. 48 (51).

idealism a premiss about which one must say a few encouraging things but to which there will not be much serious objection. It is perhaps tempting in the light of this to say that rather than finding himself convinced of the truth of idealism by argument, he took over, comparatively unreflectingly, a basic commitment to idealism that was prevalent in the philosophical climate of his day. I suggested as much earlier. But in fact Schopenhauer does give the impression that he expects idealism, for all its alleged obviousness, to be regarded as an unusual position, certainly by the general public. Thus at one point he claims that while in India the basic idealist outlook is something of a popular article of faith, in Europe it is still regarded as 'paradoxical' (a situation for which he blames the 'realism' inherent in Judaism).[14] The truth about Schopenhauer's attitude is probably that, following Kant's lead and resting to some extent on Kant's authority, he feels himself entitled to present idealism as the legitimate (if not the properly recognized) heir of the modern European tradition in philosophy.

Given the basic idealist orientation, however, there are still some questions that need to be asked. Does Schopenhauer say anything to clarify his relationships with Kantian and Berkeleian idealism, and with the idealism of Fichte and Schelling? Does he answer certain charges that can be made against idealism, in particular that it is a sceptical system of philosophy, and that it denies that there is a real external world at all? And what about some of the points of detail where he diverges from Kant? Surely he must say something about the role of the thing in itself, which (as we saw in Chapter 2) he thinks Kant mishandled by giving it a causal role. And he must explain the principles of organisation by which the subject's faculties are supposed to order the world of objects. In this, the exposition and defence of the internal workings of his own theory, Schopenhauer's grasp is surer and his writing more impressive.

There are some objections to idealism which Schopenhauer deals with by presenting them as misunderstandings of that position. The first (and according to Schopenhauer the 'chief') objection, is stated as follows:

[14] Ibid. p. 47 (50–1).

My own person too is an object for another, and therefore is the other's representation; and yet I know certainly that I would be there, even without his representing me. But all other objects stand to his intellect in the same relation as *I* do: consequently other objects too would be there, without their being represented by this other.

The reply which Schopenhauer gives reiterates an aspect of his conception of the subject which we remarked upon in Chapter 4:

The answer to this is: that other, as whose object I now regard my person, is not without qualification [*schlechthin*] *the subject*, but in the first instance a knowing individual. Thus, if he were not there, and even if no other knowing being except me existed at all, this would still not amount to the removal of the *subject*, in whose representation alone all objects exist. For I myself am this subject too, as is every knowing being. Consequently, in the assumed case, my person would by all means be there, but once again as representation, that is, in my own cognition.[15]

Thus it would be a misunderstanding of idealism, as Schopenhauer conceives it, to think that it involved linking the existence of objects to their being presented in the consciousness of any one individual. He is clearly committed to the notion that objects cannot exist unless there be *some* subject for whom they 'are there'. But we can see that his favoured expression 'The world is *my* representation' is at best a highly misleading way of putting his point if—as we should—we take seriously these remarks about the non-identity of subject and individual.

Whatever else may be said about such a position, it is not solipsistic. This is a charge that is sometimes levelled at Schopenhauer, so it will be appropriate to examine his attitude to solipsism here. Schopenhauer does not use the term 'solipsism' as such, but he does discuss it under the name of 'theoretical egoism':

But whether the objects known to the individual only as representation are nevertheless, as with his own body, appearances of a will; this is . . . the genuine sense of the question about the reality of the outside world: to deny the latter is the sense of *theoretical egoism*, which, in so doing, holds appearances apart from its own individual to be phantoms—as practical egoism does exactly the same thing in a

[15] *W*2 pp. 12–13 (6).

practical respect, treating only its own person as really a person, and all others as mere phantoms.

His view of this position is then stated as follows:

Theoretical egoism can indeed never be refuted by proofs: and yet it has never been reliably used in philosophy except as a sceptical sophism, i.e. for the sake of appearance. As a serious conviction, on the other hand, it could only be found in the madhouse: and as such it would then need not so much a proof as a cure. So to this extent we do not go into it any further, but regard it simply as the last stronghold of scepticism, which is always polemical.[16]

At the end of the same paragraph Schopenhauer compares solipsism to an impregnable fortress whose garrison can never get out to attack anybody, and concludes that, like such a fortress, we can safely pass it by. This clearly disposes of the notion that Schopenhauer openly espouses solipsism. He rather believes it to be only a sceptic's tool, to be used against other positions, and not something in which a sane person would believe. In this he is right to the extent that it is precisely the absurdity (if not insanity) of solipsism which gives it its devastating edge when used polemically. So Schopenhauer does not set out to be a solipsist (has anyone ever done so?). The charge may be brought against him that in stating that the world is *my* representation, his position must ultimately entail solipsism—but I have suggested that this would be a misunderstanding of his claim. The 'I' that is involved here is merely the self-conscious subject of representations which cannot be identified with any individual in the world. Solipsism must be a position which in some way restricts the contents of the world by tying them to a single individual. The Schopenhauerian subject cannot be an individual and so cannot fulfil this restricting role. Having said all this, however, we should note a further aspect of Schopenhauer's dismissal of solipsism in the above passage. In calling 'theoretical egoism' the view which denies that anything experienced externally to the subject is an appearance of a will, he is alluding to his own view that the will is the thing in itself of which everything is an appearance. So in a mildly cryptic way he indicates that the madness in solipsism

[16] *W*1 p. 148 (104).

is its denial that appearances are appearances of something existing in itself. His own idealism may not be solipsistic, but how will he avoid its becoming madly subjective in an analogous way unless he relies on some argument for the existence of a thing in itself lying behind appearances? For all his complaint that Kant is not a consistent idealist because he relies on the thing in itself, we have here a hint that when it comes to the crux Schopenhauer will do the same.

Another 'misunderstanding' of idealism which Schopenhauer mentions is the stubbornly persistent view that idealism 'denies the *empirical* reality of the external world'. Schopenhauer takes Jacobi to task for his claim that our belief in the reality of what we experience is purely a matter of faith, or that the world is given to us 'on credit'; rather, the world 'gives itself to us as that which it is, and delivers immediately what it promises'. The distinction must be made, for Schopenhauer, between empirical and transcendental idealism, the latter being the true kind which he himself espouses.[17] Now we saw in Chapter 2 that Kant insisted on a distinction between transcendental and empirical idealism. By the latter he meant either a *sceptical* view, which doubts the reality of external objects (his example was Descartes's scepticism of the senses), or a *dogmatic* view, which denies their existence altogether (which he took to be Berkeley's position).[18] Given Schopenhauer's professed desire to incorporate the Berkeleian view with his own, however, it is not immediately clear whether his distinction between transcendental and empirical idealism can be interpreted in the same way as Kant's.

What he explicitly says when he introduces the distinction is that transcendental idealism both (*a*) 'leaves the *empirical* reality of the world untouched', and (*b*) insists on objects being conditioned, both materially and formally, by the subject. As against its transcendental namesake, we must presumably understand empirical idealism to deny the '*empirical* reality of the world'. But what does this mean? Surely it cannot mean denying that what we experience has an existence independently of its being experienced, for making

---

[17] *W*2 pp. 14–15 (7–8).
[18] *KdrV* A491/B519, B274 (in the latter passage, Kant uses the term 'material idealism' for what he calls 'empirical idealism' in the former).

such a denial is, as far as we know, central to Schopenhauer's own position. Rather, it must mean denying that what we experience is (ever) the real world. Thus empirical idealism is a position which remains wedded to the notion that the world is something other than, and can never be attained by way of, our representations, so that the representations we have may as well be dreams or illusions. In other words, empirical idealism presupposes transcendental realism. Schopenhauer, on the contrary, is adamant that what we experience, whilst comprising only representations, is the real world of spatio-temporal objects. In this he provides a clear parallel with Berkeley, who on the one hand claimed to side with common sense in affirming the reality of what we immediately perceive, and on the other argued that 'the things immediately perceived, are ideas which exist only in the mind'.[19] Berkeley's main thrust in arguing thus was to disprove scepticism by relocating the real world of ordinary things within the mind, where there could be a guarantee that we experienced it. Like Berkeley, and in this respect like Kant too, Schopenhauer is searching for an idealist position which will be clearly distinct from, and will discredit, scepticism. Like Kant, he gives the name of 'transcendental idealism' to the kind of idealism which he thinks will do this. But (in the light of the discussion of these issues in Chapter 2, which I shall not rehearse) we can say that, unlike Kant, Schopenhauer correctly recognizes an affinity between transcendental idealism and Berkeley's enterprise.

Schopenhauer is critical of scepticism mainly on the grounds that the whole 'dispute about the reality of the external world' is 'foolish'. Scepticism is one of the unfortunate partners in this folly. The opposing disputant he calls 'dogmatism', discerning here two species: realism on the one hand, and on the other, idealism as exemplified by Fichte, or by what he takes Fichte's position to be. Transcendental idealism should be distinguished from all these positions, as can be seen here:

The whole world of objects is and remains representation, and for that very reason . . . it has transcendental ideality. But it is not because of this a lie, or an illusion: it gives itself as what it is, as

[19] *Three Dialogues*, 262 (*Philosophical Works*, p. 207).

representation, and indeed as a series of representations, whose common bond is the principle of [sufficient] reason. As such it is intelligible to the healthy understanding . . . Only to the mind twisted by sophistries can it occur to dispute about the world's reality.[20]

The underlying mistake of all positions that take the reality of the external world to be in dispute is given by Schopenhauer as their failure to realize that *causality* does not operate between *subject* and *object*. Causality is a principle of organization among objects, and may be said (in Schopenhauer's revised Kantian account, of which more below) to be 'imposed' by the subject on its representations (objects). But the subject is not, for Schopenhauer, an object. It may be regarded as the origin of causality in a suitably qualified way, but it is not linked to objects by way of causality at all. (Thus we have further confirmation that Schopenhauer is serious in his view that the subject is not a part of the empirical world of objects.) Dogmatic realism is what he calls any position which strives to make the subject, or its states, an effect of objects, while 'Fichtian idealism' is the position which 'makes the object into the effect of the subject'.[21]

Once again the assessment of Fichte here goes back to the lectures that Schopenhauer attended in 1811–12. He could not understand how Fichte's 'I' could 'posit' the 'not-I', unless what was meant by this was that it brought it about causally. If this is what Fichte meant, then Schopenhauer is right to find an instance of subject–object causality here, and right to query it. For all the absurdly complicated 'determining', 'acting', and 'positing' of which Fichte talked was supposed to take place outside of empirical consciousness. It was 'absolute' and a pre-condition of experience rather than part of its contents. But (echoing the earlier discussions of Kant) that is precisely what rendered any notion of causality inappropriate. In Schopenhauer's view, Fichte could maintain the semblance of saying anything meaningful only by presenting the antics of the absolute in terms that were applicable solely to the empirical. But what infuriated him most of all was the invention of terminology whose obscurity masked the trick

[20] *W*I p. 43 (15).   [21] *W*I p. 41 (13).

that was being played. (Fichte said of the 'I', for example, that 'through absolute creative power it posits itself as principle [*Princip*], and the representation as principiate [*Principiat*]'.[22] Schopenhauer read these words as screens for 'cause' and 'effect'; but not content with this, Fichte went still further: 'So as not to say causality he coins with impudent deceit the word *Principheit*.') Understandably, Schopenhauer cannot be sure that he has understood Fichte properly, but the impression was to remain with him that an instance of subject–object causality was being perpetrated under cloak of darkness.

Moving on from Fichte, let us look at what Schopenhauer has to say about scepticism and dogmatic realism. Both, he argues, proceed from the assumption that the subject's representations can be distinguished from objects—something that Schopenhauer himself has strenuously denied of course. The one then sets up a causal relation between object and representation, while the other (scepticism) accepts this basic framework, but points out the uncertainty of any inference from cause to effect, and argues that, in having presented to us only representations which are the effects of objects, we can never be certain about the nature or even the existence of objects outside our own consciousness.

Schopenhauer sometimes suggests that he has located here an extremely widespread and damaging philosophical error. All previous philosophies, he observes, have 'proceeded either from the object or the subject, and tried accordingly to explain the one from the other, doing so moreover by way of the principle of [sufficient] reason'.[23] His own procedure is to begin from the notion of subject and object as correlates, each distinct from and presupposing the other, and connected, not by any form of the principle of sufficient reason, but by the relation 'is there for', or 'represents'. How convincing, though, is Schopenhauer's presentation of the 'mistake' underlying the dispute about the reality of the external world? If we look carefully, he in fact gives two characterizations of the mistake. In one the mistake is that of assuming what we could call 'subject–object causality'. But according to the other the mistake is that of assuming causality between *objects* and

[22] *HN*2 p. 42. For Schopenhauer's comments, see ibid. pp. 60, 134, 143.
[23] *W*1 p. 55 (25–6).

representations. It seems fair to say that subject–object causality is a misguided notion if 'object' is taken to mean 'content' as explained in Chapter 4. The relation between a subject of mental states and the contents of those mental states is not one of cause and effect (in either direction), but is more plausibly characterized, as an initial shot at any rate, in the Schopenhauerian way. Certainly, the notion that my mental states, or their contents, cause me would be an odd one. But the realist and sceptical positions which Schopenhauer seeks to discredit use, not the notion of 'subject–object causality', but that of objects causing representations. This is only illegitimate if all objects are representations, and all representations are objects. Schopenhauer has asserted that they are, but we have noted the weakness of that assertion, and we must conclude that his attack on both realism and scepticism—and hence his claim to bypass the dispute about the reality of the external world— are no stronger. This kind of argument based on the illegitimacy of positing causality between subject and object, or between object and representation, is not found in either Berkeley or Kant. Kant, as we saw, holds fast to the notion of representations as caused by external things, even though there is deep unclarity attached to this notion for him. Berkeley, for his part, argues explicitly that there can be no causal connection between ideas and that only a spirit can be a cause,[24] so that, for him, there can be no analogue of Schopenhauer's point that it is *only* between objects/representations that causality operates. Nevertheless, there is an overall pattern common to all three philosophers, if we allow Kant to be represented by the first-edition Paralogisms section that was so admired by Schopenhauer. All of them can be seen as arguing thus: scepticism is to be disarmed by removing the gap (the distinction even) between the real object and the subject's consciously received presentation. Without this gap to exploit, scepticism about real objects would indeed collapse. But Schopenhauer's argument leaves us feeling once again that there may yet be things existing beyond our experience (or even possible experience) of them. If Schopenhauer wants to stipulate that such things are not

[24] Cf. *Three Dialogues*, 239–40 (*Philosophical Works*, pp. 189–90).

'objects', because that term is reserved for the contents of a subject's mental state, we simply have to retract that term. The sense remains that the pathways are still open to realism, or equally scepticism, about things transcending the subject's experience.

Reverting to Schopenhauer's characterization of transcendental idealism, let us consider his claim that objects are conditioned both materially and formally by the subject. Here we may recall Schopenhauer's explicit attempt to unify the doctrines of his idealist forebears:

[Transcendental idealism] holds firmly that all *object*, that is the empirically real in general, is doubly conditioned by the *subject*: first *materially*, or as object as such, because an objective existence is thinkable only over against a subject, and as its representation; secondly *formally*, in that the *mode and manner* of the existence of the object, i.e. of being represented (space, time, causality), proceeds from the subject, is predisposed in the subject. Thus to the simple or *Berkeleian* idealism, which concerns the *object as such*, there is immediately linked the Kantian, which concerns the specially given *mode and manner* of being an object.[25]

We have already said enough about the 'Berkeleian' aspect of Schopenhauer's position, the 'material' conditioning of the object by the subject. Something must now be said about the aspect of 'formal' conditioning, which, though originating with Kant, is transformed by Schopenhauer into a signifiantly different position. In accordance with his great admiration for Kant's Transcendental Aesthetic, Schopenhauer takes over its central doctrine, the ideality of space and time as a priori forms of intuition, and incorporates it virtually unchanged into his own version of idealism. Those arguments that are given are rehashes of Kant's almost without exception.[26] Space and time, then, are to be seen as necessary organizing principles of objects (i.e. representations) and as having their origin in the subject of representations. Space is an a priori form of outer sense, time an a priori form of both inner and outer sense, but the sole such form of inner sense. Furthermore, as was the case in Kant's theory, an important feature of

[25] *W*2 p. 15 (8).   [26] Cf. ibid. pp. 43–6 (32–5); *PP*2 pp. 47–54 (38–45).

Schopenhauer's conception of the thing in itself is that it is not governed by the forms of space and time.

A common objection to this notion of the thing in itself (sometimes referred to as the 'neglected alternative' charge) is that, even if space and time are subjective forms of intuition, there is nothing to prevent things in themselves, though unknown to us, from being spatio-temporal as well. According to the objection, it is a mistake to think that the following alternatives exhaust the field of possibilities: *either* (1) space and time belong to things in themselves and our knowledge of them is a posteriori, *or* (2) we have a priori knowledge of space and time, and space and time are purely subjective in origin. The reply that can be made on behalf of both Schopenhauer and Kant is that the expression 'thing in itself' is to be interpreted as equivalent to 'thing considered independently of its conforming to the forms of our intuition'. Thus, given that space and time are the forms of our intuition, to consider something as a thing in itself is to consider it as falling outside space and time.[27] Schopenhauer's all-important conception of the thing in itself can thus be safeguarded against such an objection. We may say that the Schopenhauerian thing in itself is non-spatial and non-temporal, simply on the grounds that any spatial or temporal thing would necessarily be what Schopenhauer calls an object, something that falls within the (possible) experience of the subject, and hence necessarily not a thing in itself. It is crucial to realize that whenever Schopenhauer talks of the real, the empirical, or the objective world, he decidedly does not mean the world of the thing in itself; what he means is the world of objects for a subject, the world as representation. But this, according to him, is the world which natural science can investigate empirically. The world of ordinary spatio-temporal particulars, and indeed, the world considered 'from the other side'—as it is in itself—is from the outset a world beyond the reaches of empirical investigation of any sort. (Doubt still remains as to whether anything that cannot be located in space and time can be coherently

---

[27] Cf. the discussion of the 'neglected alternative' charge in H. E. Allison, 'The Non-Spatiality of Things in Themselves for Kant', *Journal of the History of Philosophy* 14 (1976), pp. 313–21.

conceived—a doubt which Schopenhauer, I think it will be found, does no more to dispel than Kant before him.)

In our earlier discussion, we saw that Schopenhauer aligned himself with those who objected to the Kantian causal link between things in themselves and representations as incoherent. More specifically, the charge was that causality, as a category of the understanding, must by Kant's own lights have application only to objects of possible experience, and that things in themselves, which were not objects of any possible experience, could therefore be the causes of nothing at all. To infer the existence of things in themselves from the requirement that our sensations have a cause was thus wholly illegitimate. Schopenhauer agrees with all this, but comments shrewdly that none of it shows that there are no things in themselves. Schopenhauer does of course put forward a positive account of the thing in itself, various aspects of which will be dealt with in what follows. But one principle to which Schopenhauer adheres consistently throughout that account— in his views on freedom, his doctrine of the will as thing in itself underlying natural phenomena, as well as in his theory of knowledge—is that there can be no causal interaction between the thing in itself and any item in the world as representation. (Just what the relation between them is, is a question I shall raise in Chapter 7.)

If Schopenhauer is thus scrupulously free of the incoherence he detects in Kant over the role of things in themselves as causes, one can nevertheless see why Kant was driven in this direction by considering the difficulties Schopenhauer encounters over perception. 'Mere sensation', according to Schopenhauer, can give us no knowledge of an objective world; it is only when that which we are aware of as sensation is interpreted (by the understanding) as the effect of some cause that we can have experience, i.e. awareness of an objective world. He equates sensation with our organs being affected, and says that this being affected would of itself give us as little experience of an objective world as can be attributed to a plant when it receives such stimuli as light and moisture. In addition to 'merely' sensing, human beings (and animals) have an understanding, which projects back from the sensation to an object as cause of the sensation. The object is thus constructed by the understanding, though not entirely from its own resources but in response to a sensation. The account involves a major adaptation of the Kantian position. According to Kant, experience arises only out of the unification of particular intuition and general concept. Schopenhauer denies that causality, as it operates here in constituting experience, is a concept. Although his account requires the activity of the understanding to supplement the reception of sensations and convert them into objective experience, the understanding is held to operate entirely without concepts. The following shows his position quite clearly:

[Intuition] would never arise in the first place, unless there were some effect immediately known which thus served as a point of departure. But such is the effect on animal bodies. They are, to this extent, the *immediate objects* of the subject: through them intuition of all other objects is mediated. The alterations which each animal body experiences are known immediately, i.e. sensed, and as this effect is instantly connected with its cause, there occurs intuition of the latter as *object*. This connection is not a conclusion in abstract concepts, and it does not happen through reflection, or voluntarily, but immediately, with necessity and certainty.[28]

This passage raises a number of questions. First, in calling the body the 'immediate object' of the subject, Schopenhauer may invite the misunderstanding that the body itself is being put forward as an object of perception—whereas if the body has any 'immediate' role in perception, this surely lies not in its *being perceived* within any greater clarity or absence of mediating factors, or from greater proximity, but rather, in its being the body of the perceiving subject. This is not to deny that one can perceive one's own body. The point is simply that if my body 'senses alterations' as a result of which I come to experience some spatio-temporal thing, then it is that thing that is the object of my perception, and not in this case my body. Schopenhauer seems to have become aware of the possible misunderstanding, however, and rectifies it subsequently by making this very point.[29]

The most serious problem with the above passage is what

---

[28] *W*1 p. 39 (11–12).
[29] Ibid. p. 49 (20). This passage is parallel to *VW* pp. 100–1 (121), which is a later addition that is only present in the 1847 edition.

causes that 'effect on animal bodies' which Schopenhauer equates with sensation. Schopenhauer says that we take the empirical object of experience to be the cause of our sensations. Elsewhere—and here we witness the materialist trend that will be the topic of the next chapter—he claims that it is a material object which causes the alteration in our sense organs: '[matter's] effect on the immediate object [the body] (which is itself matter), is the condition of the intuition in which alone it exists'.[30] Apparently this empirical, and indeed material, object arises out of the transition from sensation to inferred cause which is carried out by the subject's understanding. It exists only in intuition. However, the sensation supposedly exists prior to (though perhaps not temporally so) the operation of the understanding which is constitutive of the object's being there for the subject—so how can the object be the cause of the initial sensation? Kant would have said that the sensation was caused in us by a thing in itself, though of such a thing we could have no knowledge. But Schopenhauer will not allow himself this option. If we assume that it is not a real option to say that our sensations are not in fact caused at all (but that we merely come to treat the object 'constructed' on the occasion of having the sensation as if it were the cause of the sensation), then Schopenhauer is in great difficulty. One way of extricating him from it might be to make a clear distinction between empirical object and objective representation. If Schopenhauer made this distinction, he could hold that empirical objects existing in space and time prior to experience cause sensations in us, and that the understanding, in positing a cause for the received sensation, has before it an objective representation, i.e. one whose content specifies a spatio-temporal object with certain causal properties. But Schopenhauer refuses to distinguish in any way between object and representation—a conscious and principled refusal, as we have seen from his definition of 'object' and from his rejection of the Kantian *Gegenstand der Vorstellung* as a meaningless hybrid.[31] Schopenhauer thus seems committed to having empirical objects as both the prior conditions and the

---

[30] *W*1 p. 35 (8–9).
[31] Cf. *VW* p. 41 (41–2), discussed in Chapter 4 above; and *W*1 p. 545 (44), discussed in Chapter 2.

consequences of the understanding's operations upon sensations.

He would contend no doubt that this is perfectly coherent,
provided one accepts the idealist doctrine that empirical
objects are representations. Within the world as representation,
empirical observation can confirm the effects of objects upon
other objects, including the human organism; but from the
subject's point of view, the object is constructed in response to
a received sensation, and this explains the nature of those
objects that constitute the empirical world. Thus (his defence
would continue), provided we distinguish the subjective from
the objective point of view there is no problem. In explaining
the nature of objects we invoke their status as mental
constructs, posited as the causes of mere sensations; but in
reporting matters of empirical fact we can assert straightforwardly that objects cause alterations in other objects.
However, the problems with this position are not so easily
dispelled. For Schopenhauer is apparently committed to the
view that the very same object has two roles: the table I see is
both the cause of mere sensations in me, and a mind-dependent
construct which transforms sensation into cognition by
featuring as an objective mental content. It is hard to see how
this is any more coherent than the Kantian version involving
things in themselves as causes.

A wider question prompted by the same passage concerns
Schopenhauer's notion of a purely intuitive, non-conceptual
understanding. The division between intuitive and strictly
conceptual representations is a major theme for Schopenhauer. Not making such a distinction properly is said to be a
'great mistake' of Kant's.[32] The following passage expresses
Schopenhauer's views quite well: 'The chief distinction among
representations is that between the intuitive and the abstract.
The latter are constituted by only *one* class of representations,
namely concepts: and these are the property on earth of
humanity alone, whose capacity for concepts, which distinguishes
them from animals, has for all time been called *reason*.'[33] So
what Schopenhauer wants is a clear difference between
perceptual awareness of empirical objects, involving their

spatial, temporal, and causal organization, and strictly conceptual thought. He thinks that Kant blurred this distintion by insisting that only the unification of intuition and concept produced experience, and by his doctrine that representation of objects requires synthesis of representations in accordance with the principles of conceptual judgement.

Schopenhauer examines the difference between these two modes of cognition at some length. He makes a close connection between reason (our capacity for strictly conceptual cognition) and language. The words of a language designate (*bezeichnen*) concepts, and conceptual thought is in principle communicable from one subject to another.[34] Only strictly conceptual cognition is capable of constituting *knowledge* (*Wissen*). Knowledge in this sense is always knowledge that . . ., where the space can be filled by a proposition that expresses a conceptual thought. But there is also cognition (*Erkenntnis*) which is not knowledge, and one of Schopenhauer's concerns is that such non-conceptual cognition is itself an adequate representation of empirical reality. The experienced billiards-player, he claims, 'can have a complete cognizance [*Kenntnis*] of the laws of impact of elastic bodies on one another, merely in the understanding, merely for immediate intuition, and he does perfectly adequately with this: in contrast, only the scientist of mechanics [*der wissenschaftliche Mechaniker*] has a genuine knowledge [*Wissen*] of those laws, i.e. a cognition of them *in abstracto*'.[35] The advantages of knowledge proper are, according to Schopenhauer, only in terms of application. If one wants to transmit one's understanding to others, or store it for wider use, or have it available to guide one's own future actions, then it must be expressed in conceptual form. Intuitive cognition can be a complete representation of parts of empirical reality, but it is rooted to the particular time and place of its occurrence and to the particular percipient. Without concepts we would be the same as animals who live in a perpetual here and now, whilst having a full cognitive grasp of the world in so far as it was presented to us in perception.

There is much that can be discussed in this. One troubling

---

[34] Ibid. p. 72 (40). Payne translates *bezeichnen* as 'express'.
[35] Ibid. p. 92 (56).

aspect implicit in the passage just quoted is the conviction that conceptual representations, which Schopenhauer holds to be ultimately derived from intuitive representations, can in some way contain nothing more than them. This view is made explicit when he says that: 'the differential calculus does not really extend our cognition of curves, and contains nothing more than the mere intuition of them already does; but it changes the mode of cognition, transforming the intuitive into the abstract, which is so full of consequences for application'.[36] This must be wrong—mathematical propositions are anything but merely useful ways of conveying and storing what any percipient can see or feel of the properties of curved (or other) objects. What distinguishes them is precisely their propositional content.

Two further points that Schopenhauer makes are (1) that conceptual knowledge is not necessary for the successful performance of many human activities, and (2) that in many cases it hinders them. Examples illustrating the second point will *a fortiori* illustrate the first—if any activity is achieved best in the absence of conceptual knowledge, then conceptual knowledge is not necessary for its achievement. The illustrations that Schopenhauer provides are varied and vivid:[37] (*a*) 'in billiards, fencing, tuning an instrument, singing: here intuitive cognition must guide the activity immediately: passing through reflection makes them unsure, by dividing the attention and confusing the person'; (*b*) 'savages' (*Wilde*) or 'primitive people' (*rohe Menschen*) can wield a bow and arrow (and perform many other activities) with a poise and precision denied to the 'reflective European'; (*c*) 'It is of no help to have the knowledge *in abstracto* of the angle at which I must apply the razor, in degrees and minutes, if I do not have intuitive cognizance of it, i.e. have it in my grasp'; (*d*) in the case of physiognomy, our understanding of features is intuitive, not something expressible in abstract concepts; (*e*) 'If the singer or virtuoso tries to guide his performance by reflection, it remains dead. The same applies to the composer, the painter, even the poet. The concept always remains unfruitful in art'.

That there is such a thing as 'knowing how', and that it does not in all cases presuppose the ability to formulate what

[36] *W*1 p. 90 (54).
[37] All the illustrations given here are from *W*1 pp. 93–4 (56–7).

one knows in propositional form, seems to be perfectly true. And no doubt there is a tendency while reading Kant to forget this, and to treat all cognition as if it proceeded by the production of theory-laden judgements such as those made by the natural scientist or the mathematician. To this Schopenhauer provides a useful corrective. (His notion of having something 'in one's grasp' finds a later echo in Heidegger's notion of *Zuhandenheit* ('readiness-to-hand'), which is similarly designed to break down traditional epistemological assumptions about our awareness of everyday objects.[38]) But there are many issues which could be developed out of this discussion. Schopenhauer is claiming that perception is non-conceptual, non-propositional, non-judgemental, non-language-dependent, non-theoretical—and all these claims need not necessarily be taken (or rejected) together as a package.

To examine these issues further, let us return to the particular case of *causality*, which Schopenhauer denies to be a concept, at least as regards its role in perception. He insists on distinguishing sharply between our concept of *cause*, which is a constituent of judgements and hence of discursive propositional thought, and our direct perceptual awareness of causal interactions. Kant held that experience requires the subsumption of sets of data under the concept *cause*, but Schopenhauer charges him with not making a clear distinction between what we might call 'explicit' judgement and the intuitive apprehension of causal connection. This, Schopenhauer alleges, led Kant to make a false claim, namely, that experience requires explicit judgements involving the concept *cause*. By an explicit judgement I mean a subject's occurrent thought that some x causes some y. On Schopenhauer's side it must be said that there is a distinction to be made between this and someone's apprehension of particular connections between causes and effects. Sticking with the hackneyed example, consider a person watching a game of billiards. This person perceives a great many instances of cause/effect relations, and her doing so certainly does not presuppose an explicit judgement that x causes y for each perceived instance. The mind seems, as it were, to perceive simply in the medium

---

[38] Cf. *Being and Time*, sect. 15, entitled 'The Being of the Entities Encountered in the Environment'.

of causality, much as it does in that of space or time, without the necessity for explicit causal judgements. Thus it is that Schopenhauer makes causality, an a priori form of the understanding, a non-conceptual form on a par with space and time.

There are perhaps two points that can be put forward on Kant's behalf. It is true that he does not make himself very clear, but there is no need (one might argue) to read him as being committed to an occurrent thought as the condition of each and every perceived causal connection. The point would be, rather, that this immediate perceptual apprehension of cause/effect relations between particular objects, while admittedly distinct from explicit causal judgement, nevertheless has as a condition of its possibility the ability to make explicit causal judgements of the kind which Schopenhauer recognizes as truly conceptual. The second point on Kant's behalf would be to argue that since a *judgement* is the combining of rep-resentations in such a way as to make them capable of referring to objects, anyone who 'apprehends' the game of billiards in the ordinary way is *ipso facto* making judgements, and doing so according to the concept of *cause* (or *cause and effect*). Schopenhauer can accept this last point, and say that if that is what is meant by using concepts in a judgement, then the understanding uses concepts in the process of ordinary perception. Still the fact remains, though, that for all Kant says, an explicit judgement must occur every time anyone perceives a causal connection. The advantage of reserving 'concept' for what can occur in discursive judgement is that we make this distinction clear, and thereby avoid any suggestion that this last claim is being advanced.

As to the Kantian point that the possibility of explicit causal judgements is a necessary condition of perceiving causal connections, Schopenhauer simply denies it. This may seem unwise, as there is clearly a strong connection between the perception of causal connections and the disposition (at least) to make causal judgements, for which Schopenhauer is apparently unable to account. However, could we hope to show that the perception of causal connections is impossible for a being incapable of explicit causal judgements? A cat or a dog would seem to be such a being, and yet they would seem to be just as capable of perceiving causal connections as human beings are. At any rate, if Schopenhauer is wrong to separate perception from explicit conceptual judgement, one of these assumptions about cats and dogs must be rejected. It is indeed a feature emphasized by Schopenhauer himself that, according to his theory, human percipients have a close affinity with other animals; in both cases the operation of the understanding yields perception of a unified world of particular objects.

So far we have treated with some sympathy Schopenhauer's claim that perception is possible without explicit conceptual judgement. But should we be in any way inclined to accept his total divorce of perception and conception? I suggest not. Since one of Kant's achievements is commonly held to be his realization that the empiricist picture of the passive reception of data required radical alteration, and that it was precisely the mind's active judging capacity that had been left out, the denial of the necessity of concepts for perception must seem today to be a retrograde step. Schopenhauer has no room for the arguably true thesis that my perceiving a table or a building is dependent on my possession of concepts, whether of the order of *table* and *building*, or that of *physical object*. Perception may not presuppose an explicit judging for each perceiving, but it is nevertheless conceptual, and may be said to have propositional content. If it does, then it is closely linked with the capacity for making explicit judgements with the same content. According to Schopenhauer, there can be entirely concept-free presentation to the mind of a particular or collection of particulars—a view that is open to the objection that experience of particulars is always of them as particular instances of some concept. However, we should at least note that Schopenhauer's position is not simply a resurrection of the pre-Kantian empiricist view. His is still a Kantian account, in that he accepts the a priori nature of space, time, and causality as organizing forms of our perception of a world of objective particulars. These forms are necessary to all objective experience, and are subjective in origin, just as they are for Kant. They serve the same function in providing the constitutive criteria of anything's belonging to objective reality; and, as with Kant, they apply *only* to the world of objects for the subject, not to things in themselves.

Let us conclude the present chapter with an assessment of Schopenhauer's idealism. I have suggested that his general arguments in support of idealism are not very strong. His attempts to show that realism is either incoherent or redundant are not very fully developed, and they are unconvincing as they stand. His historical justification of idealism as the culmination of post-Cartesian philosophy is an accurate reflection of one important line of development, but on the other hand it does nothing to show that scepticism about any real external world is not (at least) a viable alternative to idealism. Finally, the suggestion that idealism expresses an obvious, even an axiomatic, truth has been shown to rest on a reading of the slogan 'No object without subject' which in fact gives no support to the central idealist doctrine that the real objective world is mind-dependent. However, given the confidence that Schopenhauer clearly reposes in the self-evidence of idealism, along with his views about its historical justification, and the facts as we know them about the popularity and influence of idealist views in immediately preceding decades, we can readily understand why he appears to expend comparatively little energy on constructing arguments for idealism.

As regards the coherence of Schopenhauer's idealist position, he clearly recognizes that objective, empirical reality must, for a coherent idealist, be mind-dependent. The criteria of objectivity must be provided by a priori modes of organization among the subject's representations, and not by any relation that they might bear to the mind-independent thing in itself. He thus avoids the incoherence noted earlier in Kant's position. However, by losing the thing in itself in its role as cause of representations, Schopenhauer has great difficulty accounting for our perception of objects. His views about the cosntruction of the empirical object on the occasion of our organs being affected are disastrous without the assumption that things in themselves cause the affection of our organs. Jacobi's dictum (cited in Chapter 2) thus bites both ways: '*without* this presupposition I could not enter the system, and *with* this presupposition I could not remain in it'.

It is clear that Schopenhauer does not set out either to be a solipsist or to be a sceptic. There is no relativization of the world of objects to a single, individual experiencing being, nor any doubt in principle about the reality of the world of objects: the external world 'gives itself to us as it is'.[39] The dispute about the reality of the world is foolish as far as Schopenhauer is concerned. His position is clearly akin to Kant's here: from both their points of view it would be a mistake to understand 'objective reality' as equivalent to 'what exists independently of all subjects'. This notion of reality leads to the transcendental realist position, which in turn gives way to scepticism. However, Schopenhauer's way of removing the ground for scepticism is by denying explicitly that there is any causal relation between object and representation. Kant may have been muddled about the relation between representations and objects, as Schopenhauer charges. But at least Kant kept alive the sense that there must be room for such a distinction somewhere. In collapsing it completely, Schopenhauer leaves little substance to his emphatic claim that the empirical reality of the world of objects is not being denied.

I suggested earlier that Schopenhauer would ultimately have to save his idealism from being crazily subjectivist by a clear assertion of the existence of the thing in itself. This he does in fact, after developing the subjectivism to some considerable extent. For there is a side to Schopenhauer's idealism which gradually becomes apparent as his work progresses, and which makes him vulnerable to the charge of not providing any distinction between reality and appearance. This is his tendency to claim that all our experience is (or at least is like) a dream or an illusion. Delightful poetic illustrations of this theme are to hand ('We are such stuff | As dreams are made of, and our little life | Is rounded with a sleep'[40]). Schopenhauer finds that the basis of this pervasive thought is the very real difficulty of specifying any sure criterion for distinguishing dreams from waking experiences. This surely leaves him open to a kind of sceptical attack, albeit differently based from the one he has previously

<hr>

[39] *W*2 p. 14 (7).
[40] Shakespeare, *The Tempest*, IV, i, one of many literary passages quoted by Schopenhauer at *W*1 pp. 45–6 (17).

considered. Schopenhauer really seems in a way to embrace
this consequence. He rejects as criteria, first, the comparative
vividness of waking experience as against dreams (for how are
the two to be compared for vividness, unless *per impossibile*
experienced at the same time?), and secondly, the comparative
causal coherence of waking experience (since dreams can be
just as coherent in this respect). The only criterion is the fact
of waking up, he concludes, with its experience of a clean
break between the causal order of the dream and the causal
order of waking life.[41] Elsewhere Schopenhauer is prepared to
assert that the ideality of the world, the fact that it is mere
appearance, means that 'it must be regarded, at least from one
side, as related to dreams, and indeed must be placed in the
same class as them'.[42] The implication here that there might
be another side to the question, a point of view from which the
world is not akin to a dream, must be understood as an
allusion to Schopenhauer's doctrine of the thing in itself. The
world has, for him, an existence in itself beyond any subject's
experience of it, and only as such is truly real. Although this
strand of thought has been kept very much out of sight in the
main work, it picks up once again Schopenhauer's earlier
involvement with the notion of a higher Platonic reality,
opposed to the dreamlike world of becoming, that we saw in
Chapter 1.

What we find in *The World as Will and Representation* is that
when Schopenhauer comes to emphasize the notion of the
thing in itself, he is still, as in his earlier notes, prepared to
equate 'existing as the subject's representation' with 'being
akin to a dream', and 'not penetrating to the essence of things
as they really are'. Furthermore, the leitmotiv of the veil of
māyā has survived with the same significance:

The ancient wisdom of the Indians pronounces: 'It is *māyā*, the veil
of deception, which shrouds the eyes of mortals and makes them
see a world of which one can say neither that it is nor that it is not:
for it is like a dream, like the sunshine on the sand which the
traveller takes from afar for water . . .'. (These similes are found
repeated in innumerable passages in the *Vedas* and *Puranas*.) But
what all of these meant, and what they tell of, is nothing other than

[41] *W*1 p. 45 (17).   [42] *W*2 p. 10 (4).

what we are treating of even now: the world as representation, subordinated to the principle of reason.[43]

Here we may sense a serious clash to which Schopenhauer himself seems strangely blind. On the one hand we have the aspirations that crystallized early on around the notions of the 'better consciousness' and its delusive, painful, empirical counterpart; on the other hand the Kantian doctrine of appearances which in transcendental idealism (especially on Schopenhauer's reading) supposedly constitute reality. Any hope that idealism will preserve the empirical reality of the external world seems to pale in the light of the early preoccupations to which the *māyā* theme is linked. Idealism asserts that the world is the subject's representation; but when it suits him, as here, Schopenhauer treats that assertion as equivalent to the claim that the 'world' with which we are presented in experience (a world objective in the Schopenhauerian sense of being presented to us as an object of experience) is an irreparably inaccurate picture of the world as it really is. It is as if Schopenhauer sets out to reproduce the Berkeleian move of equating the world of real spatio-temporal things with mental states or their contents, hoping thereby to eliminate the gap between representation and object so valuable to the sceptic, yet at the same time he puts an unbridgeable chasm between this spatio-temporal world of objects and the world as it is in itself by calling the former an *illusion*. To make matters worse, he even attributes to Kant the view that in contrast with the thing in itself, 'time and space, and everything which fills them and is ordered in them according to causal law, is to be regarded as an unstable and insubstantial dream [*bestand- und wesenloser Traum*]'.[44] At this point I think we are justified in feeling exasperation on Kant's behalf.

Schopenhauer is a lover of paradoxes, and he sometimes seems to go out of his way to present his readers with them. His presentation of his various views about illusion is full of problems. And yet I believe that if we overlook those difficulties about the nature of the empirical object which we have already noted, there is an interpretation which saves

[43] *W*1 pp. 34–5 (8).   [44] Ibid. p. 523 (425).

Schopenhauer from outright contradiction when he says that
the world as representation is and is not an illusion. What he
is saying is roughly the following:

1. It is not an illusion that we experience a unified world of
   particular spatio-temporal objects, nor should we be
   sceptical about the existence of this world or about our
   experiencing it.
2. The real spatio-temporal world is, however, mind-
   dependent, constituted by representations which exist
   only for some subject.
3. But there is (and indeed must be) a wider perspective
   from which we can think of the world in a way unlimited
   by its experienceability. This is to think of the world in
   itself. The existence of the world in itself is not conditional
   on its falling within the forms of its experienceability by
   us.

Thus, as regards illusion, we must operate with a two-tier
system. On one level we must resist the conclusion that our
representations are mere illusions to which the real world may
not correspond. They *are* the real empirical world. So we
should not be epistemological sceptics—the world 'gives itself
to us as it is', and our everyday and scientific experience of it is
in order as it stands. All that we have to say about the thing in
itself from the point of view of epistemology is that it must be
inaccessible to us, but it must be there because, as Schopenhauer
puts it, it does not make sense to talk of appearance unless
there is something that appears.[45] If we restrict empirical
reality to a single limited perspective on the world, we must
comprehend the thought that there is a world whose existence
transcends that perspective.

On the other level, when Schopenhauer says that what is
presented to us as subjects is akin to a dream or an illusion, he
does not do so in the name of epistemological scepticism. His
point is that the empirical world itself is ephemeral and
relative only to us, and is therefore no guide to the hidden or
higher reality at the level of the 'in itself'. This supposedly
higher reality inhabits a quasi-Platonic realm, and is 'more
real' largely because it is eternally existent, not subject to

[45] Cf. *W*2 p. 569 (486), for an expression of this thought.

spatial or temporal differentiation, not causally connected with the empirical, and in some way of greater value than the empirical. We are not deceived in thinking that the empirical world exists in the way we generally take it to, but we are deceived if we put our faith in it as exhaustive of reality, or as containing what is ultimately valuable in the universe. It is not yet clear what we should make of his views about 'ultimate reality'—but this will be remedied to some extent in subsequent chapters, where his positive doctrine of the thing in itself and his advocacy of mysticism are discussed.[46]

[46] Cf. Chapters 7 and 11 below.

6

Materialism

In Schopenhauer's hands the Kantian doctrine of the categories of the understanding undergoes major surgery. Not only does he make the role of causality in ordering experience a non-conceptual one, but he excises all but one of the categories themselves: 'I demand that of the categories we throw eleven out of the window, and keep causality alone, yet realize that its activity is the condition of empirical intuition.'[1] His reason for this is that a priori forms of the understanding must fulfil two conditions:[2] (a) they must be necessary to all experience of objects, and, like space and time, 'absolutely impossible to think away, belonging rather to the being [*Dasein*] of a thing'; (b) they must not be derivable from properties of space and time. Without much detailed argument, Schopenhauer claims that causality is the only possible a priori feature to meet both these conditions: 'everything else about a thing consists either of determinations of space, or of time, or its empirical qualities, all of which reduce to its effectiveness [*Wirksamkeit*] and are thus finer determinations of causality.'[3] Whatever else fills the 'old ontologies' that are the origin of Kant's list of twelve is 'nothing more than relations of things to one another, or to our reflection, and a scraped-together farrago'.[4] We would not, I think, have much to gain by probing further into the list of categories, trying to tease out for each one a Schopenhauerian argument against its being an a priori feature of any experience of objects. But there may be some surprise at the category of *substance* going out of the window, since it is the one category besides *causality* that has continued to be thought of as of crucial importance in the Kantian scheme of things.

Schopenhauer has a fully worked-out position on substance, part of which we have met already (see the end of Chapter 3).

[1] *W*1 p. 550 (448).   [2] See ibid. pp. 546–7 (445).
[3] Ibid. p. 547 (445–6).   [4] Ibid. p. 547 (446).

He holds that the notion of subtance is a bogus one, a pseudo-genus whose only true species is matter. People only believed in substance because they needed to believe in immaterial substance; but the only backing the latter notion had came from the general notion of substance invented for that purpose. Once we realize this, we are free to abandon pseudo-genus and pseudo-species at a stroke, the result being that 'strictly speaking . . . the concept of substance must be entirely rejected, and that of matter everywhere put in its place'.[5] Why, then, is matter not retained in place of Kant's substance, alongside space, time, and causality, as an a priori organizing feature of experience? Schopenhauer's answer is simple: matter reduces to causal effectiveness. So if we think of Kant as arguing that we cannot 'think away', or have experience without our mind's applying, the a priori organizing concept *substance*, Schopenhauer's reply is: (1) *matter* must be substituted for *substance*; (2) matter is reducible to causality—its being is its acting (*Wirken*); (3) causality is an a priori organizing feature of experience, but (4) it is, in this role, not a concept.

Step (2) requires some comment. Matter, in Schopenhauer's view, is 'through and through nothing but causality', 'its being is its acting [*Wirken*]'.[6] I have given the German *Wirken* here, because of its associations. 'An effect' in German is *eine Wirkung*; thus the 'acting' that Schopenhauer has in mind is clearly an 'acting on', or being effective (cf. *Wirksamkeit*). But, equally importantly, *Wirken* is linked in German with *Wirklichkeit*, a word which is straightforwardly translatable as 'reality'. We might try to preserve the flavour of the German here by saying that the actuality of matter is its acting on something. This may give a sense of the comparative ease with which Schopenhauer can claim that matter is constituted by causality. On what, then, does matter act? 'That whereon [matter] acts is itself in all cases matter: its whole being and essence consists in the law-like alteration which *one* part of it brings about in another'[7]—or as we might put it, the actuality of a material object is its acting on other material objects. Schopenhauer also says in the same passage that matter is the

---

[5] Ibid. p. 601 (491).   [6] Ibid. p. 35 (8–9).
[7] Ibid. p. 36 (9).

perceptibility of space and time, the content that 'fills' these forms. The thought here is that while space and time are necessary forms of our experience of objects, spatio-temporal particulars could not be experienced unless there was causal interaction among them. We could not have perceptual experience of a world of spatio-temporal particulars that did not compose some kind of causal order. This is a familiar Kantian thought, though Schopenhauer is dismissive of Kant's *argument* for the principle that every alteration is in accordance with some necessary causal law,[8] and offers little in the way of cogent argument of his own apart from the considerations about the role of causality in distinguishing perception from mere sensation, which we discussed in the previous chapter and found to be highly problematic in themselves. What is required is some reason for holding that there must be a causal order pertaining among any objects that we could experience; whereas what Schopenhauer tends to offer are thoughts about the necessity for positing an object as cause of states of the subject.

Schopenhauer is fond of saying that causality 'unites space and time'.[9] He means that there being causality entails that experience be both spatial and temporal. Considering space and time as fundamental modes of ordering whatever elements make up empirical reality, it is obvious that time *per se* provides for succession of elements, space for the relative position of coexistent elements. But if there is to be alteration, then both space and time are required:

Alteration does not consist essentially in mere change of states *per se*, but rather in the fact that at *the same* place in space there is now *one* state and subsequently *another* state, and that at *one* and the same particular time this state obtains *here* and that one *there*.

In mere space the world would be rigid and immovable: no succession, no change, no action . . . Again, in mere time everything would be fleeting: no permanence, no juxtaposition, hence no simultaneity, and consequently no duration.[10]

So Schopenhauer appears to hold that any world we could experience must be one in which regular alteration occurs,

---

[8] Cf. esp. *VW* sect. 23, discussed in Chapter 2 above.
[9] *W*I p. 37 (10).   [10] Ibid. pp. 36 (9), 37 (10).

and that this explains why empirical reality must be both spatial and temporal. At any rate it is clear that, for Schopenhauer, what we perceive (what constitutes empirical reality) is a world of matter. Material objects are spatio-temporal and take part in interactions with one another, each of which instantiates some causal law uniting cause and effect necessarily. There is, according to Schopenhauer, nothing more to be said about what matter is once we have understood the roles of space, time, and causality, nor about what empirical reality is once we have said that it is parts of matter in interaction with one another.

It is because of his commitment to a fully material empirical world that Schopenhauer's attitudes to materialism are interesting. I say 'attitudes', for, contrary to initial appearances, Schopenhauer has no single stance here. What is initially striking is his attempt to ridicule materialism from his supposedly superior idealist standpoint. But he then concedes it a large measure of legitimacy by treating it as idealism's equal counterpart. We shall have to examine his attempt to strike a balance between idealism and materialism, and also begin to clarify how Schopenhauer makes full use of materialist assumptions of his own in presenting his views of the human intellect and the human will.

Schopenhauer's opposition to materialism stems directly from the discussion of subject and object with which we dealt earlier on. ' "No object without subject" is the proposition which forever makes impossible all materialism.'[11] Why? Presumably because materialism directly contradicts this Schopenhauerian principle by asserting (e.g.) that everything that exists is a modification of matter, and that matter would exist as such in the absence of any subjects of experience. Now we have seen that the objective world, which Schopenhauer equates with the world as representation, is nevertheless a material world. This explains why, in attacking materialism, Schopenhauer makes little distinction between 'the objective' and 'matter'. Consider the following passages:

nothing can be clumsier than after the manner of all materialists surreptitiously taking the objective as simply given in order to derive

---

[11] Ibid. p. 60 (29–30).

everything from it, without taking any account of the subjective, by means of which, indeed in which, it yet has its sole existence.[12]

The inescapable falsehood of materialism consists . . . primarily in its starting from a *petitio principii* . . . namely from the assumption that matter is something simply and unconditionally given, something present independently of the knowledge of the subject, and hence in fact a thing in itself.[13]

There is nothing very new here. The materialist view is criticized simply on the grounds of its realism about matter: it holds matter to exist independently of the experiencing subject, contrary to Schopenhauer's own idealist claims. Since Schopenhauer agrees that the objects making up the world are material, it is simply an alternative expression of the same point when he says that materialism takes the objective as given in independence of the subject, and is wrong to do so. Thus the first objection to materialism is that it embodies realism about matter—the objection is strong only to the extent that idealism is accepted as true.

Sometimes Schopenhauer suggests that the dispute between realism and idealism has always been over matter, and that realism necessarily leads to materialism—which he now characterizes as the view that 'there is only *one* thing in itself, matter, of which everything else is the modification'.[14] It is not clear why this should 'necessarily' be so. It may be true that a realist orientation has tended to be allied with an ontology in which only material objects figure. But the belief that things exist which are not subject-dependent does not preclude one from holding that some (or even all) things which have an existence in themselves are non-material. They could, for example, be souls or Leibnizian monads. In fact, Schopenhauer concedes this on the very page on which he asserts that realism leads inevitably to materialism. For he goes on to discuss what he calls 'spiritualism', which is the attempt to refute materialism by setting up 'a second substance, outside and alongside matter, an *immaterial substance*', and about which we already know his views. The way to oppose materialism is not to continue assuming that things in the objective world can exist in themselves independently of the subject, and to

[12] *W*2 p. 207 (177).   [13] Ibid. 367 (314).   [14] Ibid. p. 21 (13).

argue for the existence of immaterial objects among the class of things in themselves. Rather, one should abandon the initial realist assumption, which Schopenhauer calls the basic *proton pseudos* or 'false first step', and thereby render spiritualism redundant, because souls, if they were 'things in themselves', would be outside the subject's experience in the same way as material objects, and hence from Schopenhauer's point of view not objects in the empirical world at all.

In another passage he lists four different starting-points for philosophical theories of the nature of reality which are grounded not upon the subject–object dichotomy, but on the notion of objects construed realistically. Apart from matter (and various subclasses such as those favoured by 'Thales and the Ionians'), one could make the abstract concept the basis of reality (Spinoza and the Eleatics are cited here), or time and numbers (the Pythagoreans and the Chinese i ching), or the act of will of an extramundane personal being (the scholastics). Immediately following this catalogue (the accuracy of whose attributions I shall not discuss), Schopenhauer launches into one of his more protracted discussions of materialism, prefaced with the claim that realism can be most consistently and most far-reachingly developed when it is materialist.[15] I suggest that this claim is a better representation of his view than the chronologically later, and immediately qualified, claim that realism is always and inevitably materialist.

What we have seen so far is Schopenhauer attacking materialism on the grounds that it is not idealist. But there are other objections, which are contained in the following passages:

[Materialism] denies all the original natural forces, by ostensibly and apparently reducing them, and ultimately the life-force, to the mere mechanical effectiveness of matter . . . This way leads it necessarily to the fiction of atoms, which now become the material from which it proposes to construct the very mysterious manifestations of all original forces. In this it has in fact ceased to have anything at all to do with empirically *given* matter, but rather is concerned with a matter which is not to be encountered *in rerum natura*, but is a mere abstraction from that real matter—with a matter that is supposed to have no other properties than the *mechanical* ones . . .[16]

[15] *W*1 pp. 57 ff. (27 ff.).   [16] *W*2 pp. 367–8 (314).

[Atomic theories of matter] are crude, insipid, paltry, and clumsy, the offspring of heads that are in the first place incapable of imagining any reality other than a fabulous property-less matter, which is moreover an absolute object, i.e. an object without a subject, and secondly are incapable of imagining any activity other than motion and impact. These two things alone are within their grasp, and that everything should be reduced [*zurücklaufe*] to these is for them an a priori condition: for these are their *thing in itself*. To achieve this end, the life-force is reduced to chemical forces (which are insidiously and without justification called molecular forces), and all processes of inorganic nature are reduced to mechanism, to impact and counter-impact. And thus in the end the whole world, with all the things in it, would be just a mechanical trick-show, like toys driven by levers, wheels, and sand, which represent a mine or the works on a farm.[17]

Within the framework of opposition to materialism, we now find objections to atomism and to mechanism. It is not clear why Schopenhauer thinks that atoms are 'fictions', although he does object to atomic theories on the grounds that their account of matter and its ultimate properties diverges radically from 'empirically *given* matter', by which I take him to mean ordinary macroscopic material objects. He thus seems to be working on the principle that no properties or objects are empirically real unless they correspond to properties or objects as they are ordinarily conveyed to us by the senses. It would be possible for an idealist to accept atoms as real, either by using Kant's principle that something is real if we could theoretically encounter it somewhere in the progress of our empirical investigations, however remote we in fact are from experiencing it, or by accepting as real whatever we can infer as causally explaining what we do observe. But Schopenhauer is consistently at pains not to turn empirical reality into anything other than that which we perceive it to be in ordinary perception. In this connection we should recall his view that ordinary intuition provides us with our contact with reality, and his pronouncement that the world presents itself to us as it is.

His main objection is obviously to the *reductionism* he sees as inherent in the materialist enterprise. Materialism must now be

[17] *W*2 p. 370 (316).

understood to encompass the attempt to explain all phenomena in terms of the material objects, properties, and processes recognized by physics—and Schopenhauer's complaint is that this simply will not work. Many have felt an abhorrence at the presumption of such an exhaustive physicalist account of the world, and, judging from the tone of his writing, Schopenhauer felt it strongly. The vocabulary ('clumsy', 'crude', 'insipid') almost suggests that an aesthetic outrage has been perpetrated on our author's sensibilities (or does he treat it as a bad joke?). What is missing is any justification for believing that the materialist programme must fail to account for all natural phenomena.

One of Schopenhauer's more specific objections concerns the presumption that materialism will be able to give an account of the subject's consciousness. Memorably, he charges materialism with being 'the philosophy of the subject that forgets itself in its own reckoning'.[18] It might be said that Schopenhauer is reiterating here his central idealist point that the very existence of the material world posited by the materialist is conditional upon its presentation to an experiencing subject. But the point contains a more subtle line of attack. The materialist's account is produced by a conscious subject of knowledge, but in what shape or form does this subject appear in the account of the world it itself produces? The materialist must either answer that the subject appears in the account as a physical object like any other, or perhaps as a complex of physical states, or she must answer that, as such, no subject appears in this picture of the world at all. The latter is perhaps the more honest answer, since subjects are in principle beyond the terms of reference of the kind of mechanistic theory Schopenhauer is discussing. At best, the materialist can give us certain objects and states to which the subject has been reduced. While one may give (or aspire to) a seamless materialist account of the world of objects, the subjective point of view from which those objects are experienced cannot be included in the picture. Hence the picture is bound to be incomplete, not through omitting any objective states of affairs, but in a radically different and more

---

[18] Ibid. p. 21 (13); also p. 366 (313).

disastrous way, since the knowledge of material objects contained within the theory depends on the theorist's being a subject with an experiential viewpoint on the world. This is why Schopenhauer thinks that the materialist project can be equated with Baron Münchhausen's attempt to pull himself out of the river by his own hair.[19] Schopenhauer presents a difficulty for reductive materialism here which is not dependent on idealism.

For Schopenhauer, the notion that the subject of experience could be exhaustively explained in terms appropriate to physical objects ought to be particularly deplorable, since he will have no truck (cf. Chapter 4 above) with the idea that the subject could ever be any kind of object. The subject, as we saw, is not to be identified with any individual in the empirical world. It is therefore disconcerting in the extreme to encounter this: 'What is *knowledge*? It is foremost and essentially *representation*. What is *representation*? A very complicated physiological process in the brain of an animal, whose result is consciousness of a picture in that same place.'[20] Or this: 'one is justified in saying that the whole objective world, so boundless in space, so unending in time, so unfathomable in its completeness, is really only a certain movement or affection of the pulpy mass in the skull'.[21] Again, consider this far from untypical passage, which surely would have given Kant yet another opportunity for outrage: 'Kant . . . explained everything which makes genuine *intuition* possible, namely space, time, and causality, as brain-function; although he refrained from using this physiological expression'.[22] Here I can only recall Schopenhauer's own words: 'Nothing can be clumsier'; although there is an element of sheer rhetoric here, the fact is that he is pervasively committed to the notion that the intellect, the subject of representations, representation *per se*, and even (since it too is only representation) the whole world can be explained as functions of the brain and nervous system. This last combination of idealism and materialism is breath-taking. Physical objects are representations in the subject's consciousness. But representations reduce to brain-functions, so physical objects reduce to brain-functions.

[19] *W*1 pp. 57–8 (27). [20] *W*2 p. 224 (191).
[21] Ibid. p. 319 (273). [22] Ibid. p. 334 (285).

Clearly, the ambiguity of the term 'representation' is making its presence felt here. In not allowing for any distinction between a mental state and its content, the terminology makes possible the telescoping together of the claims that reality is subject-dependent and that mental states are brain-states. But the fact that the current, inherited terminology enables this move does not absolve Schopenhauer from the responsibility of making it, nor does it remove its gross absurdity.

What I would like principally to draw attention to at this point is Schopenhauer's acceptance of a kind of materialist account of all the process of representation which go on in the subject's consciousness. A whole chapter in the second volume of *The World as Will and Representation* is devoted to an 'objective view of the intellect',[23] which has a clearly stated empirical point of departure, 'zoological, anatomical, physiological'.[24] The human subject of knowledge is to be treated as an animal, the intellect 'springs from the organism', and even the 'I' or 'what Kant called the synthetic unity of apperception' is to be regarded as the 'focal point of the activity of the whole brain'.[25] While many have been afraid to admit the materiality of the subject and have fled to the notion of a simple immaterial soul 'which merely inhabits the brain', Schopenhauer's line is fundamentally opposed to this: 'We state without fear that this pulpy mass [the brain] is, like any other vegetable or animal part, an organic formation, similar to all its lesser relatives in the poorer housing of our unreasoning brothers' heads, right down to the least that are scarcely capable of apprehension.'[26] Though it is perhaps not crudely mechanistic, does not all this conflict with Schopenhauer's other objections to the project of materialism? The answer, I think, is that it does not do so directly. Schopenhauer wants ultimately to maintain the 'correlativity' of both subjective and objective views. It is not, as has been claimed, that Schopenhauer switches from an initial idealist opposition to materialism to a later reconciliatory stance.[27] The explicit concession noted earlier, that materialism is the most consistent and the most far-reaching theory that takes an objective point of departure,

[23] Ibid. ch. 22.   [24] Ibid. p. 318 (272).
[25] Ibid. pp. 324–5 (277).   [26] Ibid. p. 320 (273).
[27] Alfred Schmidt, 'Schopenhauer und der Materialismus', pp. 52–3.

was made already in Volume 1,[28] and the unequivocal
passages about the falseness of materialism are from the later
Volume 2. The fact is that what Schopenhauer chastises
under the name of 'materialism' is the view which *one-sidedly*
'forgets the subject' yet pretends to *completeness* as an account
of the world. What he is against is not the notion that an
objective account of the intellect can be given, but the notion
that all has been achieved when such an account has been
given; and, as we shall see, he is equally concerned to avoid a
one-sidedly *subjective* view of the intellect. In the following
passage he makes his position explicit:

There are two fundamentally different ways of considering the
intellect, which rest on a difference of standpoint. However much, as
a result of this difference, they are opposed to each other, they must
nevertheless be brought into agreement. The one is the *subjective*,
which, moving outwards from *within* and taking consciousness as the
given, reveals to us the mechanism through which the world
presents itself in consciousness, and how it builds itself up in
consciousness out of the materials which sense and understanding
provide.

As the last two clauses suggest, Kant is seen as the greatest
exponent of this mode of considering the intellect, though
Schopenhauer suggests that Locke should be regarded as its
originator. The passage then continues:

The way of considering the intellect which is opposed to this is the
objective, which starts from *outside*. It takes as its object not our own
consciousness [*das eigene Bewusstsein*], but beings given in outer
experience, conscious of themselves and of the world, and it
investigates what relation their intellect has to their other properties,
how it has become possible, how it has become necessary, and what
it achieves for them. The standpoint of this method of consideration
is empirical: it takes the world and the animal beings present in it
simply as given, using them as its starting-point.[29]

The exponents of this method are 'zootomists and physiologists',
of whom Schopenhauer lists a number whose works he has
studied.[30] (It is worth remembering that Schopenhauer had

---

[28] *W*1 p. 57 (27).   [29] *W*2 p. 318 (272).
[30] Schopenhauer mentions Cabanis, Bichat, Gall, Charles Bell, Magendie,
Marshall Hall, all of whom were active in the first four decades of the nineteenth
century.

attended a variety of scientific courses in his student days, and kept up a lively if somewhat distant interest in the sciences throughout his life.) Such a method becomes philosophical, Schopenhauer claims, through unification with the subjective mode of consideration and through 'the higher standpoint that is thereby achieved'. The same point is reflected in Schopenhauer's direct message for those philosophers who do not recognize the importance of the objective standpoint: 'A philosophy which, like the Kantian, totally ignores this viewpoint on the intellect is one-sided and for that very reason inadequate. It leaves between our philosophical and physiological knowledge an unbridgeable gulf, in whose presence we can never be satisfied.'[31] It is in the same spirit that, having categorized the materialist as a Baron Münchhausen engaged in an impossible task, Schopenhauer concludes: 'So, against the assertion that knowledge is a modification of matter, the opposite assertion always establishes itself with equal right, namely that all matter is only a modification of the subject, as its representation'.[32] And finally, the best statement of Schopenhauer's correlativism is perhaps the following: 'Materialism too has its justification. For it is just as true that the knower is a product of matter as that matter is the mere representation of the knower; but it is also just as one-sided. For materialism is the philosophy of the subject that forgets itself in its own reckoning.'[33]

Let us now try to gain a clear view of Schopenhauer's position on materialism. The only aspect of what Schopenhauer calls materialism that contradicts his own stated idealism is the view that reality consists of modifications of matter with an existence independent of the knowing subject. As I said earlier, it is the realism of this doctrine that brings it into conflict with idealism. The belief that some non-material items exist independently of the subject would be equally objectionable to Schopenhauer. If on the other hand materialism is restricted to the doctrine that everything in the empirical world is a modification of matter, then Schopenhauer can accept it as true without sacrificing his doctrine that the empirical world is subject-dependent. And indeed, it is his

---

[31] *W*2 p. 319 (273).   [32] *W*1 p. 58 (28).   [33] *W*2 p. 21 (13).

view that the content of empirical representation is provided by material objects, spatio-temporal particulars in causal interaction. Whatever his views about the limitations of science, Schopenhauer's idealism, like Kant's, is at least meant to leave empirical reality open to investigation by natural scientists. The point at which his position becomes particularly interesting is when he turns his attention towards the status of the subject of representation.

There is a gap between philosophy and physiology in the Kantian account of the mind. How the a priori mental structures he discerns are supposed to tally with any physiological discoveries is a question which Kant not only fails to answer, but leaves us little room even to wonder about. The transcendental subject cannot be known to be immaterial, but Kant takes no clear steps towards rooting the subject in the material world either. In line with this and in common with other post-Kantian idealists, Schopenhauer develops the notion of the pure subject that cannot be part of the world of objects. But Schopenhauer is remarkably alive to the dilemma that this leaves. This subject must—for all that the idealists have said—be something for which there is an empirical explanation in terms of material objects and processes. Again, we must be clear whether this demand could even in principle be met whilst maintaining a commitment to idealism. Schopenhauer believes that it can—all that we need to do is to state our idealism and be prepared to listen to physiologists as well, rather than being 'one-sided'. The empirical account of the workings of the brain must be accepted as falling under the umbrella of the subject-dependent, on a par with any account of empirical occurrences. That is to say, we must not assume that we are giving an account of things, or events, *in themselves* when we examine whatever processes we take to explain the workings of the subject's intellect. We can present the semblance of circularity here if we suggest that brain-processes are dependent for their existence on their (possible?) presentation to some subject, and that their presentation to some subject is dependent for its occurrence on the occurrence of brain-processes. But this would be to ignore the different levels at which Schopenhauer's subjective and objective enterprises are at work. Motivated purely by the need to give first-order empirical explanations of the phenomena of consciousness, we include as part of our story the dependence of subjective states on observable states of the brain. But, motivated by the concern for a consistent epistemology, and assuming Schopenhauer's idealism correct for the sake of argument, we explain whatever is discovered empirically as a subject-dependent representation. Either half of this pair of enterprises may in itself be questionable, but their combination is consistent.

However, suppose that we reject idealism—could we not then also reject the notion of the pure subject that cannot be an object, and thereby leave the field clear for an account of the subject in material terms, or at least an aspiration towards such an account? First, it might be suggested that the problem of the non-worldly subject is peculiar to idealism because of idealism's equation of the world with what is an object for the subject. For under this assumption the subject can be part of the world only if it is an object for itself. And if, like Schopenhauer (and Kant less blatantly), one believes that the subject cannot be object for itself, the combination of this premiss with idealism yields the impossibility of the subject's being a part of the world of objects. *A fortiori*, then, on these assumptions, the subject cannot be identified with any material object. Neither assumption alone forces the non-worldliness of the subject. So it is not idealism pure and simple which leads to the problematic conception of the subject. But if one accepts Schopenhauer's premiss that the subject cannot be object for itself, then idealism is still a central ingredient in his view that the subject is necessarily non-worldly and that it presents an insuperable problem for any materialist account. Without idealism we lack grounds for saying that the subject could not be a material object. It may not know itself as an object but instead be always the precondition of knowledge of objects, and so on, but without idealism the subject could for all that *be* something material.[34]

However, there is a broader perspective that we can take on this problem. Schopenhauer characterizes the subject of representations as that which *knows* (and is known by none).

[34] I discuss this and related issues in 'The Subject and the Objective Order', *Proceedings of the Aristotelian Society* 84 (1983-4), pp. 147-65.

But at the same time he questions Kant's apparent assumption that the subject and its relation to the world should be primarily understood in epistemological terms. We have seen the first signs of this in this chapter. Alongside the account of the subject as an 'extensionless point', never among its own objects and not to be incorporated in a materialist account, we are to take on board the fully scientific account of the subject as something objective and explicable physiologically. What the subject is required to be by Kantian epistemology is not, for Schopenhauer, exhaustive of what the subject is, even though he accepts epistemology as the starting-point for philosophy, and agrees with Kant that it should be concerned with the absolutely certain foundations of knowledge.[35] The scientific account stands as the equal counterpart of the account demanded by Kant's epistemology, creating a grave problem of 'reconciling the subjective and objective viewpoints'. Schopenhauer produces no more of a reconciliation than Kant. But his charge that Kant's philosophy ignores the objective side is surely correct; and in acknowledging the difficulty so clearly and calling for a 'higher view' to mediate between subjective and objective viewpoints he may be said to have progressed beyond Kant. This combination of adherence to Kantian epistemology and recognition of its serious limitations is at the very heart of Schopenhauer's philosophy. His questioning of Kant's account of the subject is his most important philosophical achievement. But his simultaneous inability to relinquish the terms of reference of the Kantian theory leads to some of the most serious internal conflicts of his system. I have talked of a profound questioning of Kant's account of the subject, but of this we have as yet seen only the tip. The whole iceberg is revealed in his account of the will, which is explicitly designed to undercut completely the subject–object dichotomy, to place the subject firmly in the world, and to prove that our true nature is not as pure epistemological subjects at all.

Before leaving materialism, however, it must be said that in not successfully reconciling 'subjective' and 'objective' points of view, Schopenhauer is scarcely alone. The pattern of what

---

[35] Cf. *W*2 pp. 10–11 (4–5).

he says is repeated in much more recent debates, and in particular in suggestions made by Thomas Nagel.[36] Nagel argues that materialism poses an insuperable problem for us. On the one hand we have a commitment to seek an understanding of the whole world in terms that are as objective as possible, making as little reference as we can to the peculiarities of our own nature as subjects. We must include ourselves in this objective account of the world. But on the other hand the subjective character of being ourselves, with the kinds of experience that we have, is unamenable to materialist explanation. Even an idealized materialism that was in possession of all the objective facts would be inadequate to account for the mind, according to Nagel, because the very facts that are intrinsic to conscious mental life are not among the objective facts. Nagel does not propose to resolve this clash of viewpoints; rather, he thinks that recognizing the impasse created by our necessary implication in both is the best way to clarify the nature of the problem that is involved in striving for a materialist account of the mind. These views continue to be debated and I shall return to them later. But it is impossible not to hear an echo of Schopenhauer in the debate.

---

[36] See 'What Is it Like to Be a Bat?', and 'Subjective and Objective', both in *Mortal Questions*.

7

Knowing the Thing in Itself

WE already have at our disposal some materials which will
help to place in context Schopenhauer's positive doctrine of the
thing in itself as will. First, we have noted Schopenhauer's
reference to Kant's doctrine of the noumenal will as the stem
from which his own philosophy grows. Then, we have seen how
Schopenhauer uses the appearance/thing-in-itself doctrine to
suggest that behind empirical reality there is a higher and
truer essence to things. And finally, we have noted the
widespread dissatisfaction with Kant's handling of the thing-
in-itself doctrine, centring around the problem of its causal
connection with the phenomenal—a dissatisfaction which
Schopenhauer expresses on his own behalf as well. What we
might expect, given these clues, is a doctrine according to
which (1) there is an ultimate, transempirical reality, which
(2) is a will, and (3) is non-causally related to the phenomena
that make up the empirical world. And this is, in outline, the
doctrine that Schopenhauer gives us. It is at once startling
and obscure. However, in suggesting that it is 'what we might
expect'—given Schopenhauer's adoption of certain straightforward attitudes towards aspects of the Kantian thing in
itself—I wish to play down the idea that the Schopenhauerian
metaphysic of the will is merely a dramatic and inexplicable
aberration from philosophical normality. For it clearly originates
in an attempt to sort out some of the dominant philosophical
problems with which Kant had left the German intellectual
world to wrestle.

However, having noted the roots of Schopenhauer's doctrine
of the will in Kant, we should be aware of a number of
important divergences. While Kant held the thing in itself to
be unknowable, Schopenhauer claims not only that we can
know that there is a thing in itself, but also that we can know
what its nature is. Moreover, he is prepared to use empirical
evidence to confirm his claim to metaphysical knowledge of

the thing in itself. In his doctrine of the noumenal will, Kant was careful not to claim knowledge, and he would certainly not have accepted the use of empirical evidence here. A further difference is that Kant never suggests that things in general can in themselves be thought of as will, only ourselves as subjects—whereas what Schopenhauer does is to begin with the subject, and then seek to extend the doctrine literally to the whole world. And as a final caution it must be borne in mind throughout that what Schopenhauer comes to understand by 'will' is radically different from anything Kant meant by that term.

In our discussion of Schopenhauer's idealism we encountered his view that the representations which make up the real world of our experience can never give us any acquaintance with the *essence* of things: 'On the *objective* path', he says, 'we never reach the inside of things . . . instead, when we try to find their inside from without and empirically, this inside always turns, under our hands, into an outside again.'[1] However, he believes that something available inwardly to each subject can give us knowledge of our own essence, which we can then use as a key to unlock the inner reality of everything in the world. (The metaphor here is one that Schopenhauer uses frequently in this context.) The argument designed to lead us to this important key begins once again from the account of the representing subject's self-consciousness, but, by exploiting a deficiency in that account, it proceeds to open up dramatically new ground. In terms of the representation doctrine, I can know myself only as I appear to myself, as object or as representation, like everything else in the empirical world. Of course I am, apart from this, the *subject* of experience, but I cannot as such experience myself—the subject can never become object. The related drawbacks of this 'subject + object' account are: (1) the subject cannot be identified with any individual item in the empirical world, and is left as a mere correlate of the world as a whole; (2) the subject is a mere detached observer of all objects, including its body—a situation which in fact calls into question the admissibility of talking of 'its' body at all. For if *all* bodies are

---

[1] *W2* p. 320 (273–4).

merely observed by the subject as objects, we lack any good sense in which any of them *belongs to the subject* any more than the others. There may be objective empirical facts about alterations in a particular nervous system which explain the occurrence of some representations and not others: but that concerns only what Schopenhauer would call the 'objective standpoint', and not the subjective character of the experience of the body had by the subject. (1) and (2) are related in that if the subject were to be conceived as an active influencer of objects rather than a detached observer, it would be more likely that we should have to think of it as something in the world, not something distinct from it. The conception of the pure subject distinct from all objects arises directly from the epistemological problem of the possibility of knowledge of a world 'external' to oneself. But here the very notion of the 'externality' of the world seems to contain within it the assumption of a distinctness of the subject from the world, and thereby to encourage the notion of the subject as a detached observer even of its own body.

These are drawbacks not only because of the dubious conception of an entity identical with no part of the empirical world, but equally because of the intuition that something must be said about the subject's embodiment—whatever that will amount to precisely—which meshes with facts about our ordinary cognitive contact with our own bodies. Though we treat our bodies ontologically as 'objects among objects', our awareness of them is radically different from the observational awareness we have of other physical objects, and philosophical theory out to reflect this. All along, Schopenhauer has presented the subject of representation as a necessary conception, but a highly problematic one. Now he is more openly guided by the thought that we are not, and could not be, the kind of subject that the 'representation' theory demands. And this, for him, is intimately linked with the thought that the world could not be simply what the 'representation' theory demands. Thus, towards the beginning of Book II of *The World as Will and Representation*, we find this highly important passage:

The significance I seek of the world that stands before me as my representation, or the transition from it, as mere representation of the knowing subject, to what it may also be apart from that, could never be found if the investigator himself were nothing more than the knowing subject (a winged angel's head without a body). But he himself is rooted in the world, finding himself in it as an *individual*; i.e. his knowledge, which is the conditioning bearer of the whole world as representation, is nevertheless entirely mediated through the body, whose affections, as we have shown, are the understanding's point of departure in intuition of the world. To the knowing subject as such, this body is a representation as any other, an object among objects: its movements, its actions are to this extent known to the subject in exactly the same way as the alterations of all other objects of intuition, and would be just as alien and incomprehensible to him, if their meaning were not unravelled for him in an entirely different way. Otherwise he would see his action follow on given motives with the constancy of a natural law . . . But he would not understand the influence of the motives any more than the connection with its cause of any other effect that appears to him. But all this is not the case: rather, the knowing subject that appears as an individual is given the answer to the riddle: and the answering word is *will*.[2]

Our experience of the body is the central problem here, and Schopenhauer's attempt to overcome it involves a 'two-aspect' theory in which the body 'is given to the subject of knowledge . . . in two entirely different ways: in one way as representation in the understanding's intuition [*verständige Anschauung*] as object among objects . . . but also at the same time in a completely different say, namely as that which is immediately known to everybody, and is denoted by the word *will*'.[3]

Rather than negating the view that the body appears to us as an object, then, Schopenhauer wishes to supplement it with a further account. But what does it mean to say that my body is given to me as will? In what sense is this an 'immediate knowledge' of the body? And how is this mode of knowledge 'completely different' from that through which the body is given to the subject as representation?

The rest of the passage makes it plain that it is my experience of my own body *when I act*, when my body's movements can be said to express my will, that Schopenhauer is concerned with. Just what is meant by the claim that such experience is 'immediate' is one of the questions that will be posed in some detail in Chapter 8 below. But what

[2] *W*1 pp. 142–3 (99–100).   [3] Ibid. p. 143 (100).

Schopenhauer is trying to capture is the sense in which experience of the physical object that is one's own body is fundamentally different from one's experience of other physical objects—and that this is so because it is essential to one's experience of it that one is the subject of the acts of will that are expressed in its movements. This intimate link between willing and embodiment is a theme of enormous philosophical importance, and it is one of Schopenhauer's great achievements to have opened it up with such originality and insight. His conception of the link between body and will is in fact extremely radical: for him, there is no such thing as an act of will which is not directly manifested in bodily movement. Willing and acting are one, and acting is a physical moving. This leads to a number of problems, among others, about the causal antecedents of action. But I shall leave the working out of these until Chapter 8. For the moment let us concentrate simply on the notion that there is a close connection between being a willing subject and being an embodied subject whose experience is essentially of itself as embodied.

In Schopenhauer's grand strategy it is this link between willing and embodiment that will provide the key to the mysterious thing in itself. His thinking is that if there is a way of knowing something about oneself which is not at all a matter of representation, then it is bound to provide access to oneself considered not as representation, i.e. considered as thing in itself:

It is just this double cognition which we have of our own body that gives us information about the body itself, about its acting [*Wirken*] and its movement upon motives, and also about its suffering through outside impression—in a word about what it is, not as representation, but over and above that, hence what it is *in itself*. Such information we do not have immediately about the essence, action, and suffering of all other real objects.[4]

Thus we must try to understand how the connection between willing and embodiment is supposed to take us to knowledge of the 'in itself'—and examine to what extent this is achieved.

How can there be a way of knowing about oneself which is not a matter of representation? If there cannot be such a way,

---

[4] *W*1 pp. 146–7 (103).

then Schopenhauer's grand strategy is fatally impeded—but has he himself not made the vehement assertion that there could be no knowledge (or cognition, as we have often translated the word *Erkenntnis*) which was not the being present of some representation for the subject? It seems that he can only advance to knowledge of the thing in itself by denying this central part of the representation theory. Schopenhauer never really provides a satisfactory answer to this worry. But he clearly recognizes it as one, and it is possible to discern a progression in his thought on this point. There is an initial view that awareness of one's own will is a special instance of an object coming before the subject of representation. Then there is the strong claim exemplified above, that in being aware of one's will, one has cognition in some manner totally devoid of mediation through the representing intellect. Schopenhauer claims that cognition of one's own will takes one directly to the thing in itself. And finally, there is a return to the weaker view that cognition of one's will is after all a case of representation, but a case that is *sui generis*, because it is relatively unmediated. We are now said to come as close as possible to the thing in itself, because of the relative 'thinness' of the mediation involved. In this progression, the tension between the competing accounts of the representating subject and the willing subject is keenly felt.

   In his early dissertation *On the Fourfold Root*, Schopenhauer—as we saw in Chapter 4—categorizes the objects that can come before the subject or be the subject's representation. The fourth of these classes is, he says, special and important: 'it comprises for each of us only *one* object, namely the immediate object of inner sense, *the subject of willing*, which is an object for the knowing subject; it is given only to inner sense, and hence it appears in time alone, not in space, and even then, as we shall see, with a significant limitation'.[5] There is no mention here of our awareness of will as providing access to the thing in itself. Schopenhauer reiterates the general requirement that all cognition is a relation between a subject and a distinct object. The subject of representation cannot itself be an object of representation, but the subject of willing can, and indeed he makes the claim (without offering any support for it) that

[5] *VW* p. 157 (207).

'Whenever we introspect [*in unser Inneres blicken*], we always find ourselves as *willing*.[6] Self-consciousness, then, understood as oneself becoming object for oneself, is cognition of oneself as willing subject. This is an awareness 'from within' of one's own states, such as wishing, emotions, and various 'inner movements' that can be called 'feelings'. Schopenhauer is extremely vague at this stage about what willing consists in, but he stresses its inner nature, and thus feels entitled to relate it to the Kantian conception of inner sense, whose form is time alone. Thus my knowledge of myself as willing subject is supposed to be entirely non-spatial. Although he does mention outer self-knowledge, this is not explained either. Is it really knowledge of oneself, or merely of the body as object? The most serious problem, however, is with Schopenhauer's central concern of the 'inner self-knowledge' of oneself as willing subject. How can it be *self*-knowledge, if for any instance of the schema *x* knows *y*, the subject *x* and the object *y* must be distinct?

Schopenhauer is at least aware of this problem, but his attempt to deal with it appears disingenuous:

Now the identity of the subject of willing with the knowing subject, in virtue of which (and indeed necessarily) the word 'I' embraces and designates both, is the knot of the world, and therefore inexplicable. For only the relations of objects are explicable to us: but among these, two things can be one only inasmuch as they are parts of a whole. Here, on the other hand, where we are talking about the subject, the rules for knowledge of objects no longer apply, and a real identity of that which knows with that which is known as willing, that is of the subject with the object, is *immediately given*. Anyone who properly makes present to himself the inexplicability of this identity will call it with me the miracle *kat' exochēn* [*par excellence*].[7]

Given that he accepts that (1) the willing subject is known by being an object for the knowing subject, and (2) that nothing which is an object for the knowing subject can be identical with it, the willing subject cannot, for Schopenhauer, be identical with the knowing subject. He suggests in effect that logic can be suspended, and two distinct things can be

<hr />

[6] *VW* p. 160 (211).   [7] Ibid. p. 160 (211–12).

identical, in the region where 'the rules for knowledge of objects do not apply'. Few will, in that case, be keen to follow him into that region. Schopenhauer could abandon at least one of (1) and (2). Or, consistent with both, he could settle for the distinction between willing subject and representing subject, and so explain self-knowledge as a relation between two entities rather than a relation of one entity to itself. It is arguable that, despite this passage, he does just that: later (Chapter 10) we shall see the great effort he puts into showing intellect and will to be distinct.

Part of the difficulty is that while Schopenhauer's doctrine of the will in many ways undermines the notion of a purely representating subject, he presents it within the context of his idealism, which is stated essentially in terms of the representation doctrine. The willing subject and the representating subject belong to two *competing* doctrines, which Schopenhauer is trying both to contrast and to unite into a seamless theory. The above attempt at a 'miraculous' solution—a somewhat ironic choice of word—is Schopenhauer's own work (though we may wonder how much of an echo there is here of the 'identity of subject and object' which Schopenhauer had heard about from Schelling and Fichte). However, there are also underlying problems that are by no means peculiar to Schopenhauer. We have seen how Kant wrestled with what essentially is expressed in proposition (2), and how he also in effect gave up the attempt to explain how a single subject could be both a knowing subject and an object for itself.[8] One must suspect that the difficulty is bound up with the very conception of the subject: object relation. Schopenhauer never breaks free from this conception, though his later thought about the will calls it seriously into question.

Thus, as we have seen, by the time he wrote the first volume of *The World as Will and Representation*, Schopenhauer's central thought was that while we are the representing subject and the world consists of represented objects, this is as such a deficient account. Behind both subject and object lurks the thing in itself which constitutes the essence both of ourselves and of the world as a whole. And Schopenhauer explicitly says

---

[8] Cf. *KdrV* B68, B155–6 (discussed in Chapter 3 above).

now that our knowledge of ourselves as willing is unmediated by the forms of representation, a completely different mode of awareness which take us direct to the thing in itself: 'a *way from within* stands open to us, a sort of subterranean passage, a secret connection which, as if by treachery, transports us all at once into the fortress which it was impossible to take by storm from outside'.[9] The all-but-impregnable fortress is of course the thing in itself, unknowable it seems, but for the inner access we have to our own willing. That we can know the thing in itself to be will is, and remains, his crucial thought. However, a little further on in this passage from Volume 2 he modifies his claim that we know the thing in itself directly and without any mediation, implying too that he never made that claim:

[I]t should be noted, and I have always firmly held this, that even the inner perception which we have of our own will still does not provide an exhaustive and adequate knowledge of the thing in itself. This would be the case if it were entirely immediate: but as it is mediated by the will's . . . knowing itself as the will in self-consciousness through the intellect, so this knowledge is not completely adequate. In the first place it is bound to the form of representation, is perception, and as such divides into subject and object.[10]

Then he uses another striking image: the thing in itself appears here not quite naked but covered by the very thinnest of veils! The point underlying the image is that my experience of my own acts of will is subject to the form of time alone, not those of space and causality. It belongs, as he said in *On the Fourfold Root*, to inner sense. Clearly, if he is talking about *acts* of will, they must be subject to the form of time—they must occur at some time, or perhaps have a duration. The absence of causality and space from the inner experience of willing is harder to comprehend, for Schopenhauer explicitly identifies acts of will with movements of the body (which is spatial), and goes out of his way to emphasize that human action is not exempt from causal determination. His view is that while actions *are* spatio-temporal events belonging to the empirical causal order, the agent has *an experience of* her own actions

---

[9] *W*2 p. 228 (195).   [10] Ibid. pp. 229–30 (196–7).

which is inner, in that it presupposes only temporal organization of experiences.

However, let us conclude our discussion of Schopenhauer's claim to knowledge of the thing in itself. He is, it seems, prepared to concede that strictly speaking it is impossible to have knowledge of the will as thing in itself—to try for such knowledge is to demand something contradictory.[11] If the thing in itself is as such unknowable, what can be the status of the claim that in the inner experience of our own actions we have the 'most immediate' access to the thing in itself which is possible? If the thing in itself is unknowable, we must always be ignorant about the closeness of resemblance between it and any phenomenon. Even if a clear account can be given of that inner experience of the will which is supposedly mediated only by time, there can in principle be no guarantee that a smaller number of subjective forms of the understanding takes us 'nearer' the thing in itself than a larger number does. Our experience of willing may be 'immediate' in some other sense— incorrigibly known, non-inferential, without observation (for example)—but to say that it gives us our 'most immediate' access to the thing in itself is to make nonsense of the concept *thing in itself*.

By the time he raises such doubts about our knowing the thing in itself to be will, Schopenhauer has progressed far beyond his insight about the knowledge of particular acts of will had by willing subjects. Taking that insight as his 'key', he has unlocked for us the whole of nature, and has argued that every phenomenon is a manifestation of will. Will is *the* thing in itself. If we doubt the legitimacy of the claim to immediate knowledge of the thing in itself in the case of our own actions, Schopenhauer has in fact no further argument for this conclusion. The evidence he amasses to show that the behaviour and biological structure of living things and every natural force can be given a single unifying explanation in terms of an underlying will is only meant as a corroboration of the metaphysical truth that has already been arrived at by the argument from knowledge of action.[12]

There are many questions that arise about Schopenhauer's

[11] Ibid. p. 228 (195).
[12] Cf. D. W. Hamlyn, *Schopenhauer*, pp. 81–2 and 92–4.

view that the thing in itself is will. One is: Why is there only one will underlying the whole world? Part of Schopenhauer's answer to this is that there can be only one thing in itself. This is convincing in terms of the doctrines that shape his entire thought: if there is any thing in itself, it is, by definition, outside the subjective forms of space and time that govern the relations among representations. But space and time are the *principium individuationis*—they provide the criteria for the distinctness of one individual from another—so there can be no distinct individuals at the level of the thing in itself. The will, then, is not to be thought of as a supremely mysterious individual thing, but simply as *the world as a whole*, considered apart from its appearing to us as a collection of individuatable material objects in space and time. We have to say this if we take the conception of the 'in itself' at all seriously.

Another question that arises concerns the use of empirical data to confirm a hypothesis about a supposed metaphysical reality existing beyond any possible experience. To this, Schopenhauer's reply, which we saw outlined in Chapter 1, is that the Kantian assumption that any metaphysical knowledge must be exclusively a priori is just that—an assumption. What good reason is there, he asks, for refusing to employ the data gathered by our senses in the attempt to solve 'the riddle of the world', and to arrive at knowledge of the nature of mind-independent reality? In his view, 'the solution to the riddle of the world must proceed from an understanding of the world itself; and so the task of metaphysics is not to soar above the experience in which the world is presented, but to understand it thoroughly—experience, inner and outer, being indeed the source of all knowledge'.[13] If this is so, however, what makes such knowledge metaphysical? If it is not a priori, there is surely nothing to prevent its being simply ordinary empirical knowledge. Yet there cannot, of course, be ordinary empirical knowledge of the *thing in itself*. Schopenhauer may be relying on this point to differentiate metaphysical knowledge from empirical knowledge—knowledge is metaphysical if it is knowledge of the thing in itself. But now we must be careful not to lapse into the absurdity of claiming both that

[13] *W*1 p. 526 (428).

knowledge of the thing in itself is gained by empirical means, and that it is non-empirical, metaphysical knowledge, because the thing in itself is by definition empirically unknowable. The only coherent option is to say that by examining empirical data, we can best explain them in terms of something that does not and could not itself appear among the data. It is the simplest possible kind of explanation, because it attempts to explain all the data as an expression of one underlying entity (if this is the right word)—will.

Now further questions press in on us. How does the notion of a single will constituting mind-independent reality provide an explanation for our empirical data? The two most important subsidiary questions are perhaps: What is the relation between will and empirical data? And why is the supposedly unifying explanation to be given in terms of something called *will*? The mode of explanation that Schopenhauer hopes to achieve is not really akin to an explanation of all the data concerning the material world by a hypothesis of unobserved subatomic structures, or an unobserved event such as the 'big bang'. The reason is that between thing in itself and empirical data there can be no relation of any kind which pertains between objects or events in the empirical world. The thing in itself is non-spatial and non-temporal; thus it cannot be spatially or temporally related to anything that occurs among the empirical data. Even more importantly, there can be no causal connection between it and the data. On this point Schopenhauer is consistent from first to last: having clearly criticized Kant for incoherently positing a cause–effect relation between thing in itself and representation, he never once lapses into this incoherence himself. But does he not have an even bigger problem on his hands? Is not the relation between thing in itself and the empirical data now forever obscure? What Schopenhauer himself consistently says of this relation is that the undifferentiated thing in itself 'objectifies itself' as a plurality of empirical objects. By 'objectification', he tells us, he means 'being presented in the real world of bodies'.[14] However, this is surely equivalent for Schopenhauer to 'being presented as an empirical representation for the

[14] *W*2 p. 286 (245).

subject', and hence to 'being an empirical object'. It does not provide an intelligible account of the relation that empirical objects bear to the thing in itself so much as assert of them that they are empirical objects.

In Schopenhauer's defence, it may be said that the relation between the world as it is in itself and the world inasmuch as it is knowable to us must in principle remain obscure. We may be tempted to dismiss as anodyne the thought expressed by Kant (and occasionally by Schopenhauer) that if there is appearance, there must be a thing in itself, since an appearance must be an appearance *of* something that appears.[15] But such a dismissal is perhaps over-hasty. It might be argued that even if we are confident that the whole world of individuated objects is mind-dependent, we can assert this to be the case only if we can think that there might be a totally unknowable state of the world whose obtaining is independent of the mind. If the empirical world is relative to a particular perspective, it must make sense at least to conceive of the absence of such a limitation. If so, we are committed to the intelligibility of the world's having an existence in itself—and, at the same time, to the obscurity in principle of the relation between the world as a whole, as it is in itself, and the multiplicity of objects that make up the real world of appearance. This relation could only cease to be obscure if our knowledge were that of some 'God's-eye view' which straddled the divide between appearance and thing in itself. But such a view is not possible. So, while Schopenhauer's notion of 'objectification' fails to give an account of the relation between the thing in itself and the empirical world, I suggest that there is nothing that could successfully explain that relation. All we can say here is that the world as a whole is in itself such that we are presented with an experience of it of such-and-such a kind. This concession to Schopenhauer does, however, call into question his attempt to provide the simplest explanation of the empirical data in terms of the world as will. Precisely because of the inherent obscurity of the connection between the thing in itself and the empirical world, there is no clear sense in which the data can be *explained* in this way.

---

[15] Cf. *KdrV* Bxxvi–xxvii; *W*2 p. 569 (486).

The final question to be asked is: Why is the world in itself to be called 'will'? Let us first acquire a better sense of the diversity of phenomena which Schopenhauer seeks to subsume together as instances of will objectifiying itself. First there are conscious human acts of will, which, he argues, are identical with overt bodily movements. Then, every state of mind which is such that it or its object has (broadly speaking) a positive or negative value for its subject is an instance of will too. Schopenhauer says the term is to be applied to 'all desiring, striving, wishing, longing, yearning, hoping, loving, and enjoying' and the opposites of these (whatever they are exactly). In general, 'all affections and passions' are 'only more or less weak or strong . . . movements of one's own will, which is either checked or let free, satisfied or unsatisfied'.[16] A similar but abbreviated list occurs in the *Nachlass*, prefaced by the comment: 'It is to be understood that willing is taken here in a wide sense, and means everything pertaining to well-being and woe [*Wohl und Wehe*].'[17] Beyond this, he holds that 'every movement of the body, not merely movement following on motives, but also movement following on mere stimuli', is an objectification of the will; and that 'the whole body is nothing but the objectified will'.[18] The parts and functions of the body are all expressions of will: 'teeth, gullet, and intestinal canal are objectified hunger, the genitals objectified sexual drive . . .', even the brain is the objective expression of the will to know.[19] Beyond this, Schopenhauer suggests that natural forces such as gravity and magnetism (where we do indeed talk of attraction and repulsion) should be interpreted as objectifications of the will.[20]

In view of these examples, it has often seemed that Schopenhauer wants to explain natural phenomena as stemming from the conscious or even personal direction of a universal willing subject; or, as Lukács put it, that he 'anthropologises the whole of nature'.[21] In fact, such views are incorrect, though it must be conceded that Schopenhauer's use of the

---

[16] *FMW* p. 51 (11).   [17] *HN*3 p. 428.   [18] *W*1 p. 143 (100).
[19] Ibid. p. 153 (108); *W*2 pp. 302–3 (258–9).
[20] *W*1 pp. 154 (110), 178 (130–1).
[21] *The Destruction of Reason*, p. 225 (also at Michael Fox (ed.), *Schopenhauer: His Philosophical Achievement*, p. 189).

term 'will' is, for all its importance to him, quite misleading. In the following passage he tries to clarify his usage of the term:

Until now no one had perceived the identity of every striving and active force in nature with the will, and so they had not seen the manifold appearances, which are merely different species of the same genus, for what they are, but regarded them as heterogeneous: and for this reason there could be no word available to signify the concept of this genus. Therefore I name the genus after its most advanced species, the direct knowledge of which, lying nearest to us, leads to indirect knowledge of everything else. But this would mean that someone would remain caught in everlasting misunderstanding if he could not carry out the required expansion of the concept, and instead still wanted to understand by the world *will* [*Wille*] only the single species which has hitherto been signified by it—that is to say, only the will that is guided by knowledge and expresses itself exclusively according to motives.[22]

When he is being more precise, in the second edition of *The World as Will and Representation*, Schopenhauer applies to the latter species of will, characterized by its essential presupposition of knowledge and connection with motives, the term *Willkür*.[23] *Willkür* cannot occur in the absence of the cognitive faculties. It is *Wille* that objectifies itself throughout nature, and *Wille* which—without the presupposition of cognition or even of consciousness—is the underlying thing in itself. *Willkür*, as it occurs in human beings, is nevertheless a species of *Wille*.

Thus Schopenhauer does not intend to explain all phenomena as manifestations of conscious willing. The phenomena of conscious willing are those of which we have direct inner cognition and which alert us to the inadequacy of the subject/ object model provided by the doctrine of representation. In honour of this special status, whatever lies behind the veil of representation is to be called 'will', even though the majority of its manifestations are not instances of conscious willing at all. A great many are teleologically explicable, however, and may be thought of in terms of a kind of unconscious 'striving' whose end is the propagation and maintenance of life. Others are merely the action of one thing upon another. All are manifestations of the same thing in itself that manifests itself

---

[22] *W*1 pp. 155–6 (111).   [23] *W*2 p. 290 (248–9).

in us as conscious willing. Admittedly, this argument leaves the term 'will' fairly vacuous in its application to the thing in itself. But it is important to see that Schopenhauer is not anthropomorphizing nature. In attempting to subsume human action within a wider account of 'striving and active' forces, his aspiration is as much to naturalize humanity as it is to humanize nature.

Schopenhauer's thought is that all of the rest of empirical reality must have an 'inner' nature, and that our 'inner' nature is only one instance of what underlies the whole world. We know empirically only the 'outer' nature of the rest of the empirical world, but in itself the world is what we can know ourselves in ourselves to be. We are that instance of will which is capable of consciousness that it is an instance of will; apart from this self-consciousness, we differ essentially in no other respect from the rest of nature.

I began this chapter with the observation that Schopenhauer's doctrine of the will is not as wild and unusual as it may seem, once it is seen in its context. Some writers have even been prepared to see his theory as more or less run of the mill. Thus Hannah Arendt has written:

At the turn of the nineteenth century . . . suddenly, right after Kant, it became fashionable to equate Willing and Being.

Thus Schiller declared that 'there is no other power in man than his will'. . . . Thus Schopenhauer decided that the Kantian thing-in-itself, the Being behind appearances . . . is Will, while Schelling on a much higher level of speculation apodictically stated: 'In the final and highest instance there is no other being than will.'[24]

Again Schopenhauer begins to seem more of his time than he likes to think. Fichte had tried to make a direct link between the spontaneous 'I' and the notion of a *practical* being in something like the Kantian sense.[25] But it is perhaps with Schelling's more overtly metaphysical endeavours that Schopenhauer's theory of the will is likely to be compared.

Of those philosophers who have been influential in modern times none is perhaps quite so little known in the English-

[24] *The Life of the Mind*, vol. 2, *Willing*, p. 20.

[25] Cf. *Wissenschaftslehre* (Sämtliche Werke, vol. 1, pp. 277–8). See also Patrick Gardiner, 'Fichte and German Idealism', in G. Vesey (ed.), *Idealism Past and Present*, pp. 119 ff.

speaking world as Schelling. Part of the reason for this lies in the nature of his writings. During his most productive period up to 1809 he produced a fifteen-year-long series of treatises and systems, each somewhat problematically related to those before it, in which he wrestled, for the most part abortively, with various notions of the absolute. There are very few moorings outside the immediate context of his writing for the reader to hold on to in this rarified atmosphere. Fichte—who by comparison comes to seem quite a familiar, terrestrial figure—provides one anchorage point, but the relationship between the two of them changed and was itself the subject of debates, to which Hegel's first publication was a contribution.[26] I shall not attempt a comprehensive summary of Schelling's philosophy at any of its stages, but I shall simply indicate those features of it which show strong analogies with Schopenhauer, and which Schopenhauer must have been aware of through his fairly careful reading of a number of Schelling's writings.[27]

Schelling's starting-point and preoccupation was decidedly non-Kantian, in that he sought to find an account of the absolute that was modelled on Spinoza's.[28] It was Fichtian idealism that influenced him early on, with the thought that the absolute must be subjective because the 'I' was the unconditioned ground of all objects, and nothing that was itself objective could occupy this position. But Schelling quickly moves beyond the notion that the 'I' is absolute to thinking that the absolute is something higher, with which the subject can nevertheless be united. Rather than losing oneself in Spinoza's objectively existing absolute, one can, in the highest philosophical act of intellectual intuition, 'realize the absolute in oneself through unlimited activity'. The absolute has to be conceived as something entirely unitary, prior to the split into subject and object that for Fichte is the beginning of the theoretical generation of the world of finite selves and things. But how such an absolute relates to this world is something that Schelling never really succeeds in explaining.

[26] *The Difference between Fichte's and Schelling's System of Philosophy* (1801).
[27] For evidence of Schopenhauer's reading of Schelling, see *HN*2 pp. 304–40; *HN*5 pp. 143–9.
[28] See Alan White, *Schelling: An Introduction to the System of Freedom*, pp. 5 ff.

By the time of his *Ideen zu einer Philosophie der Natur* (1797), Schelling is both searching for an account of the objective world which will provide a corrective to the one-sidedness of Fichtian idealism, and convinced that the absolute is something independent of both subjectivity and objectivity—'it is not subject, not object, but the identical essence of both'.[29] Schelling calls the absolute 'pure identity', and conceives the task of philosophy as showing how subjectivity and nature can be derived from it. On reading this in 1812, Schopenhauer was prepared to grant some credence to the notion of a 'unity beyond subject and object'. He rejected Schelling's programme as pretentious and absurd, but thought that there was a timeless, contemplative state of mind that gave an inkling of something germane to Schelling's 'absolute unity'. It was a state in which time seemed to be suspended and the distinction of subject and object was felt to disappear. Moreover, Schopenhauer added, this state was for him the 'basis of all genuine philosophical endeavour'.[30] These remarks will be seen to be of great importance when we reach Chapter 11 below.

Though he may never have fully realized it, there is a clear strategic analogy between his own project and Schelling's search for the absolute beyond subjectivity and objectivity. It would be true to say of both of them that they believed that the problematic rift between subject and object that was so characteristic of the immediate post-Kantian period could be repaired by removing to a more fundamental metaphysical realm in which the single essence and origin of subject and object could be discovered. But the analogy does not end there. Schelling's 'philosophy of nature' developed into an extensive examination of various natural processes which led him to see a continuity between the organic and the inorganic. The substratum of nature as a whole he concluded to be energy (*Kraft*). His view of nature is strongly anti-mechanistic, in that nature is to be viewed as a universal organism, and as having an essence 'which the most ancient philosophy greeted prophetically as the *common soul of nature*', as he puts it in a work entitled *On the World-Soul*.[31] Again there is some

---

[29] *Sämtliche Werke*, vol. 2, p. 63.   [30] *HN*2 p. 318.
[31] *Sämtliche Werke*, vol. 2, p. 569.

resemblance to Schopenhauer's metaphysical project and conclusion. Schopenhauer, too, wants to give a single meta-physical explanation of the whole range of natural processes, uniting human and animal, organic and inorganic. His notion of will should not be equated with that of a world-soul, but it is in its way an attempt to conceive nature as fundamentally non-mechanistic. The will stands for a dynamic end-directness in the behaviour of organisms and, Schopenhauer believes, of all natural objects.

The quote from Schelling which Arendt gives is from his essay on freedom.[32] Here he not only says that willing is the only ultimate Being, but adds that to it alone can be ascribed 'groundlessness, eternity, independence of time, self-affirmation'. Schopenhauer could have used the same words about his conception of the will as thing in itself. Schelling also talks in this work of a primal desire (*Sehnsucht*) on the part of the eternal One to produce itself. Yet for all this, the context of the discussion—as well as its style—are very different from Schopenhauer's. Not only is Schelling preoccupied with the notion of an absolute freedom in a way which Schopenhauer never is, but he is also concerned with the relation between God and the absolutely existing will. Some of his conceptions were drawn from the mystical tradition of Jakob Böhme[33]— and indeed, Schopenhauer felt that the whole essay was somewhat less than honestly derived from that source.[34] Throughout his career, Schelling relates the absolute to God with greater or lesser degrees of clarity. This is perhaps the greatest difference between him and Schopenhauer, who never had any place for God in his philosophy.

Thus in some aspects of their strategy Schopenhauer and Schelling resemble each other. In particular they do so in seeking to go beyond the differentiation of subject and object into a metaphysical realm where a primal One will be discovered, and in finding that this entity must be conceived in some way as active or willing. In one of its aspects, Schopenhauer's will may be just his version of the absolute—

---

[32] *Philosophische Untersuchungen über das Wesen der menschlichen Freiheit und die damit zusammenhängenden Gegenstände* (1809), in *Sämtliche Werke*, vol. 7, pp. 331–416.

[33] Cf. White, *Schelling*, p. 119.

[34] See *HN2* p. 314.

given the most inappropriate of names.[35] I have tried in this chapter to show how Schopenhauer argued for the knowledge of the thing in itself, and how—for all its obscurity—his argument becomes an intelligible move when one considers the problems and presuppositions with which he was working. However, I now want to leave the rather empty 'absolute' aspect of the will, and look instead at the positive use to which Schopenhauer puts this concept in explaining phenomena in the empirical world and giving an account of the self. What we shall see is that he produces a new account of the relation of self and world which radically challenges the account of the world as representation and its associated view of the self as a pure subject of knowledge. The starting-point for this development lies in what Schopenhauer himself regarded as the crux of his system—his theory of action.

[35] This is the view of A. O. Lovejoy, 'Schopenhauer as an Evolutionist', *The Monist* 21 (1911), pp. 195–7.

8

Willing and Acting

THE pre-philosophical notion of an action (to the extent that there is one) seems to include the notion of its being a publicly observable bodily movement. Some, but not all, philosophical views of action are in harmony with this way of thinking. Schopenhauer's is among those that are, since he does not distinguish 'action' from 'bodily movement', but speaks instead simply of 'bodily action'. Where Schopenhauer departs from what can plausibly be represented as ordinary thinking on these matters is in his view of willing. For there is a clear pre-philosophical notion of willing which holds it to be something distinct from the overt movement of the body. Thus it comes naturally to victims of partial paralysis to say: 'I will my arm to move, but it does not move.' Schopenhauer seems to go against this in claiming that willing *is* acting *is* moving the body. To understand the claim more precisely, we can both set it against previous philosophical theories and bear in mind some more recent treatments of action.

There are several types of theory according to which there occur acts of will or volitions, which I shall take to be conceived as mental states which cause (or at any rate can cause) a movement of the body. According to volitional theories, my making a certain bodily movement is an expression of my willing something if, and only if, a distinct event of willing occurs and is the cause (in some specifiable standard manner) of the movement. According to one type of volitional theory, my *action* (my raising my glass, my drinking a toast, or whatever) is the movement of my body that is caused by that mental act of will which can be identified as, say, 'willing to raise my glass'. According to another type of volitional theory, my action is none other than the mental act of will itself, while my bodily movements are purely effects of—and not a part of—the action.[1] The second type of theory

[1] The distinction between these two types of volitional theory is made by Jennifer Hornsby, *Actions*, ch. 4 (as well as some further refinements).

is embodied in Berkeley's view that 'when I stir my finger, it remains passive; but my will which produced the motion, is active'. For Berkeley 'can conceive no action besides volition'; the motion of the body is not action at all, but a matter of mere passively perceived sensible qualities.[2] The first type of theory is exemplified by Locke: '*Volition*, or *Willing*, is an act of the Mind directing its thought to the production of any Action, and thereby exerting its power to produce it.'[3]

Schopenhauer's view is explicitly opposed to either type of volitional theory. According to him, any willing of mine of which I may be aware is taken up with my experience *of the bodily movement itself*, because unless I make the bodily movement, I have not really willed at all. First, 'Every true act of [the subject's] will is immediately and unfailingly also a movement of his body: he cannot really will the act without perceiving at the same time that it appears as movement of the body.'[4] This is still not clearly incompatible with there being both a distinction and a causal connection between willing and bodily movement. But Schopenhauer then makes it plain that as far as he is concerned, 'The act of will and the act of the body are not two distinct objectively known states, connected by the bond of causality—they do not stand in the relation of cause and effect; rather they are one and the same, only given in two completely different ways: once quite immediately and once in intuition for the understanding.'[5] Thus for Schopenhauer act of will = action = bodily movement; the only difference, according to him, is in the point of view taken, not in the event that occurs. In this sense we might refer to his as a 'two-aspect' account. The physical moving and the willing are but two aspects of one single event.

Each of Schopenhauer's 'ways' of experiencing the body is fully intelligible, whatever precise characterization philosophers may ultimately give of them. Part of my experience of my limbs is an awareness of them as objects in space, in spatial and causal relationships with other physical objects that I perceive. But it is a familiar point that I have what is called

---

[2] *Three Dialogues*, 217 (*Philosophical Works* p. 172).
[3] *An Essay Concerning Human Understanding* II, ch. 21, sect. 28.
[4] *W*1 p. 143 (100).
[5] Ibid.

'knowledge without observation'[6] of my own overt actions. It is not merely of my pure wants or intentions that I have this kind of knowledge. There is a sense in which I do not have to discover what I am doing by observing my body or making inferences, so that when someone asks me: 'What are you doing?', and I answer: 'I'm hammering a nail into this piece of wood', the further question: 'How do you know?', is misplaced.[7] The question would not be misplaced *vis-à-vis* a claim to know how an observed physical object was moving, but it is misplaced *vis-à-vis* my own bodily movements. But could this undoubted difference in the subject's access to the body's movement in action exhaust the difference between will and movement? Is the only important distinction that between 'inner' and 'outer' points of view?

First, we should approach this terminology with some caution. It may be, as Charles Taylor has put it, that the metaphor of an 'inside' springs 'from the notion of a centre of responsibility which is inseparable from the notion of action'.[8] We may similarly be driven, with Thomas Nagel, to speak of 'a clash between the view of action from inside and *any* view of it from outside. Any external view of an act as something that happens . . . seems to omit the doing of it.'[9] But 'inside' and 'outside' are metaphors, and are used in different ways by different authors. To what are we acquiescing when we take on Schopenhauer's use of this pair of terms? A complication here is introduced by his wider aims concerning the distinction between appearance and thing in itself. Our awareness of willing is supposed to give us access to our essence, the very kernel of ourselves as opposed to the mere outer husk which presents itself in the empirical world. (Recall his saying: 'On the *objective* path we never reach the inside of things . . . instead, when we try to find their inside from without and empirically, this inside always turns under our hands into an outside again.'[10]) Having dealt with this wider argument in

---

[6] The well-known phrase is Elizabeth Anscombe's; cf. *Intention*, pp. 13 f.

[7] Qualifications are obviously needed if the question is taken to concern my knowledge that I am *successfully* hammering the nail into the piece of wood; cf. the discussion of trying below.

[8] *The Explanation of Behaviour*, p. 57.

[9] 'Subjective and Objective', in *Mortal Questions*, pp. 198–9.

[10] *W*2 p. 320 (273–4).

the previous chapter, however, we shall not now engage with that connotation of the term 'inside'. Let us take the 'inside view' to be simply that awareness of an action which is had uniquely by its subject—however precisely it is to be characterized.

Schopenhauer contends that the only distinction between someone's act of will and the movement of their body (when they act) is one of description. An event of a certain kind is described as an act of will when we consider it from the point of view of the awareness of it had uniquely by the subject. An event of a certain kind is described as a movement of the body when we consider it as a publicly observable event. But in any particular instance, the act of willing to ϕ is an identical event with the bodily movement that is the ϕ-ing.[11] The two event-descriptions are simply two descriptions of the same event. The volitional account, according to Schopenhauer, goes wrong because while it correctly fastens on the duality of descriptions, it is misled by the wide disparity between the two 'viewpoints' from which they issue into positing a duality of events. Schopenhauer, on the contrary, is in an important sense anti-dualist here: 'willing' is only the subject's-eye-view description of the physical moving. And it seems reasonable to suppose that if it is identical with the physical moving, the willing cannot be the cause of the physical moving.

There are a number of problems with this account, two of which I shall raise here. The first is over the possibility of acts of will which do not issue in overt action—of which one instance was given earlier in the victim of paralysis. If the only acts of will are to be overt actions involving the body's moving, Schopenhauer may have no way of accounting for this possibility. The second problem is this: can it really be the case that a physical movement is correctly describable as a 'willing' *solely* by virtue of its being presented to the subject in a unique way from 'inside'? Is it not more plausible to suppose that we must account for the difference between a bodily action and a mere jerk of the body in terms of differences in

---

[11] Many recent writers have argued that actions are bodily movements (e.g. Donald Davidson, 'Agency', in *Essays on Actions and Events*, pp. 58–9). Schopenhauer apparently assumes *this* identity, and then argues for the identity of action and act of will.

the way the two were brought about? A mere jerk of the body may be caused by the impact of another object, an electric shock, or some physiological process occurring within the body. But if something is an action then we must have some account of what caused it which cites events of a different kind. Typically it has been thought that actions are essentially caused by beliefs and desires of the subject—an event that is not caused by my beliefs and desires could not be an action of mine. And there is the further question of intentions to act: it is at least worth considering the possibility that every action of mine must be brought about by an intention of mine to act.

Both of these problems concern the causal antecedents of action. As we shall see, Schopenhauer does have an account of the distinctive causal antecedents of actions. His position does not in the end rest solely on the 'inner'/'outer' distinction. But first let me make two comments on the nature of the problems just raised. One is that it is possible to hold beliefs, desires, and/or intentions to be the essential causal antecedents of actions without subscribing to a theory of volitions at all. Schopenhauer could then be right that the only *willing* is the bodily action itself, even if its being presented in a unique way from 'inside' is not the sole essential feature of an action. There might, to put it briefly, be no willing among the causal antecedents of an action, even though an account of causal antecedents must be given. Secondly, even if there is willing that falls short of being overt action, this does not mean that Schopenhauer is wrong to say that bodily action is willing. Even if there is unfulfilled willing, willing does not have to be a purely mental volition that causes a wholly distinct bodily action. The bodily action itself, when there is one, can still be a kind of willing, and may indeed be the primary kind of willing, as Schopenhauer insists. It will, I hope, become clear in what follows that even if Schopenhauer allows that actions are partly constituted as such by a particular kind of causal history, and that some willing is not overt acting, he can still hold on to his claim that overt acting is willing rather than (as on the volitional account) the mere consequence of willing.[12]

Bodily actions are, for Schopenhauer objectifications of the

[12] My indebtedness to Brian O'Shaughnessy's *The Will* (esp. vol. 2), will become explicit later, if not already apparent.

will (as thing in itself). This does not tell us anything about their causal history, however, since, as we saw in the previous chapter, there is no question of a causal relation between the 'in itself' and the phenomenal. But nor does it tell us anything distinctive about actions, since every phenomenon is an objectification of will for Schopenhauer. Does this not produce for him the peculiar difficulty of not being able to distinguish that special class of events that he wishes to give prominence to—namely, actions—from all other events of whatever kind? The crucial distinction to grasp here is between an objectification of will and an act of will. All events are seen by Schopenhauer as objectifications of will; but acts of will are a special subclass of events. What distinguishes them is first their 'immediate' mode of presentation to the subject, and secondly their being caused by what Schopenhauer calls *motives*. What, then, are we to understand motives to be? Consider this passage:

[T]he act of will, which in the first place is itself only the object of self-consciousness, occurs on the occasion of something else which belongs to the consciousness of *other things*, and which, in other words, is an object of the faculty of knowledge. This object, in this connection, is called a *motive*, and is at the same time the material of the act of will, in that the act of will is directed towards it, i.e. aims at some change in it, and thus reacts to it: its [the act of will's] whole being consists in this reaction.[13]

Remembering that all objects are representations for the subject,[14] we might suggest that, according to Schopenhauer, a motive is a mental representation of a state of affairs which causes me to act. In his account, I am moved to action by an experience whose object somehow inclines me towards bringing about some change in that object. He envisages the motive as purely a representation, not as itself being an instance of willing. There is supposed to be a firm divorce between representation and willing, so that the motive is purely cognitive and the action it causes is pure willing. Nevertheless, he wants a motive to be more than just a representation of an objective state of affairs, as we see from what he says

---

[13] *FMW* p. 53 (14).
[14] *VW* p. 41 (41–2).

elsewhere in the course of a somewhat Aristotelian discussion of causes:

The *efficient* cause is one *through which* something is, the final cause one *for whose sake* it is . . . Only in the voluntary actions of animal beings do the two coincide immediately, in that the final cause, the purpose [*Zweck*] emerges as a *motive*. Such a motive, however, is always the true and authentic *cause* of the action, the preceding change which brings it about.[15]

So a motive is also a *purpose*. Is this compatible with the account of motives given so far? It might be true that someone's action is caused by a purpose that they entertain prior to acting (though this is not necessarily true of all actions). It might also be true that their action is caused by experiencing certain objective states of affairs. But how can it be legitimate to equate the purpose—or even the entertaining of it, the presentation of it to oneself in thought—with the plain representation of an objective state of affairs? It has become a commonplace point in recent philosophy of action that actions cannot be explained unless at least both the beliefs and the desires of the subject are cited. We need to know both how the subject apprehends the world as being and how the subject wants some portion of the world to be. Entertaining a purpose would seem to involve more than merely wanting something to be the case. (It is already closer to action than wanting, since if I entertain a purpose, I am disposed to try to bring about a desired change, whereas I can want without being so disposed.) But, nevertheless, entertaining a purpose entails having wants or desires. Schopenhauer says confusingly that a motive is both a purpose which causes me to act and an apprehension of an object which causes me to act. At least, then, it seems that the state occupying the place of a Schopenhauerian motive has to be a complex state, in which I (*a*) have a representation of an object, (*b*) have a desire concerning some change in the state of that object, and (*c*) am disposed to try to bring about that change in that object.

Though there is unclarity in Schopenhauer's conception of a motive, he is entirely clear that motives are the causes of acts

[15] *W*2 pp. 387–8 (331).

of will, and that it is essential to acts of will that their causes
be motives. He frequently proposes a division of causes into
three species.[16] First there is cause pure and simple, in which
action and reaction are equal, and which is to be encountered
in the physical world in general. Then there is stimulus, a kind
of causality that is found only in the case of animate beings,
plants as well as animals; it differs from cause pure and simple
in lacking equality between action and reaction. Motive is the
third species of causality, possible only in animals because it
requires the presence of understanding, or the capacity to
experience an objective world. Human beings differ from
other animals in having conceptual as well as intuitive
representations; they are able to have thoughts as the motives
of their actions, not merely the immediate impressions of the
senses. The actions of human beings can thus be distinctively
rational, but we can still speak of acts of will caused by
motives in the case of other animals. Motivation, as Schopenhauer says succinctly, 'is merely causality which passes
through cognition [*das Erkennen*]: the intellect is the medium of
motives, because it is the highest grade of receptivity'.[17]
Animals have intellect for Schopenhauer, but not reason. If
they are to be capable of having motives (and if our account of
the kind of complex state a Schopenhauerian motive must be
to do its job is correct), then animals must be able to have
beliefs, desires, and dispositions to try to bring about desired
change in the world they apprehend. This may or may not be
an acceptable consequence of his viewpoint.

   Disregarding for the moment the case of non-human
animals, we can summarize the position reached so far in the
following way. Acts of will are, for Schopenhauer, a species of
events which are identical with bodily movements, but which
must fulfil two conditions: (1) that they are experienced
'immediately' by the subject; (2) that their cause must be a
certain kind of complex mental state, involving beliefs,
desires, and dispositions to try, but called by him simply a
'motive'. David Hamlyn suggests persuasively that two such
components must be present for Schopenhauer because, while
the first may be the distinctive feature of 'knowing *that* one is

doing something', 'to *know what* one is doing one has to place the action in a context of beliefs and desires—that being what knowledge of one's motive, and indeed the very existence of the motive, comes to'.[18]

Putting these two essential features of action together in one formula, Schopenhauer remarks: 'Motivation is causality seen from within.'[19] I am the subject of, and have the unique subject's access to, not only the bodily action but also the cognitive state that causes it. But this 'inner' access to the connection between motive and act of will is compatible with the connection being an ordinary causal one. We 'see from within' a series of happenings which can also be described as an objective causal chain. The willing subject is the unique object of self-consciousness, as Schopenhauer puts it in *On the Fourfold Root*, but, just as motivation is related to causality, so the will observed within ourselves is related to the first class of objects for the subject, namely empirical spatio-temporal objects. Schopenhauer thus reaffirms that we are dealing here with two aspects of one single course of events, or a single world doubly described. He adds appropriately: 'This insight is the foundation-stone of my whole metaphysics.'

We saw in the previous chapter how the strenuous divorcing of willing from representing subject led Schopenhauer into serious difficulties in accounting for self-knowledge. Similar problems arise in his treatment of acts of will because of his insistence that, from the subject's point of view, its own states fall into at most one of the two mutually exclusive categories of will and representation. The motive belongs purely to representation, as we have seen. This may seem dubious, given that a motive has to include some specification of what the subject *wants*, and even, as I suggested, some specification of what the subject is disposed to try to do. Are we not in the realm of willing here—if we are going to countenance such a realm at all? While Schopenhauer may be at liberty to use the term 'will' as he pleases, there appears intuitively to be a continuity between desiring, deciding, intending, striving, and acting (well captured by O'Shaughnessy[20]) to which justice

---

[18] 'Schopenhauer on Action and the Will', in Godfrey Vesey (ed.), *Idealism Past and Present*, p. 137 (cf. D. W. Hamlyn, *Schopenhauer*, p. 85).

[19] *VW* p. 162 (214).   [20] *The Will*, vol. 2, ch. 17.

may not be done if one refuses to apply the term 'willing' to anything but the last one (or two[21]) in the list. But Schopenhauer does apparently want to say that anything that may precede the overt action itself, but which falls short of being an action, cannot be an instance of willing and must be merely a representation for the subject. What he says about 'resolves' (*Beschlüsse*) is instructive: 'Resolves of the will which relate to the future are mere deliberations of reason about what one is going to will at some time, not genuine acts of will: only the carrying-out seals the resolve, which until then remains only a prescription that can be altered, and exists only in reason, *in abstracto.*'[22]

There are difficulties in squaring Schopenhauer's terminology with the various terms for the characteristic antecedents of action that we have already introduced in this chapter, but what he calls a resolve is surely the arrival at a decision to act or the forming of an intention to act. Let us consider the latter. It is certainly true that the forming of an intention to act is compatible for many different kinds of reason with the intended action's failing to emerge. It is also true that failing to ϕ at a time when there are no obstacles in the way of one's doing so normally serves as evidence of the absence of one's intention to ϕ. If I claim that I intend to give up smoking on a certain date, but when the date arrives I neither do so, nor take any steps towards doing so even though the circumstances are favourable, then a likely description of the situation is that I did not really intend to give up smoking. It was not (if you like) my will so to do. Schopenhauer's claim that 'only the carrying-out seals the resolve, which until then remains only a prescription that can be altered', suggests correctly that very often my actually ϕ-ing tests the genuineness of my will to ϕ. But it does more than that. It suggests that there can be no resolve which both expresses my will and is not acted upon—which must be false. I may make an utterly sincere resolve, but be prevented by injury or some disruption of the environment from carrying it out; or I may simply change my mind. If I resolved when I was 20 years old to kill myself when I was 34, the fact that I now lack that

---

intention does not mean that I lacked it then, or that to kill myself when I was 34 was not genuinely my will. The case is thus more complicated than Schopenhauer allows. A resolve can be more than a mere deliberation, and seems to have an important continuity with the willed overt action, or type of action, that it prefigures. A resolve can in some sense be a genuine expression of will even when the action it prefigures never comes about.

At times Schopenhauer seems to recognize this. He does so implicitly in talking of 'resolves *of the will*' in the passage quoted above; but more explicitly, in a passage in his later essay *On the Freedom of the Will*, he speaks of the act of will passing through three stages: 'As long as it is in a state of becoming it is called a *wish* [*Wunsch*], when it is complete a *resolve* [*Entschluss*]; but that this is what it is, is shown to self-consciousness only by the *act* [*That*]; for until the act it can be altered.'[23] This seems to reflect much better the continuity mentioned above, while preserving the idea that the ultimate test of what I will is the emergence of the overt action prefigured in my wishes and resolves.

What this relation of 'prefiguring' is remains obscure. But part of it is surely the instantiation of the following condition: while I continue to have the intention that came into being when I made my resolve, the intended action will occur in circumstances within the scope specified by the intention, provided that I and the environment remain intact. In this sense one might suggest that the carrying-out of the prefigured action sets the seal on the resolve: if it is a genuine resolve, rather than a mere thought about what one might be going to do, it will satisfy this condition relating it to the potential carrying-out of the action. But even if all genuine resolves must conform to this condition, the intentions that are formed in making them may lapse before any occurrence of their prefigured actions. (Similarly, decisions to act can be genuine decisions without being acted upon.)

The hard and fast separation of will and representation, and the admission into the 'willing' class of overt bodily actions only, suggests a picture in which we either merely

---

[23] *FMW* p. 56 (17).

perceive objects and think in various ways, or will, i.e. spring into overt action. The thinking and perceiving causes the springing into action, but nothing mediates between the two. In practice, however, Schopenhauer's view of motives gainsays this sharp dichotomy—for, as we saw, a motive must somehow encompass a state of wanting to bring about change in the objective world, and must involve the subject's entertaining a 'purpose'. Neither of these requirements can be met if the subject's state prior to acting is to be exhaustively characterized in terms of cognition of an object and mere thoughts about future acting. Once again Schopenhauer exhibits his tendency to treat will and representation as mutually exclusive and exhaustive categories, and to simplify his subject-matter accordingly.

Another aspect of this same problem is highlighted by Patrick Gardiner, who writes:

If bodily behaviour is treated—as Schopenhauer tends to treat it— as the sole ultimately authoritative and incontrovertible mark of the character and direction of our wills, always to be assigned priority over what we may think or say about our aims and objectives, it would appear that we have been reduced to the status of mere spectators . . . of the workings of that inner nature which (he has strenuously claimed) we know in an immediate and non-perceptual manner to be ours. In other words, have we not now been presented as being *simply* objects to ourselves, in the very sense in which he insisted earlier we are not and never can be . . . For if in the last resort I have to *discover* what my will is by observing what I do . . . can I any longer feel in the full sense responsible for my will, regard it as being truly mine? It seems to have become in a manner cut off from me, in the way in which the will of another is separate from me . . .[24]

This picks up some points already touched on. We have noted the distinction between knowing that I am doing something and knowing what I am doing—and we have agreed with Hamlyn's point that, for the latter, knowledge of my motives is necessary. With this in mind, it would seem that 'discovering what my will is by observing what I do' (and by nothing else) is impossible. We have also suggested that mental states such as desires, decisions, and intentions seem to be either

[24] *Schopenhauer*, p. 168.

expressions of my will on a par with my willed bodily actions, or at least continuous with them in some important way that is hard to state precisely. But Gardiner goes further in suggesting that Schopenhauer has unwittingly argued himself into a position where my will is 'discovered' by me, as something alien from me, by my observing what I overtly do.

On Schopenhauer's behalf I would suggest that this consequence only follows if 'I' refers solely to the representating subject or intellect. Schopenhauer is prepared to concede that the intellect discovers what is truly willed by observation of the bodily expression of will.[25] But only if I am merely an intellect can it follow that *I* make such a discovery in such a way. The main stress in Schopenhauer's earlier claim that I do not merely observe my own behaviour was that I am also in addition to being an objective observer of events, a subject of willing. Schopenhauer splits the subject into active and passive elements rather than identifying it with a passive element observing the activity of a mere external body. The problem—no less a problem than that which Gardiner alleges, but a different one—is that the subject itself has to be composed of a will (which it primarily is) and a distinct intellect. I am no less 'within' the action than I am 'within' the perception I am conscious of as mine. In the previous chapter I showed how Schopenhauer regards the 'merging' of his willing and knowing subjects into one 'I' as far less problematic than it really is. Later on, when we have seen in more detail how he spurns their identification, we shall appreciate the degree to which he is prepared to accept that each of us is composite, fundamentally split into two competing facets. This does not diminish the degree of difficulty attaching to the view, but it does suggest that we should take seriously Schopenhauer's intention of saying that I am both the bodily active subject and the subject of thought and perception. For him, the will as it is expressed in overt bodily action is mine. It may be cut off from my intellect, but in no very straightforward way is it, as Gardiner proposes, cut off from me. (We shall return to the problems of compositeness later on.)

[25] See esp. *W*2 pp. 243–4 (209).

To conclude this chapter, I would like to suggest a way in which, despite the difficulties with his view that we have discussed so far, Schopenhauer's equation of willing with overt bodily action does have at the core of it an important philosophical insight, which has both a positive and a negative aspect. The negative aspect is that there need not be any such thing as a purely mental volition among the antecedents of a willed bodily action. The positive aspect is that the bodily action itself is not only an instance of willing, but the prime instance of it.

Now against this it might be contended that there is *nothing* that is an instance of willing, in the sense of a distinct event that could be called an act of will. We might talk of willed actions, but these are entirely reducible to the essential causal antecedents discussed above—belief, desire, intention, decision—and the bodily movement that they appropriately cause. O'Shaughnessy discusses such a view, which he entitles 'intentionalist extroversion', and says of it that it offers 'a tough-minded, extrovert, meagre picture' of the inner life of bodily action which is above all 'strongly counter-intuitive'.[26] From the subject's point of view, according to his account, there is an awareness of believing, desiring, and intending certain things which 'mutates' into an awareness of 'intending now to act' in a certain way, and then immediately afterwards there is an awareness of the bodily movement occurring (or, strictly, its seeming to the subject to occur). What is absent is anything corresponding to the notion that the action 'is given to us in a special way from inside' (as Schopenhauer put it), or that it is given to us 'as will'. And it is precisely this absence that is counter-intuitive. As O'Shaughnessy says: 'I think we very naturally are inclined to say that, over and above these several factors, and far more centrally significant than them all put together, is the occurrence of a single distinctive psychological event of the type of *willing*.'[27] Another way of conveying the deficiency of this account is this: what is distinctive about the agent's perspective on an action is the awareness of *doing* it, which is crucially distinct from any 'external' awareness of it as an event simply happening. But

---

[26] *The Will*, vol. 2, pp. 261–2.   [27] Ibid. p. 262.

according to the account before us, I, as agent, am aware of my bodily movement, and am aware of (am the subject of) those states which constitute its essential antecedents and appropriately cause it—and of no other kind of event. Thus the difference of perspective between 'inside' and 'outside' rests solely on the fact that I am the subject of the states immediately causing the movement. The fact that it is my body that I experience moving is irrelevant here, because I also experience it moving when it is doing so not under my voluntary control. So what we have is, in Schopenhauer's terms, an attempt to conceive the subject solely as a representating subject, not as a subject that wills. The causality that operates is 'seen from within'—but I am 'within' the action only by virtue of its being my representations that cause the movement.

It might be suggested that the counter-intuitive nature of this account springs from an unfairness in the way it has been presented. Rather than talking of 'experiencing my body moving'—as we have done so far—it would be fairer to say that what I experience besides the antecedent states of desiring, intending, and so on is 'moving my body'.[28] But what kind of event is this? It is surely an intrinsically active occurrence—'intend-able, choose-able, perform-able, done out of act-desire, for reasons that are one's reasons'[29]—but not identical with any of the causal antecedents of action we have specified. The point is that we cannot both insist that such an active event occurs, and is distinct from the specified causal antecedents, *and* say that action is reducible to the body's (passively) moving plus an appropriate causal origin from those antecedents. Better to concede the intuitions that O'Shaughnessy lays out for us, and demand that there be something which occurs and is experienced by the subject and is a *willing* of the movement that comes about. The kinds of causal antecedent mentioned in 'intentionalist extroversion' can be acknowledged as necessary constituents of an action, and as the predominant factors in explaining action—but it is implausible to suppose that they, plus the body's movement

---

[28] For the distinction between transitive and intransitive senses of 'move', see Hornsby, *Actions*, ch. 1.

[29] *The Will*, vol. 2, p. 268.

that they cause in an appropriate way, are simply constitutive of an action.

If this line of thought is persuasive, it might be taken to lead in the direction of a theory of pure volitions—acts of will which are mental, and which are the immediate causes of bodily movements, essentially present whenever an action can be said to have occurred. However, we know that Schopenhauer wants to assert the existence of acts of will, and that he is in forthright opposition to the volitional view, denying any causal connection, indeed any distinction, between act of will and bodily action. Given that we want to locate something that is an act of will somewhere in the process, we now face a choice between volitionalism and Schopenhauer's position.[30] What advantage does the latter have over the former? One is that it fits better with our awareness of willing and movement— which, when movement occurs, is almost always a single awareness. Setting aside the unusual cases where there is failure to execute what is willed—such as paralysis—we would have no grounds in our ordinary experience as agents for positing pure volitions. We are simply not aware of the occurrence of such events when we act; we regard ourselves naturally as subjects of willed movement, not as subjects of acts of will which cause movements to happen. If we posit pure mental volitions, we have to give some explanation of how the gap between mental and physical is bridged to such an extent that our experience of willing and moving is, ordinarily, one and the same.

O'Shaughnessy presents a convincing argument for the conclusion that acts of will do not cause willed movements of the body which on the way involves asserting the identity of act of will and action. First we have to accept that the essentially active occurrence which the volitionalist is right in thinking must be present is none other than an instance of *trying* or *striving*. As O'Shaughnessy puts it:

The volition is a myth and striving is not. But they each meet this same absolutely vital need of providing an event that is *so* special that . . . its happening *in* one is necessarily never its happening *to*

---

[30] The strategy here is based on O'Shaughnessy's discussion of what he calls 'theories (X), (Y) and (Z)', ibid. pp. 261–70.

one. Striving really has this very special character. For striving is willing. Necessarily, willing never happens to one. This, after all, is precisely the distinctive character of willing. This is its essence.[31]

In cases of failure to act of the paralysis type, where we nevertheless want to describe the subject as having done something, it seems to be straightforwardly the case that they have tried (or striven) to move their arm. But next we must accept that all cases of acting are cases of trying or striving. For ordinary purposes, there is only a point to describing someone as having tried to open the door, say, if there was a failure to do so or if there was a perceived likelihood of failure. But this does not alter the fact that to ϕ is to try successfully to ϕ. If we accept these two theses—that trying is the essentially active or 'willing' component that must be present in all action, and that all actions are identical with tryings—we already have the Schopenhauerian thesis that the act of the will and the action are one and the same. The qualification needed (and, as we saw, not provided by Schopenhauer) is that there can be acts of will that fail to issue in actions—mere tryings. Nevertheless, successfully performed actions are identical with tryings that would have been *mere* tryings if (through paralysis or something analogous) the requisite bodily movements had not occurred.

Next in this argument is the point that in a successful action, the movement of the body that provides the fulfilment of what the subject is trying to do is *part of* the action that is performed by the subject. The alternative is to say that the movement is distinct from and caused by the action. But this, O'Shaughnessy argues, is a highly unwelcome alternative, for a number of reasons. One is that it is absurd to think that acts of walking cause the movement of the legs, or that acts of chopping trees cause movements of arms and shoulders. Another is that in seeing someone's body moving in certain ways in the water, I see them swimming. The swimming they are doing is not something that merely causes the movement I witness. The action encompasses the bodily movement that is the fulfilment of the agent's trying. But if the act of will that we agreed must occur is a trying, and an action is identical

---

[31] *The Will*, vol. 2, p. 260.

with a trying that succeeds, and the bodily movement that fulfils the trying is not caused by the action (being encompassed in it), we must conclude that the act of will does not cause the bodily movement. If all these assumptions are accepted, volitionalism must give way to an account in which acts of will (tryings) are identical with bodily actions, not their causes, and in which the bodily movement that fulfils the willing is also not a distinctly occurring effect of the act of will but is part of it, because it is part of the action with which the act of will is identical.

Finally, O'Shaughnessy gives a difficult account of the relationship between the act of trying or striving and the purely physical bodily movement in which it results. The movement is part of the action performed—precisely that part of it whose occurrence converts a trying into a successful trying, or action. But the physical movement of the body is not itself an instance of striving or trying. It is not, therefore, to be identified straightforwardly with the act of will which O'Shaughnessy has argued must occur. But neither can the physical movement of the body be simply an event caused by the act of will: it is not an event distinct from the action, but encompassed by it, and the action *is* the act of will. O'Shaughnessy wishes to say that the act of willing 'causally develops so as to bring [the physical movement] into being', and that 'a non-autonomous part-event of striving precedes and causes' the physical movement.[32] These are difficult notions. We are to think of the act of will and the physical movement neither as identical nor as separate causally linked events. The act of will is a psychological event whose whole being is taken up with its being directed towards the occurrence of a bodily action, essential to which is the occurrence of a physical body movement; the physical movement is simply that which necessarily occurs if the act of will matures into the action to which it was originally directed. To put it crudely, in order to raise my arm all I need to do (normally) is strive to raise it—its going up is the culmination of what I instigate merely in so striving. According to O'Shaughnessy, there is both a logical and a

---

[32] Ibid. p. 286.

causal connection here. Willing to raise my arm is causally sufficient for the occurrence, in normal circumstances, of the physical movement of the body which raising my arm must encompass, but it is also logically sufficient. The connection between my striving to raise my arm and the arm's rising is not a contingent one, similar to that between my being afraid and my face turning pale: it is a priori true that an event of striving to raise my arm will be (assuming no abnormalities in my health or in the environment) a raising of my arm, and for it to be that, it is logically necessary that the event of the arm's rising occurs. So the connection between willing and embodiment is very strong: part of the essence of willing is its directedness towards the occurrence of a bodily action that includes a physical movement of the body; and willing itself is (or in normal circumstances inevitably becomes) that very bodily action.

Although I have in no way done justice to the sophistication of O'Shaughnessy's extensive arguments, I hope to have presented this account as a plausible and attractive one. What now is the relation of this account to Schopenhauer's? First, even if we overlook the different nature of the arguments in the two cases, it is clear that we do not have Schopenhauer's view to the letter. For Schopenhauer not only identifies act of will and bodily action (which O'Shaughnessy does too), but implicitly at any rate he identifies these also with the purely physical event, the body's moving, whereas O'Shaughnessy wants to regard this as a part of the bodily action which is causally and logically linked to the act of willing. Schopenhauer wants the very same event to be given to the subject both in internal experience as an act of will and objectively as a purely physical movement of an 'object among objects'. This is implausible. On the one hand it seems too fragmentary an account of the unified experience of willed bodily action. And on the other hand, anything that is a purely physical movement of the body is not an act of will, because acts of will are essentially active and psychological in their nature. Furthermore, as we noted earlier, Schopenhauer does not seem to countenance the possibility of acts of will which fail to become bodily actions, and this must be conceded if acts of will are tryings or strivings as in O'Shaughnessy's account.

Nevertheless, in terms of the two features I picked out earlier on, the two views coincide. These are the lack of any purely mental act of will distinct from and causing action; and the central notion that action itself is the prime instance of willing. Because of this overlap, we may regard O'Shaughnessy's view as a more sophisticated and rigorous adaptation of Schopenhauer's. This is confirmed by the fact that, at the culmination of his book, O'Shaughnessy invokes his predecessor thus:

Schopenhauer said: 'I cannot really imagine this will without this body.' If this wonderful remark is right—and we shall see that it is—then the psychological phenomena that occur when one engages in intentional physical action must at the very least depend on *the supposed reality* of the body. But more: we shall see that the psychological phenomena that occur in any physical action, and under howsoever psychological a description, depend in general upon *the actual existence* of the body. And this is the real sense of Schopenhauer's remark. And it expresses a position that I endorse. Then it follows that mine cannot be a Cartesian position, even though I believe that trying is a psychological event that is omnipresent in all bodily action. For what here comes to light is, the essential mutual inter-dependence of bodily strivings and of the animal body upon one another.[33]

In describing bodily striving as serving 'a crucial bridge function between mind and body' (or 'a psychic promentary [*sic*] that openly juts into the physical world'),[34] O'Shaughnessy replicates Schopenhauer very closely:

The feeling in self-consciousness, 'I can do what I will', accompanies us permanently, but testifies merely that the resolves, or decided acts of our will, although emerging from the dark depths of our inside, will always cross over into the perceptible world, since to this world our body belongs along with everything else. This consciousness constitutes the bridge between internal world and external world, which otherwise remain separated by a bottomless chasm.[35]

Schopenhauer's pivotal and most original insight, then, is that there is a psychological state—willing—of which we are

---

[33] *The Will*, vol. 2, pp. 349–50. Schopenhauer's quoted remark is at *W*1 p. 145 (102), where he actually says 'without *my* body'.

[34] *The Will*, vol. 2, p. 352.

[35] *FMW* p. 57 (18).

the subjects, just as we are of any other psychological state, and that our being the subjects of it entails our embodiment. If a subject is a subject of will, the notion of it as a pure extra-wordly knower and perceiver of objects must be wrong. Not only must the subject, *qua* willing, 'have' a body; but the whole character of its experience of itself as willing is that of being something bodily. The insight that as subjects we are essentially striving, embodied, and part of a continuum of other life-forms, is one whose ramifications never cease to spread throughout the rest of Schopenhauer's philosophy.

In this chapter we have been concerned with treatments of action in contemporary analytical philosophy. This might seem at first sight to be an excursion from the business of understanding the philosophy of Schopenhauer. After all, we have not spent much time in earlier chapters on present-day arguments for and against scepticism or materialism, or in trying to elucidate the notion of the content of a state of mind in a way that begins to satisfy the standards of today. Even though these issues have been important in our understanding of Schopenhauer, the attempt to force him too narrowly into the terms of recent debates would have been detrimental to the interpretative enterprise. However, the case of will and action is unique, in that we have found the most recent extended treatment of the topic to be genuinely continuous with Schopenhauer's—not only closely analogous in its conclusions, but clearly indebted to a reading of Schopenhauer himself. Here Schopenhauer truly comes closest to analytical philosophy. And there is a further historical reason for this. First bear in mind that it was Wittgenstein's terse question: 'What is left over if I subtract the fact that my arm goes up from the fact that I raise my arm?',[36] which to a large extent defined the programme of analytical philosophy of action, and still hangs over it. Then note that Wittgenstein's long preoccupation with willing and acting originates in his early attempts to come to terms with Schopenhauer's theory—as we shall see in some detail in Chapter 13. To someone with no knowledge of Schopenhauer, the influence is all but concealed in Wittgenstein's writing. On the surface, it is not noticeable

---

[36] *PI* i, 621.

at all in that of his disciple Elizabeth Anscombe, whose book *Intention* has been so influential on the theory of action. Nevertheless, by this route Schopenhauer's account in fact played a foundational role in the genesis of contemporary theories.

9

Determinism and Responsibility

IN 1837, almost twenty years after the completion of the first volume of Schopenhauer's main work, the Norwegian Royal Scientific Society set a prize question, which ran: 'Can the freedom of the human will be proved from self-consciousness?' In reply, Schopenhauer wrote his essay on freedom, *Über die Freiheit des menschlichen Willens*, in which he laid out clearly and ingeniously his conceptions of freedom and of self-consciousness. Schopenhauer's was judged to be the winning entry in January 1839, and was published the following year. Doctrinally there are no very significant differences from his other writings, but the essay is worthy of separate attention because it presents his views about freedom in a concise, self-contained form.

The essay begins with two definitions, one of 'physical freedom', the other of 'moral freedom'. Physical freedom is simply 'the absence of *material* hindrances of any kind'.[1] Natural objects and natural events can in this sense be said to be free, e.g. the 'free course' of a stream, but not surprisingly the main interest is in animals and human beings:

In our thinking, the concept of freedom is most frequently the predicate of animal beings, whose peculiar feature is that their movements proceed from *their will*, are voluntary [*willkürlich*], and consequently are called free, whenever no hindrance makes this impossible. Now since these hindrances can be of very different kinds, while that which is hindered by them is always *the will*, we prefer for the sake of simplicity to construe the concept from the positive side, and with it to think of everything which moves solely through its own will, or acts solely of its own will—a twist of the concept which essentially changes nothing. Consequently, animals and human beings are called *free*, in this physical sense of the concept of freedom, when neither bonds, nor prison, nor lameness, that is, when no *physical* or *material* hindrance whatsoever restricts

[1] *FMW* p. 43 (3).

their actions, and their actions proceed rather according to their *will*.[2]

Schopenhauer regards his first definition as 'subject to no doubt or controversy', and as giving the original and most frequent meaning of the word 'freedom' (he also calls this concept of freedom *populär*).[3] In this respect he resembles both Hobbes[4] and Hume,[5] whose definitions are very similar.

Schopenhauer has little to say about political freedom, but he is prepared to state that it is merely a species of physical freedom, on the grounds that 'We . . . call a people free, by which we understand that it is ruled solely according to laws, but has made these laws itself; for then it follows in all cases only its own will.'[6] The assumption behind this seems to be that only laws and physical hindrances constitute restrictions on what a people wills—hence in the sense given so far it is free if only its own laws restrict it. In discussing the political freedom either of peoples or of individuals, Schopenhauer does not consider that having a drastically reduced range of choices might constitute a lack of freedom—even though there are no obstacles to choosing between the remaining options, and though no one wants to do anything which is not one of these options. Of this sense of freedom, Isaiah Berlin's remark seems to hold good: 'If I find that I am able to do little or nothing of what I wish, I need only contract or extinguish my wishes, and I am made free.'[7] Moreover, according to Schopenhauer's definition, if someone else contracts or extinguishes my wishes for me, by whatever means, I am the freer because I can do more of what I want to do. This is highly counter-intuitive, and suggests that this first conception of freedom will scarcely provide Schopenhauer with what he is hoping for. However, it is not my aim to criticize Schopenhauer as a political theorist. Let us deal solely with the simple notion that to be free in the 'physical' sense is to be able to do, without hindrance, that which one wills.

In the context of his essay, Schopenhauer requires this first conception mainly in order to contrast it with freedom of the

---

[2] Ibid. pp. 43–4 (3–4).   [3] Ibid. p. 44 (4); cf. p. 55 (16).
[4] *Leviathan*, ch. 21, p. 110.
[5] *An Enquiry Concerning the Human Understanding*, ch. 8, sect. 73.
[6] *FMW* p. 44 (4).   [7] 'Two Concepts of Liberty', p. 139.

will, or *moral* freedom, which is after all the subject of the original question. Though it seems a relatively straightforward matter to ask whether I can (in certain circumstances) do what I will, it is clearly a different matter to ask whether my will itself is free, that is, whether when I will to do *a*, anything prevented me from willing to do *b*, which seemed a possible choice but was not my actual choice. This is to ask whether my choosing to do *a* was in fact determined by something that was not within my control—the problem to which Schopenhauer now turns.

We already know that actions, for Schopenhauer, are caused by *motives*. Motives, like physical hindrances, can intervene obstructively in what someone wants to do—examples are 'threats, promises, dangers, and such like'—but motives are never in themselves absolutely compelling. In other words, no motive is such that to have it and not to act upon it is impossible. The reason for this is that an overriding counter-motive is always a possibility, whatever motive one has. For 'even the very strongest of all motives, the preservation of life, is yet outweighed by other motives: e.g. in suicide and in the sacrifice of one's life for others, for opinions, and for all sorts of interests'.[8] No motive, then, has what Schopenhauer calls a 'purely objective and absolute compulsion' attaching to it. Quite clearly the nature of the conflict is different in cases where a motive restrains me from those in which a physical hindrance does so. I might be hindered from walking in the park, which I want to do, by the walls of a prison or by my own motivation to care for someone who is ill. In the latter case, obviously, it is something I want or value that hinders my acting on another want. One way of putting the point is to say that I have two wants, to do *a* and to do *b*, but that I make just one of these wants *my will*.[9]

If, then, I have two incompatible wants, the having of each of which is compatible with not acting upon it, am I not free to make either of them my will? Schopenhauer observes that even if there is no 'objective and absolute' compulsion attaching to a given motive, there may yet be a 'subjective and

---

[8] *FMW* pp. 45–6 (5).

[9] For this use of the term, cf. Harry Frankfurt, 'Freedom of the Will and the Concept of a Person', *Journal of Philosophy* 68 (1971), pp. 5–20. (Cf. *FMW* p. 56 (17).)

relative' compulsion—i.e. for a particular person in a particular set of circumstances. I may entertain two projected courses of action, but I myself and the circumstances in which I am may be such that, given the particular series of experiences I have, only one course of action is possible. Then it becomes irrelevant that, in general, having the motives I have does not compel all agents come what may. Thus the question of whether the will itself is free remains to be answered. But if we try to answer it in terms of the first definition of freedom, we can achieve nothing. According to that definition, an action was free if it was 'in accordance with the will'. To ask whether the will is in accordance with itself is apparently to ask: 'Can you will what you will?—which either seems to beg a merely tautologous answer, or else 'comes out as if willing were dependent on another willing which lay behind it'.[10] In the latter case, since the same question is appropriate with regard to the 'second-order' willing, there seems to be no way of avoiding an infinite regress.

The solution is to stop regarding freedom—moral freedom, that is—as defined in terms of 'accordance with the will'. Instead, as philosophers before him have recognized (Schopenhauer is very vague as to who they are, using only the impersonal *man* at this point), the more promising procedure is to define freedom in terms of the concept of necessity, namely, as 'the general absence of all necessity'.[11] In accord with what he had established in *On the Fourfold Root*, Schopenhauer states his definition of what is necessary as 'that which follows from a given sufficient ground'.[12] Although he reiterates here his division of grounds into mathematical, logical, and physical, it is clearly the latter—the occurrence of the effect as soon as the cause is present—that is relevant to the question at hand. Something free of necessity should, he continues, be called accidental (*das Zufällige*), but everything encountered in the empirical world is only relatively accidental. It is accidental with respect to events other than those which cause it, not with respect to its own cause: 'So, since absence of necessity is its characteristic, that which is free should be that which is dependent on no cause whatsoever, and hence

---

[10] *FMW* p. 46 (6).   [11] Ibid. p. 47 (7).   [12] Ibid.

should be defined as the *absolutely accidental*: a highly problematic concept, which I do not guarantee to be thinkable, but which nevertheless coincides in a strange way with the concept of freedom.'[13] The 'strange coincidence' of the concepts of freedom and accident that Schopenhauer remarks upon here suggests quite strongly the following thought: that it is not in the absence of necessity that we could ever find a satisfactory way of justifying our intuition that we will freely. The thought has been put in this way by Thomas Nagel: '[F]ree agency is not implied by the *absence* of determinism, even though it appears to be threatened by the presence of determinism. Uncaused acts are no more attributable to the agent than those caused by antecedent circumstances.'[14] In the end, Schopenhauer effectively agrees with such a line in arguing that we have a justified sense of responsibility for our actions which has nothing to do with the question of their being necessitated by antecedent causes. But first his line of attack is to accept the equation of freedom of the will with absence of necessity, and to argue that since there cannot be anything which is not subject to some causal influence, there can be no freedom of the will. It is Kant's definition of freedom as the capacity to initiate *von selbst* a series of alterations that Schopenhauer states as his chief target. *Von selbst* here means 'without preceding cause', and hence 'without necessity'.[15] (As Kant before him, Schopenhauer does not seriously countenance the question of whether a cause might not necessitate its effects—he regards this merely as a desperate and hopelessly obscure expedient to try to save some notion of freedom in the face of all odds. But whether or not we accept this, the basic issue seems to be the same: if the connection between cause and effect is not necessary, there nevertheless remains the problem of the predictability—in principle—of all effects. This is a 'problem' to the extent that it goes against our intuition of being in control of most of our actions as much as their being necessitated does.) Immediately after stating Kant's definition, however, Schopenhauer confesses that since it implies that acts of will can occur with absolute spontaneity,

---

[13] *FMW* p. 48 (8).
[14] 'Subjective and Objective', in *Mortal Quetions*, p. 198.
[15] *FMW* p. 48 (8).

determined by nothing at all—thus involving the suspension of the principle of sufficient reason—he can attach no clear sense to it.

The question set by the Norwegian Royal Society was whether freedom of the will could be proved from self-consciousness. Having explained how 'freedom' has to be understood, Schopenhauer next moves on to examine self-consciousness. 'What', he asks, 'does self-consciousness contain? or: how is a man immediately conscious of his own self? Answer: entirely as *willing*.'[16] This is familiar. We saw earlier how Schopenhauer denies that the representing subject can be an object for itself, and how from the time of his doctoral dissertation onwards he wrestled with the notion of the willing subject as object for the representing subject. That he holds this view of self-consciousness makes the question posed a very acute one for him: for if self-consciousness is entirely taken up with awareness of ourselves as willing, self-consciousness looks to be peculiarly relevant to the question of whether we will freely. The implausibility of his view of the contents of self-consciousness may be slightly dispelled by his reminder that (as we saw in Chapter 7) 'willing' is to be taken in a very wide and unusual sense, including 'all desiring, striving, wishing, longing, yearning, hoping, loving, enjoying, rejoicing, and the like, and equally not-willing or resisting, and loathing, fleeing, fearing, being angry, hating, grieving, suffering pain, in short all affections and passions'.[17] Self-consciousness, then, is not to be thought of as containing solely those *acts* of will, identical with overt actions, that were discussed in the previous chapter. However, it is these that are under discussion in posing the question of freedom, so in practice it is acts of will that Schopenhauer considers in what follows. (I shall make further comments on the restrictiveness of Schopenhauer's conception of self-consciousness below.)

When we say that a person wills, we must always assume a content to the will—the person wills *something*, the willing has an object. What that content is depends on the motive that causes the action.[18] A Schopenhauerian motive, as we saw in the previous chapter, has a fairly complex role to fulfil. It is an

---

[16] Ibid. pp. 50–1 (10–11).   [17] Ibid. p. 51 (11).
[18] Ibid. p. 53 (14).

awareness of some part of the objective world, but it also includes a desire to bring about a change in the objective world. What is clear, though, is that without motives, acts of will would not be object-directed, and would thus not be the willing *of* anything. They would not exist therefore. So whenever we are presented in our self-consciousness with an act of will, it is caused by some apprehension (or at least seeming apprehension) of an objective state of affairs, and a desire that some objective state of affairs should come about. Acts of will are essentially caused—by Schopenhauerian motives.

The question with regard to the freedom of the will is whether, given these states as causes, it was nevertheless possible for something other than the act of will they brought about (as 'reaction'[19]) to occur—could there have been, instead of the actual effect, 'either none at all, or an entirely different one, even one diametrically opposed to it'? We can attempt to answer this question either in terms of objective cognition, or by examining the data of ordinary self-consciousness. But, as Schopenhauer argues, ordinary, 'simple' self-consciousness proves to be unable in principle to answer the question:

[It] cannot even understand the question, let alone answer it. Its declaration on acts of will . . . stripped of everything alien and inessential, and reduced to its naked content, may be expressed roughly thus: 'I can will, and when I do will an action, the movable members of my body will carry it out immediately, as soon as I will, entirely without fail.' This means, in short, '*I can do what I will to do*' . . . Its declaration thus always relates to *being able to do in accordance with the will*: self-consciousness will proclaim this freedom unconditionally. But it is not the freedom we are asking after. Self-consciousness proclaims the freedom of *doing*—on the condition of *willing*: but it is the freedom of willing that we are asking after.[20]

Thus self-consciousness, which is always of oneself as willing, cannot pass judgement on whether something other than what was willed could have been willed. It does not reach back to any of the causal antecedents of the willing:

The dependence of our doing, i.e. our bodily actions, on our will,

[19] *FMW* p. 51 (11).   [20] Ibid. p. 55 (16).

which is indeed proclaimed by self-consciousness, is something completely different from the independence of our acts of will from external circumstances, which would constitute freedom of the will, but about which self-consciousness can say nothing, because it lies outside its sphere. It concerns the causal relation of the external world (which is given to us in consciousness of other things) to our resolves, but self-consciousness cannot judge the relationship of that which lies fully outside its domain to that which lies within it.[21]

The peculiarity about this argument—which is really a peculiarity about its premiss as to the nature of self-consciousness—is that *all* the causal antecedents of an act of will seem to be assigned to our 'consciousness of external things'. Schopenhauer is insistent that a motive belongs to 'consciousness of other things',[22] and we have seen that it does indeed involve an apprehension of, and a desire to effect some change in, the objective world. But is it not more plausible to hold that while such a belief–desire complex is essentially externally directed, it is nevertheless encompassed within my self-consciousness just as much as my action/act of willing? If the content of my willing is determined by its being a reaction to a motive, in Schopenhauer's sense of that term, it is surely inconceivable that self-consciousness should reveal to me my act of willing, and not the states of 'external' awareness which give it its content. Furthermore, if the willing is a 'reaction' to the motive in the way that Schopenhauer wants—i.e. by being its effect—then it is inconceivable that an awareness that the one causes the other should not also be thought to be part of my self-consciousness. Schopenhauer himself has said that motivation is 'causality seen from within'. It is surely true that self-consciousness can say nothing about the external circumstances which bring about acts of will—but how can the beliefs and desires I have which cause the act of will, and whose presence is essential to its being the act of will it is, be 'external' circumstances?

This however, does not alter the substance of Schopenhauer's point. Even allowing that self-consciousness can embrace the motives that are the causes of willing and can involve an awareness of this causal connection, it is still true that self-consciousness as such cannot adjudicate the claim that, given

[21] Ibid. pp. 55–6 (16–17).   [22] Ibid. p. 53 (14).

these conditions, the subject's act of will could have been otherwise. To think that it can is to confuse willing with wishing or wanting (*Wünschen*). One can want to do both *a* and *b*, where willing both is incompatible; one can have the sense in self-consciousness that whichever of *a* and *b* one wills to do, one can do it. But it must be clear that this is wholly different from being able to establish that I could have made *b* my will rather than *a*; to establish that, my consciousness of the states in which I am, even if it includes a consciousness of my motives and of their causing my willing, is wholly inadequate.

We must abandon self-consciousness as our guide, and take an 'objective view' of the question of freedom. If we do so, Schopenhauer argues, determinism is inescapable. Motivation is a species of causation. Throughout the empirical world, the law of causality 'holds a priori, as the general rule to which all real objects in the external world are subordinate without exception'.[23] From the objective point of view, a human being is 'along with all objects of experience, an appearance in time and space', and so must be subordinate to the law of causality.[24] Causes follow from effects with necessity—this is what the law of causality, one species of the principle of sufficient reason, says. So, Schopenhauer argues, merely from the premiss that the willing of human agents is an empirical event, we can conclude on a priori grounds that willing is always causally necessitated. Then again, on empirical grounds, we discover different species of cause in the natural world to explain the behaviour of things: cause pure and simple, stimulus, and motive—but never the absence of causality.

Thus to believe that human willing is a kind of event that escapes causal necessity is to fall prey to an illusion. Schopenhauer is an unequivocal determinist—willing is impossible without an antecedent event to cause it, but once that event is present one must will in accordance with it. Thus our ability to will is no different in principle from that of water to move in the form of a wave, shoot as a jet into the air, or boil and evaporate. We are internally conscious of willing, and the states that immediately cause our willing are conscious,

---

[23] *FMW* p. 66 (28).   [24] Ibid. p. 84 (46).

rational states of the intellect, but that does not alter the underlying principle. If water was capable of thought it might think: 'I can make high waves . . . I can rush headlong downhill . . . [etc.], but at the moment I am doing none of all that, but am staying of my own free will, quiet and clear in the reflecting pond.'[25] Nevertheless, the water could only behave in these ways if it were caused to do so; and if it were caused to do so, then it *must* do so. There occur in us conscious acts of will which proceed from rational motives and of which we are immediately conscious of ourselves as subjects. Looking at the train of events solely from the point of view of this consciousness, we are misled into denying, or overlooking, the fact that the same principle that we apply to the water must apply to us, given that we are empirical beings whose actions are empirical events. But since to decide the issue of freedom on the basis of self-consciousness is impossible, we must consider ourselves objectively—whereupon we dispel the illusion of freedom completely.

Schopenhauer's eloquent defence of determinism is both powerfully and convincingly argued. But his essay does not finish there, even though, strictly speaking, he has answered the question set. He asks principally two remaining questions: (1) How does the *character* of that upon which motives exert their influence contribute to an explanation of what is willed?; and (2) Is there after all any justified basis for our sense of *responsibility* for our actions?

'That upon which motives exert their influence' can be called a person's will. Remember that willing, according to Schopenhauer, only sets in immediately after the motive has occurred. It is the effect of the motive, and an active reaction to it. But two people in the same circumstances, having very similar experiences, beliefs, and desires, can will (act) entirely differently, so motivation can only be part of the determinist account. The qualities of the person on whom the motives work constitute the other element. This Schopenhauer calls the person's *character*.[26] The motives and the character interact, and together they determine the person's willing and action. Schopenhauer's account of character follows Kant's in

---

[25] Ibid. p. 81 (43).   [26] Ibid. p. 87 (49).

many respects. He holds, as Kant does, that having an empirical character is a property which human beings share with all other empirical objects. Thus in *Parerga and Paralipomena* he says: 'Everything which *is*, is also *something*, has an essence, a constitution, a character: in accordance with this it must operate, must act (which means operate according to motive), when the individual occasions come which draw forth its individual expressions.'[27] My actions are thus causally determined by the interaction of *what I am*, empirically speaking, with the experiences that come to me 'from outside'. More particularly, according to Schopenhauer, we must assume that the effects exhibited by each thing when acted upon by certain causal factors are determined by a *force* (*Kraft*) which lies within it. No cause 'makes' its effect 'out of nothing'. In explaining events in chemistry and physics we rely on 'natural forces', the most basic of which remains unexplained in each instance;[28] the analogous 'force' in human beings, the property they have which explains the way motives 'work', is their *will*. Thus the character with which we have to deal is the character of a person's will. Of this Schopenhauer says: 'This special and individual determinate character of the will, by virtue of which its reaction to the same motives is a different one in every human being, constitutes that which we call his character, and moreover, because it is not known a priori but through experience, empirical character.'[29] Schopenhauer makes a number of specific assertions about this character: it is individual, empirical, constant, and inborn. None of these claims is supported by anything more than anecdotal evidence. The first two are hardly contentious—that character is unique in the case of each human being seems to be trivially true, while it seems unproblematic that one learns what character is, even in one's own case, solely through experience. The other two claims, that character is constant and inborn, are hardly uncontentious, especially when taken together, but everything Schopenhauer says about them amounts only to assertion.[30]

Schopenhauer's views about character serve to reinforce his determinism. Our actions are in a sense 'nothing new',

---

[27] *PP*i pp. 140–1 (123).   [28] *FMW* p. 85 (48).
[29] Ibid. p. 87 (49).   [30] See ibid. pp. 89 ff. (51 ff.), 92 ff. (54 ff.).

because they spring from what we unalterably are, together with the equally unavoidable causal impact of motives: 'Motives do not determine the character of a person, but only the appearance of this character, in other words the acts [*Taten*].'[31] But equally, 'through what we do, we merely learn what we are'.[32] Were that the end of the story, Schopenhauer's account of human action would be for the most part a cogent exposition of determinism, but ultimately a grim and unsatisfying tale. However, he ends his essay with the acute observation that the question of responsibility is left untouched by the whole of his previous discussion:

> If, as a consequence of the above account, we have removed all freedom of human action and recognized it as thoroughly subject to the strictest necessity, then, precisely through this, we are led to the point where we are able to comprehend *true moral freedom*, which is of a higher nature.
>
> For there is another fact of consciousness, which . . . I have hitherto disregarded. This is the entirely clear, sure feeling of *responsibility* for what we do, of *accountability* for our actions, which rests on the unshakeable certainty that we ourselves are *the doers of our deeds*.[33]

It is because of this 'feeling' that the ability to point to factors which causally necessitate an action does not in general exonerate the agent: 'it nevers occurs to anyone, not even to anyone who is entirely convinced of the necessity with which our actions occur . . . to excuse himself on grounds of this necessity, and to cast the blame from himself on to the motives, on whose occurrence, after all, the deed was inevitable.'[34] In practice, determinism never is, and it is plausible to suppose it never will be, sufficient for us to lose our notions of agency and responsibility. This is a point which, as we saw in Chapter 3, is reflected in Kant's account of freedom, and which has had some currency in recent years.[35] The question that remains is how we can explain or justify this 'feeling of responsibility' which seemingly will not go away.

---

[31] *W*1 p. 187 (138).   [32] *FMW* p. 99 (62).
[33] Ibid. pp. 133–4 (93–4).   [34] Ibid. p. 134 (94).
[35] Cf. P. F. Strawson, 'Freedom and Resentment'; Nagel, 'Subjective and Objective', and *The View from Nowhere*, ch. 7.

Schopenhauer's attempt to account for this feeling involves a shift away from actions and towards oneself as the locus of responsibility. He takes the fact just mentioned—that we cannot exonerate ourselves by appeal to our motives as causes—to show that the practice of attributing responsibility for actions is only superficial. What we really do is to attribute responsibility to people for their characters, with actions serving merely as evidence, a symptom or expression of what the person is. Some support for this comes from the fact that our judgements in the wake of wrongdoings are likely to be such as: 'He is a bad man, a villain'; or: 'He is a rascal'; or: 'He is a small, false, despicable soul'[36]—judgements of the *person* in the light of the action, not of the action itself. But even if that were invariably the case, what would this contribute towards the explanation of our feeling of responsibility? Schopenhauer responds as follows:

> As this character is just as necessary a factor in every action as the motive; so in this way we can explain the feeling that our deeds proceed from ourselves, or the 'I will' that accompanies all our actions, and by virtue of which each person must recognize them as *his* deeds, for which he consequently feels himself morally responsible.[37]

Operari sequitur esse—'action follows from being'—is the phrase Schopenhauer uses to emphasize the dependence of one's actions on one's character. Given the character I have, no other action could have issued from me in the circumstances than did in fact issue from me. But, *objectively* speaking, a different action *could have* occurred in the same circumstances —if I had been someone else.[38] Schopenhauer concludes from this that I truly feel responsible *for my character*. But the conclusion seems bizarre. It is one thing to say that only if I had been other than I am could my action have been different—perhaps this could also be expressed by saying that in some sense my character is 'responsible' for my action— but a wholly different and unwarranted move to say that I feel responsible for being what I am. The sense in which my character is responsible for what I do is not substantively

---

[36] The examples are Schopenhauer's (*FMW* p. 134 (94)); the translation here is Kolenda's.

[37] *FMW* pp. 135–6 (95–6).   [38] Ibid. p. 134 (94).

different from the way in which any cause is responsible for its effects, and it has little to do with the feeling of being the doer of the deed, the person who is answerable for it. And moreover, if character is what Schopenhauer has told us it is—inborn, constant, and empirically discovered by its bearer—then it is hard to see how one could feel responsibility for it. Having intensified his determinist argument with the thought that what I unalterably am plays as much of a role in necessitating my actions as my motives do, Schopenhauer tries to justify the feeling of responsibility with essentially the same thought. The result is scarcely coherent. Nothing has yet succeeded in explaining how we come by the 'feeling of responsibility'. It is possible, for all that Schopenhauer has said, that there is no more to responsibility than a mere subjective feeling, a product of an ignorance of the causal ancestry of our actions forced upon us by our self-conscious viewpoint.

However, at the end of his essay Schopenhauer adds a further point. He reverts to Kant's distinction between empirical and intelligible characters as containing the key to 'true moral freedom'. Schopenhauer describes this distinction, and the resulting account of the compatibility of empirical necessity and transcendental freedom, as among the greatest achievements of human thought.[39] Our consciousness of responsibility is like a signpost that points in a certain direction, seemingly to a nearby object (freedom of our empirical acts of will), but really to one more distant (transcendental freedom). Schopenhauer's account of this ultimate freedom is taken from Kant, with the difference that (consistent with what we have seen before) he does not attempt to make a *causal* link between the intelligible character and the empirical world. A person's empirical character is appearance; that of which it is appearance is 'his *intelligible character*, i.e. his will as thing in itself'.[40] The intelligible character is our essence; it lies outside the empirical realm, and thus is not subject to causal necessity. Such absence of causal necessity is *transcendental freedom*: 'Consequently the *will* is indeed free, but only in itself and outside appearance':

This way leads, as is easy to see, to the point that our *freedom* is no

---

[39] Ibid. p. 136 (96).   [40] Ibid. p. 137 (97).

longer to be sought in our individual actions . . . but in the whole being and essence (*existentia et essentia*) of the person himself. It must be thought of as his free act, which presents itself merely for the faculty of knowledge, bound as this is to space, time, and causality, in a multiplicity and diversity of acts.[41]

We saw in Chapter 3 how Kant's account of freedom breaks down over the problem that an intelligible object cannot act. Here Schopenhauer comes up against the same difficulty. Given that one accepted it as coherent to say that we have an essence outside empirical reality, there would seem to be no way in which it could be a 'free act', as Schopenhauer asserts here. In general it is unclear how my essence could be an act of mine; and furthermore there are the familiar points about the impossibility of action in the absence of space, time, and causality, the forms from which here, as throughout, the thing in itself is explicitly exempted. Schopenhauer's closing remarks seem to highlight the difficulty: freedom, he comments, has not been entirely 'removed' (*aufgehoben*) by his account, but merely 'pushed out' (*hinausgerückt*), 'namely out of the area of individual actions . . . up into a region higher, but not so easily accessible to our knowledge'.[42] The original question was whether our acts of will were free. In the face of his hard determinist account, Schopenhauer nevertheless wishes to maintain some justification for our sense of responsibility. But it is for our actions that we feel ourselves responsible, not for our characters. It is for their actions, as much as for their characters, that we blame others. So if it is not coherent to say of an intelligible character that it acts, that it is an act, or that we feel ourselves responsible for it, nothing like the relevant kind of freedom can have been preserved by Schopenhauer's account, even should it make clear sense. The very consciousness of agency that is revealed to us from our subjective point of view—that awareness of being the doers *of our deeds*—vanishes once the problem is removed from the empirical realm. Despite what he says, freedom in the only clear and relevant sense is removed by Schopenhauer's account.

Thus one's immediate assessment of Schopenhauer's position is his essay on freedom is liable to be as follows. His presentation

---

[41] *FMW* pp. 137–8 (97–8).   [42] Ibid. p. 139 (99).

of determinism, and his account of the inadequacy of self-consciousness to adjudicate about the 'could have done otherwise' question, are clever and convincing. But his attempt to mark out a sense in which we are nevertheless free is a failure. With Schopenhauer the free will seems to have reached its absurd limit: explicitly banished to a realm outside the objective world, and without even the possibility—which Kant tried so hard to salvage—of any interaction with the objective world. Nietzsche's 'fable of intelligible freedom' in *Human, all too Human* seems to hit the nail on the head.[43] He pictures philosophers as searching for something on which responsibility may rest. The search begins with the action itself, but goes progressively through all the causes that comes before it: 'Thus in order one makes the human being responsible first for his effects, then for his actions, then for his motives, and finally for his essence.' But we are not responsible for our essence either—Nietzsche finds that this route reveals the belief in responsibility to be an error. Schopenhauer now enters the fable as one who resists this conclusion, arguing that because some actions produce displeasure (which he calls consciousness of guilt), there must be responsibility. Responsibility cannot be for actions (*operari*) so it must be for our non-empirical being (*esse*)—Schopenhauer reaches what Nietzsche calls 'the fantastic conclusion of so-called intelligible freedom'. But he does so by a glaring *non sequitur*: that we feel displeasure over certain occurrences, or that in general we feel ourselves to be the doers of our deeds, does not legitimate the conclusion that we are justified in so feeling. Nietzsche concludes that responsibility is an illusion, revealed as such by Schopenhauer's fantasy version. We need not follow Nietzsche to his disturbing conclusion. But it is true that Schopenhauer has no reply to this pungent attack.

On a more positive note we may say that, apart from his attempt to justify the sense of freedom in terms of the intelligible character, Schopenhauer's account of the problem of free will has much to recommend it. In skeleton form his view is as follows:

---

[43] *Human, all too Human*, vol. 1, sect. 39. It may have been to *GM* pp. 215 ff. (110 ff.) that Nietzsche was responding.

1. Human beings are part of the objective world; there is nothing in the objective world that is not subject to causes; so the actions of human beings must be subject to causes, to the extent that we consider them from an objective point of view.

2. Self-consciousness (the 'view from within') is powerless to overrule the objective view; we cannot know merely from our being the subjects of actions that something other than those actions could have come about in the same circumstances.

3. Nevertheless, from one's own subjective viewpoint one invariably considers oneself an agent responsible for certain actions.

This, I suggest, is a clear statement of the central problem of freedom. The issue is not whether or not there is anything that occurs which is exempt from causal necessity; nor is it whether or not we bring about our actions by relating to them in some quasi-causal way which corresponds to the Kantian 'causality through freedom'. Schopenhauer addresses himself to the question of whether our actions are exempt from causality, but his answer is a resounding negative. Only after that business is done does he present what he considers to be the real problem. His abandonment of any causal connection between the intelligible character and the empirical world represents in fact an advantage of his account over Kant's. For it reveals that the real problem is not one of specially privileged ways in which certain events—our actions—are brought about. It is that there are conflicting points of view from which we can consider ourselves and our actions: 'If we consider man's doing objectively, that is from outside, then we recognize . . . that, like the action of any natural being, it must be subject to the law of causality in all its strictness; and yet subjectively everyone feels that he always does only what he *wills*.'[44]

As I have already indicated, this diagnosis of the problem is closely analogous to that of some distinguished contributors to recent debate about freedom. In his latest book,[45] Thomas Nagel has argued that once we are capable of attaining an

---

[44] *FMW* p. 139 (99).   [45] *The View from Nowhere*, ch. 7.

objective view of ourselves and our actions as components of the natural order, it is inevitable that our sense of our own autonomy, and our confidence in attributing responsibility to others, should begin to be undermined. We do not thereby lose our feelings of autonomy and our attitudes of responsibility, but we come under pressure to justify our having them. The trouble is, however, according to Nagel, that once we have the objective view that instigated this search for justification, there can be nothing for us that will work as a justification. Our 'internal' sense of being agents will not, indeed *cannot* while we are self-conscious active beings, recede; but we can give ourselves no explanation of how this internal sense can be squared with the objective picture we are equally bound to retain. Thus we are very far from knowing how the problem might be solved. If Nagel is right, Schopenhauer's (as I have suggested) abortive 'solution' to the problem of determinism and responsibility is but one of a series which may never have a successful final member, while at the same time pointing to the reason behind this. Schopenhauer's essay is already a creditable achievement, given the treatments of freedom known to him, and it does not need salvaging from the depths of history by this comparison with today's debate. But for those who are tempted by the thought that the outcome of his writing looks pretty meagre, it is salutary to reflect that today's debate about free will is neither vastly different nor vastly more advanced in its view as to where the trouble lies.

10

The Primacy of Will

'MAN is a practical being,' writes Schopenhauer, 'for the primary in him, the *will*, predominates over the intellect.'[1] Tracing the line of development through Kant, Fichte, and Schelling, we have seen that this judgement can hardly be counted as wholly original. Nevertheless, there are a number of features of Schopenhauer's particular account of the primacy of the will which mark it out as an important philosophical departure. Some of those features are already familiar. The claim that the will is primary in us arises initially from Schopenhauer's unique insight into the bodily nature of striving and its intimate link with action. Equally important, the claim that our nature is fundamentally characterized by willing or striving is made independently of the preoccupation with freedom which is to be found in his idealist predecessors. In this chapter I want to go on to examine the variety of subordinate theses within Schopenhauer's claim that the will is primary, which taken together present a massive challenge to the Kantian notion of the subject as pure, non-worldly, unitary, self-conscious, and fully rational.

Schopenhauer's claim that the will is primary in us is of course only one aspect of his overall view that the will is *the* thing in itself. The general metaphysical argument for that view is one that we have discussed; and the corroborations that Schopenhauer seeks in such phenomena as gravity and magnetism can only appear fanciful, even if we are careful not to treat the concept of will anthropomorphically. Consequently I shall spend no more time on the extension of the *Willensmetaphysik* to inanimate nature at large.[2] The focus of

---

[1] *HN*3 p. 578.
[2] Bryan Magee (*The Philosophy of Schopenhauer*, p. 139) finds plausibility in the notion, on the grounds that Schopenhauer must really mean 'energy' when he says 'will'. If find no basis for that interpretation, and none for the thought that this is 'the

my greatest interest—and of Schopenhauer's—is the primacy of will in the human subject. But I shall follow Schopenhauer in his extension of the concept of will to the whole of the animate world, as this is both far less fanciful and of great significance for his account of the human subject.

The most basic manifestation of will in the animate world is what Schopenhauer calls 'der Wille zum Leben', the will to life. Sometimes the more obvious translation 'will to live' is appropriate, but I have used 'will to life' because Schopenhauer's conception covers not only an organism's in-built propensity to secure its own survival, but also its drive to *produce* life—by reproducing—and its tendency to preserve the life of the offspring it has produced. Again, the term *will* should not mislead us into supposing that Schopenhauer posits conscious, end-directed behaviour throughout the world of animals and plants. We must recall the distinctions (*a*) between stimulus and motive, and (*b*) between intellect and reason. Plants have no intellect; they have no consciousness of an objective world but merely react to stimuli. Higher animals have intellect, for Schopenhauer, in that they are able to experience a world of spatio-temporal objects. They can act on motives because they can apprehend states of the objective world and desire changes in it—all of which causes them to act. But they have no reason; they are unable to form concepts, and so are incapable of discursive thought. Human beings act on motives informed, at least potentially, by rational thought. However, what Schopenhauer seeks is a single fundamental explanation of all these diverse forms of behaviour, characterized eloquently in such passages as this:

In animal nature it becomes apparent that *will to life* is the fundamental note of its being, its sole unchanging and unconditioned quality. Consider this universal urge to life, see the unending readiness, ease, and profusion with which the will to life, in millions of forms, everywhere and in each moment, through fertilizations and germinations . . . presses impetuously into existence, grasping every opportunity, greedily drawing to itself every stuff that is capable of

same conclusion' as has been reached in twentieth-century physics. T. L. S. Sprigge would like to agree with Schopenhauer that 'things in space and time do have an inner being which is what they really are in themselves, and that this is a kind of felt striving', (*Theories of Existence*, p. 94). This, apart from the word 'felt', is closer to what Schopenhauer means—but I can at present see no reason to agree with it.

life. Then again cast a glance at its fearful alarm and wild rebellion, when in any one individual phenomenon it is to vanish from existence. . . . See for example the unbelievable anxiety of a person whose life is endangered, the rapid and deeply serious sympathy of every witness to this, the boundless joy after the person is saved. See the rigid terror with which the death-sentence is received, the profound dread with which we view the means to its being carried out, and the heart-rending pity that seizes us at that event itself. . . . In such phenomena it becomes clear that I am right to have posited the *will to life* as that which is not further explicable but is to be laid at the ground of every explanation—and that far from being an empty sound of words, like the absolute, the infinite, the idea, and similar expressions, it is the most real thing that we know, indeed the kernel of reality itself.[3]

The latter, Schellingian abstractions (a little earlier, Schopenhauer mentions explicitly the conception of a 'world-soul' in another obvious allusion to Schelling[4]) cannot provide an explanation of why the content of the vast range of phenomena in the animal world is as it is, Schopenhauer is claiming; but the conception of an underlying will to life can explain that content in all its diversity. The beautiful writing cannot be sufficient of course to establish Schopenhauer's case. Nor does he think so himself. Rather, he is constantly amassing examples from the scientific literature known to him, where observed animal behaviour can best be explained in terms of his conception of the will to life. The whole book, *Über den Willen in der Natur*, which he published in 1836, is aimed at providing detailed documentation along these lines, although in both volumes of *The World as Will and Representation* there are enough examples to give a general picture.

The principle that must be accepted before we can get any further with this conception is that behaviour can be explained as purposive or end-directed in the absence of any consciously entertained purpose or end. Schopenhauer's examples are designed to demonstrate that this is the case:

The one-year-old bird has no representation of the eggs for which it builds a nest; nor the young spider of the catch for which it constructs a net. . . . The larva of the stag-beetle bites the hole in the

---

[3] *W*2 pp. 410–11 (350–1). My translation here is heavily indebted to Payne's.
[4] Ibid. p. 408 (349).

wood where it will undergo its metamorphosis twice as large if it is to become a male beetle than if it is to become a female, in the first case in order to leave room for horns, of which it as yet has no representation.[5]

Such activities are triggered by an apprehension of the environment in which the organism is situated,[6] and may be said to be accompanied by cognition of a kind, but they are not guided by any awareness of the ends which they are explicable as fulfilling. These descriptions are relatively uncontentious. But Schopenhauer has no hesitation in describing such animal behaviour as directed to a purpose (*Zweck*)[7] unknown to the animals themselves. Should we call such behaviour purposive?

It is clear that the kind of explanation we are most likely to give of the activities that Schopenhauer uses as examples is a teleological one. It is an explanation 'in terms of the result for the sake of which the events concerned occur', or 'by laws in terms of which an event's occurring is held to be dependent on that event's being required for some end'.[8] We may wish to insist, along with Charles Taylor, that properly speaking, while all purposive explanation is teleological, not all teleological explanation is purposive.[9] Let us suppose that we do so insist, and that the basis of our distinction is that purposive explanation is only possible with respect to the behaviour of an agent capable of intentional action. Then we may say that the behaviour in Schopenhauer's examples cannot be described as purposive. But are we then in a position to say that Schopenhauer's characterization of them as purposive is unwarranted? For a number of reasons, I think, we are not. One is that the German word *Zweck*—the word Schopenhauer usually, though not invariably, uses—is equally translatable as 'end' or (clumsily) as 'result for the sake of which something occurs'. If teleological explanation is defined in terms of these notions, then Schopenhauer need be saying no more than that the explanation of these pieces of animal behaviour is essentially teleological. Another is that he makes it quite clear that the kind of 'purposiveness' or

[5] *W*1 pp. 159–60 (114).   [6] *W*2 p. 401 (342–3).
[7] e.g. ibid. pp. 400–1 (342).
[8] Charles Taylor, *The Explanation of Behaviour*, p. 9.
[9] Ibid. chs. 2 and 3 (see esp. pp. 26, 62).

'end-directedness' involved here is 'blind', in the sense that it excludes any cognition by the organism of the end-state that explains its activity. And finally, as Taylor makes clear, the dividing lines between the different kinds of explanation are very uncertain; considering the whole phylogenetic scale, '[I]t is quite possible that a continuous progression will be found, leading from inanimate non-teleological systems, through animate teleological systems to those which are not only teleological but purposive in character.'[10] The affinities between human intentional action and that of certain higher animals, and between the latter and the behaviour of those slightly lower down the order, make impossible any a priori legislation as to where purposiveness proper, as opposed to non-purposive teleology, begins. So even if the term *Zweck* were primarily associated with human intentional action, there might be a point to using it more widely for behaviour which has a greater or lesser degree of affinity with human action in its mode of explanation.

In what follows, I shall regard Schopenhauer as holding simply that the explanation of the examples he gives is esssentially teleological, and I shall use such expressions as 'blind purposiveness' to connote no more than this. I shall also assume that, for Schopenhauer, human intentional action is one species of teleologically explicable behaviour which, in being so explicable, is continuous with a whole range of behaviour in other organisms.

The claim about the will to life, then, is that it can provide the most fundamental and simple teleological explanation of a vast range of behaviour, from the lowest organisms to humanity. Whatever ends are subserved by particular kinds of behaviour—nest-building, food-seeking, mate-seeking, etc.— these are subordinate to the overarching end of the continuance and multiplication of life. Beyond this there is no further explanation, no ulterior purpose such as fulfilling a higher destiny or constituting the best of all possible worlds.[11] It is merely a rock-bottom fact that organisms manifest this end-directedness towards life itself, whatever the variety of their behaviour, and that they do so as a matter of their essence.

---

[10] *The explanation of Behaviour*, p. 71.   [11] *W*2 pp. 415–17 (354–7).

Viewed in this way, the doctrine of the will to life is readily intelligible. Every organism strives blindly for survival and reproduction, inevitably coming into conflict with other striving organisms. While Schopenhauer holds that there is a metaphysical unity, in that the same will underlies the whole world, the multiplicity of the will's manifestations in the empirical realm are in open and deadly competition: 'the will must devour itself, because apart from it there is nothing and it is a hungry will. Hence hunting, anxiety, and suffering.'[12] One further refinement, however, is that it is not the individual that constitutes the ultimate end for the will to life:

[Nature], from the level of organic life up, has only one purpose [*Absicht*]: the preservation of all species. This is what it works towards through the immeasurable excess of germination, through the urgent power of the sexual drive, . . . and through instinctive maternal love, whose strength is so great that in many species of animals it exceeds the love of self, so that the mother sacrifices her life to save that of her young. The individual on the other hand has only indirect value for nature, namely in so far as it is the means for preserving the species.[13]

Much of this is bound to strike a chord for post-Darwinian ears. We have no trouble with the thought that organisms' behaviour, including much of our own, is explicable in terms of the end of the survival of a species within a given environment. But we should not assume too readily that Schopenhauer has an evolutionary view.[14] He knew and admired Lamarck's work, though it is unclear whether he first encountered it before, after, or during the development of his own views. He is explicitly critical of Lamarck at one point in *On the Will in Nature*.[15] Lamarck held that members of a species could be in existence before developing all of their organs, and that these developed in the course of time in answer to the

---

[12] *W*1 p. 206 (154).

[13] *W*2 p. 411 (351). 'Absicht' usually means 'intention'. In my view, Schopenhauer cannot be taken to mean this literally here.

[14] Magee appears to make this assumption (*Schopenhauer*, pp. 156, 263). Schopenhauer's relation to evolutionary theories has been debated before: see A. O. Lovejoy, 'Schopenhauer as an Evolutionist', *The Monist* 21 (1911), pp. 195–222; and Maurice Mandelbaum, *History, Man and Reason: A Study in Nineteenth-Century Thought*, pp. 318–19, 504.

[15] *WN* pp. 241–3 (262–5).

animals' needs in attempting to cope with their surroundings. From Schopenhauer's point of view, this is correct only to the extent that the animal's will is held to be the primitive factor that has determined its organization. In objection to it he argues first that if animals' needs have not been met by the organs they already have they would die out before they could develop any new ones; and secondly that in order to be consistent, Lamarck ought to believe in an original primitive animal without any shape or organs but capable in diverse environments of developing into a fly or an elephant—which he rightly regards as a plain absurdity.

In fact, until late in his life Schopenhauer not only has no explanation of how the species that currently exist came to be, but he also thinks that what species there are is fixed for all time. Each member of a species is an objectification of will, for Schopenhauer, but each species itself is what he calls an adequate objectification of the will, or *an Idea* (*Idee*).[16] This use of the term 'idea' is explicitly Platonic in origin, and it is used by Schopenhauer to denote those most universal features of the natural world that are shared in by the various individuals within it. In his understanding they constitute a permanent and ordered series of 'grades' of the will's self-objectification. Even though it is still compatible with such a view that some species should at certain times have no actual living members,[17] Schopenhauer does not exploit this possibility in order to give an evolutionary account.

By the time of *Parerga and Paralipomena* (1851) and the second edition of *Of the Will in Nature* (1854), Schopenhauer had become convinced that there must be development of one species out of another.[18] This is the only satisfactory way of explaining the facts of structural similarity across so many species—one example that is particularly striking is the neck vertebrae of mammals ranging from giraffes to moles.[19] Darwin's *Origin of Species* was published a few years later in 1859, the year before Schopenhauer's death. But Schopenhauer's evolutionary view, when he did arrive at it, cannot be classed along with Darwin's. Its central notions were that of

[16] *W*1 p. 207 (155).
[17] As Lovejoy makes clear, 'Schopenhauer as an Evolutionist', p. 200.
[18] See *WN* pp. 250–2 (273–5); *PP*2 sect. 91.   [19] *WN* p. 251 (274).

an initial *generatio aequivoca*, or spontaneous generation, followed by repeated instances of *generatio in utero heterogeneo*. This was the notion that parents of one species could at times produce a mutated offspring which was the beginning of a new species. This supposed process, which notably includes the birth of humans from orang-utans or chimpanzees, must have gone on simultaneously in many different regions, Schopenhauer notes, but always stepwise, with each step one of the 'fixed, enduring *species*' that he had believed in all along. He says quite emphatically that the development from one species to another cannot have been by gradual, imperceptible transitions.[20]

Regardless of his espousal of any kind of evolutionary theory, however, Schopenhauer from the start has a well-developed notion of the adaptation of an organism to its environment which is central to his notion of the will to life. As well as seeking teleological explanations of behaviour in the terms we have seen, he also arrives at the important thought that the very growth and structure of an organism are teleologically explicable in terms of the same 'blind purposiveness'. The body itself, as well as its behaviour, is thus an expression of will in the sense I have tried to make clear here. The development of specialized organs subserves the end of adaptation, which subserves that of survival and reproduction. To take but a few examples: 'teeth, gullet, and intestine are objectified hunger, the genitals objectified sexual drive; grasping hands and swift feet correspond to the already more mediate striving of the will which they represent'.[21] In this way it is quite clear that the existence of a body with organs of digestion is as much an expression of a 'will to eat' as is food-seeking behaviour. The later can be 'blind', but it is nevertheless teleologically explicable in terms of the result of finding and consuming food, and of maintaining life. Exactly the same thing applies to the occurrence of an organism with stomach, hands, legs, and eyes.

Sexual drives understandably achieve particular prominence in such an account. Sexual desire, with its basis in the purpose of procreation, is, for Schopenhauer, the fundamental impulse in human beings—'everywhere tacitly assumed as necessary

---

[20] *PP*2 pp. 167–8 (152–3).   [21] *W*1 p. 153 (108).

and inevitable, and . . . not, like other wants, a matter of taste or mood. For it is the want that constitutes the essence of the human being.'[22] The impulse to sexual intercourse has the power, in his view, to overcome all other motives; it is 'the invisible central point of all action and endeavour, and peeps out everywhere despite all the veils cast over it'.[23] To support this claim he cites a considerable repertoire of human behaviour which is explicable in terms of sexuality, the seriousness with which it is treated, and the intense pleasure associated with it. Accordingly he is able to call the sexual drive:

the kernel of the will to life, and thus the concentration of all willing; thus in the text [of $W1$] I have called the genitals the focus of the will. Indeed, one can say that the human being is the concretion of the sexual drive, since his coming into existence is an act of copulation, the desire of his desires is an act of copulation, and this desire alone perpetuates and gives coherence to his whole phenomenal appearance.[24]

While sexual desire in humans is directed towards consciously chosen individuals, and of course need not subserve reproduction, the drive towards sexual acts nevertheless exists in us as 'blindly' and as fundamentally as it does in other animals; it is neither secondary to, nor essentially under, the control of our more sophisticated cognitive capacities. Moreover, it shows us at our closest to being instruments for the continuance of the species—it is the perpetuation and coherence of the human race as a whole that is provided by sexuality in the above passage. Even if somewhat spicily related, much of this may seem nothing out of the ordinary to the present-day reader, whose expectations are likely to have been conditioned in some way by Darwinism and, of course, by Freudianism. But in its fundamentals Schopenhauer's account remains a powerful and convincing one. As a metaphysical account of the essence of the human subject, written against the background of early nineteenth-century German philosophy, it stands out as no less than startling.

In his comment about the sexual organs alluded to above,

[22] $W2$ p. 600 (512–13).   [23] Ibid. p. 601 (513).
[24] Ibid. p. 601 (513–14).

Schopenhauer contrasted them with the brain. Brain and genitals, he said, were opposite poles, the one the focus of knowledge, the other of the will.[25] However, the two receive fully parallel treatment. It is crucial to his account of self and world that he applies unflinchingly the same principle of teleological explanation to that pinnacle of nature, the human intellect. The objective explanation of the human intellect as a manifestation of the will to life is a major plank in Schopenhauer's thesis of the primacy of will. Though he does not present it in quite such a concise form, the basic argument he uses for his view is as follows:

1. All parts and functions of the body are teleologically explicable as manifestations of a 'blind purposiveness' which is ultimately the will to life.
2. Intellect in human beings is identical to certain functions of the body, in particular to functions of the brain and nervous system.
3. The brain and nervous system are (by step 1) teleologically explicable as manifestations of 'blind purposiveness', and ultimately of the will to life.
4. Therefore, intellect in human beings is teleologically explicable as a manifestation of 'blind purposiveness', and ultimately of the will to life.

If the genitals are an objective manifestation of the will to procreate, the stomach of the will to digest, the foot of the will to walk, then the brain is simply the objective manifestation of the will to know.[26] Step 2 in the argument is supported fairly straightforwardly by empirical considerations linking the occurrence or non-occurrence of various cognitive states with the condition of the brain and nervous system. (As we saw in Chapter 6, Schopenhauer assumes *identity* as the relation between cognitive state and brain function.) But then, if we accept the general principle about the manifestation of the will to life in the animate world, and in particular in the specialized organs of animals, the primacy of will over intellect is the inescapable conclusion. We are subjects of knowledge and of other cognitive states by virtue of our having brains, and our having brains can be explained

---

[25] *W*1 p. 412 (330).   [26] *W*2 p. 302 (258–9).

teleologically as subserving the end of more accurate and extensive responsivity to the environment, resulting in greater ability to predict and manipulate it—i.e. an increased chance of maintaining life sucessfully within it. Schopenhauer puts the same point in different ways. One is to say: 'My thesis here is: *that which in self-consciousness, i.e. subjectively, is the intellect, presents itself in consciousness of other things, i.e. objectively, as the brain: and that which in self-consciousness, i.e. subjectively, is the will, presents itself in consciousness of other things, i.e. objectively, as the entire organism.*'[27] Elsewhere he puts the point thus: 'I posit first and foremost *the will, as thing in itself*, completely primitive [*völlig Ursprüngliches*]; secondly its mere visibility or objectification, the body; and thirdly knowledge, as mere function of one part of this body. This part is itself the will to know objectified (become representation), in that the will has need of knowledge for its ends.'[28]

We now see how Schopenhauer's materialist account of the intellect, and his insistence on its correlativity with the account from the 'subjective standpoint', are subsumed within his wider metaphysical theory. Earlier we discussed how from one side the subject of knowledge was primary for Schopenhauer—the necessary condition of empirical representation and thereby of there being an empirical world of differentiated material objects. Nevertheless, from the point of view of what is contained within that objective world, the subject of knowledge could be explained as a set of functions of the brain. Now, however, we see that from the objective view it is not the subject's materiality that is the primary fact, but its essentially striving, end-directed character. Because we have intellects we are capable of conscious willing. This is the distinctively human form of striving, which we may call truly purposive: *acts* of will caused by conscious cognitive states (representations which is this context function as motives). Schopenhauer's first point about the will was (as we saw in Chapter 8) that our consciousness of being the subject of acts of will can only be accounted for by acknowledging the bodily nature of the striving that they involve. Then he makes the much wider claim that the body is itself a manifestation of at

---

[27] *W*2 p. 286 (245).   [28] *WN* p. 220 (237).

least a kind of quasi-striving (what I have called 'blind purposiveness') which permeates the natural world. This move enables him to present the truly purposive acts of will as continuous, in their nature as bodily strivings, with other functions of the body, and indeed with the body's very existence in the form that it has. All are explicable teleologically, the ony difference being the essential presence of intellect in the case of truly purposive acts.

So far we seem to have an account of the subject which is split in two different ways. First there is a pure knowing intellect, and on the other hand an embodied subject of striving. Then again, the knowing subject is, from an opposed ('correlative') point of view, a mere object. We have the descriptions 'subject of knowledge', 'object of knowledge', 'willing subject', but no clear account of how they or their referents are related. But now what gives true primacy to the will is the teleological explicability of the very knowing intellect as a manifestation of blind, bodily striving. Schopenhauer offers a unified account which makes both the subject of will and the subject of pure knowing—and of course the brain as mere object—equally manifestations of the end-directedness that characterizes the animate world as a whole.

Schopenhauer locates this unified account of the self in the realm of metaphysics, as a doctrine about what we are in ourselves. In so doing he undercuts the subject–object dichotomy in terms of which he initially defined the realm of representation. In that initial account the subject was a pure extensionless point outside the world of spatio-temporal, causally connected objects, while the body was a mere object within that world. By going beyond this subject–object split, Schopenhauer presents an account in which even the subject of knowledge is securely explained as bodily, and in which both subject and object are seen as manifestations of one underlying principle.

So far we have considered what might be called the 'objective' primacy of the will, but Schopenhauer complements this with an account of what he calls 'the primacy of the will in self-consciousness'.[29] This consists of a multifarious set of

---

[29] See esp. *W*2 ch. 19.

psychological observations about ways in which will and intellect interact in the experience of a human subject. In this wide-ranging discussion, Schopenhauer throws up a number of important difficulties for any view of the subject as primarily a knowing intellect. I shall mention only a few of his more cogent observations on the 'interplay of intellect and will within us'.[30] Often our emotional reaction to some real or imagined state of affairs follows on, more or less automatically, from the presentation of the state of affairs in our thought—joy at good news, sadness and longing at the image of a long-lost love. Here 'the intellect strikes up the tune, and the will must dance to it'. But the will exhibits in many ways that it is not under the control of the intellect. Thus our interest in preserving a tolerable view of ourselves often intervenes to prevent our thinking the truth, something which Schopenhauer sees as the will exerting a kind of unconscious censorship over the workings of the intellect. Furthermore, it is possible to will in ways of which we remain ignorant but which govern our behaviour:

Often we do not know what we wish or what we fear. We can cherish a wish for years, without admitting it to ourselves or even letting it come to clear consciousness; because the intellect must not learn anything of it, as the good opinion we have of ourselves would suffer in the process. But if it is fulfilled, we learn to our delight, and not without shame, that this is what we have wished: e.g. the death of a relative from whom we inherit something. And sometimes we do not know what we truly fear; because we lack the courage to bring it to clear consciousness.[31]

Similarly, our true motives may remain unknown to us. The intellect supplies the will with motives, and to that extent all motives are conscious,[32] but the intellect does not necessarily have, and frequently lacks, insight as to which motives will be acted upon. The will, then, can act quasi-autonomously, at odds with our intellectual self-understanding. Discovering our true motivation is not simply a matter of looking at what we straightforwardly believe to motivate us; we often only

[30] Sources for this discussion are as follows: *W*2 pp. 241–5 (207–11) and 250–62 (215–24).

[31] *W*2 p. 244 (209–10).

[32] Cf. D. W. Hamlyn, *Schopenhauer*, pp. 87–8.

discover our motivations in retrospect, and sometimes not at all. All this is further evidence for Schopenhauer that the will is not under the control of the intellect: he argues that if we were primarily self-conscious thinking beings, this autonomy of our blind, striving, inner character would be inexplicable. Similar evidence is found is the fact that violent excitation of the will can either incapacitate or greatly enhance the functioning of the intellect. Hopes, misgivings, love, or hatred cloud and falsify our thoughts. (In monetary matters we are more likely to miscalculate to our own advantage, for example.) And in general the phenomenology of our ordinary experience of the objective world is shot through with the influence of those positive and negative values which we attach to portions of our environment. If we conceive ourselves as pure thinking intellects, this fact is hard to explain, but it becomes an inevitable fact of human existence if we are fundamentally the kind of striving, survival-directed beings which Schopenhauer has argued us to be.

Thus we have much evidence—informal and anecdotal, but fairly convincing—of what Schopenhauer calls a 'direct, unconscious influence' of the will on knowledge. But what conclusion should be drawn from this? Schopenhauer in fact uses the above observations to argue against two related theses. One is the thesis that will and intellect are not distinct, but (e.g.) 'equally primitive functions of an absolutely simple being [*Wesen*]'.[33] The other is that the human subject is primarily a pure intellect. Against the first thesis, Schopenhauer's examples of the interplay of will and intellect in self-consciousness can count at best as persuasive redescription. There is no argument here—for if we do not already agree to the existence of will and intellect as separate entities or elements, we will not accept the descriptions of the various struggles, conflicts, and influences as showing them to be radically distinct.

Against the second thesis, however, the phenomena Schopenhauer discusses have an arguably destructive force. If so, this is of some moment, for the thesis under attack is no straw man. As Schopenhauer sees it:

[33] *W*2 p. 251 (216).

The philosophers before Kant, with few exceptions, made their point of departure the so-called soul, an entity whose inner nature and peculiar function consisted in thinking, and indeed entirely in abstract thinking with mere concepts . . . This soul had incomprehensibly got into the body, where it merely suffered disturbances in its pure thinking . . .[34]

All philosophers before me, from the first to the last, have held the genuine essence or the kernel of the human being to be in the *knowing* consciousness, and consequently grasped and presented the I, or for many its transcendent hypostasis, called soul, as foremost and essentially *knowing*, nay *thinking*, and *willing* only as a consequence of this in a secondary and derivative fashion. . . . All of them had the intention of presenting humans as being as different as possible from animals, and yet at the same time felt dimly that the difference between the two lies in the intellect, not in the will.[35]

The first passage goes on to link 'pure thinking' with '*universalia*, innate concepts, and *aeternae veritates*'. The views of the soul under attack are those that we associate particularly with Cartesianism and with Plato. (Elsewhere Descartes is mentioned, along with Spinoza, as having considered the will to be an act of thought, or judgement, thereby reducing will to intellect.[36]) In the second passage, Schopenhauer's attribution of the view in question to 'all philosophers' is implausibly wide. Nevertheless, it is a recognizable prejudice within philosophy, against which Schopenhauer might justly complain to be taking a somewhat lonely stand. As an attack on the view that the human subject is primarily a thinking, knowledge-gaining entity, only derivatively striving and embodied, Schopenhauer's reflections on self-consciousness are surely of considerable power. Many of the phenomena of self-consciousness clearly resist assimilation to a process of what he calls 'abstract thinking'. Unless we posit as primary in human beings the kind of end-directed striving, out of the full control of conscious conceptual thought, which Schopenhauer calls 'will', much of the way in which our minds appear to work becomes alien and inexplicable.

But if this is so, then we must in some sense, however

---

[34] *W*2 p. 323 (276).
[35] Ibid. p. 232 (198–9).
[36] *W*1 p. 368 (292).

restricted, concede the distinctness of will and intellect. We are aware in ourselves both of a capacity for objective, concept-based cognition, and of the kind of autonomously existing drives, interests, and emotional orientations that Schopenhauer locates. It is hard to conceive of reducing the latter to the former. And if we add to this the objective argument concerning teleology and embodiment, we find the following explanation for the deliverances of self-consciousness: there is a distinction to be made between an essential property of organic life (will) and a mere localized instrumental feature (intellect) which is explicable in terms of a specialized organ, is present only in some organisms, and instantiates the essential property of will. Schopenhauer can rightly claim to have argued that intellect in us is not primary, that intellect and will manifest themselves in self-consciousness as distinct functions or capacities, and that there is a unifying objective explanation of this which shows the primacy of the will.

To summarize Schopenhauer's doctrine of the primacy of the will: what we are offered is an overtly metaphysical theory, but one that is grounded in a host of empirical evidence, ranging from the objective findings of physiology, to informal observation of a variety of human behaviour, and generalizations from the introspective findings of self-consciousness. According to Schopenhauer we must recognize that:

1. We are essentially striving beings: our behaviour pervasively exhibits the 'blind purposiveness' associated with all organisms which is ultimately directed towards survival of the individual and more importantly of the species.
2. Those areas of our behaviour that are dependent on, and are guided by, objective knowledge are often explicable in terms of basic drives of which we are scarcely conscious.
3. We are essentially embodied.
4. Our capacity for objective knowledge is explained physiologically and teleologically in terms of our having organs which ensure our better adaptation to our environment.
5. Our underlying drives are frequently in conflict with the functioning of our intellect.

6. Human personality is composite, consisting of will and intellect which are distinct elements.

The conception of the pure subject of knowing that Schopenhauer himself cultivated earlier on must be woefully inadequate as a conception of what we are. For according to that conception, the subject is non-composite and disembodied; it is not an object in the world, but contemplates 'from outside' a world of spatio-temporal particulars which is wholly distinct from itself. Moreover, it is concerned not with striving for ends, but with classifying and relating representations in such a way as to attain objective knowledge. That we cannot be exhaustively characterized as subjects such as this is overwhelmingly shown by Schopenhauer's account.

How, then, should we conceive the relation between the initial account of the pure subject of knowing and that of the subject as essentially striving and organically embodied? We have seen in a previous chapter how, in the early *On the Fourfold Root*, Schopenhauer refers to the identity of the subject of willing with the knowing subject as 'the miracle *kat' exochēn*'. I commented that it would indeed be a miracle if two distinct entities were identical. That they are distinct is a simple consequence of Schopenhauer's holding at this stage the undeveloped view (1) that the willing subject is object for the knowing subject, and (2) that nothing which is object for the knowing subject can be identical with it. The latter, as we saw, he continues to hold; and for all the greater sophistication of his view of the will in *The World as Will and Representation*, he never really abandons the former. Thus we would expect the same problem to haunt his philosophy throughout: are the knowing subject and the willing subject identical or distinct? In this extended passage from the second edition of his main work we find him wrestling with this difficulty in the context of his fully developed theory of the will:

The will in itself is unconscious . . . The secondary world of representation must be added for it to be conscious of itself . . . As the will, for the purpose of comprehending its relations with the outside world, brings forth a brain in the animal individual, so there arises for the first time in this brain a consciousness of one's own self, by way of the subject of knowledge, which comprehends things as existing, the 'I' as willing. For sensibility, intensified to its highest in the brain . . . must first of all bring together all the rays of its activity, and concentrate them as it were into a focal point—but this focal point does not, as with concave mirrors, fall on the outside, but rather, as with convex mirrors, on the inside . . . this focal point of all brain-activity is what *Kant* called the synthetic unity of apperception: it is by way of this that the will first becomes conscious of itself, in that this focus of brain-activity, or the knower [*das Erkennende*], comprehends itself as identical with its own basis from which it has sprung, and thus the 'I' arises. . . . As soon as it turns inwards, it recognizes the will as the basis of its own appearance, and so flows together with it into the consciousness of one 'I'. Although this focal point of brain-activity (or the subject of knowledge) is simple, being an indivisible point, it is not for that reason a substance (soul), but rather a mere state. This knowing and conscious 'I' relates to the will . . . as the image in the focus of a concave mirror relates to the mirror itself, and has, like the latter, only a conditional reality—or actually only an apparent one. Far from being the absolutely first thing (as, e.g., *Fichte* taught) it is at bottom tertiary, since it presupposes the organism, while the organism presupposes the will.[37]

Schopenhauer is in deep water here. I have dealt with many of the problems elsewhere, so I shall merely comment on the central claim of this passage—that the 'I' arises from consciousness of an identity between the knowing and willing subjects. How *can* the representing subject, or subject of knowledge, recognize the will as the thing in itself of which it is the appearance? Schopenhauer's own principles seem to militate against this possibility. First, the representing subject cannot recognize itself as appearance at all. We have been told that it is the 'correlate' of all representations, and, as such, incapable of appearing among those representations. This point is specifically supported by the strong emphasis on its being a mere 'focal point', and so on. It can recognize a brain as an appearance, but the brain is an object not a subject. Even if my brain were directly an object for me, this—in Schopenhauer's own view—should serve all the more readily to demonstrate that the 'I' that experienced it was not identical with the brain.

A second difficulty compounds the trouble for this passage.

[37] *W*2 pp. 324–5 (277–8).

In experiencing acts of will 'from the inside', not merely as externally observable movements of the body, the knowing subject allegedly has the willing subject as its object. Schopenhauer wants to make this the basis on which the knowing subject 'comprehends itself as identical with' the will as thing in itself. But it is only by abandoning the world as representation—all that the knowing subject *ex hypothesi* has access to—that Schopenhauer has been able to argue that the will constitutes our essence. So it looks as if it is only by becoming a Schopenhauerian metaphysician that the knowing subject can recognize its identity with the will. That is implausible as a theory of self-consciousness. But what is worse, if the knowing subject has constructed for itself the Schopenhauerian account outlined in this chapter, its recognition of its identity with the will can be only the realization that it is a teleologically explicable outgrowth of a blindly striving organism. And that realization seems to undermine rather than to explain the subject's self-consciousness of itself as something unitary.

Philosophers have said that the 'I' is elusive; certainly it has eluded Schopenhauer. Unless there is some basis for an account of how the same subject can be conscious of itself as a subject both of objective knowledge and of the conscious and even unconscious strivings that Schopenhauer has portrayed, or of how the 'I think' and the 'I will' are co-referential, the very notion of the intellect functioning as an adaptive aid subserving the will makes little sense. The same centre of consciousness must be apprehending the objective world as is striving to make its way within it, even if objectively speaking it is an organism many of whose drives are not under conscious control. Schopenhauer's insistence that subject of knowing and subject of will 'flow together into the consciousness of one "I"' is perfectly reasonable and correct. It is merely that in his philosophy if they do 'flow together' in this way, it still has to be by way of a miracle.

Aside from these very serious problems, which stem from some of Schopenhauer's own fundamental principles, he makes the identification of the subjects of will and knowledge even more difficult for himself by going out of his way to argue that will and intellect are distinct, and that the knowing subject is an inadequate basis for an account of the true nature of the subject. Consistent with these developments, he might easily settle for the distinctness of the two subjects, in either of two ways. One would be to stick to the line that the self is fundamentally composite, and that the idea of an identity between that in us which has knowledge of the objective world and that in us which strives for survival and all other ends is simply an illusion. There are passages, notably those in which he is discussing the unconscious influence of the will over the intellect, where Schopenhauer seems to be arguing for such a composite view of the self.

The other way of settling for the distinctness of the two subjects would be to regard them as two theoretical constructs, each necessitated by a different theory about the self. The level of resolution between the two subjects would then be shifted—we would require a resolution between the two theories in which they played a part. Schopenhauer obviously thinks that the two accounts are compatible, but in what way, if at all, can this be so? It cannot simply be that the original account of the subject of representation was correct but one-sided, and that it merely required supplementation by an account of the subject of will. For each account essentially contains what, from the point of view of the other, must be falsifications. Let us call Schopenhauer's account of the subject of representation r, and his account of the subject of will, in all its ramifications, w. According to r, that which is subject is not (cannot be) an object in the world it experiences; according to w, that very same subject is identical with the brain and its functions. On the other hand, according to r, the body which the subject regards as its own is one object among others, and one which the subject understands no differently from them, as spatio-temporally located with respect to them, and in causal interaction with them; but according to w, the individual subject's body is the manifestation of those striving forces which the individual essentially and primordially *is*.

Clearly r and w are very different kinds of theory. So we might think of exploiting the differences in order to overcome these seeming contradictions. A first approach would be to say that r and w must not be seen as competing theories of what the subject is, so much as a 'subjective' and an 'objective' theory, each of which has its legitimacy provided it is not mistaken for a theory of the other type. Thus we could say that *r* is a theory about what, from the subject's own point of view, the subject must regard itself as, while *w* is a theory about what is the case independently of the subject's point of view. This would not make the compatibility of *r* and *w* perspicuous, of course, for it is unclear in general how 'subjective' and 'objective' theories can provide co-tenable accounts of the same reality. It has been argued that on many fundamental philosophical questions, personal identity and free will among them, we are compelled to construct both kinds of account, even though we may have no inkling of how they can both be true.[38] Supposing we agree for the moment that that is the correct view to take of the nature of 'subjective' and 'objective' pairs of theories—if *r* and *w* are such a pair, they will still involve a puzzle, but we can put it down as a profound and perhaps insoluble philosophical impasse. Rather than seeking compatibility for *r* and *w*, we should, according to this view, try to articulate properly the deeper problem that Schopenhauer's progress has unearthed.

Another approach would draw attention to the fact that *r* is a component part of an epistemological theory, while *w* is overtly a metaphysical account of the subject, aiming to provide a unifying explanation for a range of empirical phenomena. Schopenhauer's argument is thus: if you enquire into the nature of our knowledge of the objective world, you are required to conceive the subject of such knowledge according to *r*, but if you enquire into what human beings are in themselves *w* is the conclusion.

It is fair to say that a combination of these two approaches represents the way in which Schopenhauer would wish to argue that *r* and *w* relate to one another. But there are problems for either approach which make the issue far from simple. The subjective/objective approach does not work, because both *r* and *w* are theories with a subjective and an objective component. For *r*, from the subjective point of view the knower is a pure extensionless point, while from the objective view it is a material object (or perhaps some

[38] Cf. Thomas Nagel, 'Subjective and Objective', in *Mortal Questions*, pp. 196–213; and id., *The View from Nowhere*, Introduction.

properties of a material object). For *w*, from the subjective point of view the subject of will is simply what we find ourselves to be *in self-consciousness*; but from the objective point of view the subject is a teleologically explicable striving organism. Any clash between the subjective and the objective occurs therefore in duplicate—both within *r* and within *w*. It begins to look as though there is indeed an inevitable rift between conceptions of ourselves as parts of the natural world and of ourselves as selves. But that rift cannot be what separates *r* and *w*.

Turning to the other approach, which tries to explain the divergence between *r* and *w* as resting solely on the fact that *r* is an epistemological theory, and *w* a metaphysical one, the immediate thought is that we should not settle lightly for an epistemology and a metaphysics which give us wholly conflicting accounts of the subject and its relation to the world. If we essentially are striving, embodied organisms, and the explanation of the existence of the human intellect is in terms of organs that enable such an organism and its species to survive in an environment, then our account of what can be known by such a being should not involve the presupposition that what does the knowing is the extra-worldly Schopenhauerian subject of representations. Unless, that is, it is inherent in the epistemological project we have undertaken that the knowing subject be conceived in such a way. Then we would have a very interesting and perplexing position. Epistemology would involve such a problematic concept of the subject of knowledge that it would be incompatible with what we took that subject to be when not doing epistemology. I shall discuss the questions raised here in my final chapter.

Ultimately Schopenhauer's theory only has unity to the extent that the pure knowing subject is, as he himself puts it, something merely conditional or apparent. The pure knowing subject reduces to brain-functions which are explicable as manifestations of will. We are embodied manifestations of will in its various guises, and the pure knowing subject can be regarded as an illusion. Whatever the problems that beset its co-ordination with the rest of his philosophy, Schopenhauer's doctrine of the primacy of the will successfully undermines any conception of the self as primarily or solely a non-worldly knowing intellect, whether Cartesian or Kantian. If we ask why in that case he persistently retains such a conception in a role that is central to his whole philosophy, there are two answers. One is that he requires the structure of Kant's transcendental idealism to express his insight about the will as thing in itself as opposed to mere phenomenon, and he clearly believes that it is only in connection with something like the Kantian notion of a pure epistemological subject that there can can be such a theory. The second reason is that Schopenhauer must retain the notion of a pure, will-less subject of knowledge, for although that would not constitute an adequate account of what we are as subjects, it is nevertheless a state towards which he thinks we can aspire, and which holds at the same time the key to the possibility of true contentment. It is to this final aspect of the relation between self and world that we now turn.

Freedom from Will

THE will that underlies the world and, as a special instance,
ourselves, is in Schopenhauer's eyes a permanent principle of
insatiable striving with countless phenomenal manifestations.
Some of his most eloquent prose[1] presents us with an
unforgettable view of the world as a place in which beings
blindly enact brief lives of suffering and violence, or of longing
and frustration, simply because it is their nature to do so.
That Schopenhauer thereby earns his title of 'the philosopher
of pessimism' there can be little doubt.[2] However, it has been
suggested that the negative value that Schopenhauer attaches
to the world has no intrinsic connection with his metaphysics.[3]
Superficially this is true. The account of the human subject as
essentially a striving organism adapted to its environment
need not incline us to the view that it would have been better
for such a being never to have been born—as Schopenhauer
often says. Schopenhauer himself seems to have been of an
increasingly gloomy disposition, and his despairing view of
the world may be explicable to some extent as a neurotic
manifestation rooted in his relationship with his mother.[4] But
it would be short-sighted to rest with that, as there are
important philosophical reasons for Schopenhauer's negative
view of the world (and the self) as will.

First, the notion of a being as striving incorporates within
it the notion of its environment's having a value for it. Not to
attain our ends is in general a bad thing for us, in the sense
that it causes displeasure, sadness, or suffering. Of course
there are no grounds for a general pessimism yet, since beings
often do attain their ends, and this must be considered prima
facie a good for them. Here, however, Schopenhauer's notion
of the will as our *essence* comes strongly into play. Having

[1] For some examples see *W*2 ch. 46; *W*1 sects. 57–9.
[2] See esp. Frederick Copleston, *Arthur Schopenhauer: Philosopher of Pessimism.*
[3] Bryan Magee, *The Philosophy of Schopenhauer*, p. 13.   [4] Ibid.

attained an end, we do not simply rest content with it as a good, for its attainment does not cause us to cease willing as such. Eating does not make us into beings who no longer strive for food. The satisfaction of a desire or appetite, or the 'blind' fulfilment of an end in an organism, leaves the organism just as disposed as before to strive towards some end or other. Now suppose we provisionally define as an *end* that in terms of which the existence, structure, or behaviour of any life-form is teleologically explicable. Then we may posit that for things to be able to go well or badly, it is sufficient for there to exist beings that have or exhibit ends. (The converse has some plausibility: that only for such beings can things go well or badly. In a universe devoid of all organic life and of all intelligent beings, could whatever happened be either good or bad? If not, it may be that things can be bad for, and only for, beings which have or exhibit ends.) In Schopenhauer's terms, the possibility of suffering springs from willing: willing is sufficient to ensure our vulnerability to suffering. And, as we have seen, the essential fact of willing as such is unchanged by the successful attainment of ends. So the possibility of suffering is an essential feature of human life which cannot be removed whichever of our strivings is successful. The fact that things go well for us never removes our vulnerability to their going wrong. This is the first plank of Schopenhauer's philosophical pessimism.

The second is the blindness of the will within us. Our fundamental drives persist and manifest themselves without our conscious rational control. We pursue them whether or not we can give ourselves a reason for doing so, and the consequent exposure to suffering and fear is essentially unchosen, and in most cases is not comprehended. Even when we have comprehended it, this in no way alters the fact that those drives exist and govern our behaviour, because it does not change our essence. That fundamental part of us which ensures the continuing possibility of suffering is not under the control of our rational intellect. So to that extent there is nothing we can *do* to make life as such any better; it is simply a matter of what we *are*, and that, Schopenhauer believes, is unalterable.

What I am suggesting is that the basic materials for

Schopenhauer's pessimism are indeed contained in his central metaphysical doctrine. It is not within our power to change what we are—essentially striving beings—and there is always the possibility of suffering for essentially striving beings. Now suppose we also accept that necessarily, given our natures, we cannot by rational effort alter things to ensure that they never go badly for us. Still we must ask: Why are these facts intrinsically bad, let alone sufficient to motivate the thought that it would have been better not to have been born? The missing assumption seems to be that life somehow might have been lived in the guaranteed absence of suffering. I shall argue that Schopenhauer's pessimism is complete and central to his philosophy because he operated initially with a premiss such as this; he assumed the possibility of a painless 'better consciousness', against which he continued to measure the value of life as he became increasingly enmeshed in the metaphysics of the will.

As we saw in Chapter 1, the notion of a better consciousness antithetical to ordinary empirical consciousness was prominent in Schopenhauer's early thought. Ordinary empirical consciousness was of an ever-changing world of individual objects existing in space and time. But the better consciousness to which Schopenhauer believed one could aspire was not bound by the forms of space and time, and penetrated beyond phenomena to an eternal reality. Initially be equated this both with Kant's thing in itself and with Plato's Forms or Ideas.[5] The connection with the latter is signifiant, because it is with the Platonic soul that Schopenhauer's conception of the subject of the better consciousness has its greatest affinity. He thinks of this subject as a *pure subject of knowledge* which somehow exists outside of time, and contemplates a realm of true existents beyond the temporal and empirical. It is detached from particular empirical objects, and it is free of all suffering, which belongs only to the temporal world: 'On the one side, the joy of contemplation . . . consists in the fact that, freed from the misery of *willing*, we are pure subject of knowledge and so celebrate a holiday from the penal labour of willing; on the other side it stems from knowledge of the true

[5] See e.g. *HN*1 pp. 286, 342.

essence of the world, i.e. the Idea.'[6] There is a clear parallel here with Plato's view of the soul as a pure, rational intellect which exists eternally, and, in separation from the body with its desires and pleasures, calmly knows 'the things that are' as opposed to the many things perceived by the senses. Schopenhauer, in common with Plato, takes the view that it is only to the extent that we are capable of this 'higher' kind of existence as pure subject of knowledge that we can be freed from the misery that attaches to our lives as bodily, striving, appetitive beings. Having made a clear distinction between pure subject of knowledge and subject of willing, he links the latter with the temporal life of suffering, and the former with a state in which true knowledge is attained and the possibility of suffering has disappeared.

As we shall see, Schopenhauer never lost this vision of the 'better consciousness', though he ceased to use that term as such. And this is the final reason why his philosophy is more than superficially or accidentally pessimistic. For Schopenhauer both retains the Platonic conception of the pure knowing subject and its unchanging real objects, thinking of it as the ideally good state for a human being to attain, *and* develops a metaphysical system in which ultimate reality is a blind, irrational will, and the subject is primarily nothing but one of that will's manifestations. One aspect of Schopenhauer's slide away from the quasi-Platonic position is that the equation of Platonic Ideas with Kant's thing in itself comes unstuck. The latter is not the object of knowledge, as the former must be; the former are plural, and the latter, as Schopenhauer argues, cannot be. Then the whole development of the conception of will from the Kantian notion of the noumenal self sets Schopenhauer even further from Plato. The final move is the demotion of the rational intellect from its position as the essence of humanity to that of a mere outgrowth of the irrational will manifesting itself in a complex organism. Schopenhauer's philosophy is basically pessimistic because it is, in a sense, Platonism turned sour. In the end, both the subject of knowledge and the ultimate metaphysical reality which it knows are explicable in terms of blind, insatiable

[6] *HN*1 p. 129.

striving. The subject is essentially something bodily, and essentially disposed to suffer.

However, Schopenhauer does not allow his pessimism to have the last word. There is release from suffering, and it is gained by achieving the state of a pure, will-less subject similar to that which Schopenhauer conceived from the beginning. The first example of this comes in his theory of aesthetic experience, where, according to Schopenhauer, we achieve such a 'pure' state briefly and elusively. The contrast is again with our normal way of regarding things (*Betrachtungsart*) in empirical experience. Normally the subject experiences material objects in terms of their relations to one another— spatial, temporal, causal. The function of the intellect in experience is to connect representations according to the principle of sufficient reason in its various guises, and it is this connecting which constitutes the principle of individuation within the empirical realm. But equally importantly, our usual empirical *Betrachtungsart* involves a relation of the objects experienced to our purposes, uses, and values. In short, it involves a relation to our will, in Schopenhauer's terms. Just as the intellect itself was explained as secondary to the will, so the intellect's empirical knowledge in all its forms is to be seen as instrumental. Given that the forms of organization of the world as representation arise from our intellect, and the intellect's existence and mode of operation are teleologically explicable in terms of the will's 'blind purposiveness', Schopenhauer argues that all empirical consciousness is subservient to the needs of control, manipulation, and survival. We may even go so far as to say that for him 'the whole phenomenal world must, in some way, be a reflection of the organism's needs, since it is a product of the activity of these organs [the sense-organs and the brain]'.[7] Thus Schopenhauer writes:

In immediate intuition of the world and of life we as a rule regard things merely in their relations, and consequently according to their relative and not their absolute being. For example, we will view houses, ships, machines, and the like with the thought of their purpose and their suitability to it. We will view people with the

[7] Maurice Mandelbaum, *History, Man and Reason: A Study in Nineteenth-Century Thought*, p. 319.

thought of their relationship to ourselves, if they have one . . . This is to regard things according to their relations, *by means of* them even, in other words according to the principle of sufficient reason.[8]

Normal empirical consciousness is a capacity we enjoy for connecting representations in certain ways which enable us to experience particular spatio-temporal objects. It is essential to such experience that its objects are experienced as connected to one another spatially, temporally, and causally. And this whole capacity exists in us to fulfil the ends of survival within our environment. Aesthetic experience, in Schopenhauer's account of it, is the antithesis of this in every respect. One abandons normal empirical consciousness 'by . . . *losing* oneself completely in the object, i.e. forgetting precisely one's individual, one's will, and remaining only as pure subject, as clear mirror of the object; so that it is as if the object alone were there, without anybody who perceives it'.[9] What one perceives then, according to Schopenhauer, is not an object in the ordinary sense, but an Idea, an eternal form or perfect representative of one of the grades of the will's objectification. The subject is no longer an individual, but rather 'pure, will-less, painless, timeless *subject of knowledge*'. This is the truth, Schopenhauer thinks, behind Spinoza's proposition *mens aeterna est, quatenus res sub aeternitatis specie concipit*—'the mind is eternal in so far as it conceives things from the standpoint of eternity'.[10] Thus, rather than a relationship between an individual experiencing being and a particular object, we are to think of a relation between a pure subject of knowing and a Platonic, or quasi-Platonic, Idea.

Aesthetic experience, for Schopenhauer, is characterized by suspension of the laws of connection between representations. Using the very perceptual apparatus produced in us by the will, we can subvert the will by refusing temporarily to see things according to their law-like connections, as we must do in empirical consciousness if we are to manipulate things successfully to meet our ends. Taking no interest in the ends it may serve for us, we can merely perceive an object for the sake of perceiving it, and in so doing we experience the object as unhooked from its spatio-temporal and causal connections

---

[8] *W*2 p. 441 (372).   [9] *W*1 p. 232 (178).   [10] Ibid. p. 232 (179).

with the rest of the world. Contemplating, say, a horse in this way brings our mind—according to Schopenhauer—into contact not merely with a particular horse, but with the eternal Idea of the horse in general. And, as before, this state of contemplation is associated with a release from the torment of life: 'we are, for that moment, relieved of the will's vile urge, we celebrate a sabbath from the penal servitude of willing, the wheel of Ixion stands still'; 'it is as if we have entered into a different world, where everything which moves our will and shakes it so mightily is no more . . . happiness and unhappiness have disappeared'.[11]

I shall not discuss here the merits of this as a contribution to aesthetic theory. Rather, I shall make some comments on the nature of the subject and the object of this supposed state of will-less contemplation. The Ideas have an uneasy position within Schopenhauer's metaphysics. Unlike Plato's Forms they are explicitly not the objects of pure thought or reasoning, but of perceptual contemplation. Plato would have found this shocking and incomprehensible. They are not the thing in itself, but they are the 'most adequate objectification' of the thing in itself in the world of phenomena. Like concepts they are general rather than particular, but unlike concepts they are supposed to be real, existing in nature prior to perception. The thing in itself is as such strictly unknowable, but by using those senses which normally suffice only to present to us the world of spatio-temporal particulars, in the absence of the laws of connection that govern empirical knowledge, we can be acquainted with the Ideas, which are as near to the thing in itself as we can come. In Kantian terms, the Ideas are thus required to repose somewhere between appearance and thing in itself, and it is deeply uncertain whether there is any such location for them to occupy. Furthermore, Schopenhauer never really explains how, in contemplating a particular object, I become equated with a general Idea. Someone reading *The World as Will and Representation* from the beginning will come upon the Ideas in their aesthetic role in the third book, and is likely to find them tenuous and ad hoc. Considering the matter in the light of

---

[11] Ibid. pp. 253, 254 (196, 197).

Schopenhauer's earlier preoccupations, we can understand his doctrine of the Ideas as a compromise between the quasi-Platonic notion of the 'better consciousness', the Kantian epistemological framework, and the doctrines of the primacy of the will which we examined in the previous chapter. The Ideas were there from the outset, but they could only be incorporated in an unsatisfactory way once the central doctrines of will and representation had been fully worked out.

As to the notion of the pure, will-less, painless, timeless subject of knowledge, it too was central in Schopenhauer's thought, and was linked with an acquaintance with Ideas from early on.[12] The contrast here is with the individual subject of experience: 'We are no longer the individual—it is forgotten—but only the pure subject of knowledge: we are now only there as the one world-eye, which looks out from all knowing beings'.[13] This 'world-eye', Schopenhauer says, is eternal, unconcerned by the coming and going of particular life-forms.

The division emphasized here is between the pure subject of knowing and the individual experiencing being. But, as we learned earlier, Schopenhauer's account of ordinary empirical consciousness involves the presentation of objects before a knowing subject that is not itself an object in the world of phenomena. How does the subject of this account relate to the subject of aesthetic experience? It is clear that initially Schopenhauer wanted the pure subject of the 'better consciousness' to experience purely *objectively*.[14] It would be able to cast off the distortions that attached to the perspective of an individual subject, and come to know things in themselves beyond their mere empirical presentation. In the second edition of his main work this aspect of his position is still essentially unchanged. The knowing subject becomes 'the pure mirror of the objective being [*Wesen*] of things', and 'one apprehends the world purely objectively only when one no longer knows that one belongs to it'[15]—all of which occurs in the state of will-less aesthetic experience. The trouble is that

[12] See *HN*ı pp. 47, 76, 136, passages written in 1813 and 1814.
[13] *W*ı p. 254 (198).
[14] Cf. *HN*ı p. 47.   [15] *W*2 pp. 435, 436 (367, 368).

none of this differentiates sufficiently the subject of aesthetic experience from the subject of ordinary empirical consciousness. While he was developing his distinction between the empirical and the better consciousness, Schopenhauer wrote *On the Fourfold Root*, in which the subject of all representations, and *a fortiori* the subject of *of empirical consciousness*, appears as that which knows objects but is never object itself, that which sees all but is not seen, and so on. So Schopenhauer has in simultaneous play both the Platonic conception of the pure knower which apprehends the essence of things in themselves, and the Kantian 'I' that is correlated with all phenomena. The latter is associated with ordinary empirical consciousness; the former with the diametrically opposed timeless and painless consciousness. But there is no room here for the contrast between the subject as 'world-eye' and the subject as mere *empirical individual*. According to both the Kantian and the Platonic conceptions of the subject, it is a non-worldly mirror, or all-seeing eye, correlated with the world of objects; according to neither is it an individual belonging to the empirical world. The only difference between empirical consciousness and that of aesthetic experience is that in the latter the subject has supposedly cast off those forms of connection among representation which in the former are constitutive of experience of objects at all. But we should be deeply uneasy about whether this is conceivable; just as we were uneasy earlier about there being a kind of experience of particular objects which was at the same time an apprehension of eternal Ideas. The two are aspects of the same problem, which presents grave difficulties for Schopenhauer's theory of aesthetic experience.

The final major part of Schopenhauer's philosophy is his ethical theory. Here the notions of suspension of the will and of the overcoming of the individual emerge once again. Goodness is to be attained by casting off a fundamental egoism, which Schopenhauer believes to be both inevitable and ultimately mistaken. There are apparently two reasons for the inevitability of egoism. First, we are manifestations of the will, and as such naturally strive to possess, to dominate, and to destroy whatever stands in our way. Secondly, each individual is the bearer of the knowing subject, which in turn is the bearer of the world—the world is my world. I find myself, says Schopenhauer, 'as a microcosm, which is to be estimated equally with the macrocosm'. Accordingly,

> every individual, who merges totally with the limitless world and is diminished to nothing, nevertheless makes himself the centre-point of the world, attends to his own existence and well-being before all else, and indeed, from the natural standpoint, is prepared to sacrifice everything else for this, is prepared to destroy the world merely in order to preserve for a little longer this drop in the ocean, his own self.[16]

Egoism is, according to Schopenhauer, 'essential to every thing in nature'. In the human world he finds evidence throughout history, with its catalogue of power-struggles, wars, despotism, and deliberately inflicted suffering, and at the other end of the scale, in the petty vanities and self-seeking actions of everyday life. It must be said that all this is merely evidence that people behave egoistically on large and small scales at many particular times and places. That egoism is 'natural', or 'essential' to us *qua* beings in nature, is a further, unsupported step beyond the evidence. Schopenhauer is clearly perturbed by social injustices:

> How humans treat each other is shown, e.g. by negro slavery, whose final aim is sugar and coffee. But one does not need to go so far: to enter the spinning-mill, or other factory, at the age of five, and from then on to sit there first 10, then 12, and finally 14 hours a day, doing the same mechanical work, is to pay dearly for the pleasure of drawing breath. But this is the fate of millions, and many millions have an analogous one.[17]

One might think that Marx would have been proud to write such passages as this, but it would be dangerous to ignore the way in which Schopenhauer treats historical circumstances as proceeding merely from our 'nature' as human beings. While Max Horkheimer may have found that twentieth-century history has made Schopenhauer's global pessimism about human nature more relevant,[18] Lukács seems nearer the mark

---

[16] *W*1 p. 415 (332).   [17] *W*2 pp. 676–7 (578).

[18] Cf. Max Horkheimer, 'Die Aktualität Schopenhauers', in Max Horkheimer and Theodor W. Adorno, *Sociologica II*, pp. 124–41, translated as 'Schopenhauer Today' in Michael Fox (ed.), *Schopenhauer: His Philosophical Achievement*, pp. 20–33; see also Max Horkheimer, *Sozialphilosophische Studien*, pp. 68–77, 135–44, 145–55.

in regarding such laments as 'indirect apologetics' for the political and economic status quo of the time (which of course Schopenhauer had no desire to change).[19] I do not suggest that this was a matter of calculation by Schopenhauer—merely that accepting the unargued assumption that such ill-treatment of human beings is explained by the human 'essence' is obviously likely to obscure the historical truth (whatever it is) about how and why such things happened.

So much for Schopenhauer's view that egoism is inevitable. Of greater importance, however, are his views that egoism can be overcome, and that it can be overcome because it rests on what, metaphysically speaking, is a fundamental mistake. From a more profound point of view it is an error to make oneself the centre-point of the world. Egoism of course depends on the possibility of being able to distinguish *myself* from others, the 'I' from the 'not-I'. But I can only be seen as thus individuated from one point of view, Schopenhauer argues. And that point of view can be progressively abandoned. It is characteristic of the non-egoistic view of life, on which Schopenhauer founds his notion of the ethically good character, that it makes less of a distinction, and ultimately none at all, between 'I' and 'not-I'. The bad character 'feels everywhere a firm barrier between itself and everything outside it. The world is for it an *absolute not-I* and its relationship to it is a fundamentally hostile one;' the good character on the other hand 'lives in an outside world homogeneous with its essence: the others are for it not "not-I", but "I once more" '.[20] The recognition of 'I' in the *other* expresses itself in sympathy (*Mitleid*), which constitutes the basis of all morality for Schopenhauer. He consistently holds to his claim that 'the concept is unfruitful for the real inner nature of virtue, just as it is in art'.[21] In the essay *On the Basis of Morality* he provides an extensive criticism of Kantian ethics, which I shall not discuss here.[22] His most obviously startling divergence from Kant, however, is his claim that being good has no essential connection with conceptual understanding or with the grasp of precepts and maxims, and that it is simply a matter of

---

[19] *The Destruction of Reason*, pp. 202–3.
[20] *GM* p. 312 (211).   [21] *W*1 pp. 456–7 (367–8).
[22] See *GM* ch. 2 for the criticisms of Kant.

attaining a certain vision of the relation between oneself and the rest of the world.

While the metaphysical foundation of the egoistic character is the view that individuation is real, that I am fundamentally distinct from others, and that I am the only genuine 'I' among the objects of my experience, that of the non-egoistic character is the supposedly higher view according to which individuation is unreal: 'Individuation is mere appearance, arising through space and time . . . Thus the plurality and differentiation of individuals is also mere appearance, i.e. present only in my *representation*. My true inner being exists in every living thing as immediately as in my self-consciousness it manifests itself to me alone.'[23] Individuation is empirically undeniable, but pertains only to appearance; what I and others are an appearance *of* is one will common to the world. Schopenhauer seems to be suggesting that it is in penetrating beyond the mere world of appearance that I am able to recognize others as 'I'. But this suggestion is both obscure and difficult.

What does Schopenhauer mean when he says that 'others are I once more'? On the one hand he is suggesting that others 'say "I" to themselves' in exactly the same way as I do.[24] To recognize another as being as 'I'-sayer like myself is presumably to recognize that other as a centre of consciousness and will, and perhaps as someone from whose 'inner' life as a self-conscious being I am not wholly excluded, someone whose interests can truly also be my own. The point will then be that a recognition of genuine *intersubjectivity* underlies the morally good, non-egoistic view of life. From the subjective point of view others may be objects for the single 'I' that I am conscious of myself as being, but from a wider viewpoint others are 'I' as well, not merely objects for this 'I'.

On the other hand, however, Schopenhauer clearly uses the expression 'others are "I" once more' to indicate a recognition of the metaphysical truth as he sees it—that in terms of our underlying essence, I and others are literally identical. The metaphysical foundation of sympathy and of morality is that we are all manifestations of the will in itself, and thus we are all, when considered in abstraction from our individuated

---

[23] *GM* p. 311 (210).   [24] Cf. *W*2 p. 547 (467).

appearance, one and the same. From the higher viewpoint, the claim 'I am the centre of all things' could survive only in the form of a claim by the will to be distinct from itself—which is plainly absurd. Thus, while in practical terms egoism can be overcome by seeing others as distinct from oneself but as equal centres of consciousness, the dominant metaphysical reading of 'others are I once more' precludes that possibility entirely. Schopenhauer cannot make morality depend on the recognition of intersubjectivity, and at the same time explain its possibility in terms of the absorption of all individuals into a single will.

Schopenhauer's aesthetic and ethical doctrines have a distinctly mystical ring to them. It is perhaps not entirely surprising that he ends with an explicit evocation of mysticism. 'My teaching,' he says, 'on reaching its summit, takes on a *negative* character, and so ends with a negation. For here it can only speak of that which is denied, given up . . . Now it is precisely here that the mystic proceeds positively, and so from here on nothing remains but mysticism.'[25] The culmination of Schopenhauer's philosophy is the absolute denial of the will, the cessation of all desire, interest, positive or negative evaluation, and of any attempt to bend what occurs towards ends of one's own. This extreme quietism, combined with rigorous asceticism (of a kind which commentators have not been slow to find lacking in Schopenhauer's own life), can lead, he maintains, to mystical experience, 'i.e. consciousness of the identity of one's own essence with that of all things, or the core of the world'.[26] This experience is incommunicable and one must live through it oneself; it is not a part of the philosophy that precedes it, but the latter can be regarded as a preparation for it. If we understand the 'loss of individuality' that occurs in aesthetic experience, we may infer from this

how blessed must be the life of a man whose will is calmed, not for moments, as in enjoyment of the beautiful, but for ever, and even totally extinguished, down to the last glowing flicker which maintains the body, and is extinguished with it. Such a man, who after many bitter struggles with his own nature has finally been completely victorious, is left only as an undimmed mirror of the world. Nothing more can worry him, nothing can move him: for all the thousand strands of willing which hold us bound to the world,

25 Ibid. p. 716 (612).   26 Ibid. p. 717 (613).

and, as desire, fear, envy, and anger tear us this way and that in continual pain—he has severed.[27]

The message is forbiddingly austere. Even death is not to be feared: the individual perishes as such, but lives on in essence—and unconsciously—as the undivided and timeless will.[28] Yet the brilliance and power of Schopenhauer's writing here testifies to the importance which he attaches to this, the attainment, as he sees it, of what he had first sought under the name of the 'better consciousness'.

It is hard to know what to say from a philosophical point of view about this final part of Schopenhauer's work. One problem that writers have remarked upon concerns the opposition between affirmation and denial of the will.[29] Schopenhauer sees the former as the source of human suffering, and the latter, the will's 'turning against itself', as the source of salvation. But since denial is an act, and in this case, it would seem, an act directed towards a certain end, it is surely as much an exercise of the individual will as anything else is. What Schopenhauer means by the will 'turning against itself'[30] is that the world-will, of which I cannot, while I exist, cease to be a manifestation, gives up those expressions of itself which pertain to the conscious ends and interests of this one individual. It is slightly paradoxical that in freeing myself from my will, I should come to find myself identical with the will in itself—that we should come to 'see the world aright' by eliminating the expression in ourselves of that which provides our point of continuity with the rest of nature. Yet again there is some lack of harmony here between the notion of self and world as will, and the 'blessed' state of a pure, passive mirroring of the objective world. But the greatest difficulty is still that unless the inception and continuance of this totally passive state were itself something that merely happened to me, as opposed to something I tried to bring about, there could be no sense in which I had escaped from my individual will at all. Instead of denying the will, I should simply witness its withering away without attaching any value to that process. But Schopenhauer does not seem to have this in

---

[27] *W*1 p. 483 (390).
[28] See esp. *W*2 ch. 41.
[29] e.g. Magee, *Schopenhauer*, p. 242.   [30] e.g. at *W*1 p. 508 (412).

mind, speaking instead of 'severing' the bonds of willing that tie us to the world, and of *voluntary* renunciation.[31]

This chapter brings to a close our discussion of the relationships between self and world in Schopenhauer's philosophy. Already intricate and problematic, these relationships are further complicated by the doctrines of the pure, will-less subject of aesthetic experience, and of the reabsorption of the individual into the world-whole. Those who expect a unified, static account (that is, to some extent all of us who are used to reading philosophy) may be disappointed not to come away with any clear answer to the questions: What is the self? and: How does it relate to the world of objects or things? What Schopenhauer gives us is no single coherent position, it will be said, but a collection of conflicting views. My presentation has borne this out to some degree, but I think it would be a mistake to write off Schopenhauer's philosophy on these grounds.

First, Schopenhauer's is a dynamic, even a dramatic, answer to those questions, and must be read as such. Earlier, seemingly secure positions are to be treated as deliberately incomplete, counterbalanced and often undermined by later ones. Secondly, the greatest inconsistencies arise not as a result of mere incompetence on Schopenhauer's part, but from tensions between large-scale intellectual aspirations which were not of his making but which were all positively alive in the intellectual climate surrounding him. Thus he took on the structure of Kant's powerful epistemology, with its distinction between appearance and thing in itself, its limitation of knowledge to what fell within the a priori conditions of appearance, and its 'empty' conception of the subject as the mere transcendental principle that unifies representations. He employed this structure to set up stage 1 of his drama: subject and object as necessary correlates; the modes of organization of objects stemming from the subject rather than existing in themselves; the subject not a part of the world of objects.

In addition he took on contemporary aspirations—which had been alien to Kant—to provide a physiological account of the workings of the mind, and to account for its existence and

---

[31] See the descriptions of asceticism in *W*1 sect. 68.

workings in a teleological way that would put it on a par with other life-forms. Out of this grew the conception of body and brain as manifestation of blind purposiveness, which I argued to be the most important aspect of his doctrine of the primacy of the will. Perhaps his greatest original thought was that which he called the 'key' to the metaphysics of the will: that as subjects of action we are predominantly aware of ourselves neither as the pure 'I' of the 'I think', nor as mere spatio-temporal objects that interact causally with others. In stage 2, then, the position of stage 1 is called into question. Kant's epistemological subject is capable of physiological/teleological explanation, and the associated split between pure subject and mere object is inadequate to explain our self-conscious awareness of bodily striving. Yet stage 2 itself relies crucially on the idealist doctrines developed in stage 1. The undermining and, as I argue, the strongly progressive insights about our nature as willing subjects coalesce around the doctrine of the will as thing in itself, which only makes sense for as long as most of the structure of stage 1 remains in place.

Stage 3 of Schopenhauer's dynamic presentation capitalizes on the limitation of the Kantian epistemological subject to knowledge of appearances, and taps into the pre-Kantian—indeed ancient—philosophical aspiration towards an un-conditioned state of knowledge whose object is an eternal and non-subject-dependent reality. But stage 3 also leans on the distinctive doctrines of the will. Because the Kantian epistemological subject has been explained as a mere outgrowth of will, its limitations are to be transcended by suspension of the will. While it functions as the instrument of the will it has been revealed by Schopenhauer to be, the Kantian subject can have no knowledge of ultimate reality, only of empirical objects which are in some way subject-dependent. Among his contemporaries, Schopenhauer's conviction of the possibility of a higher consciousness which sheds these subject-dependent forms was in general terms shared by Schelling, for whom the aesthetic also assumed a central role. For Schopenhauer, as we saw earlier, the main problem is that the thing in itself, which we have learned to be the will, has by stage 3 been rendered unsuitable as the object of pure, painless, aesthetic contemplation. Hence the compromise of the Ideas.

In stage 4 we reach a standpoint from which the very notion of distinct individuals within the world is called into question. The subject that regards itself either as a unique centre of conscious experience, or as an empirical individual, or as a distinct being whose conscious will can be imposed on the world around it is finally explained as illusory. Paradoxically, the individual subject of representation and will is capable of adopting a higher viewpoint from which it itself is absent as a distinct constituent of reality. By ceasing to strive for itself, to impose itself upon reality external to it, it loses the barriers which define it as a separate being at all; it is apprised first of goodness and then of that mystical state of nothingness, beyond happiness and unhappiness, with which Schopenhauer ends.

The four stages I have presented here correspond to the four books of Schopenhauer's main work. Some have found this work original and penetrating, but lacking a rigorous, well-integrated structure.[32] Some have come nearer to taking Schopenhauer at his word when he says that it offers the complex unfolding of a single thought.[33] Others have openly despaired of the system's inconsistencies, finding it from a purely philosophical point of view 'bizarre and fantastic in the extreme'.[34] My reading endorses something of each of these reactions. There is a clear single structure, but it unfolds dramatically as much as it does argumentatively. In the process, there are philosophical insights and innovations, but there are plenty of bizarre inconsistencies too. When an earlier position has been challenged or modified, Schopenhauer continues to apply its basic concepts unchanged. He uses terms such as 'subject' and 'object', 'appearance' and 'thing in itself', 'representation' and 'will' as if they all belonged to a single, coherent theory of the world, though this is hardly what he can claim to have provided. Schopenhauer confronts us with dynamic thought presented in a static vocabulary. He is at his most interesting when he is setting up distinct conceptions of self and world that challenge and conflict with one another. He loses most in stature as a philosopher when

---

[32] Cf. Patrick Gardiner, *Schopenhauer*, p. 301.
[33] Cf. D. W. Hamlyn, *Schopenhauer*, pp. 1–2.
[34] Copleston, *Arthur Schopenhauer*, p. 190.

he contrives to explain the conflicts away, or merely to pass over them in silence.

In Part Three I shall ask which of Schopenhauer's conceptions of the self have had, and which should continue to have, any sort of life outside the immediate presuppostions of his own system. I shall also try to examine further to what extent the conflicts we have witnessed—between 'subjective' and 'objective' viewpoints, between the self as knowing and the self as willing—exemplify important philosophical problems. For what this study has perhaps shown above all is that we cannot presuppose that there is a single problem about the nature of the self, or a single kind of relation that pertains between self and world. There are different and often conflicting philosophical motivations within which solutions to these problems have been suggested. In attempting to fulfil such disparate aspirations—epistemological, metaphysical, naturalistic, mystical, aesthetic . . . —in one single sweep, Schopenhauer was in all likelihood attempting the impossible. But in so doing he reveals in an unparalleled way just how delicately balanced and how multifarious the problems we have to face are.

PART THREE

12

Self and World

IN Parts One and Two of this book I have endeavoured to construct an account of the central strands of Schopenhauer's thought which does justice to his own aims and presuppositions, using the evidence of his philosophical writings and considering elements of his wider intellectual situation. I have not avoided criticizing Schopenhauer when he has handled his task less well than he might have done, and I have repeatedly drawn out consequences of which he was probably not aware. I have tried, however, neither to impose on him a framework of aims and presuppositions wholly alien to him, nor to judge him against a supposedly ahistorical background. Such an imposition would have been too stifling, given the task of seeking a full and accurate understanding of his philosophy. There are contradictions and tensions within his work, but some, I have suggested, could hardly have been avoided given what he set out to do; and what he set out to do is clearly intelligible against the background of early nineteenth-century thought.

It must be said, on the other hand, that I myself have aims and presuppositions. My selection of aspects for consideration, and my highlighting of particular problems, has been governed partly by a desire to make Schopenhauer accessible to a twentieth-century English-speaking audience. To the question: What in all this is relevant to us? (which some readers may be impatient to pose), this final part is designed to give a kind of answer. But I must preface that answer by saying that I am reluctant to place any very straightforward construal on the question. The 'relevance' of a historical philosopher to present-day philosophy is usually many-layered. There is room to ask whether anything Schopenhauer says is true; but to do so bluntly, as if it were the only question, without regard for the nature of Schopenhauer's very different assumptions about what philosophy was called upon to deal with and how it should proceed, is liable to be unproductive. And there are other questions to be asked. Are important problems raised and newly articulated by reading Schopenhauer? To this I shall answer that they are indeed. What influence has Schopenhauer exerted on subsequent thinkers, and through them on the shape of philosophy today? Here I shall examine the reception of some of his thought by Nietzsche and Wittgenstein. The extent to which either of these thinkers is currently an important voice, someone with whom philosophy still has to do business, are questions I do not propose to settle. Schopenhauer himself does not have such a status at present, which makes it difficult initially to know what to do with his philosophy now that we have—to the extent that we have—understood it. Showing how his thought was taken up by Nietzsche and Wittgenstein, both of whom have been highly influential in their different ways, will be part of my attempt to answer the question of Schopenhauer's continuing importance. Another aspect of my discussion will emphasize his role as critic of Kantianism. Here I shall single out his challenge to the Kantian notion of the subject of experience, a challenge that deserves as much current interest as the notion itself enjoys.

Thus in part I shall seek 'relevance' in Schopenhauer by underscoring the relations between his thought and that of other historical figures whose problems are still alive for contemporary philosophy. This, I believe, is to relate him to contemporary philosophy. I shall also indicate ways in which his articulation of problems concerning the self can still engage with present-day thought, and where I sometimes find him to be saying something that is arguably true. But to conceive the task here (or in the book as a whole) as either 'purely philosophical' or 'purely historical' would be an over-simplification.

A recognizable set of problems which is prominent in Schopenhauer's philosophy is that to which we can give the general label of 'the subjective and the objective'. Though Schopenhauer often seems naïve in his expectation that the deliverances of his subjective and objective viewpoints will sit happily alongside one another, he does show an uncommon sensitivity to this kind of problem. In the case of the subject of experience, he suggests that it is one-sided to rest with a materialist account of the workings of the brain, true though he thinks it is that these are to be identified with the workings of the intellect. The objective materialist account is deficient because it excludes the notion of a self-conscious, unified centre of experience which is crucial from a subjective standpoint—and indeed *is* in large measure what we conceive ourselves, as *subjects*, to be. We find no such entity in the world of objects. The conception of the unified centre of experience is thus both a necessary part of our self-conception as beings capable of knowledge of the world, and highly problematic, since none of our empirical knowledge of the world reveals to us anything that satisfies the description. Kant's epistemological standpoint and that of physiology are both legitimate, but one-sided. Nor can we simply tack together the two pictures they yield as two halves of one account of the subject. Some 'higher' viewpoint, as Schopenhauer puts it, would be needed for the two ever to be properly reconciled.

This paraphrase of Schopenhauer enables us to see his position as broadly similar to that taken by some contemporary philosophers.[1] It is a genuine case in which we can share an understanding of the issues with Schopenhauer. The same is true of his treatment of free will, where he argues that determinism is inescapable from the objective point of view, but does not remove our subjective sense of agency or responsibility. The problem is to know how to encompass in one coherent account what we believe to be universally true of the world of objects, and what seems to be a presupposition of our own self-conception.

Again, if we turn to Schopenhauer's centrally important views about action itself we find a similar pattern. On the one hand our actions are events that occur in space and time, and can be experienced and described objectively. But on the other hand we experience them in some sense 'from within', in that they are irreducibly what we as self-conscious subjects *do*. Some kind of 'dual-aspect' theory seems to be required if we

[1] See e.g. Colin McGinn, *The Character of Mind*, pp. 121–2; Thomas Nagel, 'Subjective and Objective', in *Mortal Questions*, pp. 201–2.

are to do justice to the equally powerful demands that action be incorporated in any objective account of the world, and that we respect the understanding of it which being agents seems to give us.

Though they require some supplementation and more detailed argument, Schopenhauer's central views about action are, I would argue, substantially right. In particular, his claim that the willing that occurs in the case of a successful action *is* the action itself has great advantages over the volitionalist account. Though mental, willing also becomes a phenomenon in the objective realm; and the relation in which we stand to the movements we make with our bodies is no longer implausibly passive. Whatever *doing* is precisely, it is essentially something of which the doer is not passively aware, something known to the doer without the mediation of inference or observation; but it is also something that is observable. The actions of which I have that elusive 'inner' awareness are events apprehended by others as occurring at some place and time, and indeed by myself as including my body's moving. There is no room for wholly dualist thinking about self and world once this is accepted, and it is to Schopenhauer's credit that he shows us this.

Schopenhauer realized too that for there to be an act of will, certain characteristic causal antecedents—what he called motives—had to be present in the mind. It is only when the causal chain 'passes through the intellect', when the subject has some objective cognition and entertains some desire with respect to the world, that an act of will can occur. My act of will could have no content if it were not caused by motives, and without content it could not even be an act of will at all. So both an 'inner' access to the body's movements and an appropriate causal history are necessary to account for acts of will—but it is a mistake to look for a distinct mental event called an 'act of will' among the causal antecedents of bodily action.

This original account of Schopenhauer's is subtle and revolutionary, and provides much fertile ground for today's theorizing about action, as we have seen in earlier chapters. Moreover, as I shall show later, it provided Wittgenstein with a stimulus for his highly influential thinking on action, and it is in that sense an important, if distant, historical origin of much recent work in the field.

In the case of free will, Schopenhauer of course leans heavily on Kant. But he demonstrates a more clear-cut awareness than Kant that the deepest problem is not one of uncaused causes, or really much to do with causality at all, but an instance of the same powerful conflict between our aspirations to objectivity and the constraints that being subjects of understanding and will places on how we can regard ourselves. In the case of the pure subject of experience, Schopenhauer works out a much starker form of a conflict that lurks within Kantianism but which Kant did little to address. Though there is a certain crudity in Schopenhauer's handling of this most delicate of Kantian issues, his very recognition of the larger-scale difficulty is an advance beyond the position that Kant reached. At least in this case and in that of free will, Schopenhauer's ability was not so much to articulate any very sophisticated response to the issue, as to state it clearly. It is not fanciful to suggest that those interested in problems of 'the subjective and the objective', or any of the issues that I have mentioned here, might derive benefit from reading Schopenhauer's statements of where the problems lie.

The peculiarly Schopenhauerian question that I wish to raise now, however, is that of the relation between his two central conceptions of the subject. We have seen how Schopenhauer argues that we must conceive ourselves both as pure subject of knowledge and as subject of will. We have seen that each of these conceptions has a number of complexities attached to it. And finally we have seen how the somewhat fraught relationships between the two conceptions provide the mainspring of his thought. If—as I shall argue— this whole problematic is one which still has a call on our attention, then we will have found a true and profound point of contact between contemporary philosophical concerns and Schopenhauer's philosophy at its most distinctive.

First let me summarize the two conceptions of the subject that are at issue. One is that of the knowing subject. Schopenhauer argues that all conscious experience must have a subject, but that this subject must always be conceived as that which knows the world of objects, and never as an item in the world that is known. The subject, then, is not be thought of as a spatio-temporal individual, nor as a special, non-material constituent of the universe, or immaterial substance. Rather, it is analogous to an 'extensionless point'—the expression of that viewpoint in general from which whatever is known objectively is known. The viewpoint itself cannot be part of the content of what is known from it. Any number of empirical individuals may exemplify this pure subject, though admittedly how they do so is difficult to explain, since individuals are identified spatio-temporally via their bodies, and all bodies that could serve in this capacity are not the subject but merely objects for the subject. The subject, according to this view of it, must be conceived as detached from everything that occurs within the world of objects it experiences.

In ordinary experience the knowing subject has access to the world of empirical objects, but these are only phenomena, not things in themselves. The experience of the subject reaches only as far as that which can be comprehended within the forms of organization that have their origin in the subject itself. However, Schopenhauer, unlike Kant, thinks that the same subject is capable of casting off this limitation, and becoming a pure, passive mirror of the way the world is beyond the merely subject-dependent forms of organization, or, as he puts it, of becoming a pure subject of knowing (*Erkennen*). In this second role the subject again cannot be identified with any empirical being. It is still a kind of principle which each of us singly can exemplify, although in so doing we now explicitly lose our sense of being an individual within the world that we mirror. The knowing subject plays its first role for Schopenhauer in his modified Kantian epistemology, and the second in his aesthetic, ethical, and mystical doctrines. The difference between the two roles can be fully stated only in terms of their relation to his conception of the subject of will, to which I shall now turn.

Despite the multifarious nature of the insights that cluster around Schopenhauer's metaphysical doctrine of the will, I shall speak in terms of a single, inclusive conception of the subject of will, which I believe I am correct in attributing to him. According to this conception the subject is self-conscious, but its primary awareness is of itself as a striving being. This covers a continuum from actions with conscious rational motives, through to instinctive acts born out of pre-rational drives. Actions, at the top of the scale, presuppose the capacity for objective knowledge, but just as importantly they are bodily occurrences, the movements of an organism, of which the subject is aware as such. Actions are on a continuum with instinctive movements for two reasons: (*a*) because the occurrence of both is explicable in terms of an end for the sake of which they occur; and (*b*) because the capacity for objective knowledge which essentially informs action is itself explained both in terms of the organism's physiology, and teleologically in terms of the ends that it satisfies for the organism within its material environment. Everything on this continuum is called 'will' in Schopenhauer's widened sense of the term. And will in all its forms has an intimate connection with embodiment. An organism's most fundamental and characteristic ends are the prolongation and propagation of life. Its existence as a self-conscious subject is fundamentally affected by its manifesting these ends. In particular it is a sexual being in whom a drive to reproduce exists regardless of whether or not it is consciously motivated towards reproduction 'or sexual intercourse. Willing, in its many forms, permeates and essentially helps to structure the subject's perception and knowledge of the world.

This conception of the subject poses a challenge to that of the epistemological subject of knowing. For one thing, it simply conflicts with it: it has the subject to be essentially embodied and essentially characterized by striving, where the epistemological conception is of a non-empirical subject concerned with pure objective knowing. But secondly, and more importantly, it is a challenge to the epistemological conception because of a built-in superiority: it offers a straightforward explanation of the presence of the very capacity for objective knowledge of the world which exhausts the former conception of what the subject is. The epistemological theory is conversely weaker in that it offers no explanation at all of the phenomena that are captured by the notion of the self as willing. According to the 'will'-theory of the self, we are knowers of an objective world because of the physiological structure and functioning of our bodies, and we have that structure and functioning for no other reason than other organisms do theirs: for the sake—though, let me emphasize again, not for the conscious purpose—of our better manipulating and surviving in our environment. Schopenhauer speaks of the primacy of the will. In part this consists in the claim that the will-theory of the self has explanatory primacy over the epistemological theory.

Schopenhauer believes that ordinary empirical knowledge is limited by the categories of the knowing subject, and that the knowing subject is explicable as an outgrowth of a particular species of organism in response to its needs within an environment. In effect he argues from this that empirical knowledge itself must therefore be bounded by the needs of that species in that environment. There is a close link for him between the knower's inability to penetrate beyond the mind-dependent forms of representation, and the knower's rootedness in a striving organism. This is the source of the contrast that he makes between the subject of ordinary empirical knowledge and the 'pure, will-less, painless, timeless subject of knowledge' which exists only as a 'mirror' of the essence of the world—or at any rate of the Ideas, a kind of mind-independent reality which is nevertheless accessible to the mind. The contrast depends on the thought that our organically produced mechanisms for apprehending objects can transcend the categories of their survival-determined operation. We can gain an eternal, absolute view of the world as a whole, as it were on the back of what is originally our merely instrumental, cognitive make-up.

One thing we should question here is the notion that empirical knowledge must be so closely circumscribed by the needs of environmental adaptation of the knower's species that it is incapable of true objectivity. What Schopenhauer says about the physiological/teleological explicability of the capacity for knowledge of objects is compatible with the Kantian position that the subject's experiencing according to the categories *constitutes the subject's experiencing objectively*. It would require some powerful argument before we could be convinced that it is possible to experience without those categories. Furthermore, to accept that this, and this alone, would enable us to slough off the limitations of our species and to 'mirror the world' in the absolute way that Schopenhauer desires, is highly questionable.

This brief résumé has already raised many difficult issues. What I shall principally be concerned to ask is: How must we conceive ourselves as subjects? Can we confidently accept or reject either the conception of the embodied subject of will or that of the pure subject of knowledge? And how does our acceptance or rejection of either conception affect what we say about the other?

It is hard, I think, to envisage rejecting the conception of the subject as will that I have outlined here, or something similar to it. It is an outline and leaves much unsettled; but it is an outline that has much to recommend it. Considering first our consciousness of ourselves as subjects, we are aware of being the subjects of striving or trying, which is arguably inseparable from an awareness of the manifestation of our strivings in the body itself. Action provides a bridge between the truly mental (a self-conscious act of striving) and the physical (the movement of the body). The link consists in the fact that the movement of the body is a non-detachable part of the action which the striving becomes and is essentially directed towards becoming.

We might pause to ask whether it would be possible for a permanently paralysed person, who had never in her life had any use of her body, to try to lift her arm, to make a cup of tea, and so on. For someone who is now the victim of total paralysis, but who at some time was not and has some kind of recall of that time, the case is different. It is possible for this person to try to move her arm, because it is possible for her to initiate that process which, if completed, would naturally be her raising her arm. The process is truncated, so she does not raise her arm, and only tries to. But the art of initiating the correct process within oneself which naturally (without physiological impediment) becomes an action is learned only in acting. Few if any of us know what the process is, other than that it is the one we set in train when we try to raise our arms. Even those who do have some extremely complex physiological description of the process can only have learned to bring it about in themselves in acting, or successfully trying to raise their arms. If in them that process had always failed to reach its completion in overt action, they might conceivably have learned by sophisticated observation that it was that process which consisted in trying to raise one's arm; but they could not have learned this in a way which would have enabled them to try to raise their own arms. This suggests that one cannot *will* without at some time having had a more or less normally functioning body.

What would strengthen the case for the primacy of the will would be a good argument for supposing that any subject must be a willing subject; more specifically, that any being in cognitive contact with the world must be equipped to strive to alter it as well. It might be suggested that if, in principle, computers can think and perceive the objective world, then it must be possible for them to do so without having anything analogous to a will at all. But the first premiss ('if computers can think') is too contentious to help us decide the issue at stake; and besides, their lacking a will might conceivably be the basis for an argument against the possibility of computers thinking and perceiving. To answer the question conclusively we must demonstrate the possibility, or impossibility, of a being which unequivocally perceives elements of its environment, but which in principle lacks any ability or disposition to *act*. I do not propose to discuss here whether there is an argument which will answer this question decisively.[2] It has sometimes been suggested that our awareness of causality stems in the first instance from our ability to bring about changes by acting upon the world. Furthermore, there seems to be a close link—which may be conceptual—between perceiving spatially and having the potential for active movement of the whole or part of the body through space. But, whether or not it is conceptually possible for there to be a wholly non-willing subject, one thing is clear, and that is that will and cognition, if both are present, must be fully integrated within a single self-consciousness. Unless the 'I's in 'I will' and 'I perceive' are co-referential, and are conceived to be so

---

[2] Brian O'Shaughnessy offers some persuasive thoughts on this (*The Will*, vol. 2, pp. 4–15); for other treatments see D. W. Hamlyn, 'Perception and Agency', in *Perception, Learning and the Self*, pp. 43–56; and McGinn, *The Character of Mind*, pp. 81–4.

by the subject that applies them, the possibility of both knowledge and action is called into question. That which strives to alter the world must be conscious of itself as being that which, perceptually or otherwise, has knowledge of it. This is because the point of acting is to change something about the world that *I* perceive, or about *my* relationship to it, while the capacity to perceive essentially informs, through beliefs and desires, the way I actively modify myself in response to what is perceived.[3]

A self that both wills and apprehends the world cannot be, in its own conception of itself, something composite. The unity of apperception extends out, if you like, to include the subject's bodily strivings. Schopenhauer is fond of saying that willing subject and knowing subject 'flow together into the consciousness of one I', and earlier I criticized him for saying of this that it constitutes 'the miracle *par excellence*'. My complaint (apart from being that Schopenhauer was very lax in accepting such a miracle) was largely that he had no right to assert the identity of willing subject and knowing subject in view of his attempts to convince us of the utter distinctness of the two subjects in question. Nevertheless, *what* he describes here as a miracle is undoubtedly a truth.

So the first points to make are: that any realistic conception of the subject must take into account the central, and perhaps necessary, presence of will in self-consciousness, and that arguably willing is inconceivable without the embodiment of the subject that wills.

But Schopenhauer's wider conception of will raises other issues. What consideration should we give in our account of the subject to the fact that we are organisms, and that much of the behaviour and structure of organisms is teleologically explicable? What difference should it make, further, that our conscious lives are permeated with the effects of unconscious urges, not least those of sexuality, whose organs are the 'focus of the will' for Schopenhauer? We may doubt whether the capacity for objective cognition, and together with it the capacity for rational action, can simply be explained in the

---

[3] Cf. O'Shaughnessy's conclusion: '[a]ll seeing is necessarily given as of "what I might in principle act upon", and all intentional physical acting upon as upon "what I might in principle perceive" '. (*The Will*, vol. 2, p. 15.)

same way as all the rest of the organism's capacities.[4] We may also doubt Schopenhauer's apparently simple reduction of sexuality to a blind urge to reproduce the species. But we cannot deny that we are organisms, much of whose behaviour is conditional on our physiology, much of whose structure and functioning is explicable teleologically as subserving the end of life itself, and who have strong pre-rational drives to survival and reproduction. Such drives persist alongside our rational behaviour, in varying degrees of integration with it. How should all this impinge on philosophical theorizing about the self?

One suggestion, well represented in Schopenhauer, is that while there must be a unitary 'I' as subject of knowledge and consciously willed action, we are nevertheless fundamentally composite beings, whose blind and organic urges are associated not with the 'I' but with a distinct component of ourselves, which for Schopenhauer is the underlying, primary, 'blind' will—the 'strong blind man who carries the lame sighted man on his shoulders'.[5] The Freudian distinction between the 'I' and the 'it'—which Freud thought 'the great thinker, Schopenhauer' had anticipated[6]—inevitably comes to mind here. But whatever ontology we commit ourselves to, Schopenhauer's 'blind strivings' (assuming that something answering to that description does exist in human beings) pose an enormous challenge.

The 'I' is an expression of the unity of self-consciousness. To recapitulate the familiar Kantian thought: the subject must be able to be aware of its own existence as that which has a variety of experiences, and undertakes, or could undertake, a range of actions. These have not only to be owned, but owned by one being, and one that is conscious to itself of their being its own, or of itself being the single subject of the collectivity of experiences and actions. This is a necessary condition of perception, knowledge, objectivity, and of conscious willed action. Conversely, a being that could have none of these but could be an 'I' to itself, that is, could think of itself self-consciously, is an impossibility. In this sense my having a

---

[4] Thomas Nagel expresses strong doubts of this kind in the context of evolutionary theory; see *The View from Nowhere*, pp. 78–82.

[5] *W2* p. 243 (209).   [6] See *Collected Papers*, vol. 4, pp. 355–6.

self depends on my apprehending and striving to influence the world. It is in being aware of being that very thing which apprehends and strives that I come to be able to think of myself as 'I' at all. This essentially Kantian thought still dominates much philosophical talk about the self. But in our theorizing, what account do we need to take of the 'blind' aspects of human psychology which Schopenhauer was the first to write about so eloquently, and indeed so convincingly? There are developmental issues: how does one grow to become a self-conscious subject of experience and action? The newborn, in Schopenhauer's view, 'who exhibit hardly the first faint trace of intelligence, are already full of their own will: in unbounded, aimless raging and crying they exhibit the urge of the will, with which they are teeming, while their will has as yet no object, i.e. they will without knowing what they will'.[7] Again we have the primacy of the will: it exists in us before we attain objectivity, before we achieve 'I'-thoughts.[8] This is not a work of developmental psychology or psycho-analytic theory—I shall make no pretensions to any account of how such thoughts are in fact reached. Nevertheless, we may surely assume that there is something the child *is* prior to its fully mastering 'I'-thoughts. By this I mean not just that the child exists, in the way that a tree or a rock exists, but that it must be something for itself, in however rudimentary a way.[9] And we surely have no alternative but to think of what it is for itself as being circumscribed, or filled out, by those pre-conscious strivings on which its survival as an organism depends. If it is out of these that intellect and true 'I'-thoughts develop—or even if it is merely the case that the two proceed in parallel with a high degree of interaction—would it not be unwise to assume that a philosophical theory of the self could get by without asking itself whether such strivings are in some sense still a part of the 'I' that each of us is? To think not, is to think that there is a peculiarly philosophical 'I', or that the 'I' must enter into philosophy in a way that is wholly unconnected with facts (whatever they are) about psychology. To this

---

[7] *W*2 p. 246 (211).
[8] I borrow the term from Gareth Evans, *The Varieties of Reference*, ch. 7.
[9] Cf. O'Shaughnessy, *The Will*, vol. 2, p. 13.

thought (and to the sources of its wording) we shall return later.

The issue of the development of self-consciousness raises, in Schopenhauer's terminology, the question of the dependence of the intellect on the 'blind' will, and in turn the question of whether the self can be exhaustively characterized as a self-conscious intellect. Schopenhauer is surely right in saying that each of us considers him- or herself to be a self-conscious subject of thought and experience. He must be right, because we could not consider ourselves to be anything if we *were not* self-conscious subjects of thought and experience, and we could not *be* such subjects unless we were capable of reflecting that we were. But Schopenhauer's further point is that what we habitually consider ourselves to be does not exhaust what we are. Of course there are all sorts of facts about me—the shape of my fingerprints, the total number of times my heart beats—which are excluded from my conception of myself as a self-conscious intellect. But, however comprehensive an inventory of such facts one chooses to imagine, Schopenhauer's further fact about what I am is not if this nature at all. The evidence he offers of the 'strange interplay within us' of will and intellect attests to my being essentially a 'blindly' willing thing, as well as a subject of knowledge and consciously willed action. It is, I think, unclear how far one can go in saying that I am the *subject of* unconscious desires, of instinctive drives, or of anything remotely like Schopenhauer's 'will to life'. Yet, given the many ways in which they interact with cognition and action, we have to see all of these as in a sense internal to the mind. In the face of this, to insist that in philosophical theory the self must be conceived as a fully self-transparent thinker of 'I'-thoughts would be no less than perverse.

Let us suppose, then, that we have reasons for retaining in some form the central features of Schopenhauer's conception of the subject as will. What now becomes of the conception of the pure, detached subject of knowing? I shall consider the subject in its Kantian epistemological guise first, leaving aside until later Schopenhauer's notion of the subject as an absolute 'mirror' of the world. Clearly the conception of the pure Kantian subject is inadequate if it is taken to provide an account of what we as subjects are and must conceive

ourselves to be. Besides the fact that it does not accommodate
the features of the self discussed above, the notion of a pure
knowing subject avowedly admits neither willing, nor embodiment of the subject, nor even its individuation as any kind of
constituent of the world. We cannot accept that such a
conception exhaustively characterizes the subject—but is
there any reason to think that we should do anything other
than reject it outright? I shall consider two basic responses.
One is that we should reject outright the conception of the
pure knowing subject; the other suggests that, hard though its
reconciliation with what we otherwise believe may be,
something fairly similar to it must be retained in order to do
full justice to the relations that hold between self and world.
This second view has to show what job a conception of the pure
knowing subject can do for us. But equally the first, rejecting
view ought to be able to explain what job the conception
accomplished for those philosophers who held it, and in
particular for Schopenhauer and Kant. It is not impossible
that they adopted their views of the subject as a kind of ad hoc
manœuvre, or by making a straightforward error. But it is
unlikely. As a strategy it might be better to ask what
philosophical aims and assumptions these theories of the pure
knowing subject support, and to attempt to gauge their worth
by an evaluation of those aims and assumptions.

It will be obvious that the views we are discussing are
embedded in a number of firm commitments: one is the
commitment to idealism, another is to the primacy of what we
have come to call 'foundational' epistemology. Less clearly
manifested by Kant, and more so by Schopenhauer, is a
commitment to account for knowledge of all kinds in terms of
the related concepts of *subject* and *object*. At this level of large-
scale theoretical assumption, any discussion is bound to be a
little schematic in character, but a number of thoughts suggest
themselves.

First, does the trouble not stem from the twin notions of
subject and *object* themselves? Are not these notions, in the way
we have seen them used, dispensable, and the problematic
conception of the 'subject that is not an object' one that need
not arise? Presumably we do not wish to give up the
distinction between that which perceives and knows, and that

which it perceives and knows. If knowledge and perception occur, there are, in this straightforward sense, subjects and objects. But there does not seem to be any good reason to build in from the start, as Schopenhauer does, the mutual exclusiveness of the two concepts. And if we do not, we remove an obstacle to thinking that the subject of perception and knowledge is at least potentially among the things known and perceived.

It has been suggested by Ernst Tugendhat that in the philosophy of Fichte and Hegel, among others, the 'subject–object model' of consciousness exerts a damaging force on their ability to account satisfactorily for self-consciousness. Progress can only be made, he argues, once we realize, as Wittgenstein came to, that self-consciousness is propositional in nature, and does not involve an immediate relation to a mysterious Something apprehended within us.[10] Does the inadequacy of the subject–object model make itself felt in Schopenhauer's thought in a similar way? On the one hand it does not, since for him the subject is in no sense an object—not really any kind of thing at all. But on the other hand, when only objects are known and the subject is not an object, self-knowledge threatens to become impossible. At this point Schopenhauer reverts to the simple suggestion that we know ourselves only as objects, and that inasmuch as we will, we are objects for the subject of knowledge. This is an attempt to account for self-knowledge on a very restricted epistemological basis: the notion of entities arrayed before the pure 'mind's eye' of the subject, which it directly apprehends. We are accustomed to thinking of this as an unsatisfactory theory of the subject's knowledge of things other than itself. How much more unsatisfactory it is in the case of self-consciousness: not only is it hard to substantiate the promised radical distinction between our knowledge of the external world and our non-observational awareness of our own acting, but the self that is knowing itself also has to disintegrate, like the rest of the world, into a pure knower and a distinct object known. Schopenhauer's attempt to account for self-consciousness in terms of the simple relation of subject and object is not one that we can be content to replicate.

[10] *Self-Consciousness and Self-Determination*, pp. 135–9.

Nevertheless, the non-objective status that Schopenhauer accords to the subject does give expression to a familiar truth: that in recognizing myself to be the subject of mental states, I do not identify myself by the use of those criteria which I must use in recognizing other things to which I apply predicates. Accounts by Wittgenstein and Strawson in particular have taught us that for certain states—including at least that class of states of which one can be said to be *the subject*—ascription of them to oneself is standardly criterionless.[11] There thus arises what has more recently been termed 'immunity to error through misidentification'.[12] In thinking that it is *I* that am perceiving such-and-such now, I cannot go wrong by making a mistake about which object I am referring to. Clearly there is something about our relationship to ourselves as cognitive subjects that is radically different from our relationship to any objects of cognition that are other than ourselves; and indeed there must be. It is not merely that I need not identify myself by the use of criteria when ascribing to myself states of which I am the subject. Rather, I cannot. It is not sufficient for such an ascription that I have a thought which refers to an object which is in fact identical with the thinker. I must think self-consciously of myself, or have 'I'-thoughts, in order to ascribe to myself states of which I am the subject. If I am to have the thought of some object that it ϕ-s, and to identify that object by using criteria in a way which allows the possibility of misidentification, then my thought that the object ϕ-s is not an 'I'-thought. An 'I'-thought, or genuinely self-conscious thought, must guarantee that that to which a property is ascribed in the thought, is what is thinking the thought. And, if Kant is right, a state's being a state of which I am the subject requires the possibility of a genuinely self-conscious thought on my part, in which I ascribe the state to myself.

Thus, despite the inadequacies of Schopenhauer's subject–object model, there is some truth in the claim that the subject is not identified as an object. However, to take the conception of the pure knowing subject further and to conclude that the subject is not an item contained within the world at all, is a

---

[11] Cf. Ludwig Wittgenstein, *The Blue and Brown Books*, pp. 61–9, and *PI* i, 404–9; P. F. Strawson, *Individuals*, ch. 3, and *The Bounds of Sense*, part iii, ch. 2.
[12] See especially Evans, *The Varieties of Reference*, ch. 7.

wholly new step which requires new assumptions. And it is here that idealism comes into play. We have agreed, to put the point in convenient but avoidable terminology, that the subject is not, and cannot be, straightforwardly an object for itself. But if we want to conclude that the subject is therefore not an object in the world at all, we must introduce the premiss that something can only be an object in the world if it is an object for the subject. This is accomplished most readily if one treats as equivalent the concepts *object* and *object for a subject*, as Schopenhauer does. What is in the world is what is a representation for the subject, the subject is not a representation for itself, therefore the subject is not in the world. But if we are not idealists, and do not force together in this way the notions of an object existing in the world and an object for the subject, there is no ground for the conclusion that the subject is not a part of the world. Though I do not (in the sense discussed), and even cannot, identify myself 'as an object' when ascribing to myself the states of which I am the subject, there is, without idealism, no reason to suppose that I *am not* an object existing in the world. It could simply be that (*a*) I am one of the objects in the world, and (*b*) none of the objects in the world can have the same mode of cognitive contact with itself as it has with objects other than itself.

Suppose, then, that we jettison idealism. Remaining with the same terminology, we are content from now on to allow that something can be an object in the world—say, a spatio-temporal individual—without having to be an object for the subject. What reason remains for believing in a pure, non-empirical, knowing subject of the kind advocated by Schopenhauer? I believe there is a further reason, which is closely connected with the kind of epistemological enterprise from which this conception of the subject issues. It is after all a pure subject mainly because it is purely a knowing subject. Within the confines of Kant's epistemological enterprise, the 'I' is to be considered first and foremost as that which has knowledge. He does not ask primarily what is the nature of the human being, of the self, or of the soul. He asks what can be known, and seeks a transcendental answer. Similarly Schopenhauer's subject of representation is 'that which knows', and is called upon to play a one-dimensionally epistemological role.

The Kantian epistemological project, inherited in outline by Schopenhauer, is foundational in its aspiration: it aims to find a basis for knowledge which is immune from doubt, and on which the whole edifice of knowledge can be securely set. Just as Descartes found in the 'I think' the absolute certainty of his own existence which provided the base for the rest of knowledge, so Kant relies on the existence of the subject of apperception to unify the data of the senses in accordance with the categories. One cannot argue (as Descartes is sometimes taken to[13]) from the impossibility of doubting one's own existence to one's existing only immaterially. Nevertheless, there is a sense in which Kant's task can only be accomplished by treating the 'I that knows' other than as an object in the empirical realm. He must use its necessary modes of operation as the fixed point on which to found the possibility of knowledge of objects in general. These modes of operation are to define the knowable world. There would be no way of proceeding if their bearer, the subject, were conceived to be an ordinary member of that empirically knowable world. Besides, it is questionable whether the assumption of empirical status for the subject would allow Kant to claim anything more than a posteriori knowledge of the classifications it imposes on its data. Since it is a priori conditions of all experience that are sought, a non-empirical consideration of the subject of experience is called for. The subject must be treated transcendentally, and to treat the subject transcendentally is precisely to treat it non-empirically.

I have talked here of 'treating the subject transcendentally'. Kant's account should not be taken as an attempt to describe an entity called 'the transcendental subject'. As we saw earlier, he leaves open the possibility that the subject has an empirical 'realization', and of course decidedly does not require that the subject be immaterial. But the point is that his epistemological enterprise constrains him to enquire of the subject only what the conditions of any objective experience necessitate it being—not what kind of thing it is. This leads to a gap, which is not successfully bridged by Kant, between

---

[13] For a clear account of this issue in Descartes, see Margaret D. Wilson, 'Descartes: The Epistemological Argument for Mind–Body Distinctness', *Nous* 10 (1976), pp. 7–8.

oneself treated transcendentally and oneself treated empirically, as a thing of some kind existing in the world.

All of this suggests the following answer to the question of whether we must retain the conception of the pure knowing subject: if the nature of the subject and its relation to the world are primarily to be understood in epistemological terms, and if we are to seek the foundations of the subject's knowledge in an essentially Kantian way, then we shall have to reckon with something like the Kantian conception of the subject of knowledge. We shall at least have to take a non-empirical stance towards the subject, and consider it primarily according to the a priori conditions of the knowability of objects. And this central part of our theorizing will not explain for us how that which knows is at the same time a part of the knowable world of objects. If, on the other hand, these assumptions are challenged and rejected, there will seem little reason so far to hang on to the conception of the pure knowing subject. If, that is, we do not accept that the primary and overriding relation of the self to the world is that of *knowing* it, or, even if we accept that but do not believe that we can give a fixed, universal account of the a priori conditions that are foundational for all knowledge on the part of any being that knows,[14] then, the thought goes, we can dispense with the pure Kantian subject.

So, if we progress beyond Kant's conception of the centrality to philosophy of foundational epistemology, we progress beyond the need to conceive the subject as he did; but if we remain with his conception of epistemology, we are bound in some measure to conceive the subject as he did. It would take more argument than is possible here to establish that the choice presented by this conditional response is a fair one. Clearly, however, it is apposite in terms of assessing Schopenhauer's position. For Schopenhauer—remarkably— offers to embrace both options at once. He protests that Kantian epistemology is deficient, that the subject as conceived by Kantian epistemology is explicable as a secondary outgrowth of organism and of will, and that it is in willing, now knowing, that our essence lies. And yet his whole strategy depends on

[14] Strictly speaking: for any being that knows by way of both a capacity for receiving intuitions and a capacity for active classification.

the retention of that very conception of the pure subject securely embedded in the foundational project, the subject–object model of consciousness, and the idealist view of the world as representation. It is as if we are to believe that philosophy, and the self of philosophy, must be fundamentally as Kant's *Critique of Pure Reason* indicates, but yet to allow the insights about the thing in itself and the will to cast profound suspicion on Kant's conception of the self and at least call into question his philosophical method.

While immersed in the *Critique*, it is possible to take it for granted that it is as pure knowers of the world that we must primarily conceive ourselves. After reading Schopenhauer, it is difficult to take that proposition at all seriously. His problematic treatment of the knowing subject prompts the thought that we are dealing here with a notion that belongs solely to Kantian epistemology, and which can be left behind as a local (if highly influential) product of the history of thought. But suppose we want to keep Kant's enterprise central to our conception of the way philosophy should proceed, and suppose that this approach necessitates a non-empirical treatment of the 'I that knows'—what else are we committed to? Does any of this legitimize the view that the subject is 'not a part of the world'? I suggest that it does not. Even if there must be a transcendental mode of enquiry which seeks to delineate that which must hold a priori of any conceivable subject of experience, it is not thereby precluded that some or all individual subjects of experience are empirical things, accessible in principle to empirical enquiry. It is simply that the theory of the pure 'I', arrived at a priori, contains no account of its instantiation by empirical beings. We can call this, if we like, the problem of how the subject can be equated with any object in the world. It is a serious enough problem. But it is not the same as claiming that the subject *must not be* an object in the world. Nor, after Schopenhauer, can it be considered *the* problem of the self.

We should be under no illusion of having dispelled altogether the theoretical difficulties involved in locating ourselves as subjects within the realm of empirical things. If we accept that the theory of the pure subject of knowledge is inadequate and unnecessary, and that we must think of ourselves as essentially embodied, striving, organic beings, with some or all of the Schopenhauerian corollaries discussed earlier, we still do not really know how an organism can be a subject even of willed action, let alone of knowledge. I shall briefly discuss two remaining difficulties, both of which arise in recent work by Thomas Nagel.

The first might be called the problem of being a subject at all. We have the concepts of knowledge, belief, perception, desire, willing, action, emotion, all of which we have to take into account in thinking about ourselves, and at least some of which presuppose embodiment and a place within the objective order. But what is it to be a subject of any of these states and occurrences? Can subjects ever be accommodated in our description of what the objective order contains? On the one hand, if being a subject of will and (say) emotion entails being bodily, and being bodily entails being contained in the objective order of things, then subjects must be accommodated within the objective order. But, as Schopenhauer put it, 'on the purely *objective* path, we never attain to the inner nature of things, but if we attempt to find their nature from outside and empirically, this inner always becomes an outer in our hands'.[15] Part of what this means, or can be taken to mean, is that empirical investigation of spatio-temporal individuals and the causal laws according to which they operate cannot reveal to us what a subject is. The often misleading metaphor of the 'inner' is linked with the thought that any facts there are about *what a subject is* are wholly taken up with what it is *to be a subject*. It seems plausible, and perhaps inescapable, that in *being* what I am for myself—that which has all my experiences —I gain an understanding of what it is I am that is irreplaceable by any kind of information gathered by objective investigation of things other than me. It also seems right to say that such an 'inner' self-understanding—gained essentially by being that which is being understood—is irreplaceable by any objective investigation of whatever empirical thing I am. If investigation of the world is conceived as increasingly objective the more it tends to presuppose independence of any particular viewpoint (such as mine) or kind of viewpoint (such

---

[15] *W*2 p. 320 (273–4).

as the human), and if the objective order of things is that revealed to us by our most objective investigation, then, given what I have said about an irreplaceable self-understanding, attaining knowledge of the objective order will never tell us what a subject is. This is not a problem if one is content to say that there are no facts of the matter about what a subject is. But since there is clearly such a thing as being a subject, that is not a comfortable option.[16]

The other problem I referred to is this: how is an objective account of what the world contains to be achieved by the mind of one individual contained in it?[17] If we can envisage a complete and centreless account of what the world contains, it will have to comprehend within it *everything* that is the case concerning every individual, whether object or subject. At the same time, it will be an account whose contents in no way depend on the location or constitution of any one individual or kind of individual. Nagel believes that we can, and must, envisage such an extremely objective account. He calls it the 'centreless' or 'perspectiveless' conception of reality. The problem that arises once we start thinking in these terms can be put as follows. Everything about myself as an individual is encompassed within the centreless conception. In this sense I am completely accounted for in the conception of what—from no perspective at all—is the case. Nagel suggests that this can become puzzling: 'How', he asks, 'can I be anything so *small* and *concrete* and *specific*?'[18] How can I be a particular person?

This appears to assume that what I am is something other than this, something about which there can then be a question of its identity with a particular person in the world. Nagel suggests that this is in part true. Inasmuch as I am the subject of the perspectiveless conception of the world (the conceiver of that conception), I must, he argues, be a self that is not limited by attachment to any mere being in the world, and is in a sense impersonal: 'I am both the logical focus of an objective conception of the world and a particular being in that world who occupies no central position whatever.'[19]

[16] Cf. Nagel, 'Subjective and Objective'.
[17] Ibid. p. 208: 'Problems arise because the same individual is the occupant of both [subjective and objective] viewpoints.'
[18] *The View from Nowhere*, p. 61.   [19] Ibid. p. 64.

Schopenhauer's great problem re-emerges, even down to the metaphor of the 'focus'. Nagel says further of the 'objective conception':

This conception does not itself imply anything about who its subject is, or even that he exists at all inside the world being described. So far as the content of the objective view goes, it might be of a world in which I, its subject, never have existed and never will. But since the objective conception *has* a subject, the possibility of its presence in the world is there, and it allows me to bring the subjective and objective views together.[20]

This is not, then, the same as Schopenhauer's view that the subject can never be an object. It is not impossible for the subject to be a part of the world of objects. Nevertheless, each of us must, according to Nagel, conceive him- or herself as being a subject such that its existence as a pure 'logical focus' is possible, and its identity with an individual person (which each of us also is) philosophically troubling. (In the next chapter we shall examine Wittgenstein's notion of the 'metaphysical' subject, and consider its Schopenhauerian origins. But without encroaching too much on that discussion, we may note Nagel's comparison of his own view with Wittgenstein's. The two have, he says, 'something in common', though unlike Wittgenstein he stops short of excluding the objective self from the world entirely.[21])

If what Nagel attempts to describe really is a problem, it is one of the greatest generality. It cannot be brushed aside as a product of idealism, foundational epistemology, a crude subject–object model of consciousness, or a refusal to acknowledge truths about our nature as active, embodied subjects. Rather, it stems from our being particular parts of the world whilst conceiving of what the world contains as not being bound by any partial perspective.

We should at this point remind ourselves that ultimately Schopenhauer's analogue of the 'objective self', or the subject of a perspectiveless view of the world, is to be found in his aesthetic, ethical, and mystical doctrines. The Kantian knowing subject, regarded purely transcendentally, poses a similar problem initially: 'each of us finds himself as this

---

[20] *The View from Nowhere*, p. 61.   [21] Ibid. p. 62 n.

subject', Schopenhauer claims, and the consciousness of so being flows miraculously together with that of willing, into the consciousness of one 'I'. But the Kantian subject is rendered unsuitable as the focus of a perspectiveless point of view, because it, and the categories with which it operates, are understood as merely advanced capacities of a particular kind of organism, inseparably linked with that organism's ends, and incapable of providing knowledge with that degree of detachedness from self which the perspectiveless view demands. Thus, only in a casting-off of those categories through which we ordinarily know and manipulate the world can we hope for the status of a pure mirror of everything that reality contains. Only in abandoning the cognitive structures on which our survival depends, only by total absence of self-imposition on the world, can we attain a state in which we cease to treat ourselves as individuals within the world, and genuinely refuse preference to *any* one part of the world over another. There is an argument here which says that we will not be able to be anything like Nagel's 'objective self' whilst we persist in acting through particular bodies (particular manifestations of will), and whilst we continue to use cognitive modes of classification which have instrumental value in our lives as individual human beings. It is an argument which should be taken seriously. If we believe that it is impossible to cast off our ordinary modes of acting and classifying in this way, then Schopenhauer's problem of how we can be the 'perspectiveless subject'—'the pure, painless, will-less, timeless subject of knowing'—is one that we do not have to face. But if at the same time Schopenhauer is right—that we could fulfil our potential to be such a perspectiveless subject only by abandoning those modes of acting and classifying, and by entering a rarified aesthetic-cum-mystical realm—then we must ask to what extent Nagel's problem is a genuine one.

Both Nagel and Schopenhauer, in their different ways, argue that we have to conceive ourselves as being something which in principle could exist outside the totality of what the world contains. A different response would be to acknowledge the same general problem of the centreless conception and the particular worldly subject, but to suggest that we are not driven to such an extravagant conclusion. Perhaps we must think of what there is as 'contained within a perspectiveless view', but we can do so without needing the supposition that this 'view' has its own peculiar subject—without, therefore, having to think of ourselves as anything other than particular embodied subjects of action and knowledge, occupying a single perspective within the world. The problem of how this is possible may not have gone away, but it will no longer take the form of how a pure subject or an objective self meshes with this or that empirical individual.

That is the outline of one imaginable response. There are, however, two ways in which one might attempt to remove the alleged central difficulty altogether. One is to insist that any particular being in the world is simply not the true referent of 'I' at all, that the 'I' is the subject of the centreless view, and that this or that body, mind (or whatever) is merely one of the contents of the world correlated with the 'I'. The other is to deny the intelligibility of the centreless view of the world, and thereby to do away with any suspicion that we require a conception of the pure perspectiveless self. With these thoughts we move on to Wittgenstein and to Nietzsche.

13

Remarks on Wittgenstein and Nietzsche

IT is by now fairly well known that Wittgenstein's early work owes much to Schopenhauer. A number of writers attest to the fact that Wittgenstein had read Schopenhauer thoroughly at an early age, though there is less of a clear consensus as to precisely which elements of it most impressed him and how long the impression lasted.[1] Wittgenstein himself wrote in 1931 that he had been merely 'reproductive' in his thinking, passionately seizing other people's trains of thought for his own purposes: 'In this way I have been influenced by Boltzmann, Hertz, Schopenhauer, Frege, Russell, Kraus, Loos, Weininger, Spengler, Sraffa.'[2] The length of the list reminds us of what we should know already, that it would be wrong to interpret Wittgenstein predominantly—let alone solely—in the light of Schopenhauer. On the other hand, his presence in the list calls for a serious attempt to discover what it was that Wittgenstein had seized upon.[3]

If one approaches Wittgenstein's writings with a systematic

---

[1] The primary sources are: G. E. M. Anscombe, *An Introduction to Wittgenstein's Tractatus*, pp. 11–12; P. T. Geach, review of G. C. M. Colombo's translation of *TLP*, *Philosophical Review* 66 (1957), p. 558; G. H. von Wright, 'Biographical Sketch', in Norman Malcolm, *Ludwig Wittgenstein: A Memoir*, pp. 5, 20–1. Some discussions of the nature of the influence have been: Patrick Gardiner, *Schopenhauer*, pp. 275–82; Allan S. Janik, 'Schopenhauer and the Early Wittgenstein', *Philosophical Studies (Ireland)* 15 (1966), pp. 76–95; P. M. S. Hacker, *Insight and Illusion* (2nd edn.), ch. 4 (also 1st edn., ch. 3); A. Phillips Griffiths, 'Wittgenstein, Schopenhauer, and Ethics', in *Understanding Wittgenstein* (Royal Institute of Philosophy Lectures, vol. 7 (1972–3), pp. 96–116); S. Morris Engel, 'Schopenhauer's Impact on Wittgenstein', *Journal of the History of Philosophy* 7 (1969), pp. 285–302; Bryan Magee, *The Philosophy of Schopenhauer*, pp. 286–315.

[2] *Culture and Value*, pp. 18–19.

[3] Bryan Magee has written of 'Schopenhauer's all-pervading influence on Wittgenstein' (*Times Literary Supplement*, 14 Oct. 1983, p. 1126). This is an exaggeration. Michael Tanner has replied that: 'It certainly does not pervade even the *Tractatus*, which, as a classic text in logical atomism, is totally independent of it; and it is wholly irrelevant to the later work' (*Times Literary Supplement*, 28 Oct. 1983, p. 1189). This, on the last two points, is also much too extreme, as will become clear in subsequent pages.

knowledge of Schopenhauer's philosophy, many parallels stand out plainly. In the *Tractatus* alone the following propositions find correspondences—often extremely close ones—in Schopenhauer:[4] 'It is clear that ethics cannot be put into words. Ethics is transcendental. (Ethics and aesthetics are one)' (6. 421); 'There is indeed what is inexpressible. This shows itself. It is the mystical' (6. 522); 'The view of the world *sub specie aeterni* is the view of it as a—limited—whole. The feeling of the world as a limited whole is the mystical feeling' (6. 45);[5] 'If good or bad willing alters the world, then it can alter only the limits of the world, not the facts; not what can be expressed by means of language. In short the effect must be that it becomes an altogether different world . . . The world of the happy man is different from that of the unhappy man' (6. 43); 'So too at death the world does not alter, but comes to an end' (6. 431); 'If we take eternity to mean not infinite temporal duration, but timelessness, then he lives eternally who lives in the present' (6. 4311); 'The temporal immortality of the human soul, that is its eternal survival after death, is not only in no way guaranteed—above all this assumption completely fails to achieve what people have always wanted from it. Is some riddle solved by my eternal survival? Is not this eternal life as much of a riddle as the present one? The solution to the riddle of life in space and time lies *outside* space and time' (6. 4312).

We may have forgotten over the years just how unusual, unexplained, and unsupported these remarks are. They must provoke speculation. Why cannot ethics be put into words? In what sense are ethics and aesthetics one? Why try to say

---

[4] Corresponding passages in Schopenhauer: *W*1 pp. 456–7 (368) (ethics incommunicable in words, the concept unfruitful in both ethics and art); *W*2 pp. 715–16 (611–12) (the mystical incommunicable, at most expressible by a negation); *W*1 pp. 231–5 (178–81), 481–3 (389–91) (the aesthetic view *sub specie aeternitatis*, and mysticism as an extension of it); *W*2 p. 442 (373) (the smiling or gloomy aspect of the whole world when we are happy or unhappy shows that only in not willing do we see objectively); ibid. p. 586 (500) (the world vanishes at death); ibid. pp. 571–2 (487–8) (our true eternity is non-temporal, not a continued duration); *W*1 pp. 351–3 (278–80) (the present as the form of all life); ibid. p. 356 (282) (both will and subject of knowledge are outside time, but their survival does not console the individual who seeks assurance of immortality).

[5] Note 'das mystische' (i.e. *das mystische Gefühl*), not, as in 6. 44, 6. 522, 'das Mystische'.

anything about 'the mystical'? What is it to live timelessly, or view something *sub specie aeterni*? In what possible sense does the world come to an end at death? Why would eternal survival not give us what we wanted? And so on. Has Wittgenstein simply strung together some oracular pronouncements (many taken straight from his notebooks) in order to sound impressive? The alternative to this interpretation is to seek some unifying sense to the remarks—a more advisable approach in view of Wittgenstein's statement that the sense or point of the book 'is an ethical one'.[6]

To someone who has thoroughly absorbed Schopenhauer's system—as Wittgenstein himself had done ten years before starting to compose the *Tractatus*—the speculative questions above can be readily answered. Ethics, for Schopenhauer, is a matter of taking the right stance to the world as a whole, of viewing correctly the relation between self and world. It is not a matter of conceptual or discursive knowledge. Aesthetic experience is closely linked with this, since it too involves the pure, incommunicable experience of 'regarding' the world without imposing conceptual categories on it, and without awareness of one's own separateness from it. This is, as Schopenhauer says, to view the world *sub specie aeternitatis*. The mystical is outside philosophy, and consists in the complete and heightened awareness of one's non-separateness from the world as a whole. Such an awareness cannot be communicated, but philosophy can and should lead us to the brink of its comprehension. To live timelessly is to achieve one of the states of consciousness that strip away the forms of connection that govern empirical knowledge of the world. The world ceases with the death of the representing subject because the world is its representation. We fear death because we *will* life—but in attempting to conceive of my surviving death as an individual, I make a fundamental mistake. I as an individual centre of consciousness perish, but the underlying will (that whose manifestation in me accounts for my fear of extinction) lives eternally, outside of space and time. If my will to life is independent of my comprehending it, so that why

I am, and continue to want to be, alive remains from a rational point of view a mystery, then if I lived for ever the situation would be no different.

Furthermore, it is very difficult not hear some echo of the final pages of the *Tractatus* when one reads Schopenhauer's account of the relationship between philosophy and mysticism:

The mystic starts out from his inner, positive, individual experience, in which he finds himself as the eternal and only being, and so on. But none of this is communicable, except assertions for which we have to take his word: consequently he cannot convince. The philosopher on the other hand starts out from what is common to all, from objective appearance that lies before all, and from the facts of self-consciousness which are present in each of us. His method is thus that of reflection on all this and the given data it contains: for this reason he can convince. So he should avoid getting into the way of the mystic, and . . . wanting to project the image of a positive knowledge of that which—forever inaccessible to all knowledge—can only be signified through a negation. . . . Philosophy's theme must restrict itself to the world: pronouncing in all aspects *what* the world *is*, what it *is* in its innermost nature, is all that it can honestly achieve. Now it is in keeping with this that my teaching, on reaching its summit, takes on a *negative* character, and so ends with a negation. For here it can speak only of that which is denied, given up . . . Here is precisely the point where the mystic proceeds positively, and from here on nothing remains but mysticism.[7]

The correspondences are not always exact, and obviously we are dealing here with extracts from very different philosophical enterprises. Wittgenstein has apparently adapted central elements of Schopenhauer's aesthetic, ethical, and mystical doctrines to suit his own purposes. It is hardly surprising that he should do so, given his career up to 1916, when, as his notebooks show, he began to wrestle with these topics. Since giving up engineering a few years earlier, his work had been narrowly focused on the problems of logic and the foundations of mathematics. When it comes to writing his book he aspires to give it an 'ethical sense', and so he returns to the systematic treatment of such issues that had impressed him ten years before, and the only such treatment, apparently, of which he had any great knowledge. The process by which

[7] *W*2 pp. 715–16 (611–12).

he attempts to utilize the basic Schopenhauerian conceptions to express his own thoughts is revealed in the *Notebooks 1914–1916*, starting with the entry for 11 June 1916. Here we find him using the notion that the relation of self to world is like that of an eye to its visual field, discussing the relation of the will to the world, and in particular the notion that the will's being good or bad gives sense to the world. The final sentence reads like a direct commentary on Schopenhauer's doctrine of the denial of the will: 'I can only make myself independent of the world—and so after all master it in a certain sense—by renouncing any influence on happenings.'

As he pursues the same theme, Wittgenstein only once mentions Schopenhauer by name: 'One could say (in a Schopenhauerian way [*Schopenhauerisch*]): it is not the world of representation that is either good or evil, but the willing subject.' Then he adds: 'I am conscious of the complete unclarity of all these sentences.'[8] It is as if he possesses Schopenhauer's vocabulary, but is unclear what he really wants to do with it: 'Just as the subject is not a part of the world, but a presupposition of its existence, so good and evil are predicates of the subject, not properties in the world. Here the nature of the subject is completely veiled'; 'The I, the I is what is deeply mysterious!'; 'What my will is, I do not yet know'.[9]

One set of entries where Wittgenstein achieves some clarity corroborates the view I have given of the *Tractatus* passages above:

The work of art is the object seen *sub specie aeternitatis*; and the good life is the world seen *sub specie aeternitatis*. This is the connection between art and ethics.

The usual way of regarding things [*gewöhnliche Betrachtungsweise*] sees things as it were from in their midst, the view *sub specie aeternitatis* from outside.

In such a way that they have the whole world as background.

Is this it perhaps—that it sees the object *with* space and time instead of *in* space and time?[10]

[8] *NB* p. 79.   [9] Ibid. pp. 79, 80, 74.
[10] Ibid. p. 83. 'Gewöhnliche Betrachtungsweise': cf. Schopenhauer's own 'gewöhnliche Betrachtungsart', which he also contrasts with the view *sub specie aeternitatis* to be had in 'peaceful contemplation of the present natural object' (*W*1 pp. 231–2 (178)).

There can be little doubt that when Wittgenstein wrote this he was either reading Schopenhauer's text, or reconstruing it accurately from memory. Many other instances occur where in greater or lesser degree we find an allusion to Schopenhauerian doctrines, notably the claims: 'It is true: the human being is the microcosm: I am my world'; and 'I can speak of a will common to the whole world. But this will is in a higher sense *my* will. Just as my representation is the world, so my will is the world-will.'[11]

Thus the *Notebooks* establish clearly what is slightly less apparent in the *Tractatus* itself, that it was partly by thinking through Schopenhauer's views on ethics, aesthetics, and the relation of the self to the world that Wittgenstein came to write these famous propositions. But whether a clear and systematic position emerges from this collection of notes is debatable. To complete our task we must give an interpretation of those passages in the *Tractatus* where the 'I', the subject, and the will are explicitly discussed.

The few remarks on the 'I' in the *Tractatus* are often quoted, and too often merely quoted. But once we apply an overall frame of reference closely analogous to Schopenhauer's, they become more amenable to interpretation. Of particular interest to us are such remarks as these:

The subject does not belong to the world, but is rather a limit of the world (5. 632).

Where *in* the world is a metaphysical subject to be found?. . . (5. 633).

Thus there really is a sense in which in philosophy there can be talk about the I in a non-psychological way.
The I enters into philosophy in that 'the world is my world'.
The philosophical I is not the human being, not the human body, or the human soul with which psychology deals, but rather the metaphysical subject, the limit—not a part—of the world (5. 641).

Here Wittgenstein appears to defend something analogous to the Schopenhauerian notion of the subject of knowledge. As he says in the *Notebook*: 'The I is not an object'—'I stand

---

[11] *NB* pp. 84, 85.

objectively in confrontation with every object. But not the I.'[12] This is clearly *Schopenhauerisch*. However, the remarks about the philosophical 'I' require careful treatment, and must be seen in the context of the continuous presentation of points that runs from 5. 6 through to 5. 641.

The fundamental preoccupation of the *Tractatus* is with the relation between language and the world, which is a crucial influence on the way in which the 'I' or subject must be conceived. Propositions picture facts; or at least 'We make pictures of facts for ourselves' (2. 1). What then of the relationship between the world and the individual subject of thought? This is the question which Wittgenstein seems to begin raising at 5. 6: '*The limits of my language*', he writes, 'mean the limits of my world.' There follows a reminder that the limits of *the* world are the limits of logic. Elsewhere he refers to logic as a 'mirror-image of the world' (6. 13; cf. 5. 511, where logic is called 'the great mirror'). Logic 'fills out' the world—the limits of the world and the limits of logic coincide (5. 61). This is because logic (which comprises tautologies) does not picture any facts in the world, but makes manifest the fundamental structure of language, and in the process the structure of the world that propositions in language picture. The limits of *the* world, then, are the limits of logic. But Wittgenstein has also introduced the notion of *my* world. What is the relation between *my* world and *the* world? The answer comes in another much-quoted passage: 'That the world is *my* world is shown in that the limits of *the* language (the language which alone I understand) mean the limits of *my* world' (5. 62).

Apparently, then, the world is my world because *my* language is *the* language, and because the limits of logic that are manifested in that language also indicate the limits of the world. So I relate to the world by making *the* language my language, thereby partaking in its mirroring relation to the structure of the world as a whole. My world is, we might say, no more and no less than the world. While Schopenhauer sought a pure subject that would mirror the world, Wittgenstein, using the same metaphor, finds the primary 'mirroring' to

---

[12] Ibid. p. 80.

occur in logic itself, and in the language whose structure logic shows. I as subject mirror the world only to the extent that I am the user of a language. But to that extent my mirroring of it exhibits the same structure as that of the language itself, which in turn is the structure of the world.

The first question raised by this interpretation is why Wittgenstein links these remarks about the limits of my language, my world, and the world so closely to the issue of solipsism. The passage quoted above follows these two sentences: 'this remark provides the key to the problem, to what extent solipsism is a truth. For what solipsism *means* is quite correct, only it cannot be *said*, but rather shows itself' (5. 621). P. M. S. Hacker has recently contended that Wittgenstein was in some serious sense a solipsist in the early stages of his development. The only textual basis for this in the *Tractatus*, it seems, comprises the claim: 'what solipsism *means* is quite correct . . .', and the ensuing remark that 'the world is my world'. However, against reading Wittgenstein as a solipsist, at least on the face of it, is the later claim that 'solipsism, when its implications are followed out strictly, coincides with pure realism' (5. 64). Unless there are good reasons to the contrary, this must surely be taken to mean that solipsism is an apparent philosophical position which undermines itself when one attempts to state it—and hence not the kind of position to which Wittgenstein could have conceived himself to be adhering. Hacker is right to see many of the thoughts in this section of the *Tractatus* (5. 6 ff.) as having a Schopenhauerian origin. But his interpretation of their significance is clouded by a conviction that Schopenhauer's chief influence on Wittgenstein was to predispose him towards solipsism. Before giving my own interpretation, let me briefly deal with this view.

Hacker is keen to argue that it was reading Schopenhauer that inclined Wittgenstein towards solipsism, but the question is why anybody should think this. True, Schopenhauer is an idealist who gives prominence to the thought that 'the world is my representation', and who talks of the subject as a microcosm which is the 'bearer' or presupposition of the macrocosm. But this, as I have tried to make clear, is never intended to be a solipsistic claim. The subject that I am, all others are equally. The world cannot be restricted to that which is representation for one individual as opposed to others, because the subject whose representation the world is said to be cannot be empirically individuated. We must also take into account Schopenhauer's stated position on solipsism ('theoretical egoism')—that it is irrefutable but close to insanity. Hacker notes this, but goes on to wonder how someone who writes the following can 'be so sanguine in dogmatically brushing aside' solipsism:

the whole of nature outside the knowing subject, and so all remaining individuals, exist only in his representation; that is, he is conscious of them always only as his representation, and so merely indirectly, and as something dependent on his own inner being and existence . . .

every individual, completely vanishing and reduced to nothing in a boundless world, nevertheless makes himself the centre of the world . . .[13]

Hacker says that 'in the grip of a misconceived picture' it is tempting to take such a view as this. But what he does not emphasize sufficiently is that *in Schopenhauer's view* someone who thinks like this is in the grip of a misconceived picture. For this is Schopenhauer's characterization of practical or ethical *egoism*, which, as we saw in Chapter 11, for Schopenhauer involves the fundamental metaphysical error of regarding oneself as in principle separate from the rest of the world. Egoism may be all but inevitable for each of us, and may stem from the 'identity of microcosm and macrocosm' which is part and parcel of Schopenhauer's idealism, but egoism is an error for Schopenhauer none the less. Solipsism is perhaps tempting to human subjects for reasons similar to those which make

---

[13] Hacker, *Insight and Illusion* (2nd edn.), p. 94. The passage quoted is from *W*1 pp. 414–15 (332), in Payne's translation. In his first edition (p. 70) Hacker said that this passage and many others 'make it difficult to grasp how solipsism can be avoided'—wrongly assuming that this was a statement of Schopenhauer's own metaphysical view. The only other passage he referred to specifically came from Schopenhauer's anti-Hegelian discussion of history, which made the point that it was each person's own life that was really of significance. It had nothing to do with solipsism (though it does have a Wittgensteinian parallel in *NB* p. 82: 'What has history to do with me?' etc.). Happily, these mistakes are eliminated from the second edition. But as I argue, Hacker has now lost even the semblance of a case for regarding Schopenhauer as a solipsist.

practical egoism tempting—but the most that Schopenhauer is ever prepared to concede to it is that it is irrefutable. His theory is that as individual subjects of representation and will we are strongly disposed to be egoistic—but on that basis he should not be accused either of covertly espousing solipsism or of 'dogmatically brushing it aside'. Thus when Hacker ends by saying that 'such passages' in Schopenhauer 'evidently struck a deeply resonant chord in Wittgenstein', we may readily agree. But that does not go any way towards supporting the view that Wittgenstein ever adhered to solipsism. If he thought he found solipsism in Schopenhauer he was misinterpreting him, and while that cannot be ruled out, I do not think we have to assume it either. Hacker's other main consideration—that in later years Wittgenstein spent much energy trying to explain the error behind solipsism—does not require that he ever held the view himself. His later preoccupation is just as intelligible if at the time of writing the *Tractatus* he thought solipsism was something which gave the illusion of being a statable philosophical position without really being so.

If we dispense with a solipsist Schopenhauer in the background, can we finally dispense with a solipsist Wittgenstein?[14] If solipsism were something that 'could be said', it would have to be a putative picturing of some fact or facts pertaining within the world. It would have to be a case of saying: 'the world has this in it, and this, but not that'. In particular, it would have to consist in saying that the world has in it what *I* picture to be in it—what there is, is limited by *my* understanding. So not only would solipsism propose to give an inventory of what was factually in the world, but it would attempt to do so by tying the contents of the world to one pre-eminent constituent of the world, namely, the individual making the solipsist claim. If it were true that the contents of the world were restricted in this way to that which was comprehended by one individual, this would substantiate the claim 'the world is my world', and would mean that solipsism

---

[14] For discussion of this issue, see David Pears, 'Wittgenstein's Treatment of Solipsism in the *Tractatus*', in *Questions in the Philosophy of Mind*, pp. 272–92. Pears emphasizes something I have omitted: the extent to which Wittgenstein was criticizing Russell's view of the self.

is not only 'quite correct', but something that 'can be said'. The something that 'shows itself' is different from this, however; it concerns not what facts obtain, but the structure of the language I use. And because I make the language my language, it is my language which shows me the structure of the world that is mirrored in it. The structure of the world as a whole is limited by what I understand—in this sense the world is my world—but only by virtue of my understanding being in a language whose structure is isomorphic with that of the world. Because of Wittgenstein's confidence in the complete isomorphism of language and world, he thinks that in adopting a language (which I make mine), my understanding is bound to be isomorphic with the world. This is the extent to which solipsism is 'quite correct'.

The 'I' enters into philosophy in that 'the world is my world' (5. 641). We have now distinguished the reading of 'the world is my world' which takes it as something that can be said—a proposition about facts in the world—from the reading of it according to which it merely shows itself. With this in mind we can turn more directly to the question of the nature of the 'I'. What is beyond contention is that, for Wittgenstein, the 'I' that concerns philosophy is not an individual entity within the world. It is not the human being, not the human body, not even a particular soul, whose multiple states are facts within the world, and as such provide the proper study for empirical psychology. It is not a part of the world, but a limit of it. All this we are told explicitly. On the other hand, it is clear that the 'I' *does enter into philosophy*. It is neither a mere illusion,[15] nor something which is of no philosophical concern.

We start, then, with the assumption that Wittgenstein's 'I' (or, as he also calls it, 'the metaphysical subject') is meant to be a legitimate philosophical conception, something which, though not present in the world of facts, is nevertheless not illusory. Can we gain any further understanding of this by turning to Schopenhauer?

The Schopenhauerian conception of the representing subject as the 'necessary correlate' of the world of empirical objects is

---

[15] Hacker presents a good case against the view that the 'I' is dismissed as illusory (*Insight and Illusion*, 2nd edn., p. 89).

clearly analogous in important respects to Wittgenstein's 'I' as it appears here. Wittgenstein writes in 5. 631 of 'the thinking, representing subject [*das denkende, vorstellende Subjekt*]', which suggests something like the Schopenhauerian conception. However, he says of this subject that it 'does not exist [*Das denkende, vorstellende Subjekt gibt es nicht*]'. Hacker takes this to show that the 'thinking, representing subject' is dismissed as illusory. This is very plausible, given that in the *Notebooks* Wittgenstein asked: 'Is not the representing subject mere superstition?', and a day later he gave himself the answer that 'the representing subject is surely an empty illusion'.[16] But the accompanying thoughts, which are the basis for *Tractatus* 5. 633–5. 6331, use the comparison of the eye and its visual field, Schopenhauer's commonest image for the relation between the representing subject and the world, and are taken up with a simple statement of the non-encounterability of the subject in the objective realm. The conclusion from these thoughts should not be that the subject in question is an illusion. For the point made by the eye image is that the subject is not included in its own experience of objects ('I stand objectively in confrontation with every object. But not the I'), but yet must exist as a presupposition of that experience. The conclusion of the non-encounterability argument is similarly not that there is no such thing as the subject, but that the subject is not a part of the world that the subject encounters. No one with a Schopenhauerian background would think that the non-objective status of the subject entailed its illusoriness.

To the extent that there is an argument in *Tractatus* 5. 631–5. 6331, it too has not the illusoriness, but the non-worldliness of the subject as its conclusion. Wittgenstein imagines the book *The World as I Found it* containing a report on my body (an 'object among objects' in Schopenhauer's sense), and (interestingly) on which parts were subordinate to my *will*. This he says would be a method of isolating the subject, 'or rather of showing that *in an important* sense there is no subject' (my emphasis). Not 'there is no subject', but 'in an important sense' there is none. In what sense? The next sentence tells us: 'it alone could *not* be mentioned in that

[16] *NB* p. 80.

book'. The sense in which the subject does not exist is simply that in which it is not part of the world as I find it—as the next four sentences, recapitulating the eye image and the notion of 'a limit, not a part', clearly confirm. Thus, though Wittgenstein seems to believe that the thinking, representing subject is to be dismissed as an illusion, he gives us no reason for this belief. It may be that the 'metaphysical subject' is supposed to be distinct from the 'thinking, representing subject', but as yet it has been left obscure why this is so.

What Wittgenstein does give us reason for believing is that to think that the subject was an object within the world would be to fall prey to an illusion. And this is sufficient to explain what he goes on to say about the collapse of solipsism: 'Here one sees that solipsism, strictly followed through, coincides with pure realism. The I of solipsism shrinks together to an extensionless point, and there remains the reality co-ordinated with it' (5. 64). Solipsism is inherently unstable as a position putatively statable in a meaningful proposition. It could only be statable as the claim that the world is limited to that which falls within the understanding of one individual. But because the 'I' with which the world *is* correlated is *not* any individual item within the world, to say that the world is what is correlated with the 'I' is not to restrict the contents of the world at all. The putative subject to which solipsism attempts to anchor the world yields to the Schopenhauerian (Kantian) conception of the self as an extensionless point.[17]

What has, I think, been overlooked about Wittgenstein's claim that the subject is not a part of the world is its implicit reliance on a kind of idealism. The interrelationship of the various propositions is not transparently clear, but the premiss of the argument seems to be as follows: the subject does not occur as one of its own objects (does not occur in the world as the subject finds it). And the conclusion seems to be: the subject is not a part of the world. What is missing is the premiss that the subject is a part of the world only if the subject is an object for itself (occurs in the world as the subject finds it). But why should we accept that only what is object for the subject, or is 'found' by the subject in the world, is in the

---

[17] Cf. Pears, 'Wittgenstein's Treatment of Solipsism', p. 287.

world? Might I not be a physical entity, and hence something in the world, despite the fact that I do not confront myself as I do objects in general? For Schopenhauer this is simply ruled out by the equation of 'object in the world' with 'object for the subject'. If Wittgenstein tacitly makes this equation, as he needs to do to have any semblance of an argument, he is tacitly an idealist about the world.[18] If we allow Wittgenstein this idealist claim, a coherent position emerges: the 'I' is not encountered as an object within the world. Only what is encountered as an object within the world is part of the world. Therefore the 'I' is not a part of the world. But, just as the eye which is not seen constitutes a 'limit' of what is seen, so the 'I' which is not encountered in the world is a limit of the world. Thus we must be able to talk about the 'I' in philosophy, though in so doing we are not talking of any empirical human being, body or mind. If solipsism is thought of as a statable position, it collapses altogether, because it falsely takes the 'I' to be some factual entity, to associate the world with which is to place a genuine restriction on what the world contains. Once it is seen that the 'I' is not a part of the world, solipsism's claim that the world is the world of the 'I' is transformed into the empty claim that there is the world of objects, because under the presupposition of idealism, 'the world of objects for the subject' is equivalent to 'the world of objects'.

To the extent that there is a coherent position in this section of the *Tractatus*, then, it is one so thoroughly imbued with Schopenhauer's thought that it is almost hard to know how to assess it as a separate contribution to philosophy. The major difference is that the metaphysical 'I' is by implication closely linked with the discussion of the limits of language. But because Wittgenstein uncritically, as it would seem, takes over so much from Schopenhauer, he does not succeed in spelling out this linkage very clearly.

I commented on Wittgenstein's half-realized thought that the thinking, representing subject is illusory, saying that the ensuing propositions could show only the different point that

---

[18] I shall not attempt to deal with this question with regard to 'the world' throughout *TLP*. For the argument here cf. my paper 'The Subject and the Objective Order', *Proceedings of the Aristotelian Society* 84 (1983–4), pp. 151–4.

no subject was part of the world. In fact, however, there is good reason aside from this for thinking that the metaphysical 'I' in the *Tractatus* ought not to be conceived as a thinking, representing subject. For if we pursue this thought, which is not spelled out by Wittgenstein, we shall be able to suggest how the 'I' connects both with the general claims about language, and with the ethical pronouncements with which we began.

The prime difference between the subject in the *Tractatus* and the subject in Schopenhauer's philosophy is that while in the latter it is the unifying focal point for the multiplicity of mental states that make up experience, and hence knowledge, Wittgenstein envisages a subject whose relation to the world is essentially mediated by its possession of a language. His concern is not primarily with the question: What do I know of the world?, but with the question: How does language mean something about the world? To the extent that he is concerned with the individul subject it is primarily as a language-user who partakes of the relation of language to the world; hence it is only derivatively from this relation that the 'I' can enter into philosophy. As we have seen, the 'I' enters into philosophy in that 'the world is my world'; but the world is my world only in that my language limits the world, and this is so, I suggested, by virtue of a structural isomorphism that shows itself between the world and *the* language which is the one I understand.

The 'I' is supposed to enter into philosophy in a 'non-psychological' way. Psychology deals with facts about the processes of thought, and so on, but Wittgenstein is quite clear (despite the surface appearance of 'the human soul' in 5. 641) that none of the propositions concerning these facts needs to make reference to any unitary entity that could be called the soul, or the 'I':

It is clear . . . that '*A* believes that *p*', '*A* has the thought that *p*', and '*A* says *p*' are of the form ' "*p*" says *p*': and here it is not a question of a correlation of a fact with an object, but rather of the correlation of facts through correlation of their objects (5. 542).

This shows too that the soul—the subject, etc.—as it is conceived in today's superficial psychology, is a non-entity (5. 5421).

A thought, as Wittgenstein explained somewhat inadequately to Russell, is composed of 'psychical constituents' that have 'the same sort of relation to reality as words'. (He adds: 'What those constituents are I don't know', and clearly he does not care either, since 'It would be a matter of psychology to find out.')[19] What all this shows is that Wittgenstein is quite content to account for thinking, and, one presumes, everything that Schopenhauer would have called *Vorstellung* or representation, in terms of relationships pertaining within the world between different sets of facts. So despite his use of Schopenhauer's terminology, images, and argument in the passages following 5. 631, the 'I' that he wants to play a role in *his* philosophy has a very different function from that of Schopenhauer's subject of representation. It is not a unifying centre of experience, not the 'I that thinks', not 'that which knows all and is known by none'. Furthermore, in the *Tractatus* there is no call for a subject that acts as the source of necessary modes of connection between objects. The only law-like connections, the only necessities, are *logical*,[20] and these are supposed simply to show themselves in the structure of language.

'(This thought thrusts itself up): the thing seen *sub specie aeternitatis* is the thing seen with the whole of logical space.'[21] Though Wittgenstein does not spell it out, there is an un-mistakable coincidence between the 'mystical' view of the world as a limited whole, seen from no point within it, and the view of it which he thinks logic affords us. Logic mirrors the

---

[19] *NB* Appendix III, pp. 129–30. The issues here are much more fully discussed by Hacker, *Insight and Illusion* (2nd edn.), pp. 83–6, and by Pears, 'Wittgenstein's Treatment of Solipsism'.

[20] See 6. 3–6. 3751. It is has been argued with some plausibility by A. Phillips Griffiths that the structure of Wittgenstein's case for the elimination of all necessary connections other than those of logic also shows the influence of Schopenhauer. In *VW*, the four kinds of necessary connection that Schopenhauer discerns, each corresponding to a distinct expression of the principle of sufficient reason, are: physical (causal), logical, mathematical, moral. It appears to be something like these supposed forms of necessity that Wittgenstein discusses; but the correspondence is not exact. Schopenhauer's 'logical' necessity is an epistemic notion (see *VW* pp. 171 (226–7) and 121 (156)); and his 'moral' necessity concerns the connection between action and its antecedents, not the connection between willing and its effects, which is what preoccupies Wittgenstein (see A. Phillips Griffiths, 'Wittgenstein on the Fourfold Root of the Principle of Sufficient Reason', in *Proceedings of the Aristotelian Society*, suppl. vol. 1976, pp. 1–20).

[21] *NB* p. 83.

structure of the world without concern for particular facts. All facts are, from the point of view of logic, of equal value (cf. 6. 41). But that point of view is available to me to the extent that, as a language-user, I picture the world in a way which embodies or shows logical structure. Wittgenstein's sublime and surely drastically over-ambitious thought—the 'point of the book'—is that by making clear to myself that I can occupy this logical standpoint towards the world as a whole, without preference to any fact or object over all others, I can come to 'see the world aright' in a profound ethical sense. It is the 'I' as possessor of the a logic-manifesting language that is the limit of the world, and hence capable of the view *sub specie aeternitatis*, the possession of which constitutes the 'good life'.

To support this interpretation, let us look at the central place occupied in Wittgenstein's conception of the 'I' by his description of it as 'the bearer of good and evil', or (6. 423) 'the will as bearer of the ethical'. In the *Notebooks* Wittgenstein is much troubled by the problem of good and evil. He finds it hard to reach a settled view, continually asking himself questions and on occasion chiding himself for making 'crude errors'. One problem that seems to haunt him is whether willing can alter the world at all. The dominant view, which is also carried over directly into the *Tractatus*, is that it cannot: 'The world is independent of my will'; 'Even if everything we wish were to happen, this would be, as it were, a favour of fate'; 'The world is *given* to me, i.e. my will enters into the world entirely from outside as into something that is already complete'; 'I cannot steer the happenings of the world according to my will, but am completely powerless'.[22] In Wittgenstein's world, everything other than logical structure is accidental. The logical framework of the world remains fixed, but any single fact or occurrence could obtain independently of all others. The only kind of willing or not-willing that is appropriate if the world is like this, is a kind which takes up an attitude to the world as a whole. Wittgenstein makes a connection between this attitude and the happiness or unhappiness of one's life, and again between happy/unhappy

[22] Ibid. pp. 73, 74 (cf. *TLP* 6. 373-4).

and good/bad. Sometimes he wants to settle for Schopenhauer's solution: 'In a certain sense not wishing for anything seems to be the only good'; 'I can make myself independent of the world . . . only by renouncing any influence on what happens'; 'Supposing that someone could not activate his will, but had to suffer all the misery of this world, what then could make him happy? How can man be happy at all, since he cannot ward off the misery of this world?'—a profoundly Schopenhauerian question, which receives a Schopenhauerian answer: 'Through the life of knowledge [*Erkenntnis*]. . . . the life of knowledge is the life which is happy in spite of the misery of the world. The only life that is happy is that which can renounce the comforts of the world.'[23]

So the will on which the goodness or badness of my life hangs is what Wittgenstein calls 'an attitude of the subject to the world', adding that 'the subject is the willing subject'.[24] Hence the following important passages:

Good and evil enters only through the *subject*. And the subject does not belong to the world, but is a limit of the world.

One could say (in a Schopenhauerian way [*Schopenhauerisch*]): it is not the world of representation that is either good or evil, but the willing subject.

I am conscious of the complete unclarity of all these sentences.

According to the above then, the willing subject must be happy or unhappy, and happiness and unhappiness cannot belong to the world.[25]

And:

The representing subject is surely an empty illusion. But there is the willing subject.

If there were not the will, then there would not be that centre of the world which we call the I, and which is the bearer of ethics.

What is essentially good or evil is the I, not the world.

The I, the I is what is deeply mysterious![26]

The confessions of deep mystery and unclarity should remind

---

[23] *NB* pp. 77, 73, 81.   [24] Ibid. p. 87.
[25] Ibid. p. 79.   [26] Ibid. p. 80.

us that these are highly exploratory notebook jottings. However, Wittgenstein was prepared to inflict this same mystery, heightened by the even terser format of the *Tractatus*,[27] on the reading public, so it is legitimate to take the *Notebooks* seriously as a guide to the thoughts he may have hoped to express there. And it is tolerably clear that the 'philosophical I' that is a limit, not a part of the world is meant to be the bearer of value. It is the subject which is capable of taking an attitude towards the world as a whole. If this attitude is one of acceptance, of renunciation of any influence over, or gain from, what happens among the world's facts, then the subject can be said to partake of a happy, or a good, life. Whichever attitude is taken, the facts of the world will not alter, but according to Wittgenstein the world must then 'wax or wane as a whole' (6. 43). The significance of *everything* that is the case is profoundly altered for me by virtue of my good or bad willing towards it.[28]

The parallel with Schopenhauer here is easy to see. For Schopenhauer the 'I' that is a limit, not a part of the world is the subject of knowledge. However, this subject is ordinarily constrained to experience the world according to categories that subserve the interests of one single embodied being with the world. The subject experiences at the behest of the individual will, and in this state it is inevitably liable both to suffer and to be egoistic, placing a division between itself and the rest of the world. But by denying rather than affirming the will that subserves the individual, it can attain the pure 'life of knowledge', and come to exist as an undimmed mirror which reflects the world *sub specie aeternitatis*, first in aesthetic experience, then in leading the good life, and finally by progressing to the complete renunciation and asceticism which is said to engender a mystical view of the world as a whole. For Wittgenstein the counterpart of affirmation and denial of the will is 'good or bad willing' (6. 43). The subject of this willing is simply what he calls the 'I'. And, as I maintain, it is the same 'I' that by making a language its own, finds the structure of the whole world mirrored in itself.

---

[27] See esp. *TLP* 6. 373, 6. 374, 6. 423, 6. 43.
[28] Cf. A. Phillips Griffiths, 'Wittgenstein, Schopenhauer, and Ethics', in *Understanding Wittgenstein*, p. 107.

Simply to submit oneself to that unalterable structure of the world that shows itself in one's language is to become indifferent to any of the facts within the world. This is what Wittgenstein means by 'seeing the world aright'. He suggests with enormous boldness that it is by comprehending just what logic shows about the world that one can attain that view of it from outside that constitutes the only true happiness. If the boldness, or indeed the enormity, of this position seems too great for my interpretation to be correct, it should be borne in mind that, though not in the context of logic and language, Schopenhauer's great philosophical ambition was to say something very similar.

Thus I argue that the influence of Schopenhauer on Wittgenstein was considerable and systematic, and that reading him against this background gives a degree of overall coherence to parts of his early work which are otherwise all but inexplicable. However, it has also been apparent that Wittgenstein was neither very original, nor very clear-headed, in the way in which he took over terminology, images, and arguments from Schopenhauer, nor very eager to reveal his sources.

We shall now revert to the theme of the previous chapter: can Wittgenstein's famous remarks about the 'I' in the *Tractatus* give any more substance to the thought that we must conceive the subject as in some way external to the world of objects? It is difficult to see how they can advance the argument very much. First, his reasons, to the extent that they are clear, for wanting the 'I' to be 'not a part of the world' are so similar to Schopenhauer's as to give us no really fresh input. What we have in Wittgenstein is *another instance* of the view that since a subject is primarily something that does not encounter itself as an object among objects, it is therefore not a part of the world at all—a view which, as I have said, presupposes for its intelligibility the idealist assumption that what is in the world is co-extensive with what is an object for the subject. We also have another instance of the view that the world's reality is only to be fully grasped by being comprehended as a whole from some point of view outside of it, by a metaphysical subject that is beyond the boundary constituted by the world's facts. And finally we have another instance of the view that the subject's attaining such an external view coincides with its coming to see what is of true value and significance in life, or with a certain attitude of 'the will' towards the world.

Of course the context of these thoughts is sufficiently different from that of their Schopenhauerian counterparts that we may want to regard them as having gained in significance by their reoccurrence. But this just points to another difficulty: what Wittgenstein says about the 'I' is so hard to extricate from his views about the nature of logic and language, which in some respects are peculiar to the *Tractatus*, that it is difficult to be confident that they can exert any great abiding influence. Confidence is further diminished by a consideration of Wittgenstein's own subsequent philosophical progress, in which he completely abandoned his early views about '*the* I', to concentrate on describing how the expression 'I' was used in language. This is not the place to discuss again that important and difficult piece of philosophy; but before leaving Wittgenstein I would like to say something about one particular view which he was disposed to hold in later years, and which somewhat surprisingly was first developed in the early notebooks alongside the material we have discussed above. It is the view that willing is acting.

This is one of the most distinctively Schopenhauerian views to be found anywhere in Wittgenstein, but it conflicts dramatically with the dominant conception of the relation between self and world which Wittgenstein developed from Schopenhauerian sources also. The notion that the will is manifested in action is wholly suppressed from the published *Tractatus*, and the reason seems to be precisely its conflict with the view that the will is external to the world and can affect only its limits.[29]

What do we say of the human body if we conceive the 'I' as distinct from the body, and as a 'limit of the world'? In one strand of Schopenhauer's thought, the body is left behind as a mere 'object among objects'; in another, it is an individual manifestation of will from which one must turn away as much as possible to gain salvation. Both these (compatible) strands

[29] Here I agree with Peter Winch, 'Wittgenstein's Treatment of the Will', in *Ethics and Action*, pp. 110–29.

find an echo in Wittgenstein, who, on first formulating the thought that 'the philosophical I is not the human being, not the human body', and so on, adds the following reflections: 'The human body, however, *my* body in particular, is a part of the world among other parts of the world, among animals, plants, stones, etc. Whoever has this insight will not want to secure a privileged place in the world for his body or the human body.'[30] A month later the same thought acquires ethical significance: 'A stone, the body of an animal, the body of a human being, my body, all stand on the same level. For that reason, what happens, whether it happens from a stone or from my body, is neither good nor bad.'[31]

Paradoxically, and again parallel with Schopenhauer, Wittgenstein's 'I', in viewing the world *from outside*, comes to see that the individual human being *belongs to* the rest of the world.[32] I, as an individual subject, am capable of occupying a 'viewpoint' on the world from which I myself am revealed as merely one of the contents of the world; but to have such a viewpoint seems to presuppose something more than the position of an individual part of the world. For Schopenhauer, as for Nagel,[33] there is a tension between this demand and the facts about our life as individual active and embodied subjects. Wittgenstein, to judge from the *Tractatus*, has escaped this tension. There is no mention of the body except to deny its identity with the 'I', and no mention of human action as something occurring within the world. But there is mention of the will, of which the world is said to be completely independent (6. 373). Merely *wanting* (*wünschen*) something to be the case is connected only accidentally with whatever happens as a matter of fact (6. 374). This is consistent with the notion that the 'I' or willing subject takes up a stance towards the world as a whole, and that the only significance of willing is its showing me the whole world in a different light. In the *Notebooks* Wittgenstein wrote that it would be 'intolerable' if any part of the world (including presumably my body) should 'stand nearer to me than another'. Similarly, he

---

[30] *NB* p. 82.
[31] Ibid. p. 84.
[32] Cf. ibid. p. 85.
[33] *The View from Nowhere*, ch. 4, as discussed in Chapter 12 above.

thought, it 'must be impossible' for the will not to 'confront the world as its equivalent'.[34]

However, Wittgenstein had been led to precisely this 'intolerable' conclusion by his own discussion of willing and acting. What is the difference, he asks himself, between the will as 'bearer of good and evil'—what he primarily wants to call 'will'—and the will that 'sets the human body in motion'?[35] A person without the use of her limbs would in one sense lack a will, but could, Wittgenstein suggests, think and communicate her wants to another person who could carry them out. Our subject would then be 'in the *ethical sense* a bearer of *will*'. One problem not mentioned by Wittgenstein is how the wishes of such a person could be communicated if she were not capable of some action. Perhaps by using some form of telepathy—but then (the objection that Wittgenstein does consider), why should we not include thinking itself as 'an action of the will'? In some sense, he concludes (addressing our earlier question), it seems impossible for there to be a being that can only represent, and not will.

Later he argues that we cannot conceive the occurrence of something called an 'act of will' unless it has some, as yet ill-defined, relation to a body. We can imagine that someone wills to move their arm, and the arm does not move. But we must imagine at least that a sinew moves, or that something bodily occurs higher up the causal chain, otherwise 'we would come to the position that the act of will relates in no way at all to a body, that in other words there is no act of will in the ordinary sense of the word'.[36]

So, while on the one hand it is true that the world of facts is independent of my wanting or wishing for things to happen, Wittgenstein edges towards the establishment of a close link between willing and the body. The position he arrives at finally is that a distinction has to be made between wanting or wishing (*wünschen*), and willing (*wollen*), and that the latter is identical with acting:

The act of will is not the cause of the action, but is the action itself.

One cannot will without doing.

[34] *NB* p. 88.   [35] Ibid. pp. 76–7.   [36] Ibid. p. 86.

If the will must have an object in the world, then it can be the intended action itself.

And the will must have an object.

Otherwise we would have no foothold and could not know what we willed.

And could not will different things.

Does the willed movement not then happen just like everything that is unwilled in the world, except that it is accompanied by the will?

But it is not accompanied merely by a *wish*! But by the will.

We feel ourselves, so to speak, responsible for the movement.

My will fastens on to the world somewhere, and does not fasten on to other things.

Wishing is not doing. However, willing is doing.[37]

Clearly, if, as Wittgenstein earlier thought, the will manifested itself merely in the form of wishing that such-and-such were the case, what he said about it before[38] would be true: the world would be independent of my will because nothing guarantees the occurrence in the world of that which is wished for. But what he comes to see is that the will manifests itself also as 'willed action of the body'. The body is after all singled out among the objects as the place where my will 'grasps on to' the world. Rather than merely wanting my action to occur and watching to see whether it does, I must will it in the very doing of it; Wittgenstein speaks of the will accompanying the action in a 'compelled' sense. In contrast, a wish that accompanied my action of ϕ-ing, even if it were a wish that I should ϕ, would be gratuitous.[39] As Wittgenstein said later in *Philosophical Investigations*: 'When I raise my arm, I have *not* wished it might go up. The voluntary action excludes this wish.'[40]

His writings from the 1930s onwards return continually to the theme of will and action. Wittgenstein once refers to 'the will in the Schopenhauerian conception' in the course of a discussion of the distinction between what I do and what

---

[37] *NB* pp. 87–8.   [38] Ibid. p. 73.
[39] Ibid. p. 88.   [40] PI i, 616.

merely happens.[41] He associates Schopenhauer with the claim that the will is not any phenomenon, because there is a fundamental distinction between what I do and anything that I simply observe or experience happening. (This is half right as an interpretation of Schopenhauer, who does claim that will is wholly distinct from representation—but who also thinks that there are observable phenomenal manifestations of the will.) I shall not attempt to give a full account of Wittgenstein's later thoughts about action. In the light of our present discussion, however, it is relevant to note first that Wittgenstein consistently opposes the notion that a mental volition is necessary to account for that which is distinctive in acting; and secondly that he continues to allow in a qualified way that willing is, if anything, what we ordinarily call action: 'speaking, writing, walking, lifting a thing, imagining something. But it is also trying, attempting, making an effort,—to speak, to write, to lift a thing, to imagine something etc.'[42]

While he obviously continued to worry about the problem of willed action, Wittgenstein excluded from the *Tractatus* any such thoughts as he expressed in the notebooks. Will manifests itself there as either an ineffective wishing that something be the case, or as the 'good or bad willing' which alters the limits of the world, but not any facts. I said earlier that the view arrived at in the notebooks conflicts with the view published in the *Tractatus*. It does so because it sees willing itself as one of the facts of the world, and thereby presents great difficulty for the idea that the willing 'I', whether 'bearer of the ethical, or not, is a purely metaphysical subject, not rooted in any part of the world. Whether Wittgenstein arrived at Schopenhauer's view that willing is acting by reading Schopenhauer is a question to which we may never have a conclusive answer. But in arriving at that view he clearly experienced a tension—between it and the conception of a pure metaphysical subject that 'sees the world aright'—that is directly analogous to the central tension we found in Schopenhauer. Schopenhauer fights through to his conception of the pure, will-less, timeless subject that mirrors

---

[41] *Philosophical Grammar*, 97; passages in other writings include: *Zettel*, 576–601; *The Blue and Brown Books*, pp. 150 ff.; PI i, 611–32.

[42] PI i, 615.

the world only after explaining that as subjects we are material embodiments of will. Wittgenstein had decided in his notebooks that through expressing my will my body has a privileged status for me as a subject, which must threaten the notion of a pure, non-worldly 'I'. If he had admitted this into the *Tractatus*, his final position there would have been openly even more Schopenhauerian than it already appears. For it would have been that it is solely by denying our status as embodied subjects of willing that we attain the perspective of the metaphysical subject from which the world is 'seen aright', and in adopting which we find happiness. The alternative is to retain either the pure metaphysical subject or the bodily nature of willing, suppressing or abandoning the other. Wittgenstein appears to have resolved this highly Schopenhauerian dilemma in one way in the *Tractatus*, and in the other in his later works.

Within the confines of this book it is not possible to embrace Nietzsche's thought sufficiently to assess his many-sided debt to Schopenhauer. I shall merely indicate how some of Nietzsche's most radical views spring in part from his understanding of Schopenhauer's conceptions of the subject as willing and as knowing. That these radical views are there, further shapes the map on which we have to plot the significance of the conceptions under scrutiny. If Wittgenstein's early reaction to Schopenhauer was at one extreme of the territory, Nietzsche's, eventually, was at the other.

Nietzsche was, according to his own later description,[43] a directionless and despairing 21-year-old when he came across *The World as Will and Representation* in a second-hand bookshop. This was in 1865, five years after Schopenhauer's death. The book gave him a sense of direction, both intellectually and personally. His letters over the next few years demonstrate the fervour with which he approached Schopenhauer—whom he came to call his 'master'—and his desire to form a movement of like-minded people. As well as sharing this passion with close friends, he notes with great joy the influence of Schopenhauer on Paul Deussen, Eduard von Hartmann, and

---

[43] Quoted in Volker Spierling (ed.), *Materialien*, p. 253.

Jacob Burckhardt, while the supreme moment comes with his acquaintance with Wagner and the discovery that the great man is also a devotee of the same philosophy.[44]

It might appear from this that Nietzsche's use of Schopenhauer was solely as a spiritual guide, and that his attitude was uncritical. However, a set of notes written in 1868[45] shows that he was engaging argumentatively with the central theme of Schopenhauer's philosophy, the claim that 'the groundless, knowledge-less will reveals itself, when brought under an apparatus of representation, as world'. He argues that Schopenhauer's conception of the thing in itself is indefensible. In attempting to give content to the Kantian 'object = x', Schopenhauer succeeds in showing only that 'it = x, i.e. that he has not found it'. The attachment of the name 'will' to the thing in itself is unmotivated by the argument Schopenhauer gives for it. Moreover, he has no right to the predicates —unity, eternity (or timelessness), and freedom (groundless-ness)—which he wishes to attach to this will.

A totally obscure, inconceivable x is draped with predicates, as with bright-coloured clothes which are taken from a world alien to it, the world of appearance. Then the demand is that we should regard the surrounding clothes, that is the predicates, as the thing itself: for that's what is meant by the sentence: 'If it is yet to be objectively thought, it must borrow name and concept from an object.'[46]

Nietzsche has further points: if Schopenhauer argues for his positive account of the thing in itself on the grounds that it must contrast with the world as appearance, this is illegitimate, since even the notion of such a contrast is inapplicable to something truly unknowable. Schopenhauer, confronted with the 'riddle of the world', is left with the prospect only of a guess, hoping that in a moment of genius the right word will pass his lips: 'Could this be the word *will?*'

Nietzsche's final criticism in these early notes concerns the account of the intellect as instrument of the will. If we are to take Schopenhauer's idealism seriously, then it is only for an

---

[44] See letters in G. Colletti and M. Montinari (eds.), *Nietzsche Briefwechsel: Kritische Gesamtausgabe*, I/2, nos. 599, 625, and II/1, nos. 58, 107, 111.

[45] 'Zu Schopenhauer: Philosophische Notizen', as reprinted in Spierling (ed.), *Materialien*, pp. 255–61.

[46] Cf. ibid. p. 259.

intellect that the will manifests itself as an objective world. But then how can the will have produced the intellect as an instrument for some pre-existing end? It is in the organism that the intellect is produced. But unless the intellect existed already, no such organism could have existed as an objectification of will. These points show both that Nietzsche had understood Schopenhauer, and that he never swallowed the whole of his philosophy uncritically, even when his admiration was at its greatest height.

In 1872 Nietzsche's first book, *The Birth of Tragedy*, appeared, and two years later the essay *Schopenhauer as Educator*. These works both give Schopenhauer special importance. In the essay Schopenhauer is lauded less for his philosophical ideas than as a type of writer from whom the German world could learn. His independent, truth-seeking character, his contempt for the State, and his divergence from the stereotypical academic philosopher are particularly emphasized. In *The Birth of Tragedy*, however, a version of Schopenhauer's dichotomy between self as pure representing subject and self as will is introduced to help establish the work's central distinction: that between Apollo and Dionysus, the two Greek gods who preside over artistic productions, and who symbolize opposed poles of the human personality:

To Apollo applies in an eccentric sense what Schopenhauer says of the person caught in the veil of *Māyā* . . . 'Just as the boatman in a stormy sea boundless in every direction, rising and falling in mountains, sits in his small boat, trusting the frail craft; so in the midst of a world full of misery and suffering the individual man calmly sits, supported by and trusting in the *principium individuationis*.' It could indeed be said of Apollo that in him the unshaken trust in that *principium* and the calm sitting of the man caught up in it have received their highest expression. And one would like to call Apollo himself the noble divine image of the *principium individuationis*, whose looks and gestures radiate to us the full delight and wisdom of 'appearance' [*Schein*], along with its beauty.

In the same passage Schopenhauer has portrayed for us the tremendous awe which seizes a man when he suddenly begins to doubt the cognitive forms of appearance, when the principle of sufficient reason in any one of its versions seems to suffer an exception. If we add to this awe the ecstasy which rises up out of the innermost depth of man, and even of nature, at this same shattering of the *principium individuationis*, then we get a glimpse of the *Dionysian*, whose closest analogy is with *intoxication*. Either through the influence of a narcotic drink . . . or at the powerful approach of Spring joyously penetrating the whole of nature, Dionysian stirrings awake and in their intensification the subjective disappears to the point of complete forgetfulness of self.[47]

Two obvious comments on this passage are that its train of thought is uniquely Nietzsche's, and that at almost every turn he has learned how to express it from Schopenhauer. The work's central dichotomy applies to the Greek world, and to tragedy one aspect of the distinction we have centrally discussed: the contrast between self as individual subject of knowledge and self as the point of expression for blind, unindividuated will. This dichotomy, some vestige of which Nietzsche never gave up, was to bear great fruit, and reach a wider audience, in the writings of Thomas Mann. Nietzsche meanwhile moved on from Schopenhauer. By 1877 he was proclaiming in his letters that Schopenhauer's metaphysics was false,[48] and that all those writings that bear its stamp would soon become unintelligible. Of Paul Deussen's *Elemente der Metaphysik*, a book thoroughly imbued with Schopenhauer, Nietzsche wrote to its author that it was 'a fortunate *collection of everything which I no longer hold as true*'.[49] For the remainder of this chapter I shall examine some of the ways in which Nietzsche, in his writings from this time on, makes objections to Schopenhauer's thinking about the self and the world, and advances the themes discussed earlier in this book.

Nietzsche is greatly concerned to explain the existence of those categories of thought about the world which we, philosophers included, commonly take for granted. One of his consistent claims is that we conceive reality as we do because it is useful to do so, because it preserves us: 'a species grasps *so much* reality as to become master over it, to press it into service'.[50] We 'fabricate' our world of objects according to the laws of logic and the 'categories of reason'. The only 'criterion of truth' we should expect is what Nietzsche calls 'the *biological usefulness of a system of in principle falsification*'.[51] The fundamental

---

[47] *The Birth of Tragedy*, 1. The passage Nietzsche cites is at *W*1 p. 439 (352–3).
[48] *Briefwechsel*, II/5, no. 640.
[49] Ibid. no. 642.   [50] *WM* 480.   [51] Ibid. 584.

classifications we employ are fundamental not because they correspond with reality, but because they fulfil the most important of functions for us. Here we can see that Nietzsche is spelling out the consequences of Schopenhauer's position. If we take seriously the view that the thing in itself is unknowable, and wish to place objective reality wholly within the grasp of the modes of classification stemming from the subject, we must give up any thought of these modes of classification delivering to us a picture of the world that corresponds with a subject-transcendent reality. In that sense the world as we experience it has to be seen as a fabrication. But if we add, as Schopenhauer does, that our having the classifying, objectively experiencing minds we do is explicable biologically in terms of the will to life, we have to acquiesce in the conclusion that what we call 'reality' is a fabrication that fulfils a quite specific end for the subject. It is 'our reality', but it is real for us because of its inescapability, not because it corresponds to something with an interpretation-free existence. Nietzsche thinks that we should accept this conclusion, though the end which he sees all our classifying behaviour as fulfilling is not *life*, but *power*. What motivates us is not continuing to be alive as such ('there is much that life values more highly than life itself'), but what he calls 'mastery' over things, 'pressing them into service' ('out of the valuing itself speaks the will to power'[52]). The will to power might also be said to be the fundamental tendency to seek the greatest *effect* on the rest of the world, or 'an activity that consists in expanding a particular sphere of influence, physical or mental, as far as it can possibly go'.[53] For Nietzsche it manifests itself in every species, every class of individuals, and every individual.

Nietzsche continues to be suspicious of the notion of the 'thing in itself' or of any form of 'intelligible object'. We can conceive just enough of such a thing to know that it is inconceivable to our intellect. That there could be a thing that was something in itself once all its properties, relations, and activities had been subtracted is, for Nietzsche, a nonsensical

---

[52] *ASZ* ii, 12 ('On Self-Overcoming').
[53] Alexander Nehamas, *Nietzsche: Life as Literature*, p. 80. I am often indebted to this work in the present chapter.

suggestion.[54] Nevertheless, he sometimes speculates in a distinctly Schopenhauerian manner about the role of his central conception of the will to power:

Suppose . . . we succeeded in explaining our entire instinctive life as the development and ramification of *one* basic form of will—namely of the will to power, as *my* proposition has it; suppose all organic functions could be traced back to this will to power, and one could find in it the solution of the problem of procreation and nourishment —it is *one* problem—then one would have gained the right to determine *all* efficient force univocally as—*will to power.* The world viewed from inside, the world defined and determined according to its 'intelligible character'—it would be 'will to power' and nothing else.[55]

(See also the exclamation: '*This world is the will to power—and nothing besides!* And you yourselves are also this will to power— and nothing besides!'[56]) Nietzsche does not, and cannot consistently, say that we could think of will to power as the thing in itself. Nevertheless, he speculates that we might reach a position where will to power is viewed as *what there is.* If our need to dominate our environment explains our ordinary, and indeed our philosophical, systems of classification, we might suppose that the existence of that need in us must have a kind of priority over those systems of classification. The will to power must be 'the given' in terms of which our fabrications can be accounted for. Nietzsche is aware of the temptation to convert one's own fundamental conception of things into a 'truth' by claiming its correspondence with a reality beyond all interpretation. But rather than treating the conception *will to power* as the description of an ultimate metaphysical reality, Nietzsche must regard it too as a fabrication, its supremacy arising from its usefulness in allowing us to be in control of whatever it enables us to understand. This is to account for the primacy of one's ultimate explanatory principle in terms of that very principle itself—but it is not as such an inconsistent position. As a recent commentator on Nietzsche has put it: '[w]hat there is is always determined from a specific point of view that embodies its particular interests, needs, and values, its own will to power'; yet 'the will to power is not a general

---

[54] *WM* 558.   [55] *JGB* 36.   [56] *WM* 1067.

metaphysical or cosmological theory. On the contrary, it provides a reason why no general theory of the character of the world and the things that constitute it can ever be given.'[57]

Consistent with this line of thought, Nietzsche decisively rejects Schopenhauer's conception of the subject of knowing that can step outside of its will-bound classificatory stance towards the world:

From now on, my dear philosophers, let us guard ourselves better against the dangerous old conceptual fabrication which set up a 'pure, will-less, painless, timeless subject of knowledge'. . . . Here the demand is always for us to think of an eye that cannot be thought of at all, an eye that is supposed to have no direction, one in which the active and interpreting powers that are a condition of seeing's being a seeing *of something*, are supposed to be suppressed, or absent. Thus what is demanded here is always a nonsense and an inconceivability of an eye. There is *only* perspectival seeing, *only* perspectival 'knowing'; and the more affects we allow to have their say over something, *the more* eyes, different eyes, we are able to engage on the same thing, the more complete will be our 'concept' of this thing, the more complete our 'objectivity'.[58]

The argument here is that we could not be the kind of pure subject of knowledge which Schopenhauer requires. To be a subject is to experience *something*. To experience *something* always presupposes active interpretation on the part of the subject. Hence a subject that actively imposes no interpretation on whatever confronts it is inconceivable. So far the argument has a Kantian ring to it. However, Nietzsche accepts a modified form of Schopenhauer's own view that *how* we interpret and classify is always explicable as a manifestation of will. It is our 'affects' which interpret;[59] or, elsewhere: 'It is our needs that interpret the world; our drives and their For and Against.'[60] Consequently the subject is never an undimmed mirror of the world. In *every* experience of something, any subject can achieve only a partial reflection—a perspective on the world that is limited by its own drives and affects. Hence, though Nietzsche allows himself a conception of 'objectivity', it is radically different from that to which Schopenhauer aspires—to be understood 'not as "disinterested contemplation

---

[57] Nehamas, *Nietzsche*, pp. 81, 80.
[58] *Gen.* iii, 12.   [59] Ibid.   [60] *WM* 481.

[*Anschauung*]" . . . but as the capacity to have one's For and Against *in one's control*, and to cast them off and on: so that one knows precisely how to make the *variety* of one's perspectives and affect-interpretations useful for knowledge'.

The latter notion is radically new, but it has emerged out of thinking with a solid Schopenhauerian basis. If (*a*) the real world is what falls within our subjective modes of classification, and (*b*) what Nietzsche calls our 'For and Against'—the value things have in fulfilling or failing to fulfil our needs and drives—fundamentally determines those modes of classification; and if (*c*) a subject to which (*a*) and (*b*) do not apply is inconceivable—then there is no possibility of *objective* experience, if this is understood as a state of which one is the subject, but which is attained only by transcending one's own need- and drive-related schemes of classification. Here (*a*) and (*b*) are modifications of Schopenhauer's theories of representation and will, while (*c*) is an argued denial of Schopenhauer's notion of the pure subject of knowing.

Nietzsche's conclusion is not that there is no objectivity. Objectivity cannot be reached by escaping from will; but, he suggests, by affirming it however it manifests itself in one, by multiplying the limited perspectives one can achieve on any object, and by somehow *controlling* one's 'For and Against', one can aspire to objectivity in the only genuine sense that is left. The idea seems to be that by recognizing one's classifications of reality to be mere partial interpretations whose origins are found in drives within oneself, one opens the door to a way of progressing beyond partiality, or at least of mastering it. That *my* way of understanding the world can encompass a multiplicity of perspectives supposedly frees me from the tyranny of a single, partial perspective which I have not recognized for what it is.

However, it is crucial to this idea that I affirm all the drives and needs which Nietzsche holds to determine my interpretation of reality. I cannot claim a perspective as mine unless I embrace as mine the will that shapes its scheme of classification. Thus Nietzsche's conception of objectivity coincides with another aspect of his conception of the will to power. For he believes that greatness of character is to be achieved by the affirmation and harnessing of all one's drives and affects, however much in conflict they are.[61] This is the path which can take humanity beyond itself to something higher, the *Übermensch*. While Schopenhauer aspired to a will-free state of passive objectivity and painlessness for the human subject, Nietzsche may be said to aspire to the reverse: an active affirmation and harnessing of will which explicitly includes among its desiderata the embracing of any resulting pain and destructiveness.[62] In offering respectively the safety of total denial and the greatness of total affirmation, both Schopenhauer and Nietzsche produce a kind of therapeutic vision which attempts to show human beings that what they are is far from desirable, and that they can become in some sense better. In both cases, the therapies may strike us as worse than the condition they treat, which is after all the ordinary human condition. Yet their positions are intelligible as responses to the same set of problems of the self.

The other trend in Nietzsche's thought that is germane to our discussion concerns the overall conception of a subject, of an 'I' that thinks, knows, and wills. However problematic we have found this conception, we have not asked so far whether it is one that we should jettison altogether. Of all philosophers, Nietzsche poses this question in its starkest form.

Nietzsche seems unavoidably to prefigure Wittgenstein in his suggestion that those who believe in a *substance* as referent of 'I' make an error that arises from misplaced trust in grammar.[63] Nietzsche holds too that the very notion of substance 'is a consequence of the concept of the subject: not the reverse!'[64] In his view, we come to think of there being enduring things, as distinct from properties and activities, only as a result of our prior conviction that we ourselves are something over and above our own properties and activities. Material things and thinking things are equally fictional, the former fiction depending on the latter. I shall not discuss this claim of dependence; what concerns us here is the notion of the subject, about which Nietzsche says: 'Hitherto one believed as ordinary people do, that in "I think" there was something of immediate certainty, and that this "I" was the given *cause* of thought . . . However habitual and indispensable this fiction may have become by now—that in itself proves

---

[61] Cf. *WM* 966, 928.   [62] Cf. *JGB* 44; *WM* 702, 1027.
[63] Cf. *JGB* 54.   [64] *WM* 485.

nothing against its imaginary origin: a belief can be a condition of life and nevertheless false.'[65] Our belief in an 'I' that thinks, or as Nietzsche recasts it, an 'I' that is what brings about thinking ('the *cause* of thought'), may be so useful as to be indispensable. We would no doubt say this too of our beliefs in time, space, and motion; but in these cases, Nietzsche remarks bitingly, we could admit their *necessity* 'without feeling compelled to grant them absolute reality'.[66] They are necessary only in the sense that we could be masters over nothing, not even sufficiently to survive, unless we held these beliefs. If we admit this, why make an exception in the case of the 'I'? There can be no reason to see the 'I' as anything other than a fiction we have grown used to, and that we are powerless to give up.

Once again, it is against the background of Schopenhauer's philosophy that the dialectical movement of Nietzsche's thought is best appreciated. Schopenhauer agrees that space and time are subjective classifications, and that (at the very least) there is no warrant for attributing space and time to reality 'in itself'. He agrees too that biological usefulness ultimately determines the nature of the classifications made by a subject. He rejects the notion that there is any immaterial substance that thinks. Nevertheless, he holds on to the conception of the subject as distinct from its states and activities. All such occurrences are the objects of the subject's awareness. It itself is a pure non-object which somehow remains when abstraction is made from all specific objects, all specific states and activities. Nietzsche's point is that to think of ourselves in this way is an interpretation like any other, serving particular ends.

People have often wondered whether in place of the 'I think', Descartes was entitled only to 'there is thinking' as his certainty. It has been argued recently that this objection is not ultimately coherent.[67] The point I wish to stress, however, is that Nietzsche's attempt to undermine the 'I' that thinks is different from this. For he suggests that what is *predicated* of the 'I' in the traditional formula is equally a fabrication:

---

[65] Ibid. 483.
[66] Ibid. 487.
[67] See Bernard Williams, *Descartes: The Project of Pure Enquiry*, pp. 95–101.

'Thinking', as epistemologists conceive it, simply does not occur: it is a quite arbitrary fiction, arrived at by selecting one element from the process and eliminating all the rest, an artificial arrangement for the purpose of intelligibility.

The 'spirit', something that thinks . . . this conception is a second derivative of that false introspection which believes in 'thinking'; first an act is imagined which simply does not occur, 'thinking', and secondly a subject-substratum in which every act of thinking, and nothing else, has its origin: that is to say, both the deed and the doer are fictions.[68]

So, Nietzsche is not attempting to hold that thinking occurs but is wrongly predicated of an 'I' that thinks. Rather, more radically, his view is that the pair of concepts *I* and *think* must be rejected together. There is one fiction here, he is claiming, which is of a thing and of those distinct acts predicated of it.

There are two important questions to ask here: Why is 'thinking' a fiction?, and: How can we undeceive ourselves, and start believing in neither thoughts nor thinkers? Nietzsche's answer to both will require some explication of 'the process' from which he says some features are arbitrarily selected to produce the conception of 'thinking'. The process in question is, for Nietzsche, ultimately the will to power. It is the functioning of a multiplicity of drives or forces, each of which is directed towards greater effect on, mastery over, whatever it encounters. The course of experience—if we are allowed that term—is always characterized by its content having, in some degree, a positive or negative value from the point of view of each of the drives. The content of experience is always interpretation-bound, but 'One may not ask "Who then interprets?", for the interpretation is itself a form of the will to power'.[69] For Nietzsche, no segment of our mental life is correctly described as an instance of an activity called 'thinking'. Its content is ever-changing, multiple in its sources, often internally conflicting, and always value-related —propelled by our needs and drives. To conceive of there being many discrete, separable episodes, each of which has its content, as it were, entirely within itself, and all of which are commonly classifiable as 'thinking' (or for that matter

---

[68] *WM* 477.   [69] Ibid. 556.

'willing', which as a general psychological classification he also rejects) is thus, for Nietzsche, a denial of the complex interweaving and evolving flux that he finds our mental life to be. I have striven merely to make Nietzsche's view clear, and to show how it addresses the two questions posed: Why is the conception of 'thinking' a fiction?, and: How otherwise should we conceive what occurs? I make no claim to defend one view or the other as a superior view of our mental life.

We are to rid ourselves, then, of the notion that there is a type of event such as an 'act of thinking', or an 'act of will', and of the prejudice that individual episodes of our mental life are, regardless of their content, classifiable as events of a certain type. Where does this leave the notion of the subject? We will not require a subject *of thinking*, nor a subject *of willing*. There is merely a continuous process of becoming, with overlapping multiple strands whose nature, it must be said, remains fairly obscure. There is nothing that is conceptually distinguishable from this flux which we have to think of as bringing it about, or as doing the thinking. There is nothing that interprets, no subject that imposes a unitary set of classifications. Rather:

perhaps it is just as permissible to assume a multiplicity of subjects, whose interaction and struggle is the basis of our thought and our consciousness in general? A kind of aristocracy of 'cells' in which dominion resides? to be sure, an aristocracy of equals, used to ruling jointly and understanding how to command?

My hypothesis: The subject as multiplicity.[70]

Nietzsche's claim, then, is that if we remove the classification of parts of our experience as acts of thinking, acts of willing, and so on, we remove the need for a single agent to perform these acts. If it is better to interpret the mind as the perpetual state of 'becoming' of a multiplicity of sub-personal, power-directed drives, we falsify when we conceive it as a unitary centre in which consciousness concentrates, and out of which action emanates.

In the case of action, Nietzsche's view has far-reaching consequences from which he does not flinch:

---

[70] Ibid. 490.

Just as ordinary people separate lightning from its flashing, and take the latter as an *action*, as an effect of a subject called lightning, so popular morality separates strength from the manifestation of strength, as if behind the strong there were a neutral substrate which was *free* to manifest strength or not. But there is no such substrate; there is no 'being' behind the doing, the acting, the becoming; 'the doer' is merely a fictional addition to the doing—the doing is everything.[71]

Consequently, it is foolish to expect that strength will not manifest itself as strength. The attempt to found morality on the assumption of responsibility for actions must fail, according to Nietzsche, since that to which responsibility is supposed to be ascribed—the agent—is a fiction. There is only 'drive, will, activity', manifesting itself in varying degrees of strength, and achieving different degrees of mastery. With perfect consistency Nietzsche locates the origin of the belief in free will and responsibility in the drive of the weak to dominate over the naturally strong: 'The doctrine of the will was essentially invented for the purposes of punishment, that is, of the *will-to-find-guilty*. . . . People were thought "free" in order to be judged and punished—so that they could become *guilty*: and as a consequence every action *had* to be thought of as willed, and the origin of every action as lying in consciousness.'[72] If the will to power explains all our behaviour, then it also explains and, Nietzsche thinks, explains away, our belief in ourselves as conscious centres of willing in the more traditional sense.

   Briefly, we must ask whether Nietzsche's proposed dissolution of the self into a multiplicity of drives—whatever these are supposed to be precisely—is even coherent. Suppose one were prepared to accept that all our supposed objective knowledge is perspectival, that we cannot 'mirror the world' without imposing selective classifications on it, and that the selection of those classifications is always explicable as fulfilling some end of growth, mastery, or enhanced capacity to influence that which is other than oneself. Still, must there not be a single subject *of* the perspective, *of* the classification, *of* the drive to mastery? Nietzsche explicitly tells us not: it is needs, drives, instincts, their For and Against, the will to power, and so on,

---

[71] *Gen.* i, 13.   [72] *Twilight of the Idols*, vi ('The four great errors'), 7.

that interprets. There are only interpretations, but there is no 'I' that is the subject of the interpretation. The 'I' is a fiction whose author is an aggregate of manifestations of the will to power.

This is unsettling—but why exactly? One problem, which takes us back to Kant, is that the very existence of a picture of an objective world, such as we have, whether partial or indeed a complete fabrication, seems to presuppose a single conscious-ness in whose possible experience all elements of that world are united. Nietzsche appears merely to deny this, without convincing us of its falsity. It might further be suggested that the notion of needs or drives without a subject is dubious. Yet one can speak of my brain's need for oxygen, and, not too misleadingly, of the drive of my entire body to secure a sufficient flow of oxygen. This, once again, is close to Schopenhauer's notion of the 'blind' will. Other drives, such as the drive to eat or to have sexual intercourse, are not subjectless, yet here there is a sense in which I make *mine* what otherwise exists without presupposing a self-conscious 'I'.

But how can Nietzsche account for *my* desiring sex? He has to say that there is at work a sub-personal manifestation of will to power, a drive directed towards an increase of a form of power, whose success involves pleasure. But *whose* power, *whose* pleasure? What seeks and is gratified is merely the sub-personal drive itself, he will reply. Yet, clearly, even if there is a sub-personal drive at work here, I can appropriate it as mine, and any resulting pleasure can only be mine. So even drives that have a sub-personal basis *can* be personal drives, and some associated states such as pleasure (not to mention desire or intention) can, it seems, *only* be personal. Can a collection of sub-personal drives fabricate a unitary self that comes to regard those drives as its own? Or must there be a presupposed unitary self as author of the fiction? If the latter, then Nietzsche must hold paradoxically that I am a fiction that is the author of itself; if the former, that I am a fiction whose author is a sub-personal complex of drives, in which case whence comes the unity that is required for the production of the single coherent story of one self and the world of its experience?

Nietzsche's answer to the last question is that the body

provides the unity of my drives. In *Thus Spoke Zarathustra* we find the highly Schopenhauerian thought that 'The creating body created spirit for itself as the hand of its will', and the claim that the true self [*das Selbst*] is the body: ' "I" say you and are proud of this word. But the greater thing is what you will not believe in—your body and its great wisdom: it does not say I, but does I.' This suggests that it is the integration of drives within one *organism* that gives me a truly unified self. The ability to say 'I', to think of myself self-consciously as the subject of experience and action, presupposes the existence of a pre-conscious organic unity of drives, is explicable as part of the fulfilment of those drives, and is far from being the most important feature of oneself: 'Your self laughs at your I and its proud leaps. "What are these leaps and flights of thought to me?" it says to itself. A roundabout way to my ends. I am the leading-string of the I, and the prompter of its concepts.'[73]

That this chapter has left many open ends is in a way a testimony to the enduring philosophical importance of Schopenhauer. Wittgenstein in the *Tractatus* seeks a truly perspectiveless account of the world. The world is mirrored without remainder in language; seeing its structure in this way, *sub specie aeternitatis*, provides us both with objectivity and with the clue to value. But the 'I' whose view this is must be the purely philosophical 'I'—the metaphysical subject, excluded from any place within the world. It is just such a subject, metaphorically conceived by both Schopenhauer and Wittgenstein as an unseen eye on the world, that Nietzsche banishes as 'a nonsense and an inconceivability of an eye'. No account of the world, for him, can be perspectiveless. No value can be absolute. Needs, drives, ends, affects are ineliminable, and pervasively determine all interpretations, beyond which there is no world 'in itself' for them to match or fall short of. Objectivity has to be redefined as the maximizing and harnessing of one's indwelling will to power; value likewise. The self is either a mere interpretation—a fabrication with usefulness for our preservation—or it must be accounted a mere sum of manifestations of will to power, unified only by their occurrence in one organism.

[73] *ASZ* i, 4 ('Of the despisers of the body').

It is clear by now that in the trains of thought which led to these extreme and contrasting views, Schopenhauer was the chief catalyst. From Schopenhauer's standpoint, the two resolve in opposite ways the tension he deliberately generates between self as pure, unitary subject of knowledge, and self as organic, vulnerable, and destructive manifestation of will. Yet the attempted resolutions, for all their contrast, are equally troubling. Neither appears to leave room for what each of us ordinarily conceive ourselves to be: a single, unified centre of self-conscious thought and action existing at one location within the material order of things. This deepening of the problem ought not, I think, to reflect badly on Schopenhauer. We have accepted Kant's view of the self as a progress beyond Descartes and Hume, and Schopenhauer's view as a significant reappraisal of Kant. It is an apposite, if disruptive, intervention in a wider debate, and one which had a profound effect on the debate's future. Those who in this century have worked on such issues in those philosophical traditions which claim Wittgenstein or Nietzsche as ancestors have not thought it necessary very often to debate directly with Schopenhauer. Nevertheless, he is a secure part of their own history.

14

Conclusions

WE have seen that Schopenhauer's philosophical exploration of the relations between self and world has a dramatic, or dynamic, structure within which the same general theme is illuminated from many angles. The unity of his thought is a unity built out of tensions carefully sustained: between self as subject and self as object, self as knower and self as actor, self as rational centre of consciousness and self as 'blind' organism. Looked at in this light, his work is a brilliant achievement. Yet he set out to persuade us of the truth of a single thought in all its ramifications, and to produce a lasting metaphysical edifice that would embrace coherently all the tensions we have discerned. It is in the philosophical management of his insights, their deployment as a fully integrated system, that Schopenhauer very often falls down.

It is not mere ineptitude that brings this about. If we consider in strategic terms what Schopenhauer was trying to do, the failure of integration comes to seem inevitable. He was attempting to subvert some of the central features of Kant's transcendental idealism, using mainly the ruling conceptions of that very position itself.[1] Having accepted as fundamental the dichotomies of subject and object, representation and thing in itself, it is difficult to go on to show that we can know what we are in ourselves, and that the primary relation of self to world is not at all that of the objectively knowing 'I' of Kant's epistemology. With the odds thus against him, Schopenhauer's greatness partly lies in failing so elegantly in pursuit of his task, and in persevering so ruthlessly in it that he comes near to success.

At the same time, he shows a strange degree of blindness in not questioning his initial assumptions when massive inconsistencies threaten, and in sometimes not even seeing them

---

[1] For this view, cf. Patrick Gardiner, *Schopenhauer*, pp. 301–2.

threatening. That awareness of our own bodies which we have as a component of our awareness of willing, so memorably captured by Schopenhauer, suggests that the Kantian model of the pure 'I' confronted by its manifold of objective representations is seriously inadequate in accounting for our experience in general. Yet Schopenhauer subordinates his insight to the terminology of subject and object which he should be leaving behind: the self as willing is a special kind of object, distinct from, and apprehended by, the self as pure subject of knowledge. That 'the world as representation' is dependent on the need-related structure and functioning of a particular species of organism, as Schopenhauer maintains, ought at least to raise the question of whether it was right at the outset to equate it with empirical reality. But Schopenhauer carries on insisting that the whole empirical world is subject-dependent, even when he has identified the subject with the functioning of an organism's brain.

Then again, although he would probably never have conceived his doctrine of the will at all were it not for the dichotomy of representation and thing in itself, it does hamper Schopenhauer at crucial points in his argument. Having established that the subject that applies its Kantian categories achieves only a limited perspective on the world, determined by the particular manner in which the will to life has manifested itself in one kind of cognitive apparatus, Schopenhauer's argument really demands that a true Platonic knowledge of 'what is' can be attained by casting off those categories altogether. Unfortunately, however, he cannot say that this casting-off lends the subject access to the thing in itself, since that is unknowable. But nor is it Kantian empirical representations that suffice. For the kind of pure knowledge Schopenhauer wants, the Kantian conceptions of representation and thing in itself are both manifestly unsuited.

Finally, when it comes to his account of action, Schopenhauer needs to be able to say that the Kantian realm of spatio-temporal representations cannot explain our knowledge of ourselves as embodied agents. But given the initial dichotomy of representation and thing in itself, this amounts to holding that action gives us knowledge of the thing in itself. This, indeed, is what Schopenhauer says; it is the 'key' to his metaphysics as a whole. Yet the willing of which we are 'internally' aware—as a genuine mental state of ours inseparable from its manifestation in the body—is at least a type of event, and is something known to us. There seems to be no ground for assuming here that we are touching the tip of the atemporal, unknowable thing in itself.

To Schopenhauer the authority of Kant in certain respects was irresistible. No more than any other thinker could he avoid accepting a framework of assumptions from an earlier source; and the great Kant is perhaps particularly hard to shake off once one has internalized his central ideas. So we cannot lightly suggest that Schopenhauer could have bypassed transcendental idealism altogether. At the same time, Schopenhauer was well aware, because of the deficiencies his immediate predecessors had found, that Kant could serve only as a starting-point from which new ways must be found. I am not suggesting that his system of thought, with its mix of Kantian and anti-Kantian elements, was inevitable, merely that it is understandable how he should have been caught in the half-way position which, I allege, explains many of his larger-scale inconsistencies.

Because he undertook this task of undermining Kant with Kantian tools, and because as a result he played his part in shaping some of the new preoccupations of the late nineteenth and twentieth centuries, Schopenhauer provides us with a unique opportunity. If we want to confront Kant's notion of the self with embodiment, action, the living organism, environmental adaptation, the unconscious, sexuality, Schopenhauer's philosophy is an arena in which we can do so most pointedly. We will not call upon his metaphysical system to solve the resultant problems, but to guide us towards their identification and articulation. By showing us how polymorphous the problem of 'the self and the world' can be, he enables us to redraw the map on which we plot our own philosophical questions.

So, what position have we reached? I offer the following as a summary of the main Schopenhauerian points that can be abstracted from our whole discussion. I suggest that points 1–7 and point 10 are true; the others I have presented as intelligible claims which raise substantive issues and provoke further debate.

1. All experience requires a subject, which is self-conscious, and conceives itself to be the unifying point, or centre, of a multiplicity of experiential states.

2. Thinking of oneself as such a subject does not require the identification of oneself by the kind of criteria that are applicable in the case of thought or experience of empirical objects.

3. Thinking of oneself as a subject of experience presupposes that one regards oneself as something that is not exhausted simply by the totality of the experiences one has—rather, one must think of oneself as what has them.

4. We understand ourselves also as objects within the empirical world.

5. Neither the 'subjective' nor the 'objective' understanding that we have of ourselves is complete; yet harmonizing the two into one account is difficult to conceive, since each claims explanatory primacy over the other.

6. The problems of personal identity and of free will both rest ultimately on this dichotomy of viewpoints.

7. The close connection between the mental state of willing and the willed movement of the body presupposes the embodiment of the 'I' inasmuch as it is an 'I' that wills.

8. We will, act, or strive towards ends primarily; our capacity for knowledge is derivative from our capacity to will.

9. The classificatory schemes that characterize our cognitive apparatus are explicable in terms of the ends that they serve for the survival and increased prospering of ourselves as organisms.

10. Many of the ends that our behaviour and bodily constitution subserve are pre-rational and unconscious.

11. Wholly objective knowledge of the world is possible only if we cease to apply to experience the classifications on which our existence and prospering as organisms depends.

12. When we cease to apply these classifications we must

regard ourselves as simply a pure knowing subject which is not identifiable with any individual item within the world.

In some sense I am both subject and object—but Schopenhauer is right to think that the simple subject–object model of experience does not provide us with an adequate account of the self. I have to conceive myself as part of the world I objectively experience, but without being for myself a mere empirical 'object among objects'. My body is an object among objects, but it is encompassed in my 'inner' awareness of willing. I have to think of myself as a unified centre of consciousness which I do not 'confront objectively'. (It must be that something about me is not within 'the world as I find it'.) Yet I am also the subject of states which involve my having a body.

According to Schopenhauer, I am the kind of subject I am because of the kind of object I am. We should ask ourselves, as he does, how my being an organism with certain essential pre-conscious drives influences the imposition of categories which I must make if I am to be a subject of objective experience at all. One answer that it is tempting to give is that understanding ourselves as organic products of nature makes us recognize the perspectival nature of all our experience. My capacities for forming beliefs about, and acting upon, the world are conditional on the workings of a particular organism, and those workings are as they are because of what they achieve for the species of organisms to which this one belongs. So (the thought goes), I can only ever achieve a 'worm's-eye view', however sophisticated a worm I become.[2]

Yet there remain two mysteries, which it would be better to confess are mysteries to us. Namely, that 'blind' nature should produce a self-conscious 'I'-saying being; and that this being should be endowed with the capacity to understand itself, at least in principle, to be a product of 'blind' nature. The dark, impersonal will manifests itself as conscious intellect, which

---

[2] No such line of thought as is sketched here could work if it were true both that our cognitive abilities have enabled us to survive, and that their having done so would be a guarantee of their being a channel for objective truth about the world. For suggestive scepticism about both these claims, see Thomas Nagel, *The View from Nowhere*, pp. 78–9.

can illuminate its own origins in the will—this is Schopenhauer's central thought about the self, which, although
mysterious, seems to contain a fundamental truth about
ourselves. The problem, however, is that the ability to
understand oneself—this self-conscious centre of experience
—as a product of nature can lead us in two directions, either
towards an undermining of the status of the subject, or to a
loss of the sense of rootedness in the world.

There is no *self* as such, we may sometimes be inclined to
think, only a great number of facts about bodily states and
processes, including possibly something like the 'drives' of
which Nietzsche talks, organized to function, for the most
part, towards collective ends. At best I am a fabrication
thrown up by these sub-personal processes. Yet this 'fabrication'
is one that can be responsible for understanding itself not to be
explanatorily basic. And only a unified, self-conscious consciousness could attain such an understanding, since such an
understanding could only exist for some being that can claim
it as its own. If having or being a self amounts to having or
being a unified, self-conscious centre of experience, then even
thinking that the self is in some sense a fabrication presupposes
having or being a self.

On the other hand, our understanding ourselves in principle
to be products of 'blind' nature may be thought to show that
we can transcend the perspectival limitation of a particular
organism or species.[3] A cat's perceptions are circumscribed by
the mechanisms that have developed in its species, and are
explicable, we suppose, in terms of the functions that they
perform for that kind of organism. But a cat, or any animal,
cannot understand itself objectively to be an organism, a
natural product, whose perceptions are so circumscribed. As
Rilke put it:

<blockquote>
sein Sein ist ihm
unendlich, ungesfasst und ohne Blick
auf seinen Zustand, rein, so wie sein Ausblick.[4]
</blockquote>

[3] In *The View from Nowhere*, Nagel uses a similar reflection to cast doubt on the
possibility of explaining our cognitive capacities in terms of environmental
adaptation.

[4] 'its own being for it / is infinite, inapprehensible, / unintrospective, pure, like its

The animal looks purely 'out of' nature, not at it. We, by contrast, in comprehending nature and ourselves as part of it, are paradoxically forced to consider ourselves as separate from that which we observe:

> Und wir: Zuschauer, immer, überall,
> dem allen zugewandt und nie hinaus![5]

I am, and must recognize myself to be, the *subject* of a single, objective understanding of nature, in which facts about 'the human body, and the human soul with which psychology deals' are, in principle, included. It seems that to be able to understand myself as a part of nature on a part with the rest, I have to be able to transcend the 'worm's-eye view'. Yet how can I do this while being a finite member of a particular species? Occupancy of a partial perspective upon reality seems a necessity for me.

Thus the conflict that gives Schopenhauer the most trouble as a systematic metaphysician, and which gives his thought its dynamism, is a very fundamental philosophical problem. There seems little choice but to think of oneself as a unitary, objectively experiencing intellect, and as a product of organic nature. But how, in one coherent theory, do we account for our looking 'at' and 'out of' nature at the same time? If I am a natural product, looking 'out of' nature, my intellect ought to have a natural explanation too. But if I truly am an objectively experiencing intellect, all the natural facts and explanations in the world apparently do not add up to the single being in whose thinking they are comprehended. Schopenhauer's genius is shown by his unequalled ability to dwell in, elaborate, and give human significance to this most human of problems.

The figures whom we regard as great philosophers are often paradigms for us of what philosophy is, what its aims are, how it should be conducted. In this sense, Schopenhauer is unlikely, I think, ever to be placed among the greatest, at any rate by philosophers. His grasp of his methods is too insecure,

---

outgazing.' (*Duino Elegies*, Eighth Elegy, ll. 38–40, translation by J. B. Leishman and Stephen Spender.)

[5] Ibid. ll. 66–7: 'And we, spectators always, everywhere, / looking at, never out of, everything!'

while his lack of self-criticism, and perhaps even his kind of elegance, are too great. But he is a brilliant and wide-ranging thinker, with a keen eye for deep philosophical problems, a talent for presenting them crisply and memorably, and above all a great courage in holding on to them. In his account of the will he is unique; and few, if any, have shown such awareness of the complex set of questions that arise in the attempt to explain the nature of the self and its relation to the world. We cannot accept his metaphysical solution, any more than we can accept that of Descartes, Leibniz, Berkeley, or Plato. Yet as an heir and critic of Kant and the immediate post-Kantian philosophers he occupies a position we should not neglect, especially in the light of the overwhelming importance currently afforded to Kant. And to the extent that twentieth-century philosophy still needs to come to terms with Wittgenstein and Nietzsche, it often has to do so—I have argued—within the context of questions that Schopenhauer raised most pointedly. We partly choose our history in the light of what we now conceive and re-conceive philosophy to be, and, in turn, we partly owe such conceptions to the way we have written its history. I have suggested both that Schopenhauer is part of our own past, and that we should encompass him in our living sense of that past, as an important articulator of great problems which, in some manner, we still need to address.

BIBLIOGRAPHY

Works by Schopenhauer

(a) German editions

Schopenhauers sämtliche Werke, ed. Arthur Hübscher, 7 vols. (3rd edn.; Wiesbaden: Brockhaus, 1972).
Zürcher Ausgabe: Werke in zehn Bänden, 10 vols. (Zürich: Diogenes, 1977).
Der handschriftliche Nachlass, ed. Arthur Hübscher, 5 vols. (Frankfurt am Main: Kramer, 1970).
Arthur Schopenhauer: Mensch und Philosoph in seinen Briefen, ed. Arthur Hübscher (Wiesbaden: Brockhaus, 1960).

(b) Translations

On the Basis of Morality, trans. E. F. J. Payne (Indianapolis and New York: Bobbs-Merrill, 1965).
On the Freedom of the Will, trans. Konstantin Kolenda (1st edn.; Indianapolis and New York: Bobbs-Merrill, 1960; 2nd edn.; Oxford: Blackwell, 1985).
On the Will in Nature, trans. Mme Karl Hillebrand (London: Bell, 1915).
Parerga and Paralipomena, 2 vols., trans. E. F. J. Payne (Oxford: Clarendon Press, 1974).
On The Fourfold Root of the Principle of Sufficient Reason, trans. E. F. J. Payne (La Salle, Ill.: Open Court, 1974).
The World as Will and Representation, 2 vols., trans. E. F. J. Payne (New York: Dover, 1969).

Works by Other Authors

Adickes, Erich, *Kant und das Ding an sich* (Berlin: Pan, 1924).
Allison, H. E., 'Kant's Critique of Berkeley', *Journal of the History of Philosophy* 11 (1973), pp. 43–63.
—— 'The Non-Spatiality of Things in Themselves for Kant', *Journal of the History of Philosophy* 14 (1976), pp. 313–21.

—— 'Things in Themselves, Noumena, and the Transcendental Object', *Dialectica* 32 (1978), pp. 41–76.

Ameriks, Karl, *Kant's Theory of Mind* (Oxford: Clarendon Press, 1982).

—— 'Recent Work on Kant's Theoretical Philosophy', *American Philosophical Quarterly* 19 (1982), pp. 1–24.

Anscombe, G. E. M., *Intention* (2nd edn.; Oxford: Blackwell, 1963).

—— *An Introduction to Wittgenstein's Tractatus* (4th edn.; London: Hutchinson, 1971).

Arendt, Hannah, *The Life of the Mind*, vol. 2. *Willing* (New York: Harcourt Brace Jovanovich, 1978).

Berkeley, George, *Philosophical Works*, ed. M. R. Ayers (London: Dent (Everyman), 1975).

—— *Siris*, in A. A. Luce and T. E. Jessop (eds.), *The Works of George Berkeley*, vol. 5 (London: Thomas Nelson, 1953), pp. 1–164.

Berlin, Isaiah, 'Two Concepts of Liberty', in id., *Four Essays on Liberty* (Oxford: University Press, 1969), pp. 118–72.

Bracken, H. M., *The Early Reception of Berkeley's Immaterialism* (The Hague: Martinus Nijhoff, 1965).

Copleston, Frederick, *A History of Philosophy*, vol. 7/ii. *Schopenhauer to Nietzsche* (New York: Image/Doubleday, 1963).

—— *Arthur Schopenhauer: Philosopher of Pessimism* (London: Search Press, 1975).

Dauer, Dorothea W., *Schopenhauer as Transmitter of Buddhist Ideas*, (European University Papers, Series I, vol. 15; Berne: Herbert Lang, 1969).

Davidson, Donald, 'Agency', in id., *Essays on Actions and Events* (Oxford: Clarendon Press, 1980), pp. 43–61.

di Giovanni, George, and Harris, H. S., *Between Kant and Hegel: Texts in the Development of Post-Kantian Idealism* (New York: State University of New York, 1985).

Ebeling, Hans, and Lütkehaus, Ludger (eds.), *Schopenhauer und Marx: Philosophie des Elends—Elend der Philosophie?* (Königstein/ Ts.: Hain, 1980).

Engel, S. Morris, 'Schopenhauer's Impact on Wittgenstein', *Journal of the History of Philosophy* 7 (1969), pp. 285–302; repr. in Michael Fox (ed.) *Schopenhauer: His Philosophical Achievement*, pp. 236–54.

Engelmann, Paul, *Letters from Ludwig Wittgenstein: With a Memoir* (Oxford: Blackwell, 1967).

Evans, Gareth, *The Varieties of Reference* (Oxford: Clarendon Press, 1982).

Fichte, Johann Gottlieb, *Sämtliche Werke*, ed. J. H. Fichte (Leipzig: Mayer & Müller, 1834–46).

Fichte, Johann Gottlieb, *The Science of Knowledge*, ed. and trans. Peter Heath and John Lachs (Cambridge: University Press, 1982).

Förster, Eckart, 'Kant's Refutation of Idealism', in A. J. Holland (ed.), *Philosophy: Its History and Historiography*, (Dordrecht: Reidel, 1985), pp. 287–303.

Fox, Michael (ed.), *Schopenhauer: His Philosophical Achievement* (Brighton: Harvester, 1980).

Frankfurt, Harry, 'Freedom of the Will and the Concept of a Person', *Journal of Philosophy* 68 (1971), pp. 5–20.

Freud, Sigmund, *Collected Papers*, vol. 4 (London: Hogarth Press/ Institute of Psychoanalysis, 1949).

—— 'History of the Psychoanalytic Movement', in *Historical and Expository Works on Psychoanalysis* (Pelican Freud Library, vol. 15; Harmondsworth: Penguin, 1986).

Gardiner, Patrick, *Schopenhauer* (Harmondsworth: Penguin, 1963).

—— 'Fichte and German Idealism', in Godfrey Vesey (ed.), *Idealism Past and Present*, pp. 111–26.

Geach, P. T., review of G. C. M. Colombo's translation of Wittgenstein's *Tractatus*, *Philosophical Review* 66 (1957), pp. 556–9.

Griffiths, A. Phillips, 'Wittgenstein, Schopenhauer, and Ethics', in *Understanding Wittgenstein* (Royal Institute of Philosophy Lectures, vol. 7 (1972–73); London: Macmillan, 1974), pp. 96–116.

—— 'Wittgenstein on the Fourfold Root of the Principle of Sufficient Reason', *Proceedings of the Aristotelian Society*, suppl. vol. 1976, pp. 1–20.

Hacker, P. M. S., *Insight and Illusion* (1st edn.; Oxford: University Press, 1972; 2nd edn.; Oxford: Clarendon Press, 1986).

Haffmans, Gerd (ed.), *Über Arthur Schopenhauer* (2nd edn.; Zürich: Diogenes, 1978).

Hamlyn, D. W., *Schopenhauer* (London: Routledge & Kegan Paul, 1980).

—— 'Schopenhauer on Action and the Will', in Godfrey Vesey (ed.), *Idealism Past and Present*, pp. 127–40.

—— 'Perception and Agency', in *Perception, Learning and the Self* (London: Routledge & Kegan Paul, 1983), pp. 43–56.

Hartmann, Eduard von, *The Philosophy of the Unconscious*, trans. William Chatterton Coupland (London: Kegan Paul, Trench, Trubner, 1931).

Hegel, Georg Wilhelm Friedrich, *The Difference between Fichte's and Schelling's Systems of Philosophy*, trans. H. S. Harris and Walter Cerf (Albany: State University of New York Press, 1977).

Heidegger, Martin, *Being and Time*, trans. John Macquarrie and Edward Robinson (Oxford: Blackwell, 1978).

Heller, Erich, *Thomas Mann: The Ironic German* (Cleveland, Ohio: World Publishing Co., 1961).

Hobbes, Thomas, *Leviathan* (London: Dent (Everyman), 1914).

Horkheimer, Max, *Sozialphilosophische Studien* (Frankfurt am Main: Fischer, 1972).

—— 'Die Aktualität Schopenhauers', in Max Horkheimer and Theodor W. Adorno, *Sociologica II* (Frankfurt am Main: Europ. Verlagsanstalt, 1962), pp. 124–41; trans. in Michael Fox (ed.), *Schopenhauer: His Philosophical Achievement*, pp. 20–33.

Hornsby, Jennifer, *Actions* (London: Routledge & Kegan Paul, 1980).

Hübscher, Arthur, *Schopenhauer: Biographie eines Weltbildes* (Stuttgart: Reclam, 1967).

Hume, David, *Enquiries Concerning the Human Understanding and Concerning the Principles of Morals*, ed. L. A. Selby-Bigge (3rd edn.; Oxford: Clarendon Press, 1975).

—— *A Treatise of Human Nature*, ed. L. A. Selby-Bigge (2nd edn.; Oxford: University Press, 1978).

Jacobi, Friedrich Heinrich, *David Hume über den Glauben, oder Idealismus und Realismus: Ein Gespräch*, in id., *Werke*, vol. 2 (Leipzig: Gerhard Fleischer, 1815), pp. 1–310.

Janaway, Christopher, 'The Subject and the Objective Order', *Proceedings of the Aristotelian Society* 84 (1983–4), pp. 147–65.

Janik, Allan S., 'Schopenhauer and the Early Wittgenstein', *Philosophical Studies (Ireland)* 15 (1966), pp. 76–95.

——, and Toulmin, Stephen, *Wittgenstein's Vienna* (New York: Simon & Schuster, 1973).

Jones, Ernest, *Sigmund Freud: Life and Work*, vol. 2 (London: Hogarth Press, 1955).

Kant, Immanuel, *Gesammelte Schriften*, ed. Königliche preussische Akademie der Wissenschaften (Berlin: Reimer/de Gruyter, 1903–).

—— *De mundi sensibilis atque intelligibilis forma et principiis*, in Kant, Immanuel, *Gesammelte Schriften*, vol. 2, pp. 385–419; trans. in G. B. Kerferd and D. E. Walford (eds.), *Kant: Selected Pre-Critical Writings and Correspondence with Beck* (Manchester: University Press, 1968).

—— *Grundlegung zur Metaphysik der Sitten*, ed. Karl Vorländer (Hamburg: Meiner, 1965); trans. as *Groundwork of the Metaphysic of Morals*, in H. J. Paton, *The Moral Law* (London: Hutchinson, 1948).

—— *Kant: Philosophical Correspondence 1759–99*, ed. and trans. Arnulf Zweig (Chicago: University of Chicago Press, 1970).

370   *Bibliography*

Kant, Immanuel, *Kritik der reinen Vernunft*, ed. Ramund Schmidt (Hamburg: Meiner,1971); trans. as *Immanuel Kant's Critique of Pure Reason* (London: Macmillan, 1929).
—— *Prolegomena zu einer jeden künftigen Metaphysik, die als Wissenschaft wird auftreten können*, ed. Karl Vorländer (Hamburg: Meiner, 1976); trans. as *Prolegomena to any Future Metaphysics* by L. W. Beck (Indianapolis: Bobbs-Merrill, 1950).
Kitcher, Patricia, 'Kant on Self-Identity', *Philosophical Review* 91 (1982), pp. 41–72.
—— 'Kant's Paralogisms', *Philosophical Review* 91 (1982), pp. 515–47.
Locke, John, *An Essay Concerning Human Understanding*, ed. Peter H. Nidditch (Oxford: Clarendon Press, 1975).
Lovejoy, A. O., 'Schopenhauer as an Evolutionist', *The Monist* 21 (1911), pp. 195–222.
Lukács, Georg, *The Destruction of Reason*, trans. Peter Palmer (London: Merlin Press, 1980).
McGinn, Colin, *The Character of Mind* (Oxford: University Press, 1982).
Magee, Bryan, *The Philosophy of Schopenhauer* (Oxford: Clarendon Press, 1983).
—— letter to the *Times Literary Supplement*, 14 Oct. 1983, p. 1126.
Mandelbaum, Maurice, *History, Man and Reason: A Study in Nineteenth-Century Thought* (Baltimore and London: Johns Hopkins Press, 1971).
Mann, Thomas, 'Schopenhauer', in Gerd Haffmans (ed.), *Über Arthur Schopenhauer*, pp. 87–132.
Marx, Karl, 'Theses on Feuerbach', in Karl Marx and Friedrich Engels, *Collected Works*, vol. 5 (London: Lawrence & Wishart, 1976), pp. 3–5.
Mattey, G. J., 'Kant's Conception of Berkeley's Idealism', *Kant-Studien* 74 (1983), pp. 161–75.
Matthews, H. E., 'Strawson on Transcendental Idealism', in Ralph C. S. Walker (ed.), *Kant on Pure Reason*, pp. 132–49.
Nagel, Thomas, 'Subjective and Objective', in id., *Mortal Questions*, pp. 196–213.
—— 'What Is it Like to Be a Bat?', in id., *Mortal Questions*, pp. 165–180.
—— *Mortal Questions* (Cambridge: University Press, 1979).
—— *The View from Nowhere* (Oxford: University Press, 1986).
Nehamas, Alexander, *Nietzsche: Life as Literature* (Cambridge, Mass.: Harvard University Press, 1985).
Nietzsche, Friedrich, *Werke in drei Bänden*, ed. Karl Schlechta (München: Carl Hanser, 1954–6).

—— *Beyond Good and Evil: Prelude to the Philosophy of the Future*, trans. W. Kaufmann (New York: Vintage Books, 1966).

—— *The Birth of Tragedy*, trans. W. Kaufmann (with *The Case of Wagner*) (New York: Vintage Books, 1967).

—— *The Will to Power*, trans. W. Kaufmann and R. J. Hollingdale (New York: Vintage Books, 1968).

—— *Thus Spoke Zarathustra*, trans. R. H. Hollingdale (Harmondsworth: Penguin, 1969).

—— *Twilight of the Idols*, trans. R. J. Hollingdale (with *The Anti-Christ*) (Harmondsworth: Penguin, 1969).

—— *The Genealogy of Morals*, trans. W. Kaufmann and R. J. Hollingdale (with *Ecce Homo*) (New York: Vintage Books, 1973).

—— *Nietzsche Briefwechsel: Kritische Gesamtausgabe*, ed. G. Colletti and M. Montinari (Berlin and New York: de Gruyter, 1975–84).

—— 'Schopenhauer as Educator', in *Untimely Meditations*, trans. R. J. Hollingdale (Cambridge: University Press, 1983).

—— 'Zu Schopenhauer: Philosophische Notizen', in Volker Spierling (ed.), *Materialien zu Schopenhauers 'Die Welt als Wille und Vorstellung'*, pp. 253–62.

—— *Human, all too Human: A Book for Free Spirits*, trans. R. J. Hollingdale (Cambridge: University Press, 1986).

O'Shaughnessy, Brian, *The Will*, 2 vols. (Cambridge: University Press, 1980).

Pears, David, 'Wittgenstein's Treatment of Solipsism in the *Tractatus*', in id., *Questions in the Philosophy of Mind* (London: Duckworth, 1975), pp. 272–92.

Popper, Karl, *The Open Society and its Enemies*, vol. 2. *Hegel and Marx* (London: Routledge & Kegan Paul, 1966).

Prauss, Gerold, *Kant und das Problem der Dinge an sich* (Bonn: Bouvier, 1977).

Rilke, Rainer Maria, *Duino Elegies*, trans. with introd. and commentary by J. B. Leishman and Stephen Spender (London: Chatto & Windus, 1975).

Royce, Josiah, *The Spirit of Modern Philosophy* (Cambridge, Mass.: Riverside Press, 1892).

Schelling, Friedrich Wilhelm Joseph von, *Sämtliche Werke*, 14 vols. (Stuttgart and Augsburg: J. G. Cotta'scher Verlag, 1856–61).

—— *System des transzendentalen Idealismus* (Hamburg: Meiner, 1957); trans. as *System of Transcendental Idealism* by Peter Heath (Charlottesville: University Press of Virginia, 1978).

Schmidt, Alfred, 'Schopenhauer und der Materialismus', in id., *Drei Studien über Materialismus*, pp. 21–79.

—— *Drei Studien über Materialismus* (Frankfurt am Main: Ullstein, 1979).

Schulze, Gottlob Ernst, *Aenesidemus, oder über die Fundamente der von dem Herrn Prof. Reinhold in Jena gelieferten Elementar-Philosophie* ([Helmstädt], 1792).

Smith, Norman Kemp, *A Commentary to Kant's Critique of Pure Reason* (2nd edn.; London: Macmillan, 1923).

Spierling, Volken, *Materialien zu Schopenhauers 'Die Welt als Wille und Vorstellung'* (Frankfurt am Main: Suhrkamp, 1984).

Spinoza, Benedict de, *The Ethics*, trans. R. H. M. Elwes (with *On the Improvement of the Understanding, Correspondence*) (New York: Dover, 1955).

Sprigge, T. L. S., *Theories of Existence* (Harmondsworth: Penguin, 1985).

Strawson, P. F., *Individuals: An Essay in Descriptive Metaphysics* (London: Methuen, 1959).

—— *The Bounds of Sense: An Essay on Kant's Critique of Pure Reason* (London: Methuen, 1966).

—— 'Freedom and Resentment', in id., *Freedom and Resentment and Other Essays* (London: Methuen, 1974), pp. 1–25.

Stroud, Barry, 'Transcendental Arguments', *Journal of Philosophy* 65 (1968), pp. 241–56; repr. in Ralph C. S. Walker (ed.), *Kant on Pure Reason*, pp. 117–31.

Tanner, Michael, letter to the *Times Literary Supplement*, 28 Oct. 1983, p. 1189.

Taylor, Charles, *The Explanation of Behaviour* (London: Routledge & Kegan Paul, 1964).

Tugendhat, Ernst, *Self-Consciousness and Self-Determination*, trans. Paul Stern (Cambridge: Mass.: MIT Press, 1986).

Turbayne, Colin, 'Kant's Refutation of Dogmatic Idealism', *Philosophical Quarterly* 5 (1955), pp. 225–44.

Vesey, Godfrey (ed.), *Idealism Past and Present* (Royal Institute of Philosophy Lectures, vol. 13; Cambridge: University Press, 1982).

Volkelt, Johannes, *Arthur Schopenhauer: Seine Persönlichkeit, seine Lehre, sein Glaube* (4th edn.; Stuttgart: Fromann, 1910).

Walker, Ralph C. S., *Kant* (London: Routledge & Kegan Paul, 1978).

—— (ed.), *Kant on Pure Reason* (Oxford: University Press, 1982).

Weininger, Otto, *Sex and Character* (London: Heinemann; New York: Putnam, 1906).

Weldon, T. D., 'Kant's Perceptual Vocabulary', in Terence Penelhum and J. J. MacIntosh (eds.), *The First Critique: Reflections on Kant's Critique of Pure Reason* (Belmont, Calif.: Wadsworth, 1969), pp. 34–7.

White, Alan, *Schelling: An Introduction to the System of Freedom* (New Haven: Yale University Press, 1983).

Williams, Bernard, *Descartes: The Project of Pure Enquiry* (Harmondsworth: Penguin, 1978).

Wilson, Margaret D., 'Descartes: The Epistemological Argument for Mind–Body Distinctness', *Nous* 10 (1976), pp. 3–15.

Winch, Peter, 'Wittgenstein's Treatment of the Will', in id., *Ethics and Action* (London: Routledge & Kegan Paul, 1972), pp. 110–29.

Wittgenstein, Ludwig, *Philosophical Investigations* (3rd edn.; Oxford: Blackwell, 1967).

—— *Zettel* (Oxford: Blackwell, 1967).

—— *Briefe an Ludwig von Ficker*, ed. G. H. von Wright (Salzburg: Otto Müller, 1969).

—— *Notebooks 1914–16* (Oxford: Blackwell, 1969).

—— *Tractatus Logico-Philosophicus* (2nd edn.; London: Routledge & Kegan Paul, 1971).

—— *The Blue and Brown Books* (Oxford: Blackwell, 1972).

—— *Philosophical Grammar* (Oxford: Blackwell, 1974).

—— *Culture and Value / Vermischte Bemerkungen*, ed. G. H. von Wright, trans. Peter Winch (Oxford: Blackwell, 1980).

Wolff, Christian, *Psychologia rationalis*, in *Gesammelte Werke*, II/b (Hildesheim: Georg Olms, 1972).

Wolff, Robert Paul, 'Kant's Debt to Hume via Beattie', *Journal of the History of Ideas* 21 (1960), pp. 117–23.

Wright, G. H. von, 'Biographical Sketch', in Norman Malcolm, *Ludwig Wittgenstein: A Memoir* (London: Oxford University Press, 1958).

INDEX

action, 3, 7, 191–2, 196–7, 208–29, 232–
  3, 235, 239–47, 258, 293–5, 297,
  299–301, 337, 338–41, 353–4
Adickes, Erich, 70 n.
aesthetic experience, 8–10, 275–7, 278–
  9, 283, 319, 335
Allison, H. E., 59 n., 61 n., 72 n., 156 n.
Ameriks, Karl, 43–4 n., 91 n., 102 n.
Anscombe, Elizabeth, 210 n., 229, 317 n.
appearance, 5, 21, 72–4
  Kant on, 72–8, 169
Arendt, Hannah, 203, 206
asceticism, 11, 283, 335
Asiatic Researches, 29

Beck, J. S., 62, 63, 71, 74, 77
Bell, Charles, 182 n.
Berkeley, George, 53–67, 69, 73, 74, 75,
  76, 77, 78, 79, 117, 118, 143, 144,
  147, 150, 151, 154, 155, 169, 209,
  365
Berlin, Isaiah, 231
'better consciousness', 27–8, 30, 169,
  273–4, 278, 284
Bichat, Marie François Xavier, 182 n.
body, 125–6, 158–9, 189–92, 196, 201,
  208–10, 211–12, 218–20, 221–8,
  255, 258–9, 294, 299–300, 337–40,
  335–6
Böhme, Jakob, 206
Bracken, H. M., 56 n.
brain, 125, 180–1, 184–5, 257, 258, 293
Buddha (Buddhism), 26, 28, 29
Burckhardt, Jacob, 16, 343

Cabanis, Pierre Jean Georges, 182 n.
categories, 79, 172
  Kant on, 42, 46–8, 50, 172–3
  Transcendental Deduction, 43–7,
    104–6, 110–11
causality, 48, 51–3, 126–7, 152–4, 157,
  163–5, 172–5, 214, 215
  Kant on, 51–3, 77, 95–6, 97, 157,
  163–5, 172–4
character, 239–44

Christianity, 21, 33, 111–12
concepts, 41–2, 44–6, 48–51, 160–5
Copleston, Frederick, 16 n., 271 n.,
  287 n.
correlativism, 136–7, 181–3

Darwin, Charles, 254
  Darwinism, 256
Davidson, Donald, 211 n.
death, 284, 318, 319
Descartes, René, 1, 15, 35, 58, 61, 99,
  100, 106, 143, 150, 227, 262, 270,
  309, 351, 357, 365
determinism, 234, 238–41, 246, 247
Deussen, Paul, 342, 345
di Giovanni, George, 142 n.
dreams, 167–9, 170

Ebeling, Hans, 3 n.
egoism, 10, 279–83, 325–6
Eleatics, 177
Engel, S. Morris, 317 n.
epistemology, 35, 185–7, 268–9, 305,
  308–11
Eschenbach, J. C., 56 n.
ethics, 11, 279–83, 318, 320–1
  Kant on, 11, 87, 88–9, 281
Evans, Gareth, 303 n., 307 n.
evolution, 2, 253–5

Feder, Johann Georg Heinrich, 55
Fichte, Johann Gottlieb, 26, 31, 32, 33,
  35, 71, 82, 83, 110, 119, 120, 121,
  130, 131, 142, 143, 147, 151, 152,
  153, 195, 203, 204, 205, 248, 265,
  306
Förster, Eckart, 82 n.
Frankfurt, Harry, 232 n.
freedom, 96, 230–47, 293, 295, 354
  Kant on, 84–97, 234–5, 241, 243–5,
  246, 295
Freud, Sigmund, 16, 302
  Freudianism, 259

Gall, Franz Joseph, 182 n.
Gardiner, Patrick, 16 n., 35 n., 203 n., 219, 287 n., 317 n., 358 n.
Garve, Christian, 55
Geach, P. T., 317 n.
Griffiths, A. Phillips, 317 n., 332 n., 335 n.

Hacker, P. M. S., 317 n., 324–6, 327 n., 328, 332 n.
Hall, Marshall, 182 n.
Hamlyn, D. W., 35 n., 138 n., 197 n., 215–16, 219, 220, 260 n., 287 n., 300 n.
Harris, H. S., 142 n.
Hartmann, Eduard von, 16, 342
Hegel, Georg Wilhelm Friedrich, 13, 33, 34, 204, 306
Heidegger, Martin, 163
Heller, Erich, 12 n.
Herbart, Johann Friedrich, 32, 130
Hindus, 25, 28, 29, 35, 112
Hobbes, Thomas, 231
Horkheimer, Max, 280
Hornsby, Jennifer, 208 n., 222 n.
Hübscher, Arthur, 12 n., 26 n., 27 n., 58 n.
Hume, David, 1, 15, 102, 103, 104, 105, 107, 123, 231, 357

'I', 1, 2, 7–8, 120–3, 129, 131, 149, 152–3, 181, 204, 220, 265–6, 281–3, 300, 301, 302–4, 307, 308, 311, 315, 316, 322–3, 327–9, 330–3, 334–5, 336, 337, 338, 341–2, 350–2, 355, 356
   Kant on, 84, 99–100, 102, 106–9, 279, 286
i ching, 177
idealism, 2–3, 67, 117, 137–9, 140–71, 175, 180, 183, 184–5, 305, 308, 329–30
   see also transcendental idealism
Ideas, 9–10, 27–8, 31, 254, 273–4, 276–8, 279, 298
India (Indians), 147, 168
intuition, 25–6, 48–51, 158, 160–3
   and concept, 42, 48–51, 158, 160–5, 215
Ionians, 177

Jacobi, Friedrich Heinrich, 32 n., 71 n., 150, 166
Janik, Allan S., 16 n., 317 n.

Jones, Ernest, 16 n.
Judaism, 147

Kant, Immanuel, 4, 5, 15, 21–4, 25, 26, 27, 30, 31, 32, 33, 34–6, 37–83, 84–114, 117–18, 126, 135, 141–2, 144, 146, 147, 152, 154, 155, 163, 178, 180–1, 182–6, 194, 239–40, 248, 270, 278, 285–6, 296, 298, 358–60, 365
   relation to Berkeley 53–67, 155
   see also under appearance; categories; causality; ethics; freedom; 'I'; metaphysics; object; representation; scepticism; self; self-consciousness; space and time; thing in itself; transcendental idealism
Kitcher, Patricia, 102 n., 109 n.

Lamarck, 253, 254
Leibniz, Gottfried Wilhelm, 41, 146, 176, 365
Locke, John, 61, 182, 209
Lovejoy, A. O., 207 n., 253 n., 254 n.
Lukács, Georg, 11, 13, 201, 280–1
Lütkehaus, Ludger, 3 n.

Magee, Bryan, 16 n., 29 n., 35 n., 248 n., 253 n., 271 n., 284 n., 317 n.
Magendie, François, 182 n.
Mahler, Gustav, 16
Majer, Friedrich, 29
Mandelbaum, Maurice, 253 n., 275 n.
Mann, Thomas, 9 n., 15–16, 345
Marx, Karl, 2, 3, 13, 280
materialism, 2–3, 137, 175–87, 258, 293
matter, 48, 112, 138, 173–5, 176–8
Mattey, G. J., 65 n.
Matthews, H. E., 72 n., 74
Mauthner, Fritz, 16
māyā, 29–30, 168, 169
McGinn, Colin, 293 n., 300 n.
metaphysics, 22–4, 26, 188–9, 198–9, 268–9
   Kant on, 44–6, 198
motive, 213–16, 232, 235–42, 249, 260, 294
music, 10, 27
mysticism, 11–12, 283, 319, 320, 332, 335

Nagel, Thomas, 187, 210, 234, 241 n., 246–7, 268 n., 293 n., 302 n., 312–15, 338, 362 n., 363 n.

Nehamas, Alexander, 346 n., 347–8

Newton, Isaac, 41, 56, 61

Nietzsche, Friedrich, 15, 17, 111, 245, 292, 316, 342–56, 357, 363, 365

O'Shaughnessy, Brian, 212 n., 216, 221–7, 300 n., 301 n., 303 n.

object, 5–6, 66, 79–81, 132–9, 141–3, 152–5, 158–60

'No object without subject', 54, 118, 124, 133–4, 136–7, 138 n., 139, 166, 175

in Kant, 78–81, 167

Oupnek'hat *see* Upanishads

Pears, David, 326 n., 329 n., 332 n.

perception, 157–60, 163–5

person, 125–6

pessimism, 8, 271–5

physiology, 2, 180–3, 184–5, 263

Plato, 9, 14, 25, 27, 28, 30, 31, 35, 168, 170, 254, 262, 273, 274, 276, 277, 278, 279, 365

Popper, Karl, 34

Prauss, Gerold, 70 n., 72 n.

principium individuationis, 127, 198

Puranas, 168

Pythagoreans, 177

reason, 50–1, 160–1, 215, 249

Reinhold, Carl Leonhard, 32, 141, 142

representation, 141–3, 152–4, 158–60, 180, 192–3

Kant on, 37–8, 54, 74–7, 79–80, 81, 132

world as, 5–6, 34, 67, 140, 146, 148–9

responsibility, 241–3, 244–5, 246, 247, 357

Rilke, Rainer Maria, 363–4

Rosenkranz, Johann Karl Friedrich, 58

Royce, Josiah, 12 n., 16 n.

Russell, Bertrand, 326 n., 332

scepticism, 144, 150–2, 153–4, 167, 170

Kant on, 59–60, 81

Schelling, Friedrich Wilhelm Joseph von, 31, 32, 33, 35, 82, 110, 119, 120, 143, 147, 195, 203–6, 248, 250, 286

Schleiermacher, Friedrich Ernst Daniel, 32 n.

Schmidt, Alfred, 3 n., 181

Schulze, Gottlob Ernst, 27, 31, 32 n., 71, 142

self, 1–5, 6, 12, 15, 16, 17, 24, 110–13, 128–32, 189–97, 235, 240, 242–3, 257, 259, 261–70, 271, 285–8, 292–316, 322–4, 327–31, 336–8, 344–5, 348–56, 358–65

Humean conception, 1, 102–5, 107

Kant on, 1, 2, 84, 90–1, 93–5, 98–114, 120–4, 128–30, 184–6, 286, 292, 293, 308–11, 314–15, 329, 355, 357

objective (Nagel), 314–15

self-consciousness, 83, 110–11, 121–5, 129–32, 189, 192–5, 230, 235–8, 239, 246, 259–61, 262–3, 301, 304

Kant on, 44–6, 104–5, 107–9, 194, 195, 265, 302–3, 307

sexuality, 7, 16, 255–7, 301–2, 355

Smith, Norman Kemp, 59 n.

solipsism, 6, 148–50, 167, 324–6, 327

space and time, 41, 126–7, 155, 174–5, 198

Kant on, 37–41, 58, 60–2, 155–6

Spinoza, Benedict de, 9, 177, 204, 262, 276

Sprigge, T. L. S., 249 n.

Strawson, P. F., 43, 44, 109, 241 n., 307

Stroud, Barry, 47 n.

subject, 5–6, 17, 33, 66, 112, 117–39, 141–3, 152–5, 179–87, 189–96, 248, 264–70, 273, 293, 295–316, 322–3, 327, 334, 344–5, 350

'No subject without object', 133, 136–7

metaphysical (Wittgenstein), 314, 327–31, 341–2, 356

of will, 33, 128–9, 130, 193–6, 220, 264–9, 295–301

pure, will-less, 9–10, 270, 275–6, 278–9, 296, 298, 315, 323, 341–2, 348

substance, 47–8, 111–13, 172–3

immaterial, 1, 102–4, 107–9, 111–13, 176

synthetic a priori, 22–3, 38–9, 40

Tanner, Michael, 317 n.

Taylor, Charles, 210, 251, 252

teleology, 202, 250–3, 255, 257, 263, 272, 275, 301–2

Thales, 177
thing in itself, 5, 21, 31, 67–9, 69–74, 83,
    96–7, 156–7, 166, 170–1, 176–7,
    188–9, 192–3, 195–203, 210, 259,
    343, 346–8
  in Kant, 67–74, 75–8, 90–7, 133, 150,
    156–7, 159, 166, 188–9, 199, 200,
    273–4
Toulmin, Stephen, 16 n.
transcendental idealism, 5, 34, 66, 82,
    150–2, 155, 270
  in Kant, 37, 40–1, 53–78, 82, 84, 150–
    1, 155
trying, 223–7
Tugendhat, Ernst, 306
Turbayne, Colin, 59 n.

unity of apperception, 46, 105–6, 110–
    11, 123–4, 129
Upanishads, 29, 30, 119

Vaihinger, Hans, 16
Vedas, 30, 168
volition, 208, 223–5, 341
Volkelt, Johannes, 136

Wackenroder, Wilhelm Heinrich, 27
Wagner, Richard, 15, 343
Walker, Ralph C. S., 43 n., 98 n.
Walter, Bruno, 16

Weininger, Otto, 16
Weldon, T. D., 74
White, Alan, 204 n., 206 n.
will, 6–8, 24, 29, 35–6, 96, 97, 129, 186,
    188–9, 191–7, 199, 201–4, 230, 232,
    235–8, 248–70, 271, 272, 273, 274–
    5, 296–304, 343
  and intellect, 7–8, 16, 129, 248–9,
    257–8, 260–3, 264, 275, 343–4
  as bearer of good and evil
    (Wittgenstein), 17, 333, 339
  denial of, 11, 284–5, 321
  world as, 6–7, 10, 188–9, 197–9, 201–
    3, 206–7, 248–9
will to life, 249–50, 252–3, 255–7
will to power, 17, 346–8, 349–50, 354–5,
    356
Williams, Bernard, 351 n.
willing, 131, 208–13, 216–28, 236–8,
    248, 337, 338–41
Wilson, Margaret D., 309 n.
Winch, Peter, 337 n.
Wittgenstein, Ludwig, 15,16, 17, 119,
    228, 292, 294, 306, 307, 314, 316,
    317–42, 350, 356, 357, 365
Wittgenstein, Margarete, 16
Wolff, Christian, 56, 134
Wolff, Robert Paul, 102 n.
Wright, G. H. Von, 317 n.
Wundt, Wilhelm, 16